CYPRESS

UNIVERSITY PRESS OF FLORIDA

Florida A&M University, Tallahassee

Florida Atlantic University, Boca Raton

Florida Gulf Coast University, Ft. Myers

Florida International University, Miami

Florida State University, Tallahassee

New College of Florida, Sarasota

University of Central Florida, Orlando

University of Florida, Gainesville

University of North Florida, Jacksonville

University of South Florida, Tampa

University of West Florida, Pensacola

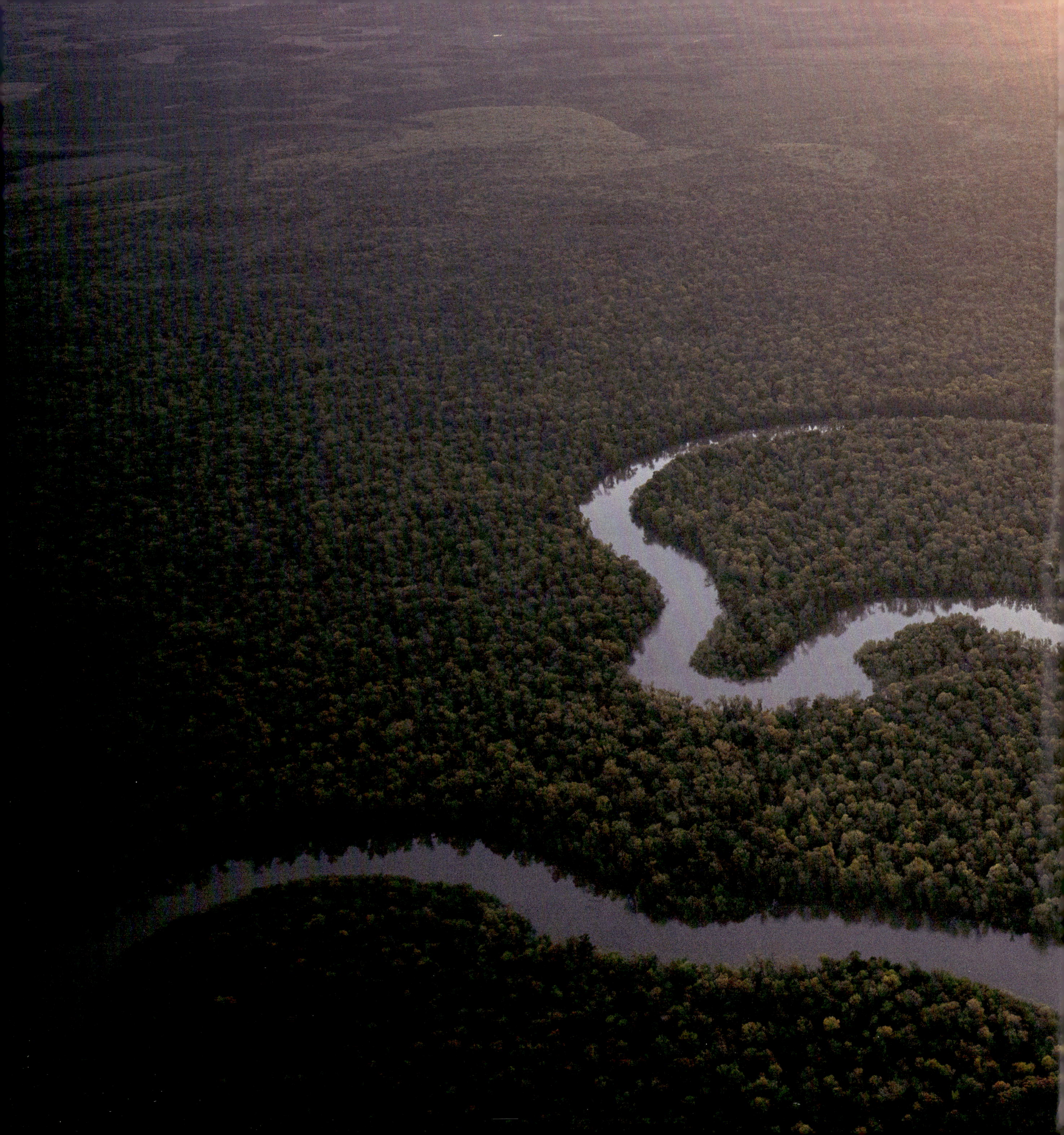

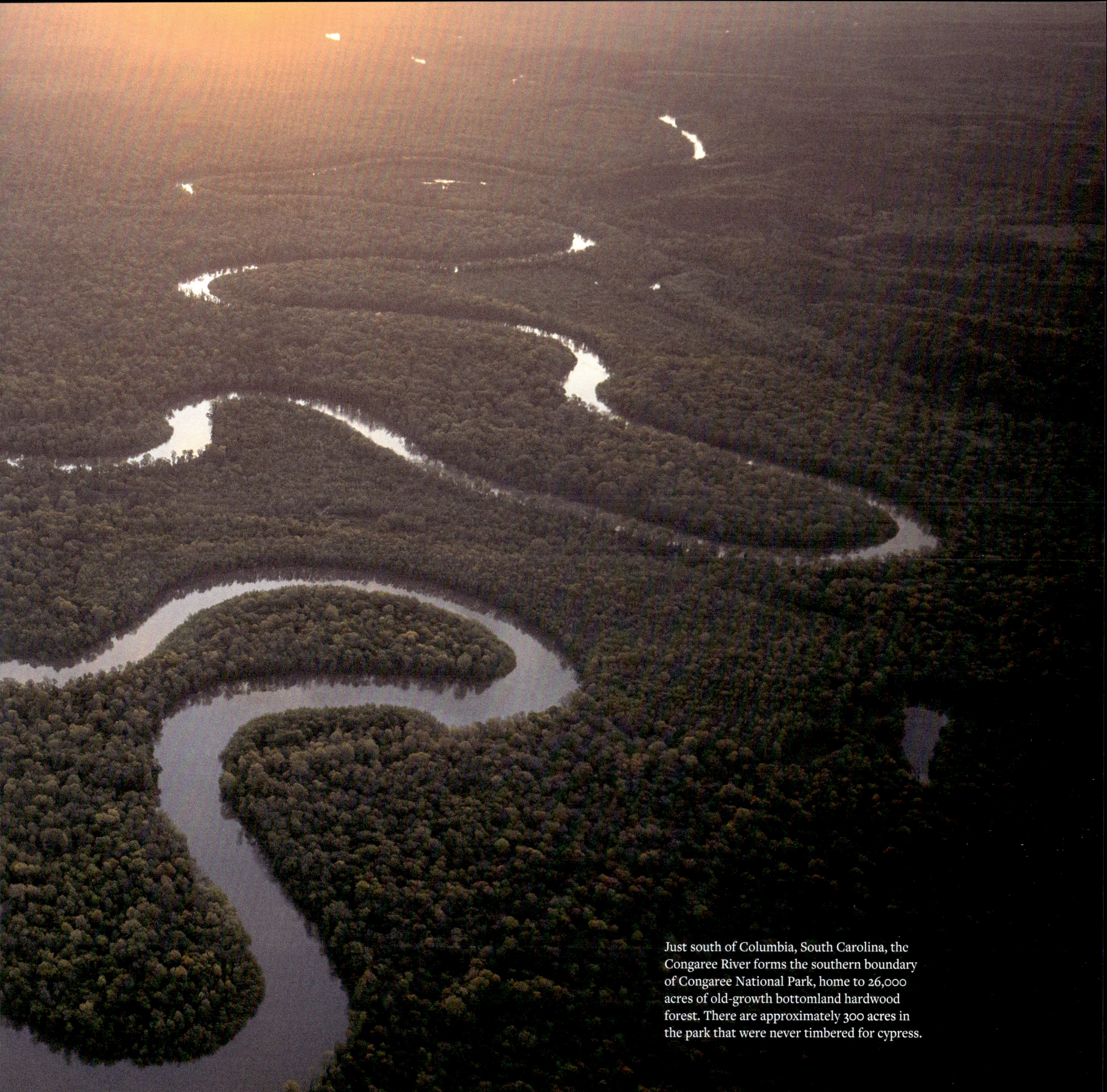

Just south of Columbia, South Carolina, the Congaree River forms the southern boundary of Congaree National Park, home to 26,000 acres of old-growth bottomland hardwood forest. There are approximately 300 acres in the park that were never timbered for cypress.

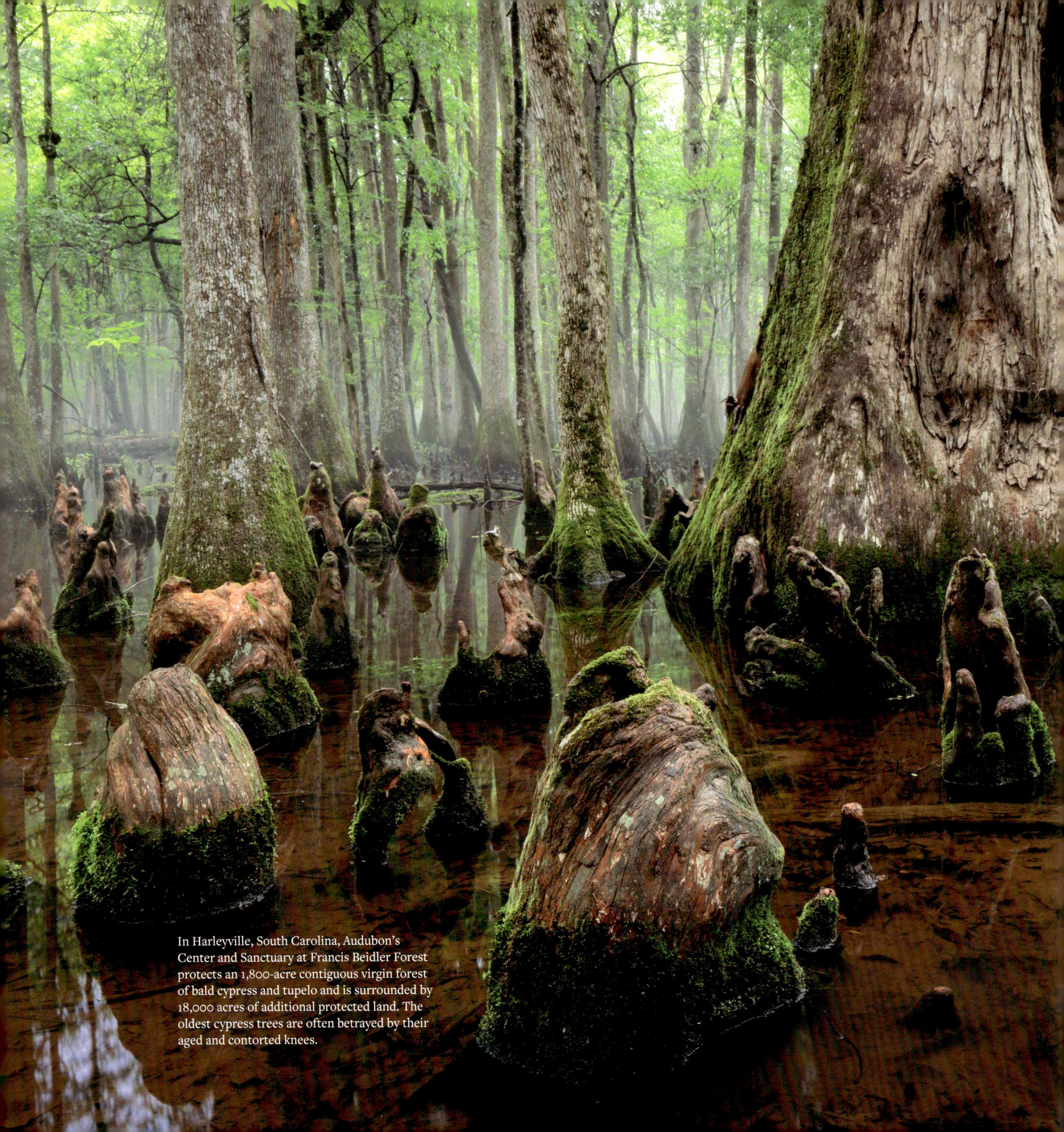

In Harleyville, South Carolina, Audubon's Center and Sanctuary at Francis Beidler Forest protects an 1,800-acre contiguous virgin forest of bald cypress and tupelo and is surrounded by 18,000 acres of additional protected land. The oldest cypress trees are often betrayed by their aged and contorted knees.

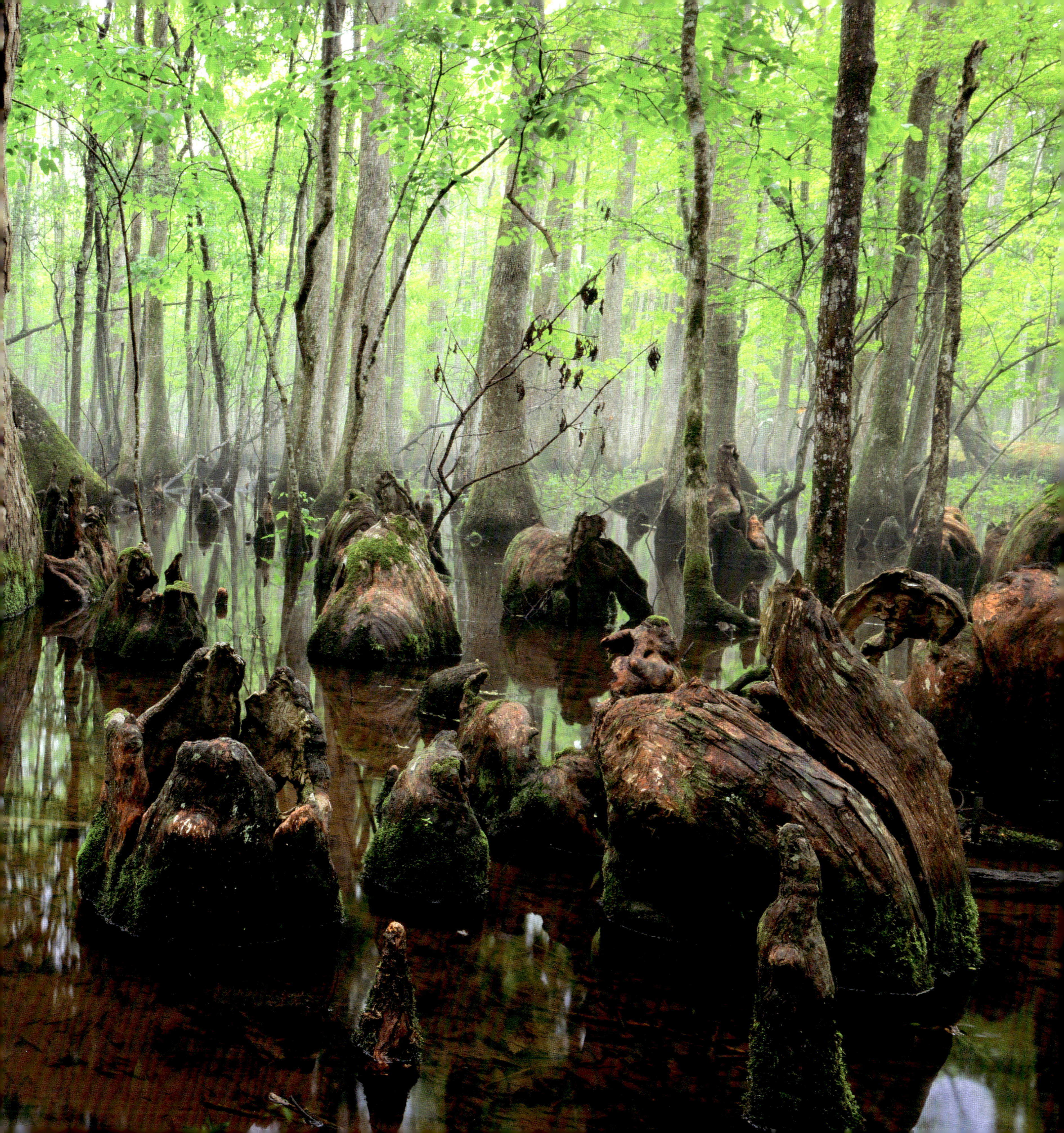

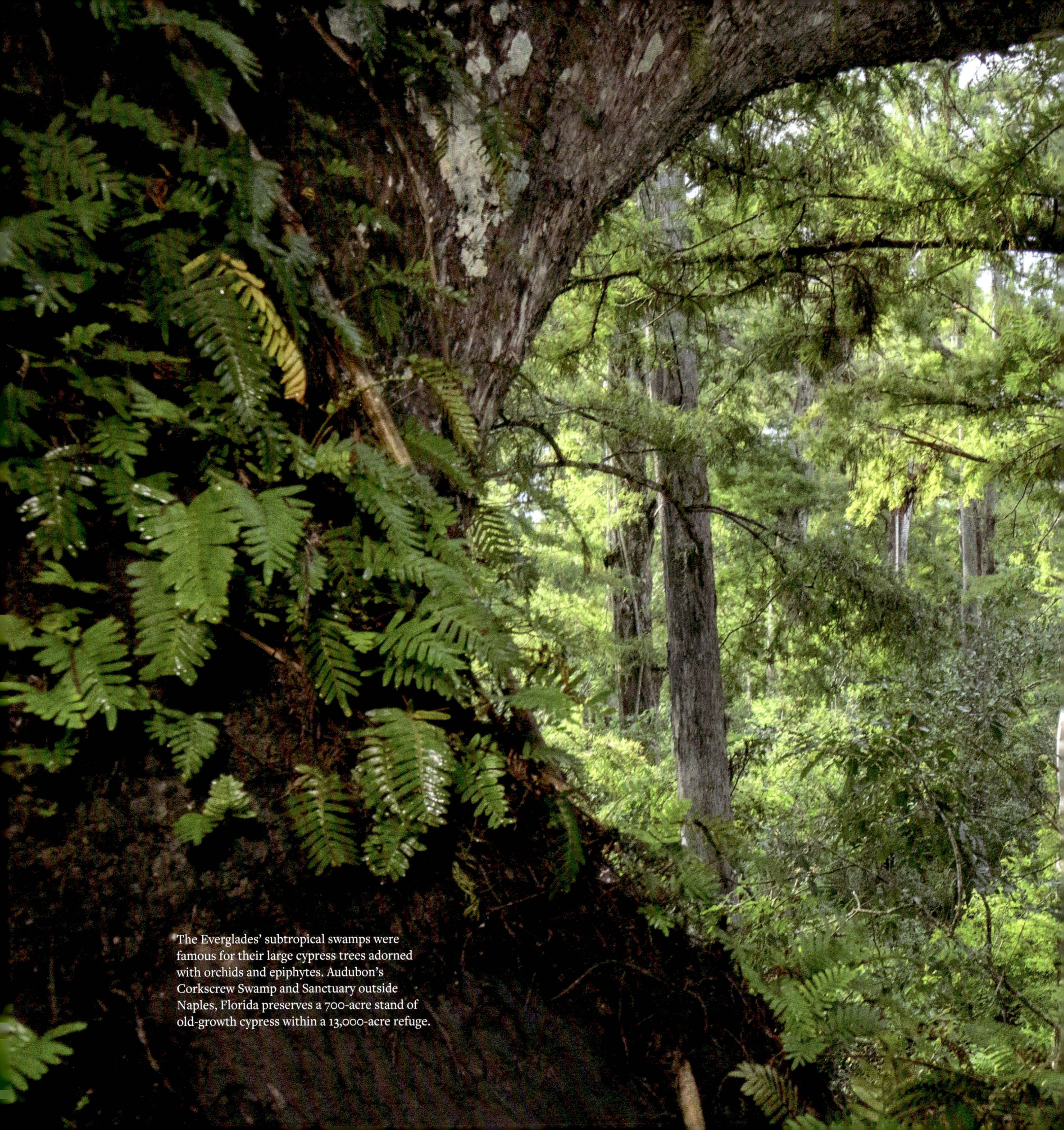

The Everglades' subtropical swamps were famous for their large cypress trees adorned with orchids and epiphytes. Audubon's Corkscrew Swamp and Sanctuary outside Naples, Florida preserves a 700-acre stand of old-growth cypress within a 13,000-acre refuge.

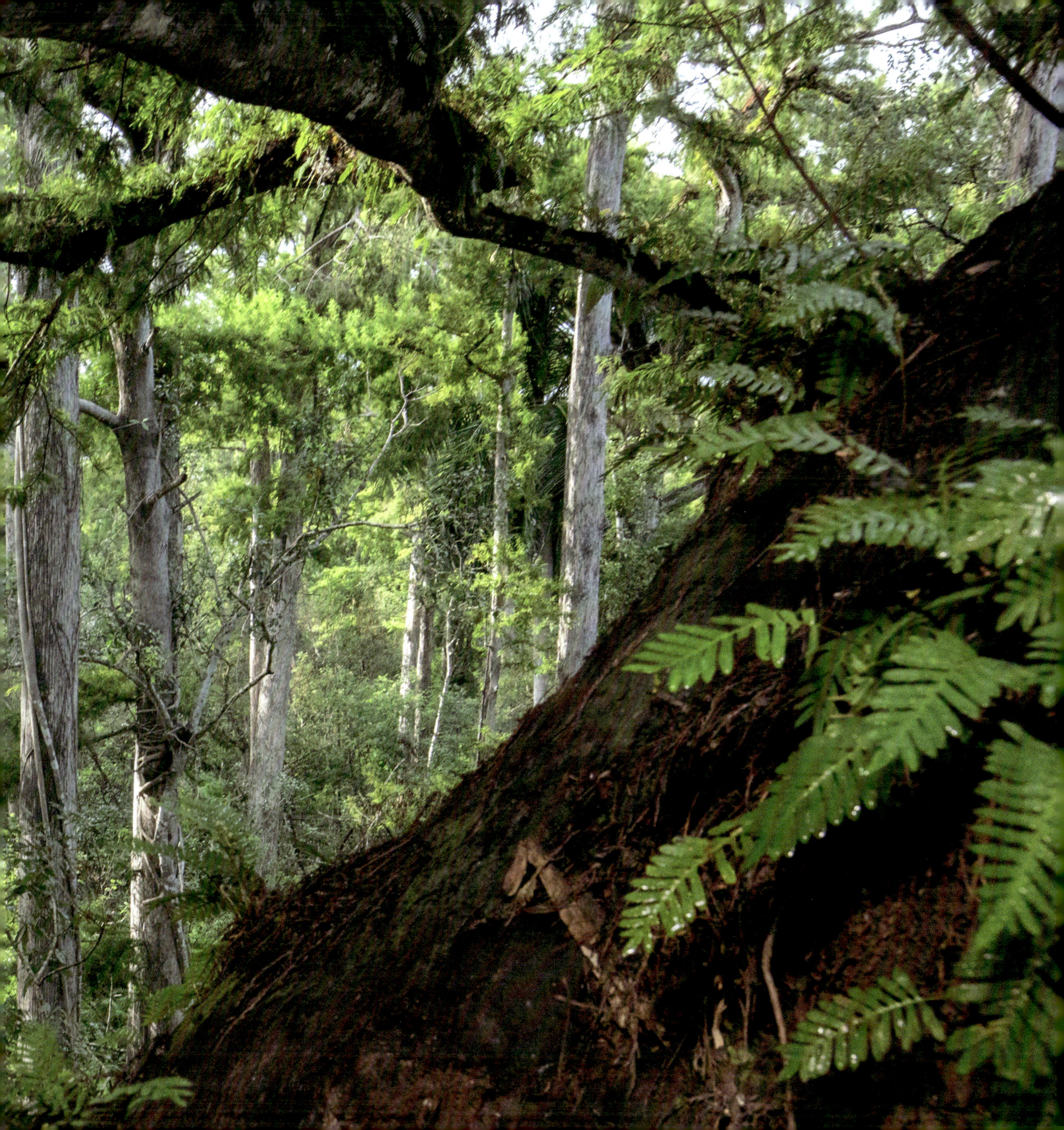

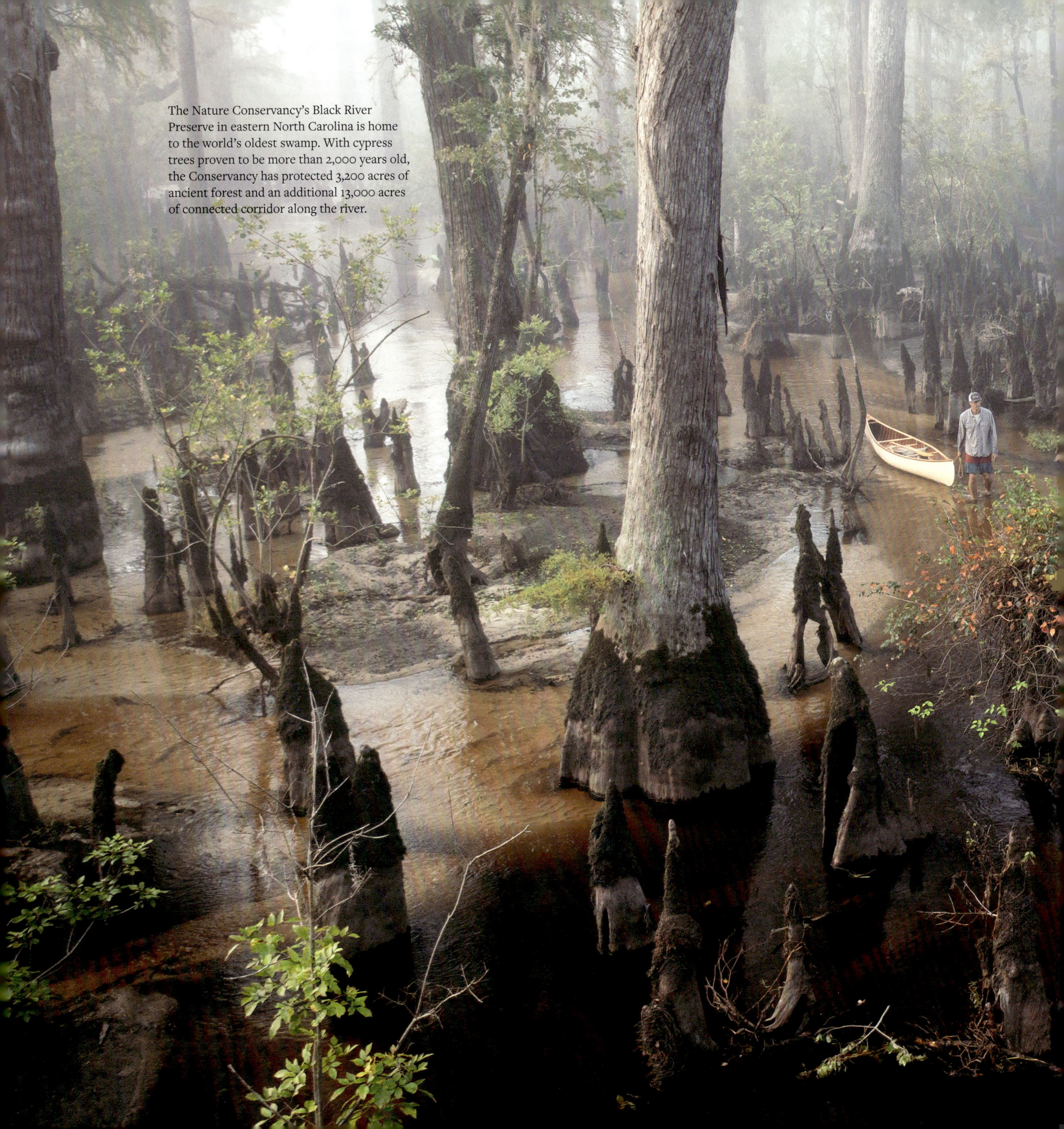

The Nature Conservancy's Black River Preserve in eastern North Carolina is home to the world's oldest swamp. With cypress trees proven to be more than 2,000 years old, the Conservancy has protected 3,200 acres of ancient forest and an additional 13,000 acres of connected corridor along the river.

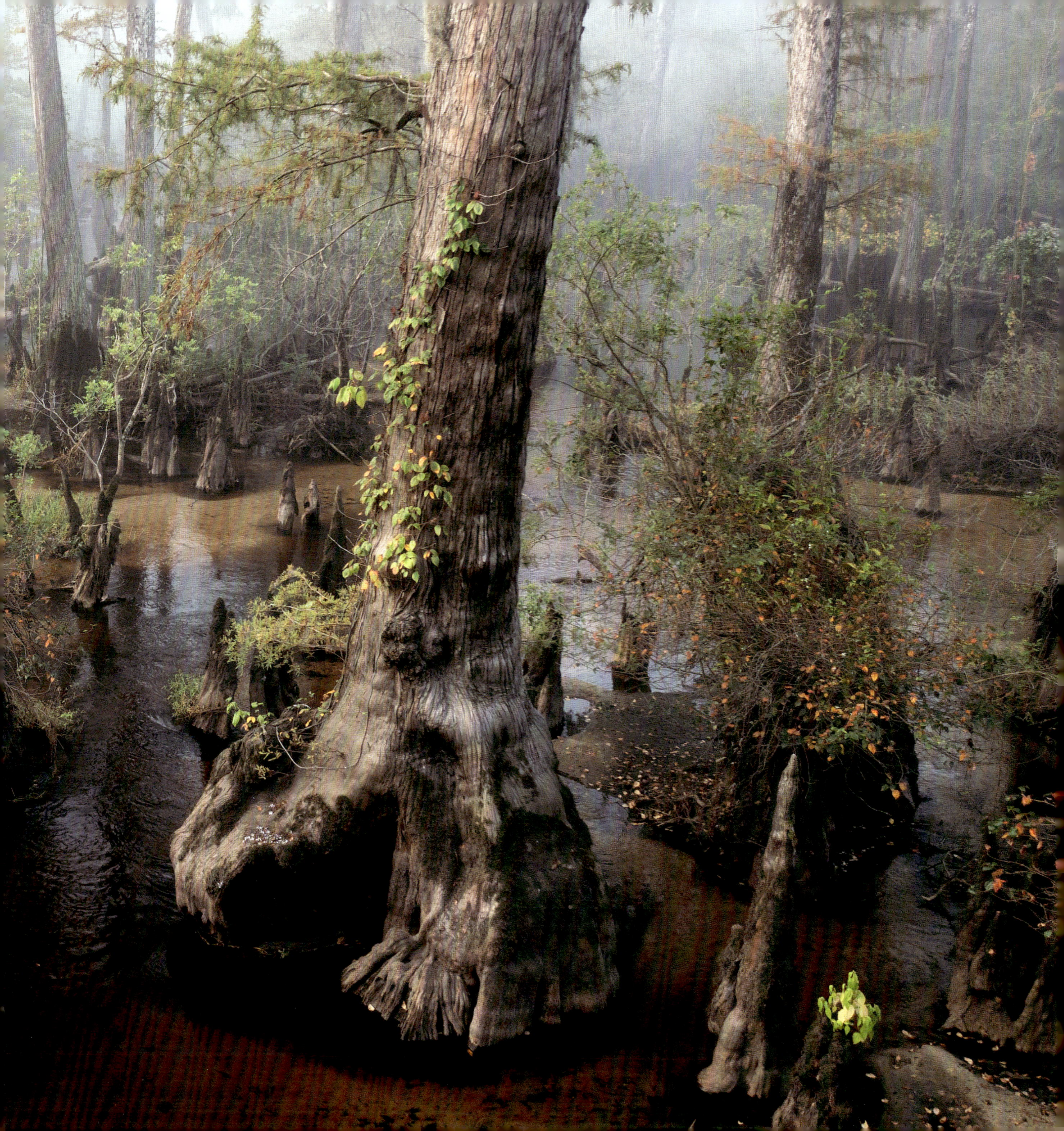

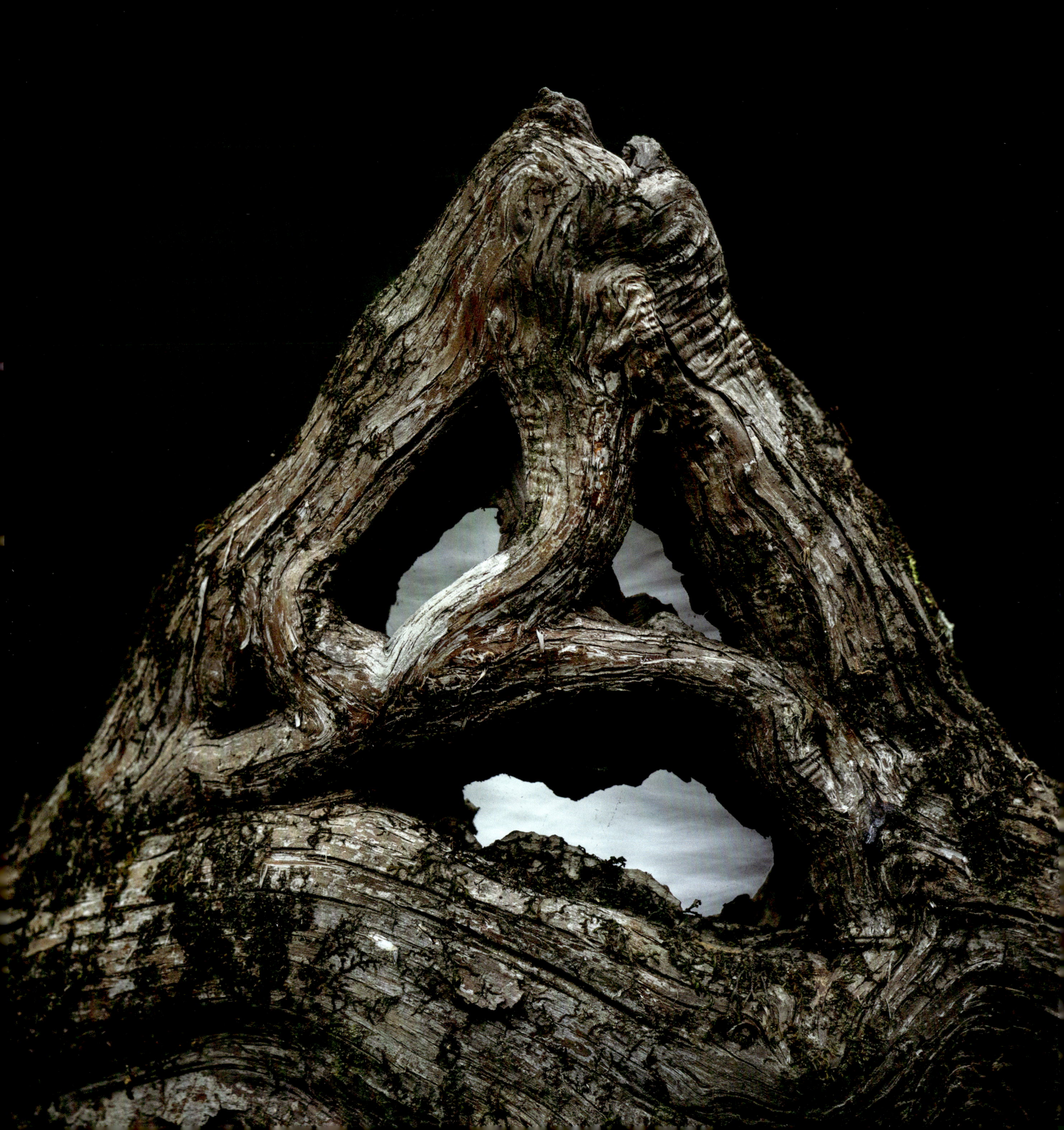

CYPRESS

THE LAST OLD-GROWTH SWAMPS

MAC STONE

UNIVERSITY PRESS OF FLORIDA

Gainesville/Tallahassee/Tampa/Boca Raton

Pensacola/Orlando/Miami/Jacksonville/Ft. Myers/Sarasota

Cover: North Carolina's Black River shelters the oldest known cypress swamp on Earth.

Published in the United States of America

Printed in Canada

31 30 29 28 27 26 6 5 4 3 2 1

Library of Congress Cataloging-in-Publication Data
Names: Stone, Mac, author.
Title: Cypress : the last old-growth swamps / Mac Stone.
Description: Gainesville : University Press of Florida, 2026.
Identifiers: LCCN 2026008599 | ISBN 9780813079639 (hardback)
Subjects: LCSH: Cypress—Southern States. | Old growth forests—Southern States. | Cypress swamp ecology—Southern States. | Nature photography. | Landscape photography. | LCGFT: Illustrated works.
Classification: LCC QH541.5.C95
LC record available at https://lccn.loc.gov/2026008599

The University Press of Florida is the scholarly publishing agency for the State University System of Florida, comprising Florida A&M University, Florida Atlantic University, Florida Gulf Coast University, Florida International University, Florida State University, New College of Florida, University of Central Florida, University of Florida, University of North Florida, University of South Florida, and University of West Florida.

University Press of Florida
PO Box 140239
Gainesville, FL 32614

floridapress.org

GPSR EU Authorized Representative: Mare Nostrum Group B.V., Doelen 72, 4831 GR Breda, The Netherlands, gpsr@mare-nostrum.co.uk

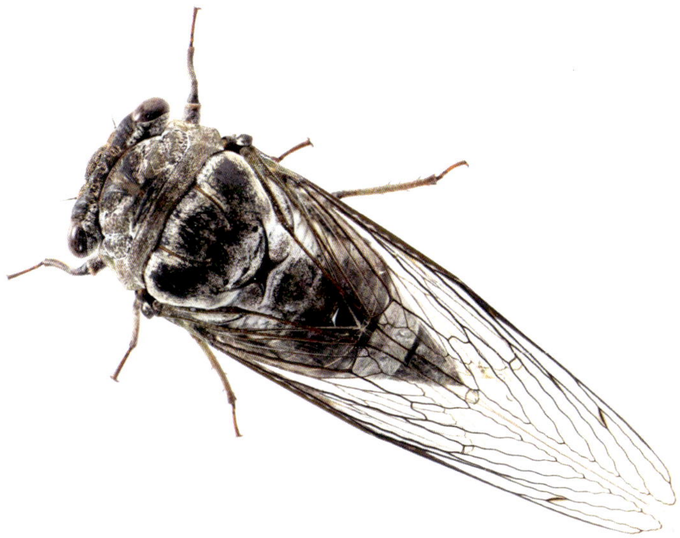

For McAllen and Hinton—my greatest adventure.

May the wild always feel like home.

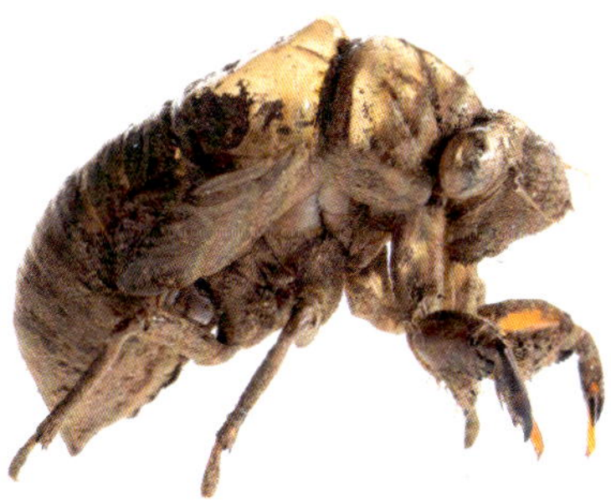

CONTENTS

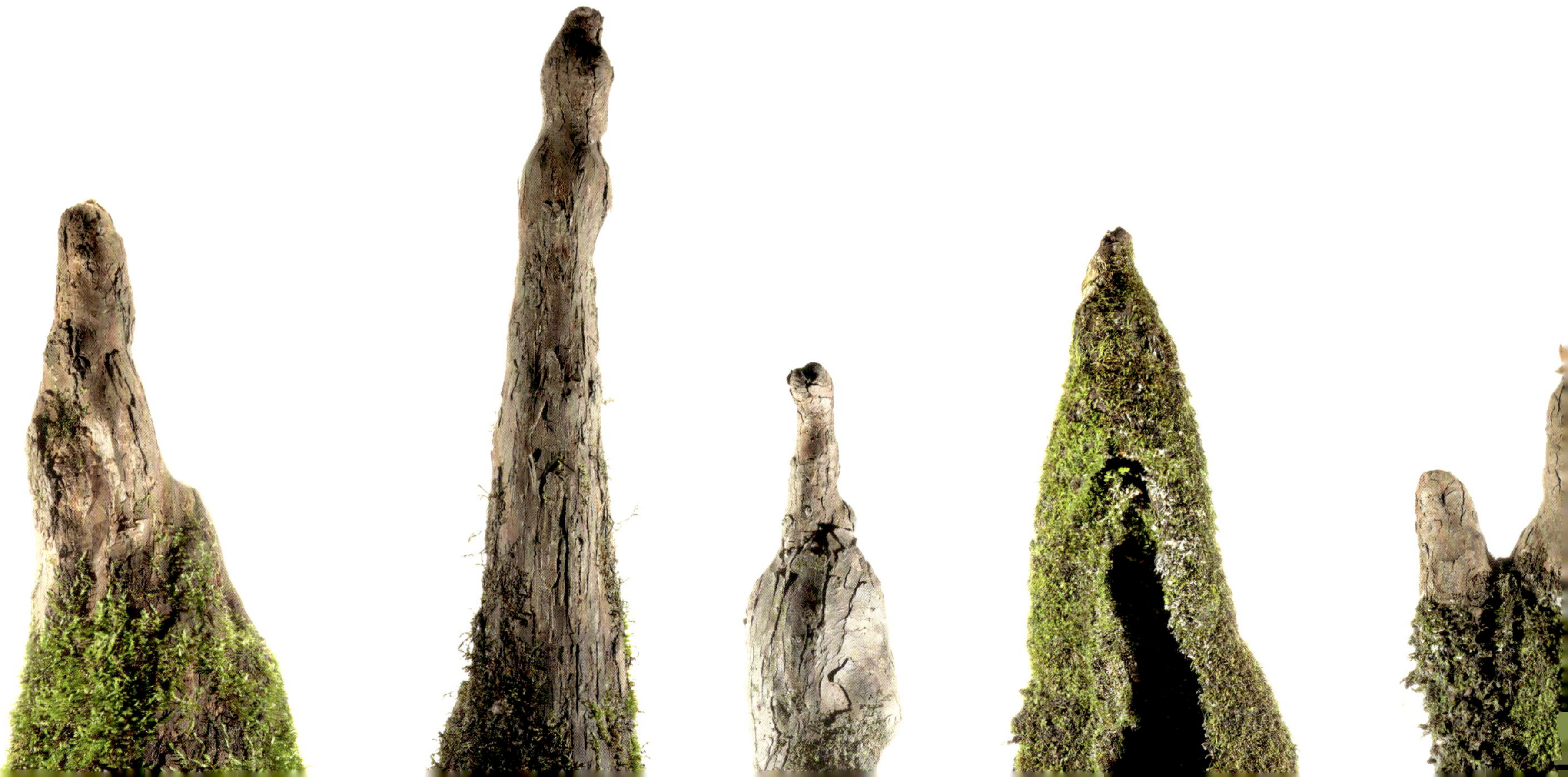

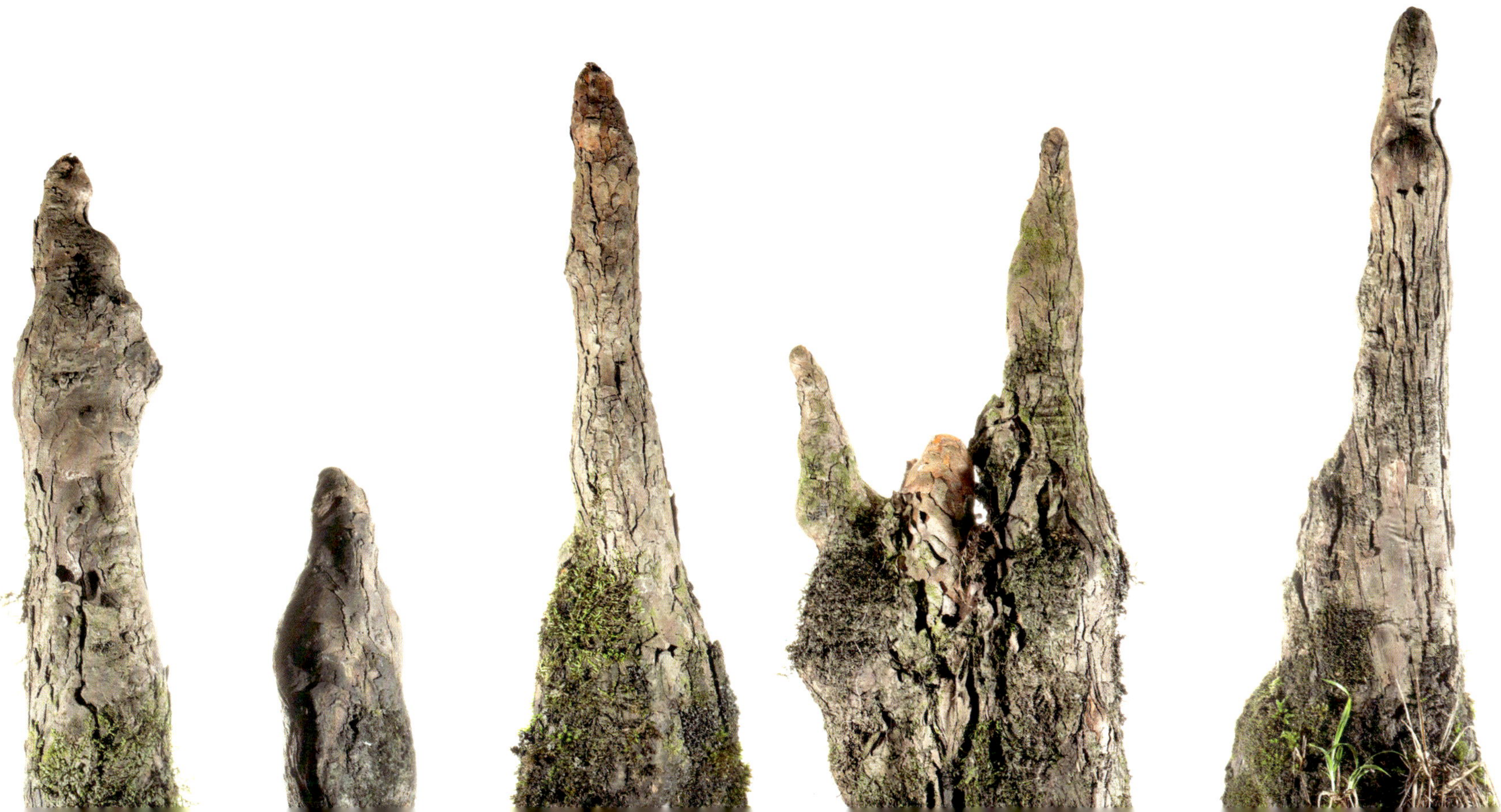

PREFACE

For two decades, I explored what I believed were the pristine swamps and floodplains of my hometown in North Central Florida. Under the cypress and oak canopies that presided over blackwater sloughs, I learned to compose, expose, and interpret this southern brand of wilderness at an early age. These ecosystems imprinted themselves on my impressionable heart, sending roots deep into my identity and forming the foundation of what I found beautiful.

The way fluted cypress trunks and limbs draped with Spanish moss created sinuous frames for prairies and rivers made me feel as though I was documenting ancient, sacred places. What I didn't know then was that these towering trees—even the centenarians—were as adolescent in their lifespan as I was in mine. In fact, nearly all the forests and mountains of the Southeast I explored and admired were merely the second- and third-generation canopy of a landscape once ravaged by industrial might and federal decree.

From Florida to Delaware, west to Illinois and south to Texas, bald cypress (*Taxodium distichum*) once dominated the floodplains and rivers of the Atlantic Coastal Plain and Mississippi Alluvial Valley. Iconic for their wide buttresses and towering knees, marooned in open water yet obstinately thriving where little else could survive, cypress trees represented the wild heart of the American South. Approximately 40 million acres of cypress forests once connected the freshwater arteries of the southeastern United States like a vast, living network.

But swamps were seen as a nuisance—an obstacle to progress for early settlers. In 1850, Congress passed the Swamp Land Act to incentivize states to cut, drain, and transform their flooded forests into "productive" agricultural land.

Unlike in the vast longleaf pine savannas and dry Piedmont forests of oak and hickory, harvesting bald cypress proved exceedingly difficult. Before the Civil War, this back-breaking work was carried out primarily by enslaved laborers who toiled and died in the southern heat, converting flooded forests into pastures and rice paddies by hand.

After the Civil War, toward the end of the nineteenth century, cypress logging turned industrial. The scale required engineering feats of tram roads, railways, and canals to move tens of thousands of acres of gargantuan trees through expansive wetlands.

Each tree represents 10,000 acres of virgin cypress forest once found across the Atlantic Coastal Plain and Mississippi Alluvial Plain. Of the historic 40 million acres, less than 0.1 percent of old-growth cypress swamp remains.

Cypress was coveted for two compelling reasons: the underlying land was cheap, and the raw lumber was the equivalent of modern pressure-treated wood—naturally insect-, water-, and rot-resistant. Early marketing campaigns touted it as "the wood eternal." This cypress gold rush attracted industrialists and land barons from Chicago, Philadelphia, and New York, who bought up millions of acres for pennies on the dollar. Entire towns sprouted around enormous 800,000-square-foot sawmills that produced a quarter million board feet daily in the formerly quiet backwoods of the southern states.

In only half a century, by the 1930s, nearly all the last remote lowcountry wildernesses were penetrated and indiscriminately logged. The Great Dismal Swamp, the Atchafalaya Basin, the Mississippi Delta, Okefenokee Swamp, Big Cypress, Mobile Delta, the ACE Basin, Pearl River Swamp, and the Waccamaw River—all were laid flat. Trees 15 feet in diameter at the base, which had stood for thousands of years, provided tens of billions of board feet to become the decking, pilings, trestles, fences, shingles, siding, and coffins of a burgeoning nation.

In their wake, even ambulatory species that could find no other refuge vanished forever, including the Bachman's warbler, the Carolina parakeet, and the "lord god bird" itself—the ivory-billed woodpecker.

Today, less than one-tenth of 1 percent of old-growth swamp remains—a mere 10,000 acres scattered across various states

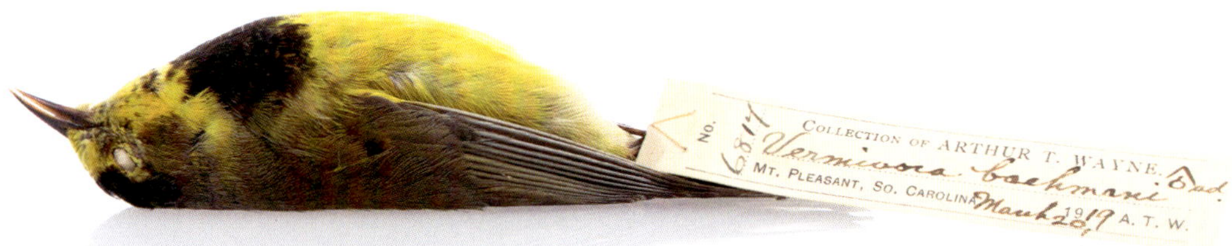

The Bachman's warbler was a specialist that nested in the canebrakes and edge ecosystems of cypress swamps.

and sanctuaries. These precious pockets of ancient trees, protected by thoughtful organizations and heroic individuals, weathered by hurricanes, floods, and fires, guarded by alligators, moccasins, panthers, and bears, and adorned with ferns and orchids, are our last glimpses of how the South once looked and functioned.

The geographical guardrails for this body of work were fairly specific. Loggers often left solitary trees behind—hollow, bent, or misshapen specimens known as "cull trees"—because they held no commercial value. Many are certainly old, but they stand alone. The artistic intent of this book was not to portray isolated relics, but to reveal a living, breathing forest. *Cypress* takes a deep dive into the functioning ecosystems of ancient swamps and bottomlands, where soils, understory, blackwater, and upland margins interact to form a web of life that is complex, unique, and enduring.

In a world where ecosystems have been so thoroughly compromised by human interference—their slow collapse masked by shifting baselines—there are vanishingly few places left where we can step back thousands of years without using our imagination. The old-growth swamps described in this book are not only national treasures but also vital touchstones to our natural heritage. It is in these primal wildernesses that we discover surprising and sacred rhythms of life, along with irreplaceable clues about our ecological past that can serve as blueprints to guide future conservation efforts.

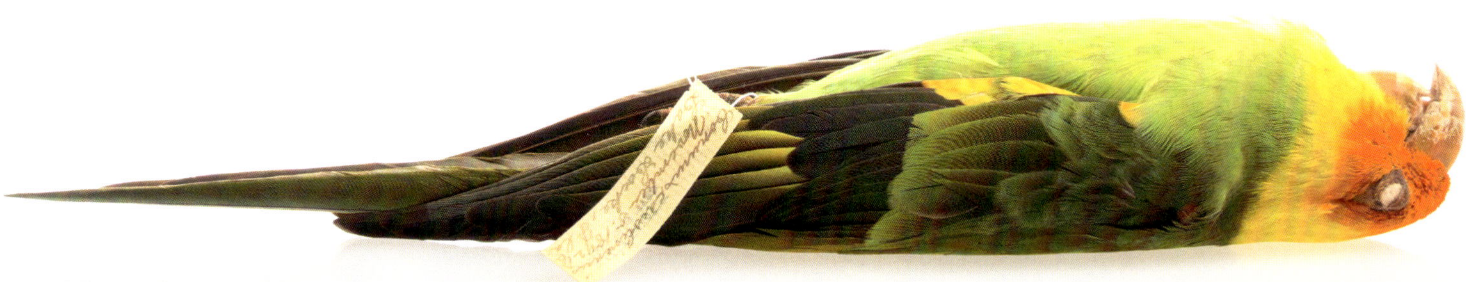

The only parrot native to the United States, the Carolina parakeet was last seen in Florida in 1904.

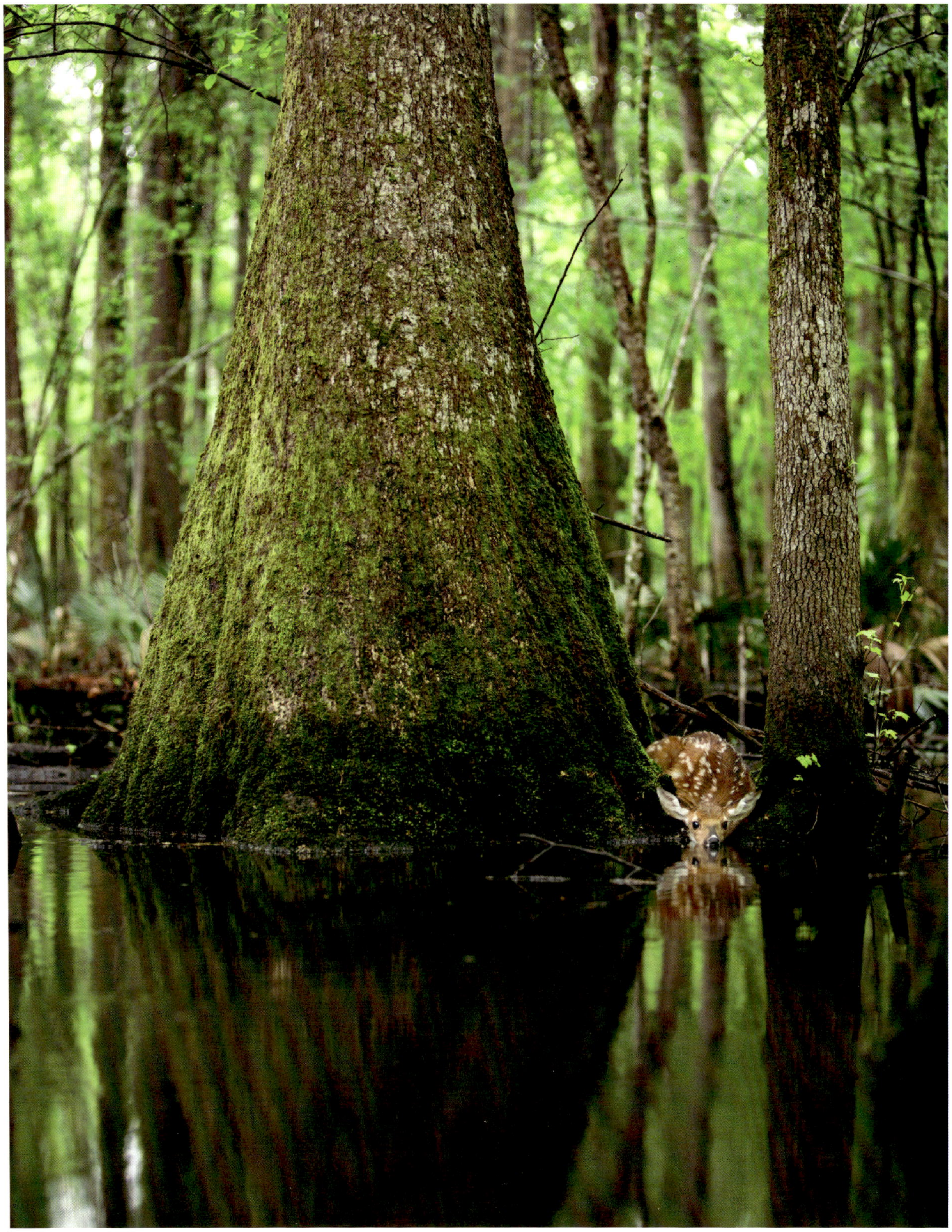

INTRODUCTION

My quaint idea of an afterlife has always been a kind of wormhole passenger train, one that transports my conscious soul to any place in time. As a chrononaut, I would witness the building of the pyramids, see the Mayan and Aztec empires at their zenith, and watch woolly mammoths and saber-toothed cats roam the United States. I'd marvel at the great bison herds of the plains, the elephant migrations of Amboseli, the Everglades during the Tequesta and Calusa civilizations, and the oceans before the hunt for whale oil. I would watch evolution unfold, unfettered, and glimpse the mysterious rise and fall of empires.

The more shadows I encounter of once-vibrant landscapes, the more I long to rewind the clock. After 24 years and without breaking these earthly chains, I finally found the time capsule I'd been longing for.

After college, I accepted a naturalist position at Audubon's Francis Beidler Forest in Harleyville, South Carolina. The 18,000-acre preserve protects 1,800 acres of old-growth cypress and tupelo gum in Four Holes Swamp. I had never seen a virgin swamp before, but my first day was revelatory.

The understory was open, giving way to fields of knobby knees and elephant-footed trunks of 1,000-year-old cypress. Their crowns spread overhead and vanished into the shade of maple and tupelo. Tea-colored water meandered around palmetto islands, carrying a rainbow sheen of pollen. Snakes coiled on fallen limbs, otters scavenged for crayfish, and brilliant prothonotary warblers skittered through the branches, foraging for caterpillars and spiders. Even the poison ivy—climbing the tall knees and, finding no other purchase, umbrellaing out in a canopy of greens and reds—was awe-inspiring. In all my years exploring southern swamps, I had never encountered anything like this. I had found Eden.

While I lived there, I recruited other believers. I brought dozens of acolytes to the swamp: my parents, my brothers, my high school teacher and their students, my oldest friends, my newest friends, their friends, even strangers who blindly followed me to what I proclaimed was a southern Mecca. My girlfriend—who, by no coincidence at all, would later become my wife—came too. I shepherded them through the braided sloughs, marveling at the massive trees, counting snakes, and confronting fishing spiders the size of my hand. It was a seminal time. A seed took root that would grow into a years-long obsession.

Whenever anyone mentioned forests near me, I'd find my way into the conversation and commence my sermon on the one true swamp: Beidler Forest. And then I visited Audubon's Corkscrew Swamp in South Florida—and my tent grew a little larger.

Corkscrew became my second home for several years. Where Beidler's understory was clear, the western Everglades were riotous with growth. Even where there was no soil, ferns, tillandsia, and orchids created their own, clinging to the smallest fissures in bark and bough. Wildlife was abundant—frogs, owls, lizards, wading birds, otters, and snakes.

In the backcountry, among pond cypress sloughs, wet prairies, and oak hammocks, I scattered camera traps—DSLRs paired with speedlights, tripped by infrared beams—to document larger animals: bears, panthers, bobcats. I'd leave the setups for months, usually in vain. My success rate hovered around 5 percent. Bears chewed up cameras, mice gnawed through cables, ants built nests inside my housings, strobes misfired, and floodwaters claimed entire kits. I lost six cameras to the swamp. But when everything worked, checking those memory cards felt like being seven years old again on Christmas morning.

The true revelation came when I looked up. Hurricane Irma had just torn through western Florida as a Category 4 storm, snapping giant cypress trees like matchsticks and scattering their crowns across the forest floor. As in the Amazon, much of a subtropical forest's biodiversity lives in the canopy—and now it lay at eye level: hundreds of orchids and massive epiphytes, suddenly within reach.

I knew I had to get higher. Lacking my own climbing gear, I called a local arborist with a wild proposition: rent me your rig, and I'll hold you harmless. Roped up and safety-spotted by an Audubon intern, I ascended a cypress where a "super ghost" orchid bloomed 50 feet up the trunk.

When I reached it, my heart was pounding and the golden hour was fading. Dangling from a rope, I strained to compose a shot with the orchid backlit by the rising sun. I held my breath, contorted around branches, and stared through the wide-angle lens. All the while, the tree swayed in the breeze. Then, sweat turned cold. Nausea overtook me. Barely able to speak, I warned my assistant—"MOVE!"—before I vomited onto the swamp below. It was his first and last time assisting me. But I had found my next obsession: a new way to explore and adore these sacred giants. The following summer, with a camera rigged high in the canopy and aimed at the ghost orchid, fellow National Geographic Explorers Peter Houlihan, Carlton Ward Jr., and I made a discovery that would upend generations of scientific conjecture about the orchid and its mysterious pollinator.

Unbeknownst to me, the summer before, in a little-known stand of ancient cypress along the Black River in North Carolina, Dr. Dave Stahle was making his own groundbreaking discovery. Climbing a ladder to take a core sample from his last tree in the transect with his swamp compadre, Charles Robbins, he would change everything we thought we knew about how long these trees can live. The core revealed the tree, famously known as BLK227, to be 2,624 years old at the time, making it the fifth-oldest tree species on Earth and one of only two known trees east of the Rockies to have surpassed 2,000 years.

The following summer, during the height of the COVID-19 pandemic, Congaree National Park—home to the largest remaining virgin bottomland hardwood forest in the United States—shut its gates in its busiest month. Only the park staff, two scientists from the University of Colorado Boulder, and I were permitted inside the 26,000-acre forest. The scientists, Julie Hayes and Rafael Sarfarti, were studying how *Photuris frontalis* fireflies synchronize their flashes across hundreds of individuals and seemingly impossible distances. Every night with them felt like a dream: fulfilling a childhood fantasy of catching fireflies, professionally. While markets plummeted, hospitals overflowed, protests filled the streets, and the world shut down around us, we stood in a timeless swamp immersed in the ancient, silent rhythm of thousands of pulsing synchronous orbs.

It's in these old forests that we find new wisdom. E. O. Wilson said it best: "A lifetime can be spent in a Magellanic voyage around the trunk of a single tree." As someone who spent two summers consumed by a single square foot occupied by an orchid, I can vouch for this. The following pages are the fruits of that pursuit and I hope they are enough to entice the reader to visit these hallowed grounds.

Seeing these places is believing. They are sacrosanct and singular in their aura and energy. Every visit fills me with gratitude and a profound sense of connection to the real world. Corkscrew Swamp, Beidler Forest, Congaree, and the Black River have given me a deep reservoir of memory and inspiration. While these sanctuaries preserve a vital part of our past, they've also unlocked in me a vast well of hope for the future. Just a few hundred years after I'm gone—a mere wink of time for a bald cypress—the forests we protect today will become the old growth of tomorrow.

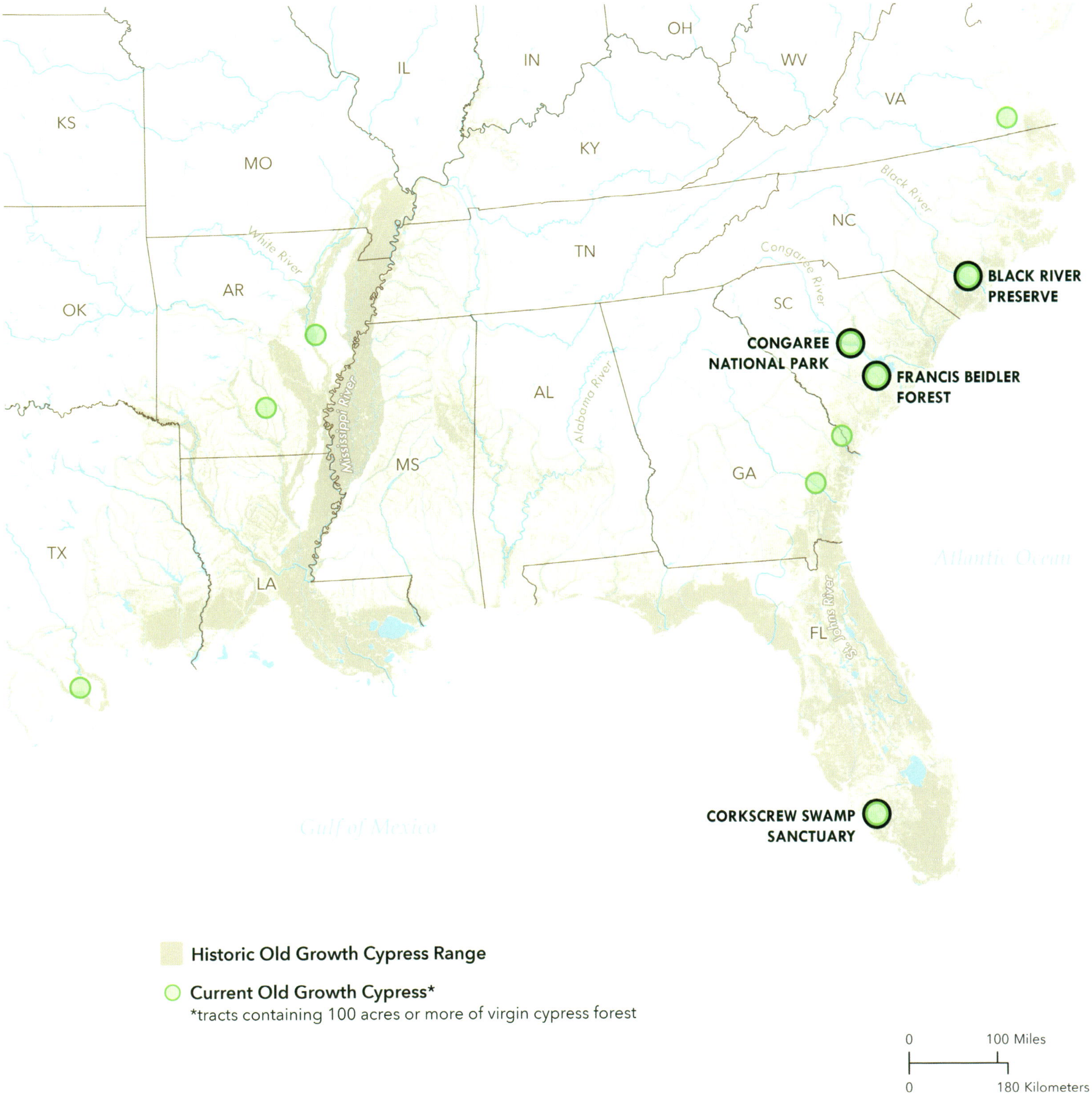
KS
MO
IL
IN
OH
WV
VA
KY
OK
AR
TN
NC
SC
TX
LA
MS
AL
GA
FL
White River
Mississippi River
Alabama River
Congaree River
Black River
St. Johns River
BLACK RIVER PRESERVE
CONGAREE NATIONAL PARK
FRANCIS BEIDLER FOREST
CORKSCREW SWAMP SANCTUARY
Atlantic Ocean
Gulf of Mexico
Historic Old Growth Cypress Range
Current Old Growth Cypress*
*tracts containing 100 acres or more of virgin cypress forest
0
100 Miles
0
180 Kilometers

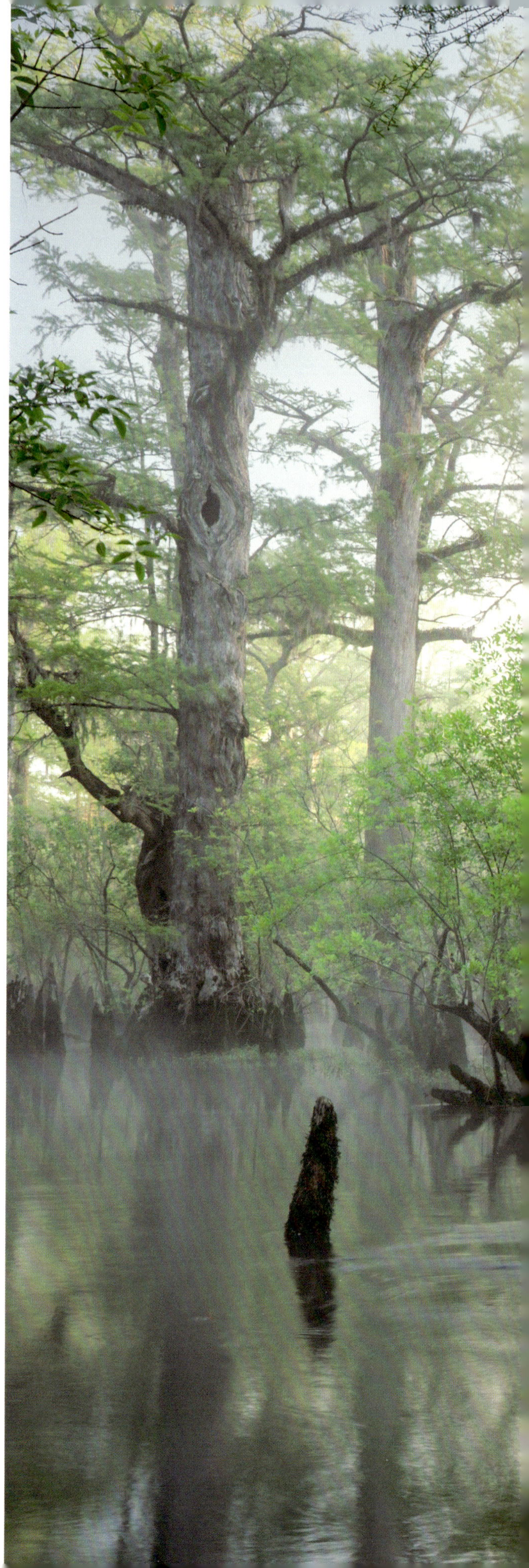

Though many ancient cypress trees are hollow and their true age unknowable, their living outer bark can thrive for thousands of years.

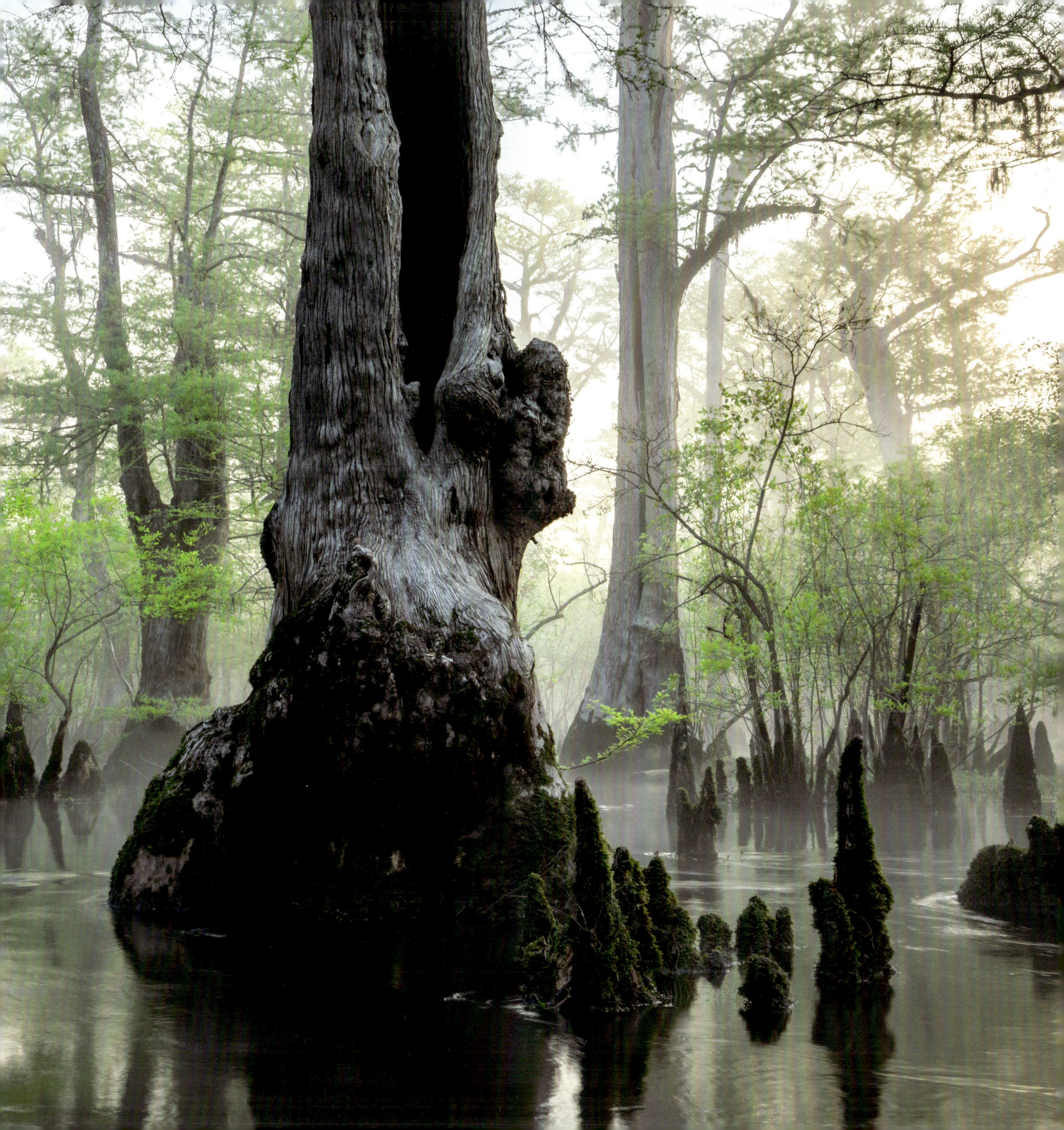

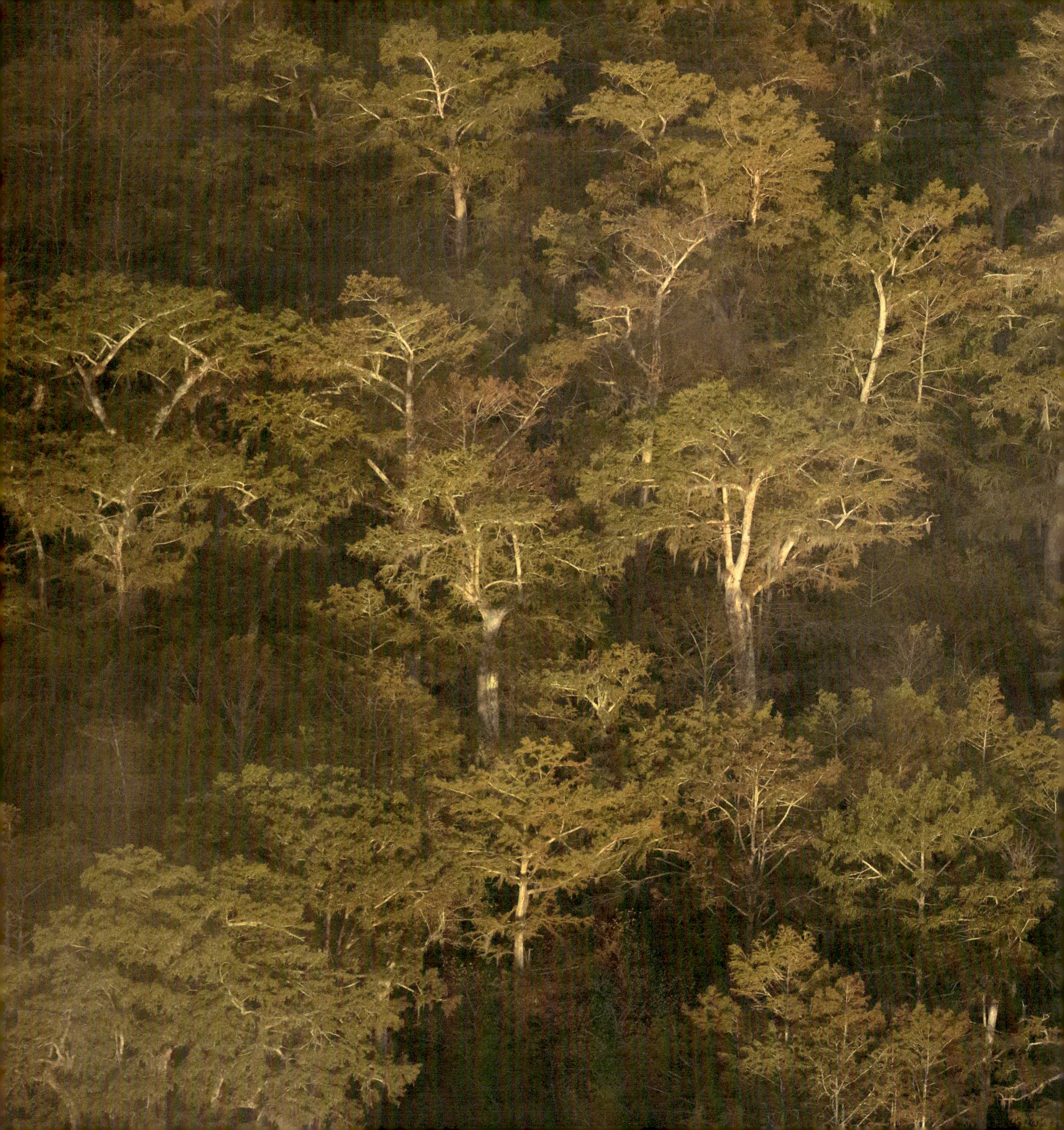

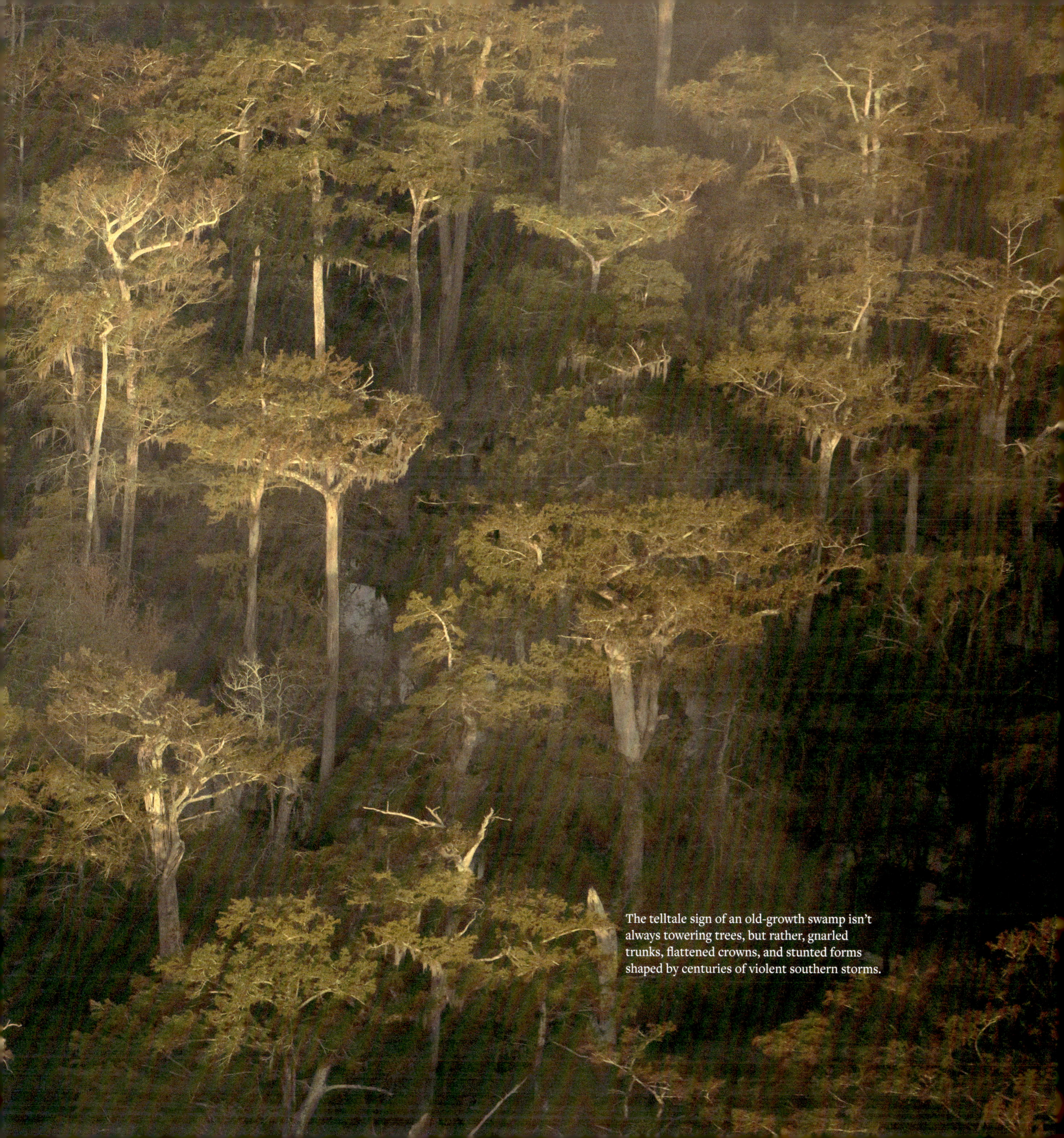

The telltale sign of an old-growth swamp isn't always towering trees, but rather, gnarled trunks, flattened crowns, and stunted forms shaped by centuries of violent southern storms.

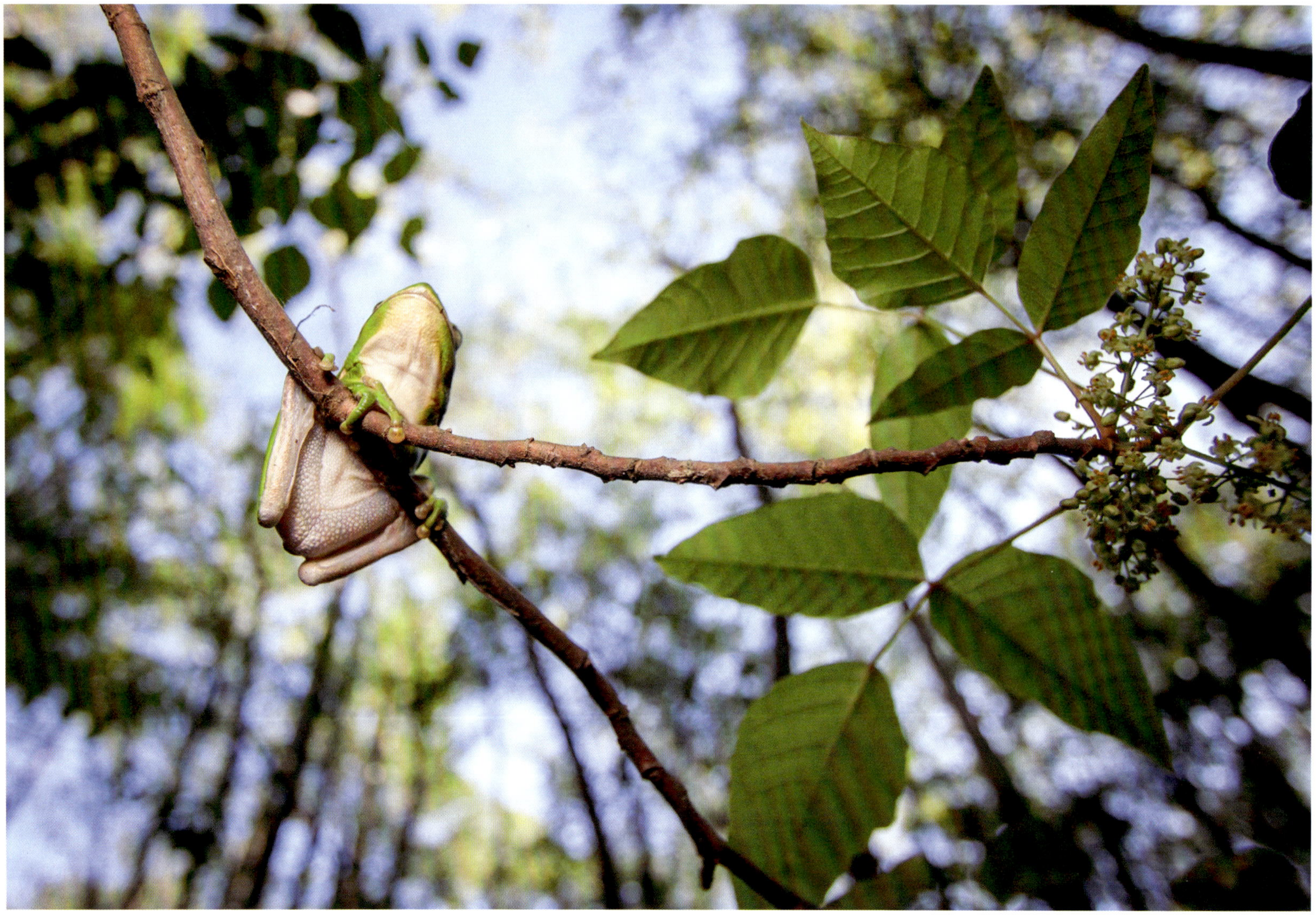

Green tree frogs often perch next to flowering plants,
even poison ivy, to ambush potential pollinators.

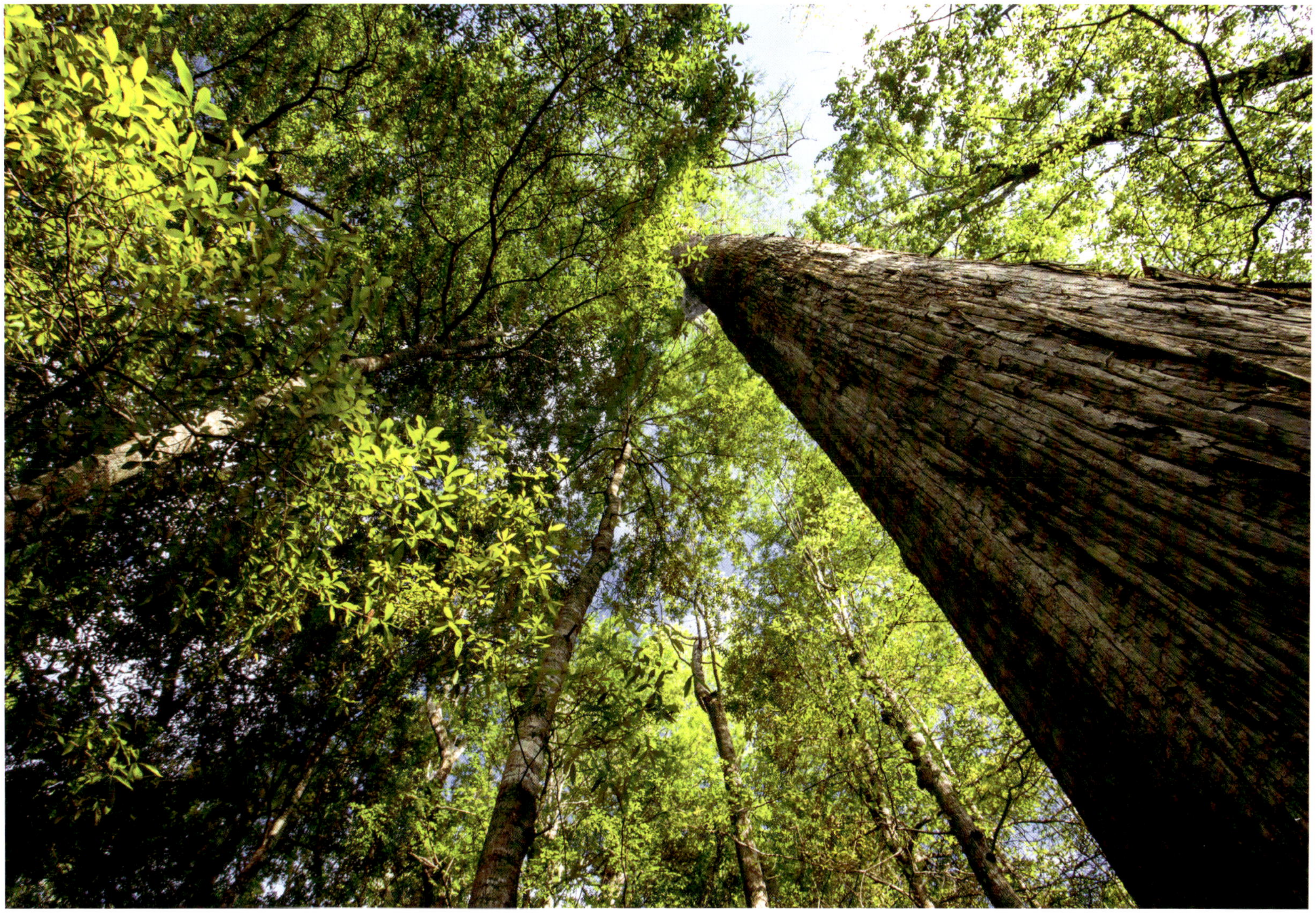

Valued for its natural weatherproofing and remarkably long, knotless trunks, cypress provided ideal lumber because it often grows 60 feet before branching.

Anaerobic microbes consume organic debris beneath the surface, releasing gases and oils that spread to form shimmering, moonlike sheens.

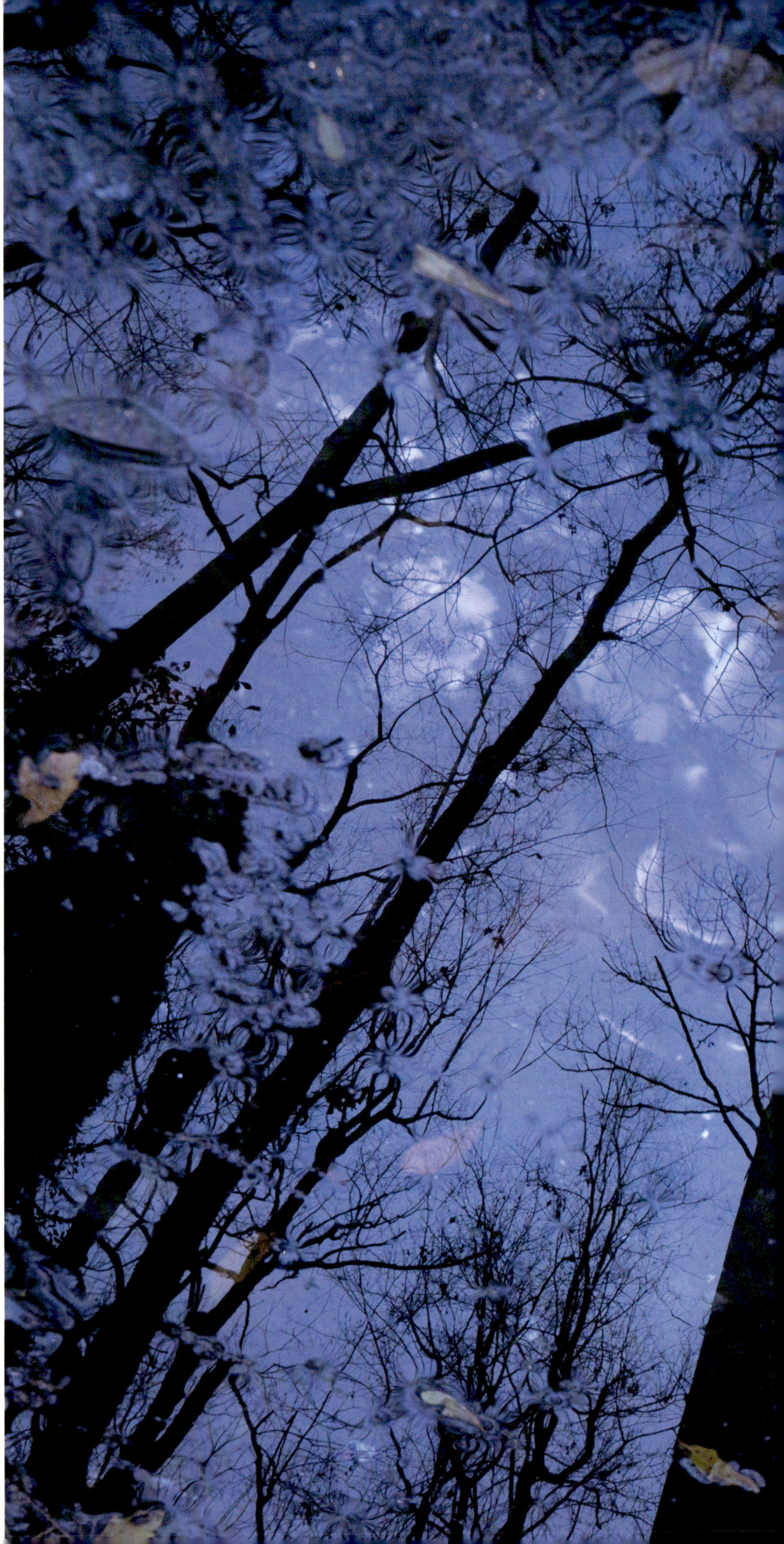

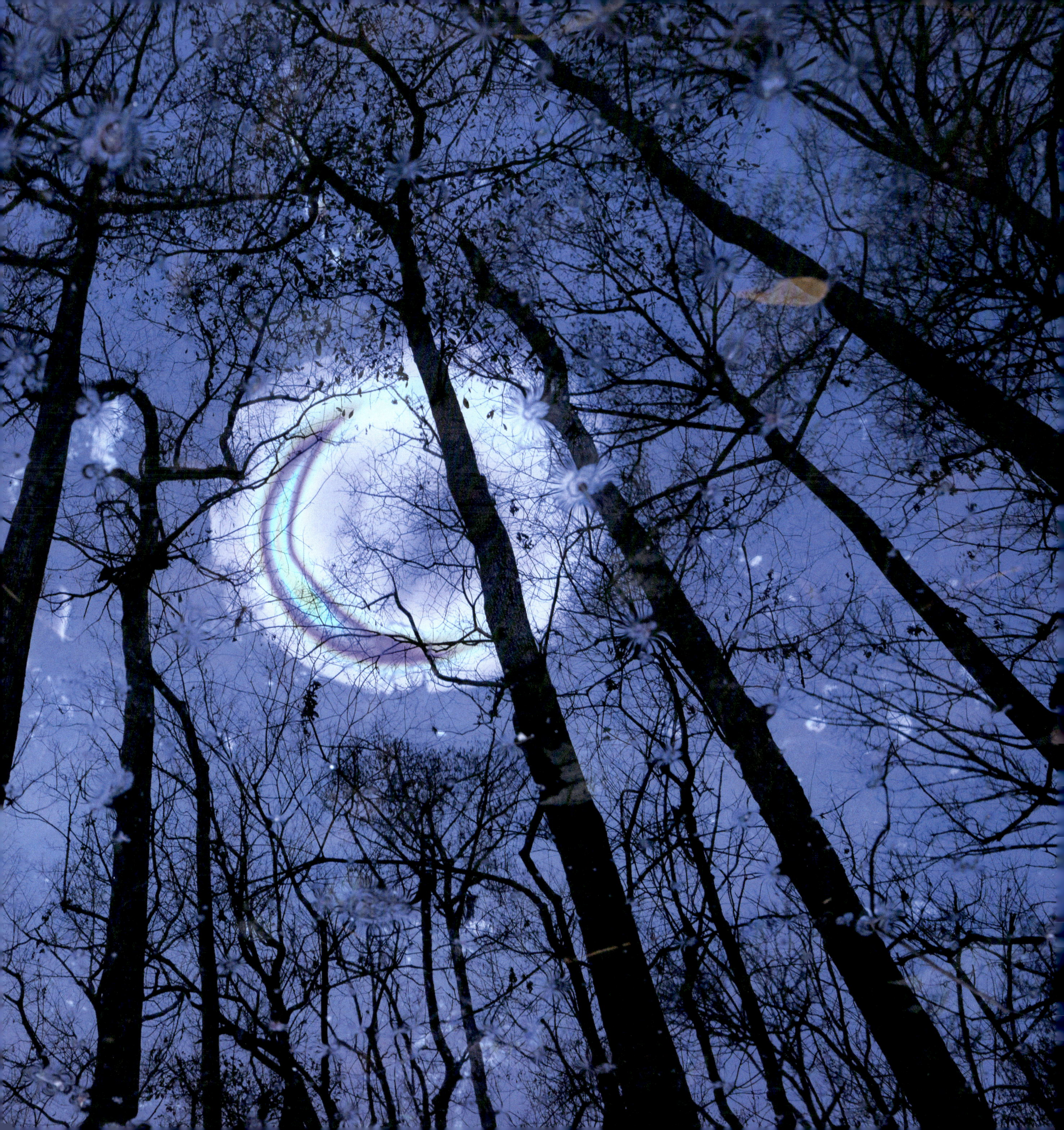

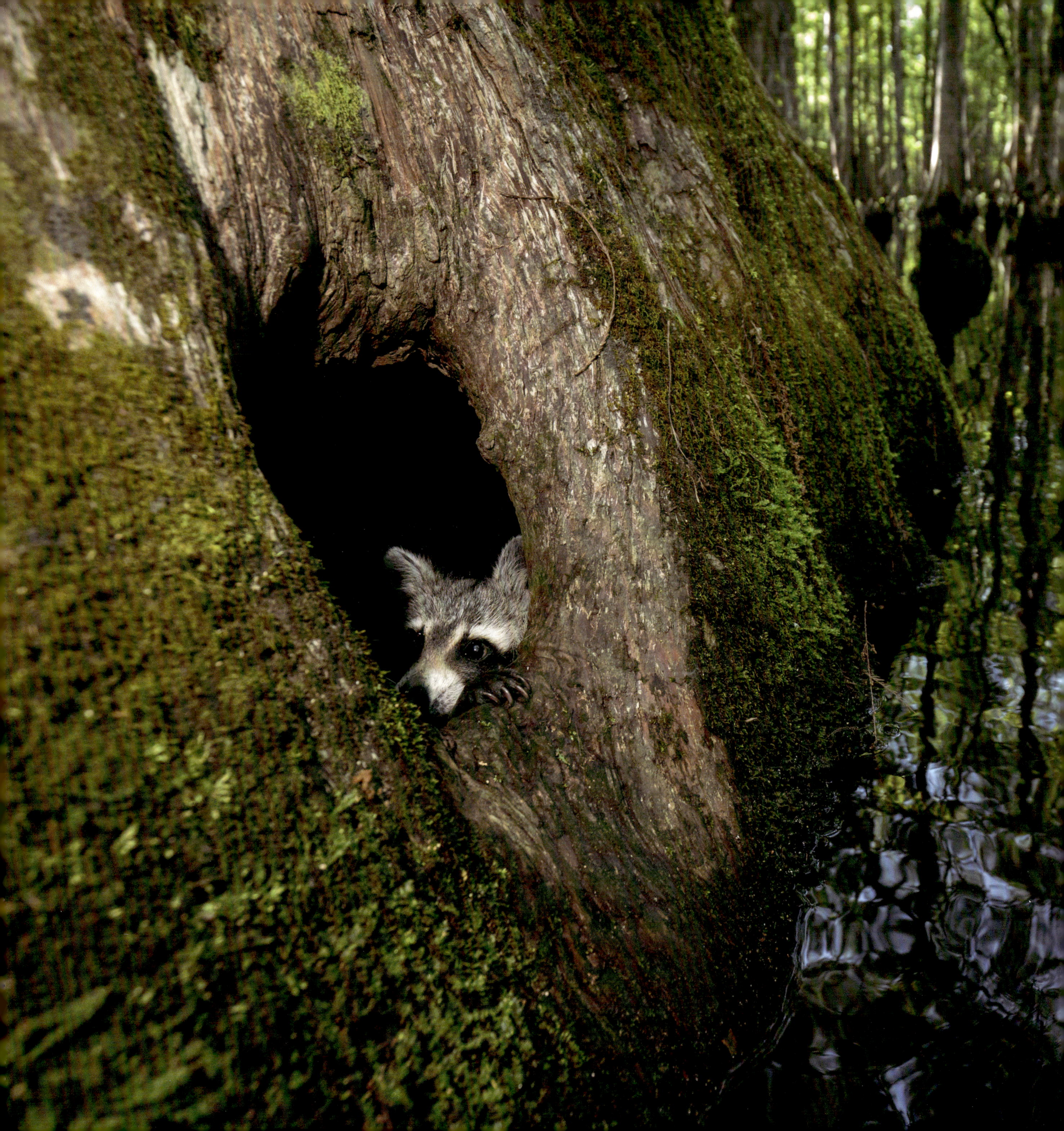

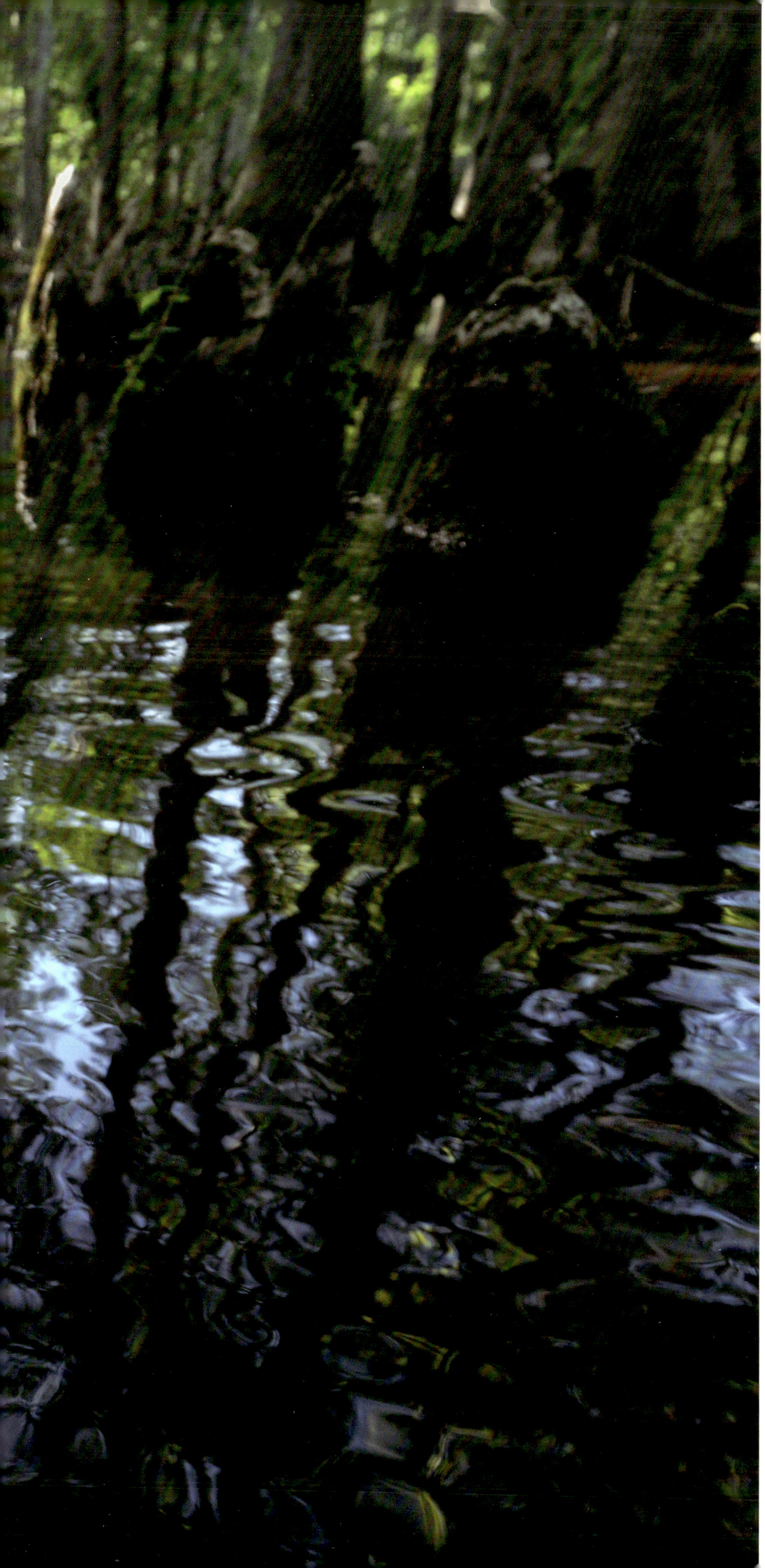

Hollow trees offer important refuge for myriad species including raccoons, otters, bats, and birds.

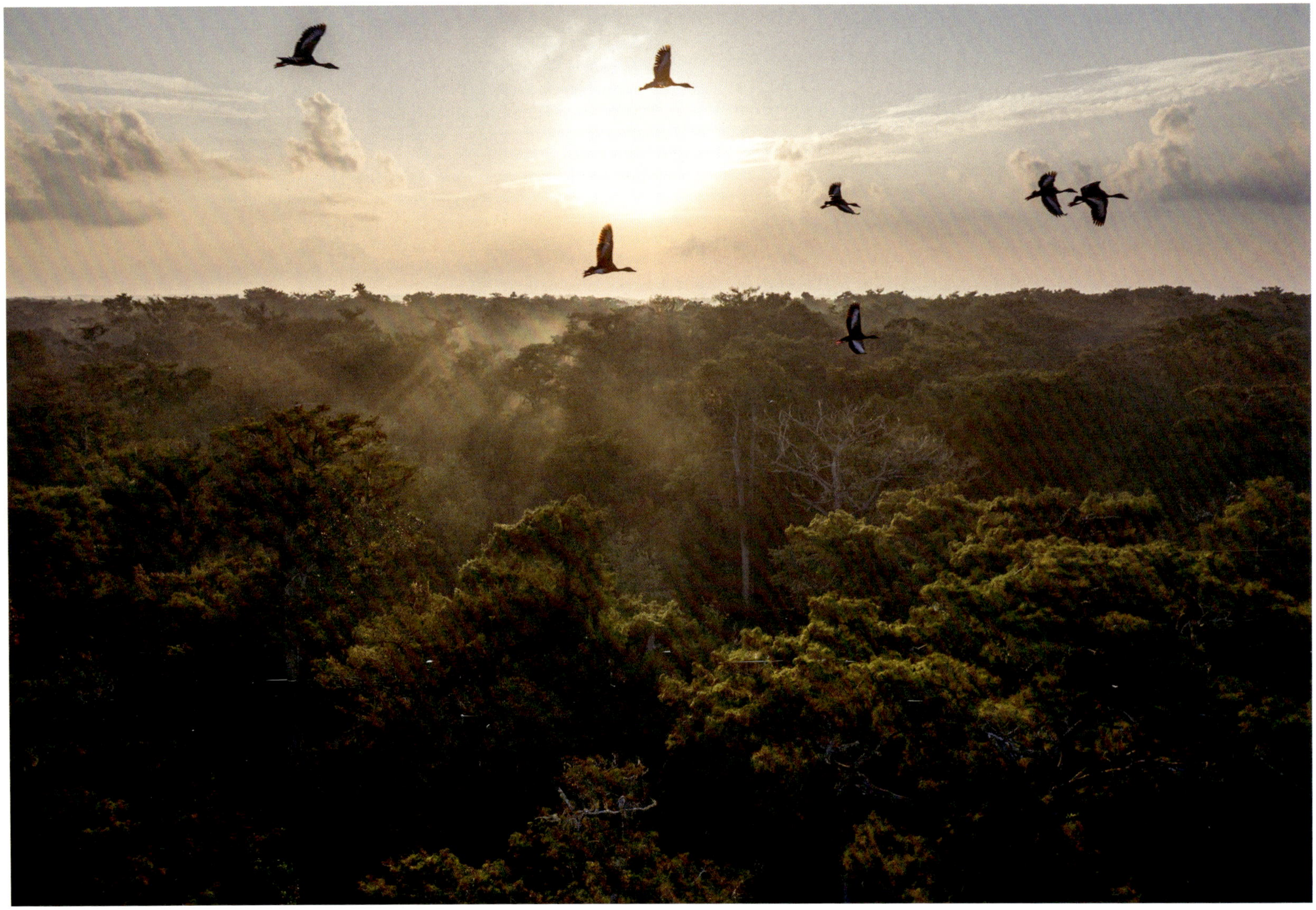

Once limited to Central America and southern Texas, black-bellied whistling ducks have dramatically expanded their range over the past century, now breeding as far north as the Carolinas and even the Midwest.

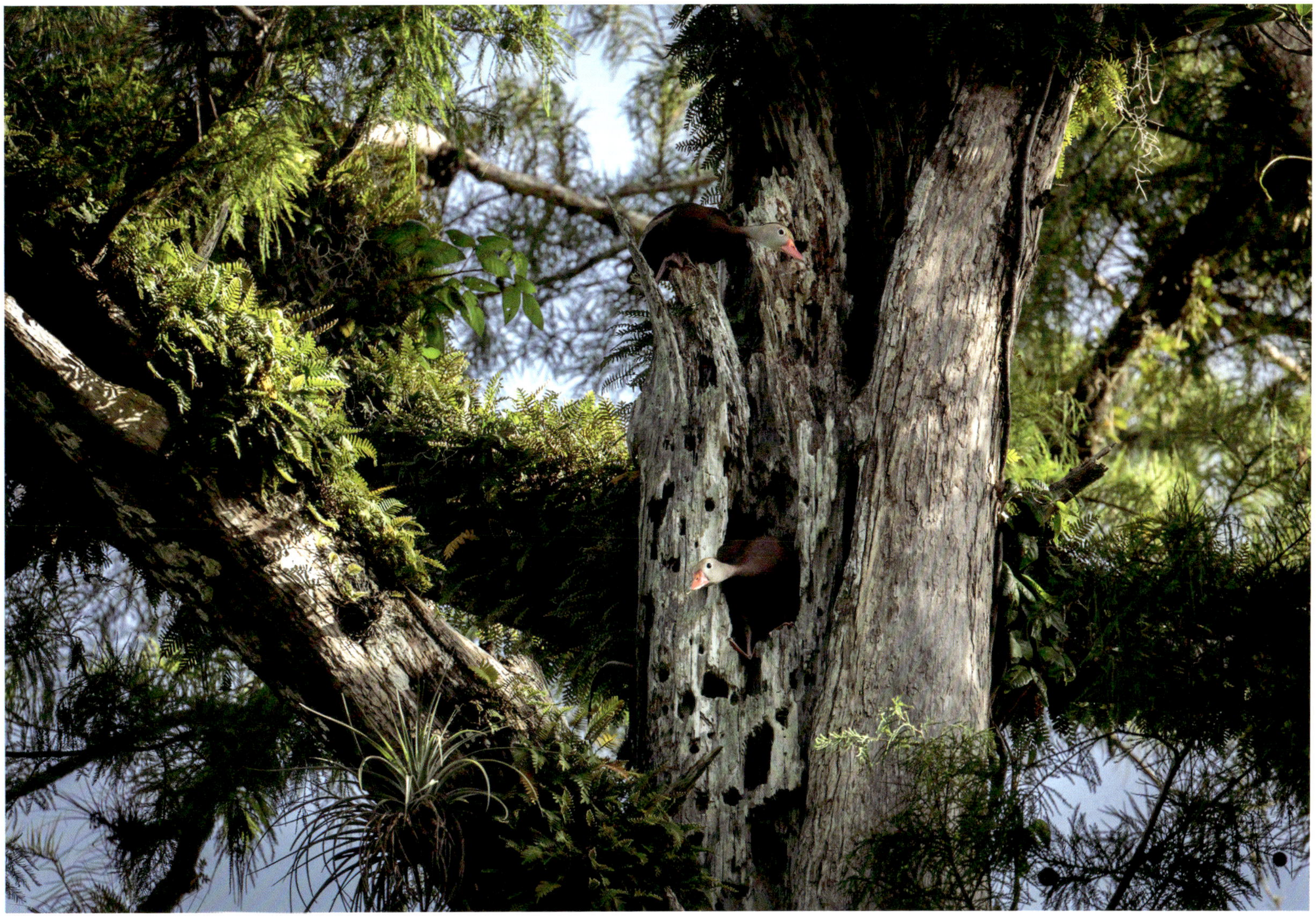

Today, whistling ducks occupy the nesting cavities of ancient cypress trees—spaces that may once have sheltered ivory-billed woodpeckers and Carolina parakeets.

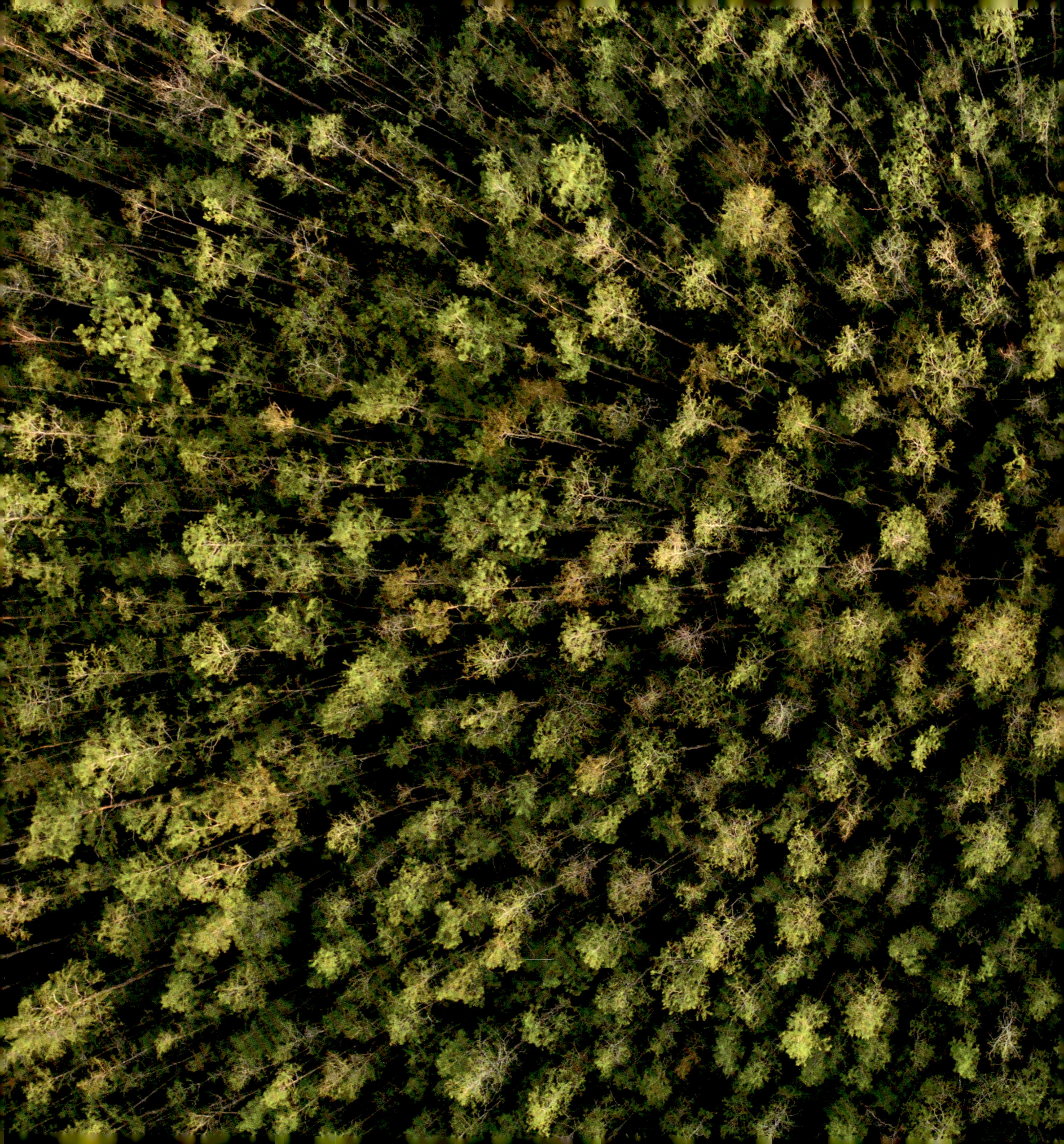

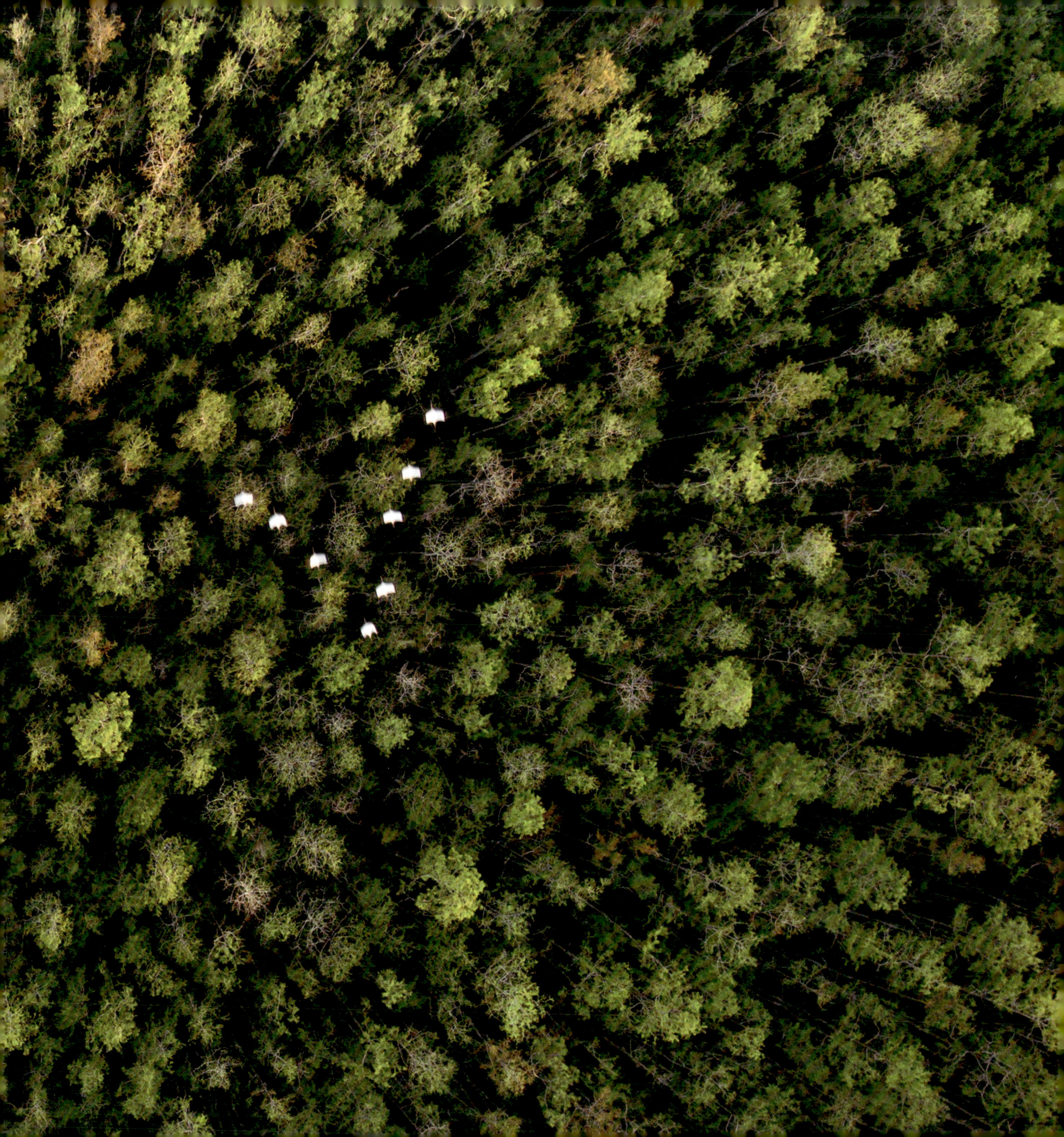

Corkscrew Swamp was home to the world's largest wood stork nesting colony from the 1940s to the 1970s, making it a vital stronghold for the species' survival.

PREVIOUS PAGE

Cypress swamps are important flyways and nesting grounds for wading birds like white ibis who benefit from patrolling alligators who help limit potential predators.

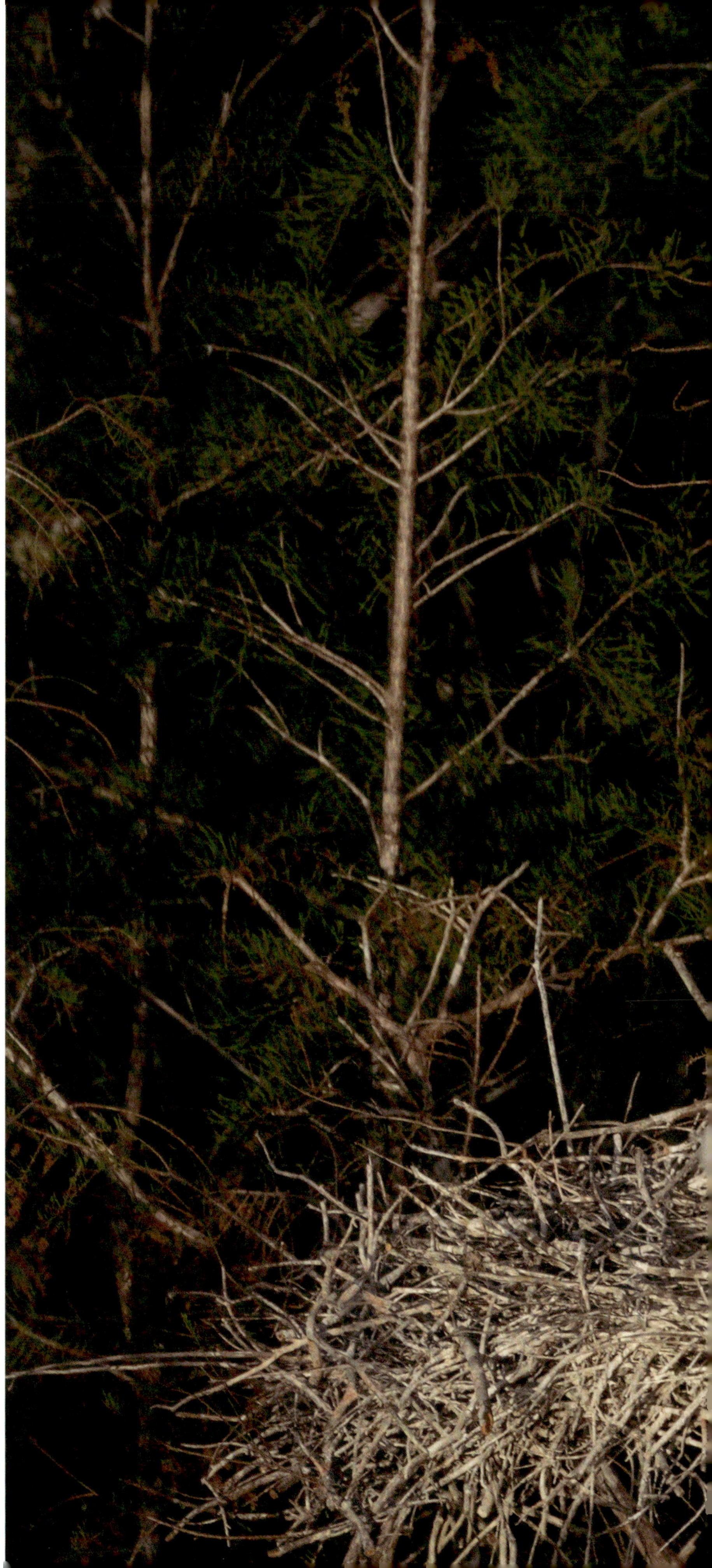

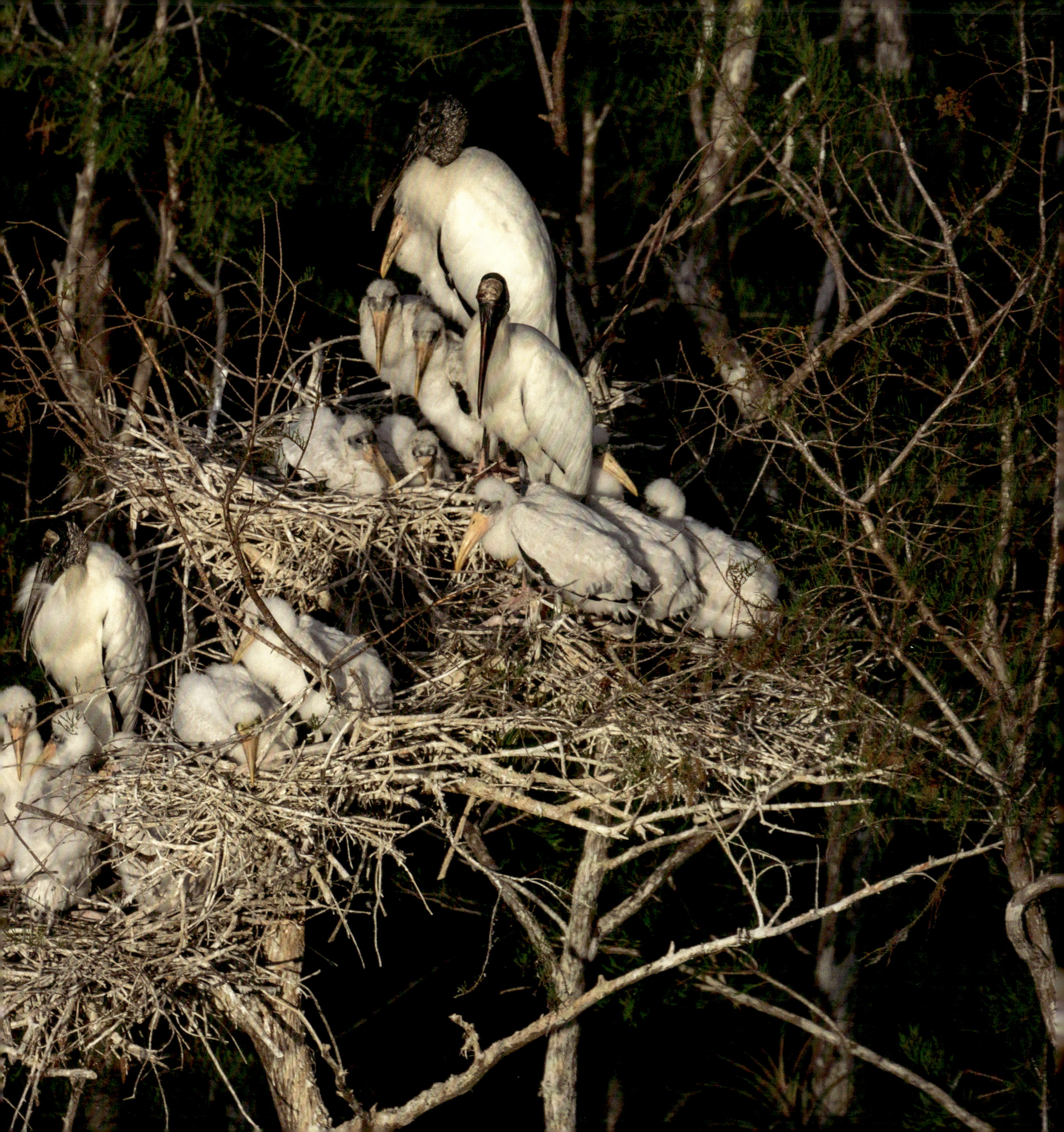

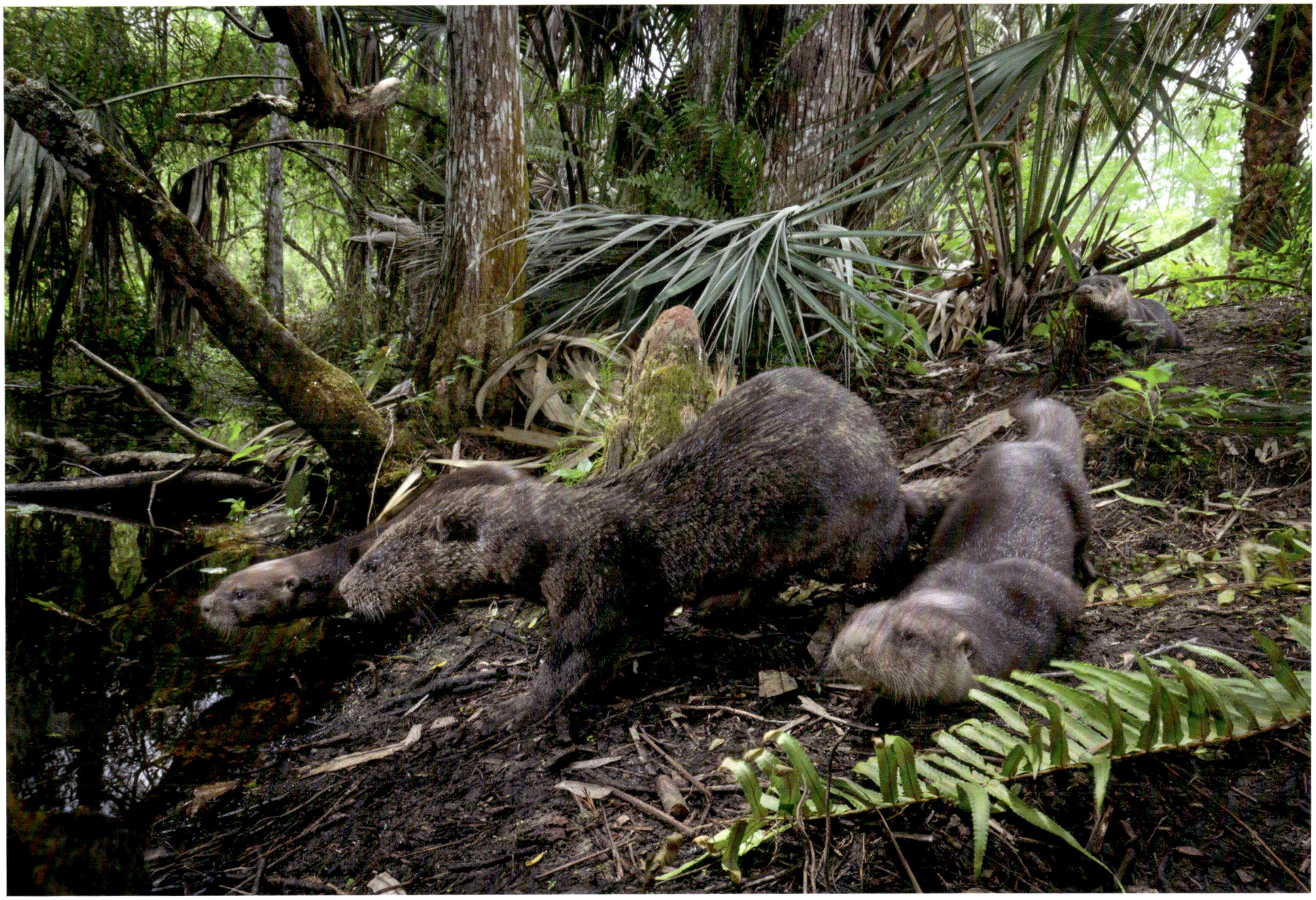

In the height of the nineteenth-century fur trade, swamps became a last refuge for river otters, offering a lifeline from near-extinction.

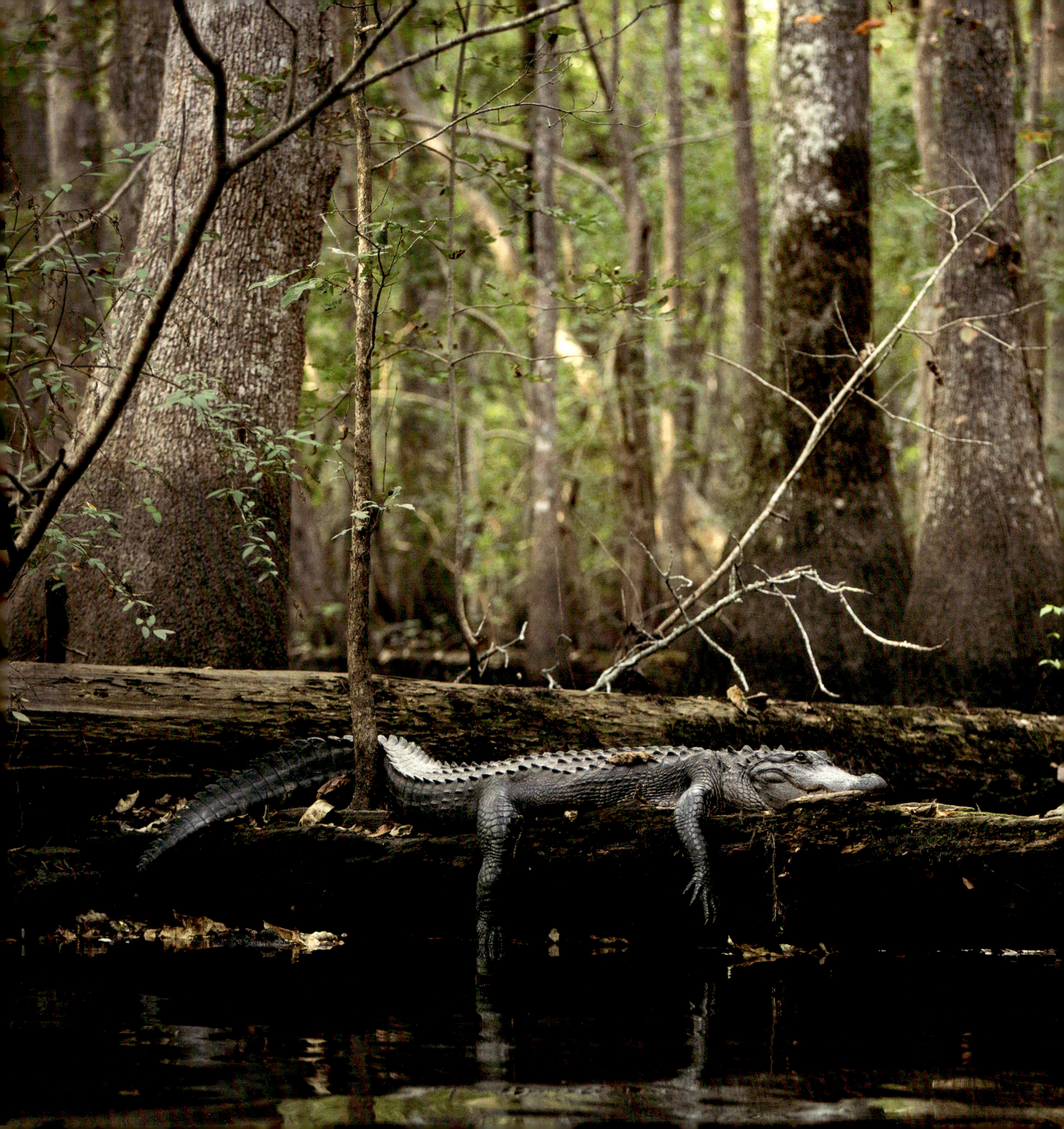

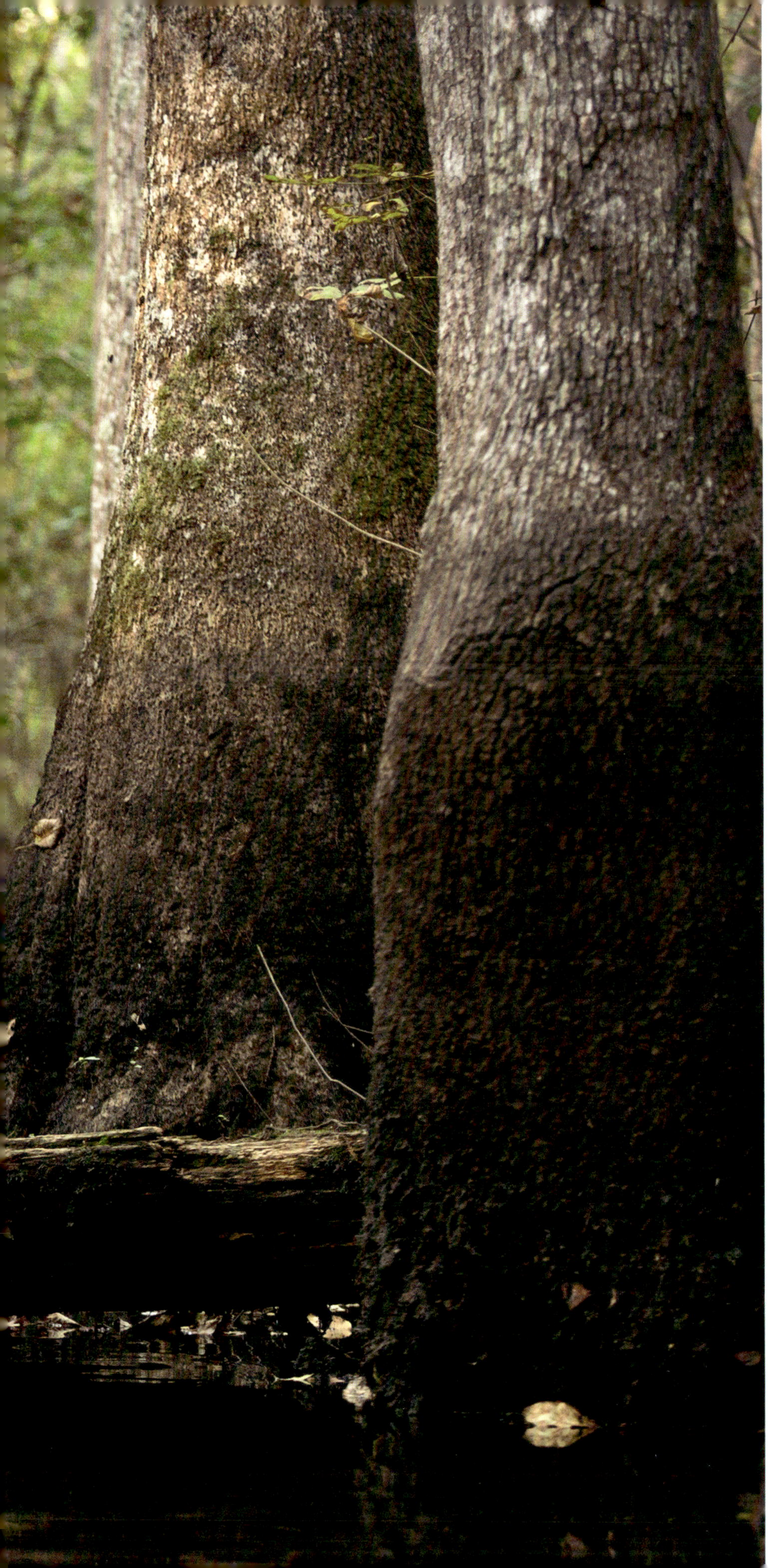

Canopy breaks along wide streams and lakes allow sunlight to reach basking ectotherms like alligators and turtles.

FOLLOWING PAGE

Darkened bands of moss often trace the swamp's high-water line, soaking up moisture like sponges when rivers and sloughs overflow.

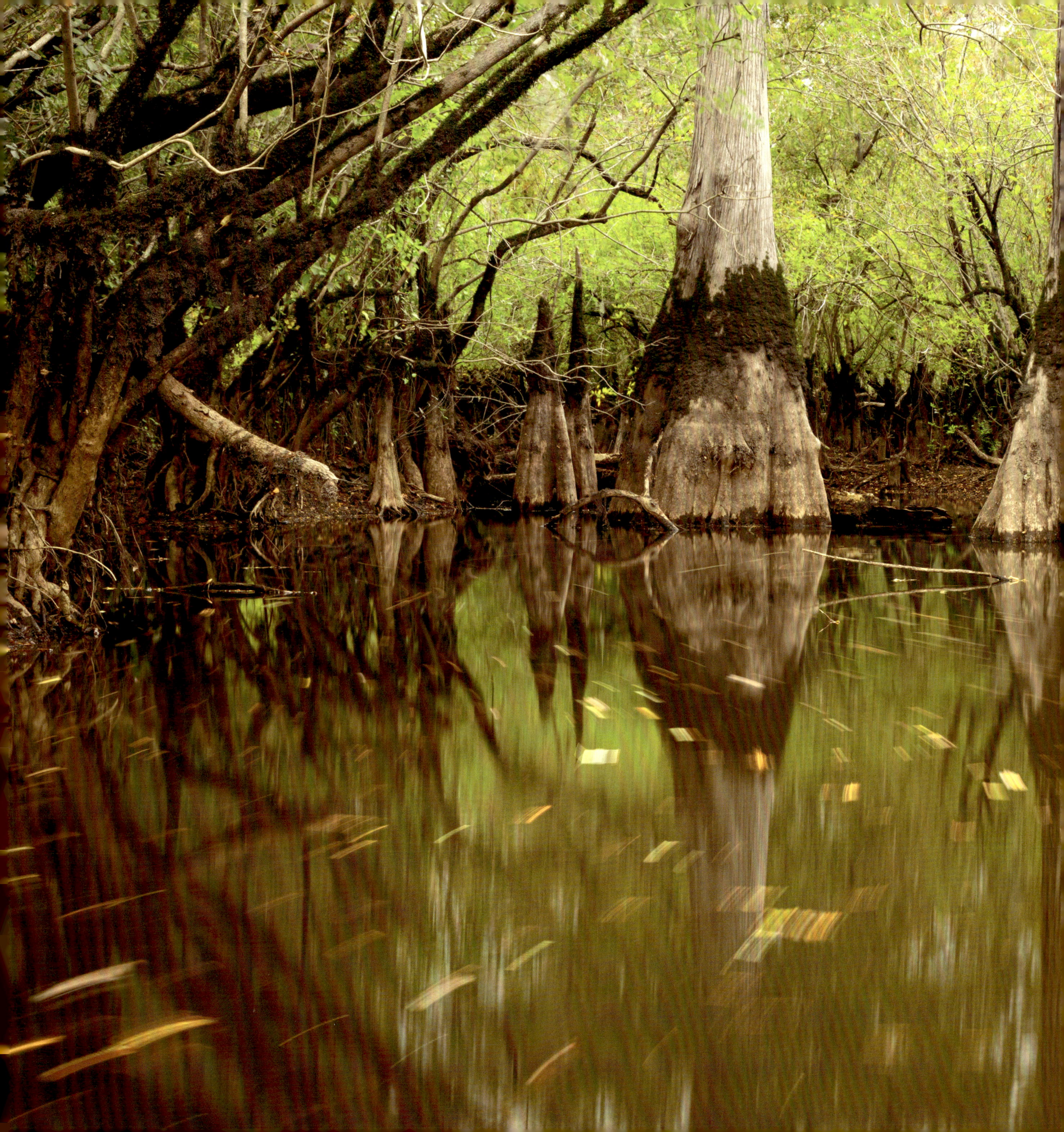

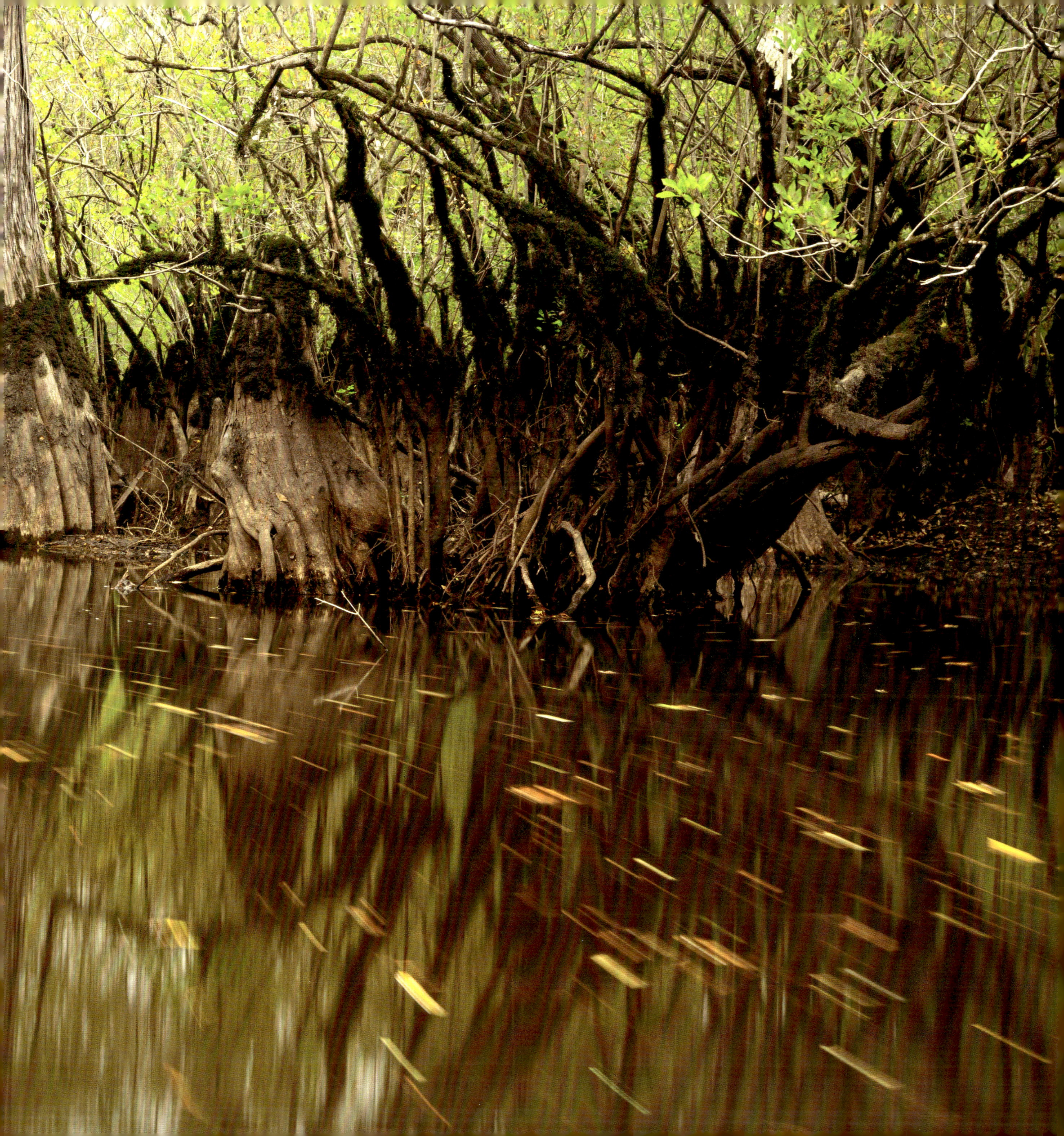

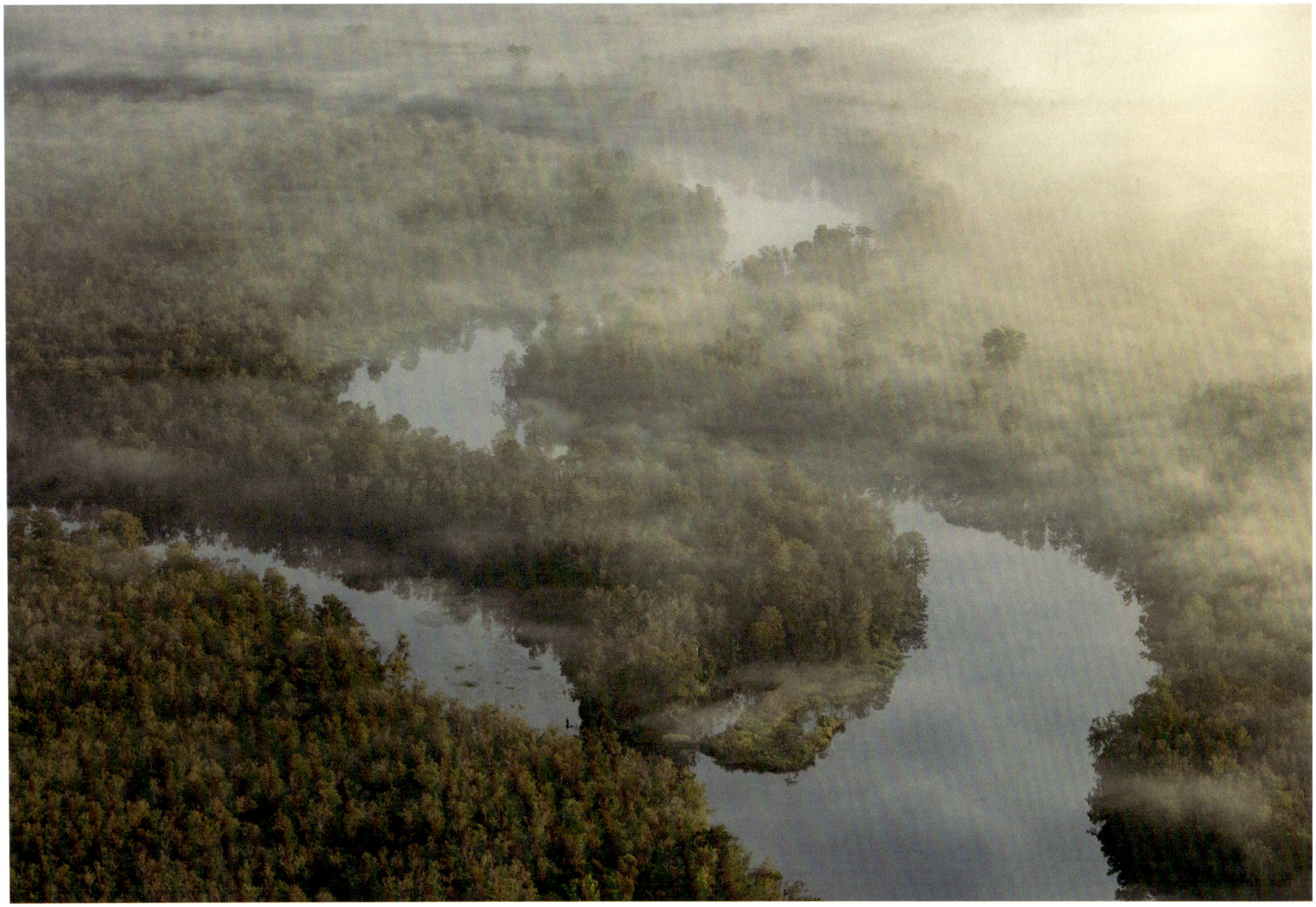

For 66 miles, North Carolina's Black River winds past the oldest trees in eastern North America before merging with the Cape Fear River.

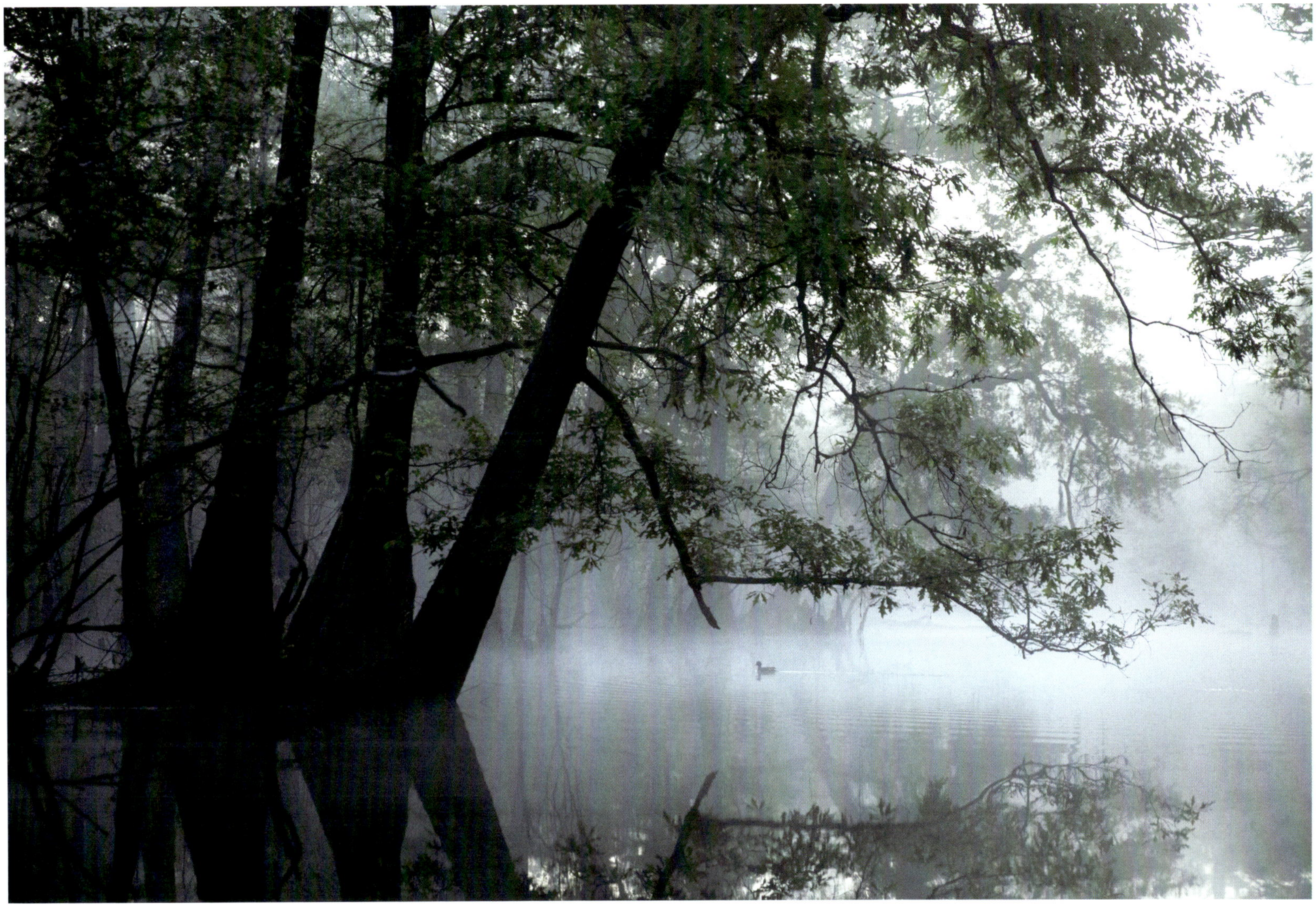

Named for their woodland haunts, wood ducks are uniquely adapted to nest in tree cavities, sometimes dozens of feet above the swamp.

FOLLOWING PAGE

As drought shrinks the swamp, a flathead catfish faces an impossible choice: abandon the eggs it guards beneath its tail—or stay and risk death to protect them.

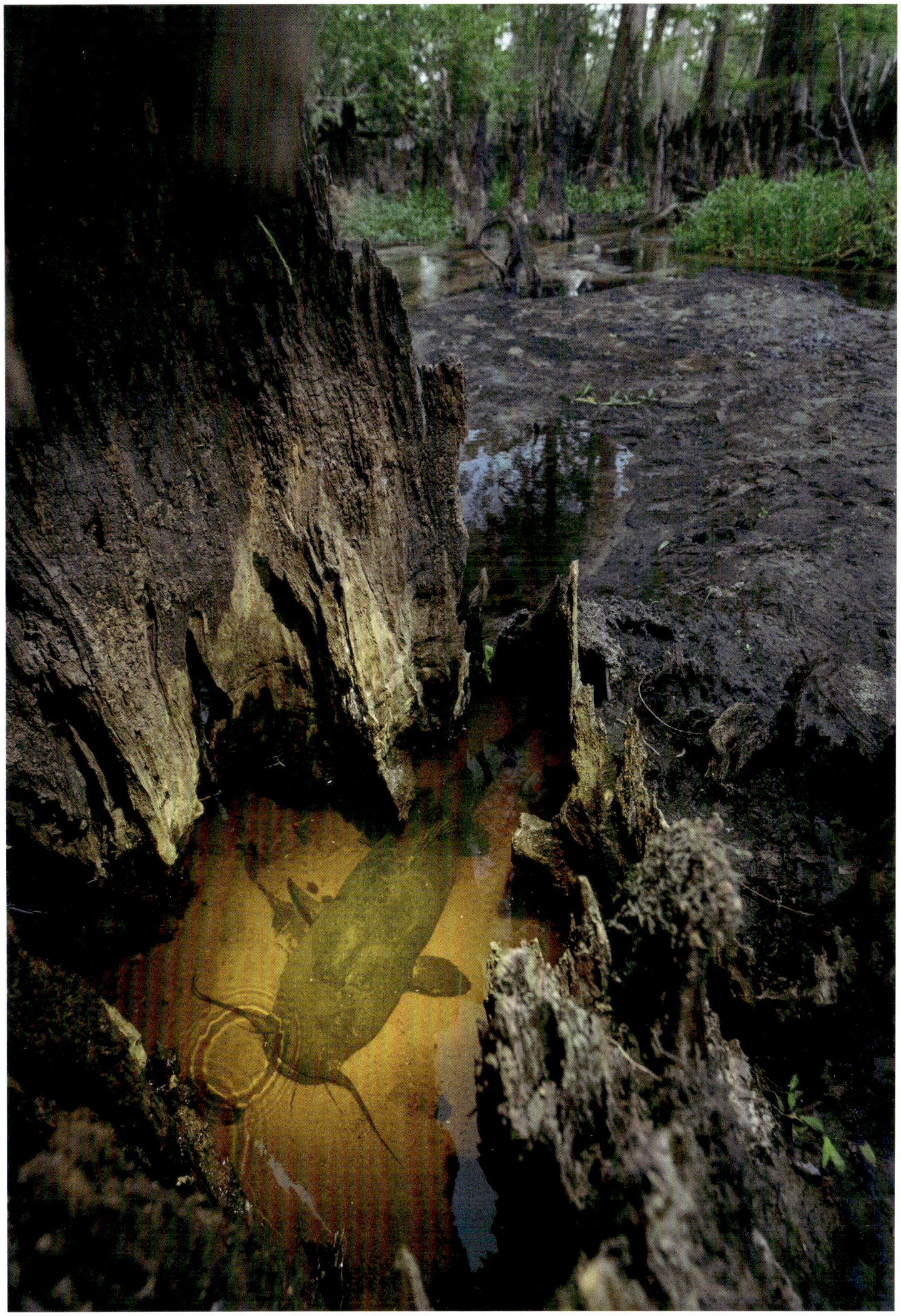

OLD MAN *of the* WATER

DAVE STAHLE

I have studied ancient bald cypress forests for half a century now. We have developed tree-ring chronologies at 50 old-growth bald cypress forests, taking small core samples from hundreds of trees, including some at Black River, Francis Beidler Forest in Four Holes Swamp, Congaree, and Corkscrew Swamp. Bald cypress wetland forests like these have become exceptionally rare, and they include trees that are astonishingly old. Using dendrochronology (tree-ring dating) we have documented bald cypress more than 1,000 years old at Four Holes Swamp and one ancient cypress that is currently 2,632 years old at Black River. Very few trees live to this age.

For some context, there are 64,088 taxonomically described tree species on Earth.[1] An estimated 10,000 more have yet to be discovered by science. Only 22 species include individual trees that have been proven with dendrochronology to have lived for more than 1,000 years.[2] Just nine species have been proven capable of reaching two millennia in age. Most 2,000-year-old trees are bristlecone pines in high-elevation forests of the Great Basin. These bristlecones likely number in the hundreds. A much smaller number of 2,000-year-old trees are giant sequoias in California.

There are roughly three trillion trees on the planet.[3] If we do not count bristlecone or sequoia, there may be fewer than 100 individual trees that are at least 2,000 years old among the other seven longest-lived tree species in the world. For bald cypress there are only two. Both are in the Three Sisters area at Black River, North Carolina, and they are the oldest-known trees in the three billion acres that comprise eastern North America. So, 2,000-year-old trees are incredibly rare.

There are likely a few more 2,000-year-old bald cypress at Black River, probably even a couple that are more than 3,000 years old. Unfortunately, many ancient bald cypress are partly hollow, so we cannot know their true age. But the exact age of these ancient trees is honestly not important, because 1,000-year-old trees are remarkable anywhere they exist, especially in the long-settled landscapes of the Southeast.

Bald cypress are phylogenetically related to the sequoias, so it is not surprising that they grow large and very old. What *is* surprising, however, is the climate response of these swamp-grown trees. Remarkably, bald cypress ring-width chronologies are positively correlated with rainfall during the spring and early summer growing season, despite living in frequently flooded wetland forests. In other words, the more it rains, the better they grow and the wider the ring. We observe a similar precipitation signal in trees growing on dry upland sites like pines and oaks in the Carolinas, or conifer species in the arid American West.

Without harming the living trees, we take pencil-thin core samples to build "proxy" ring-width chronologies that represent precipitation changes over the centuries. In doing so, we can identify major drought episodes of the past, including

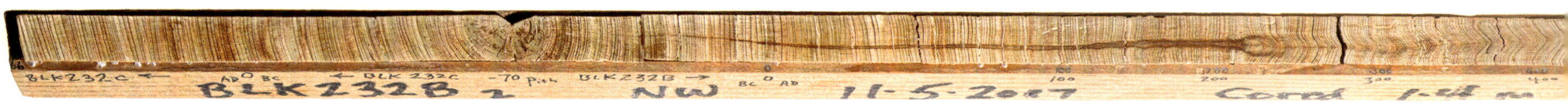

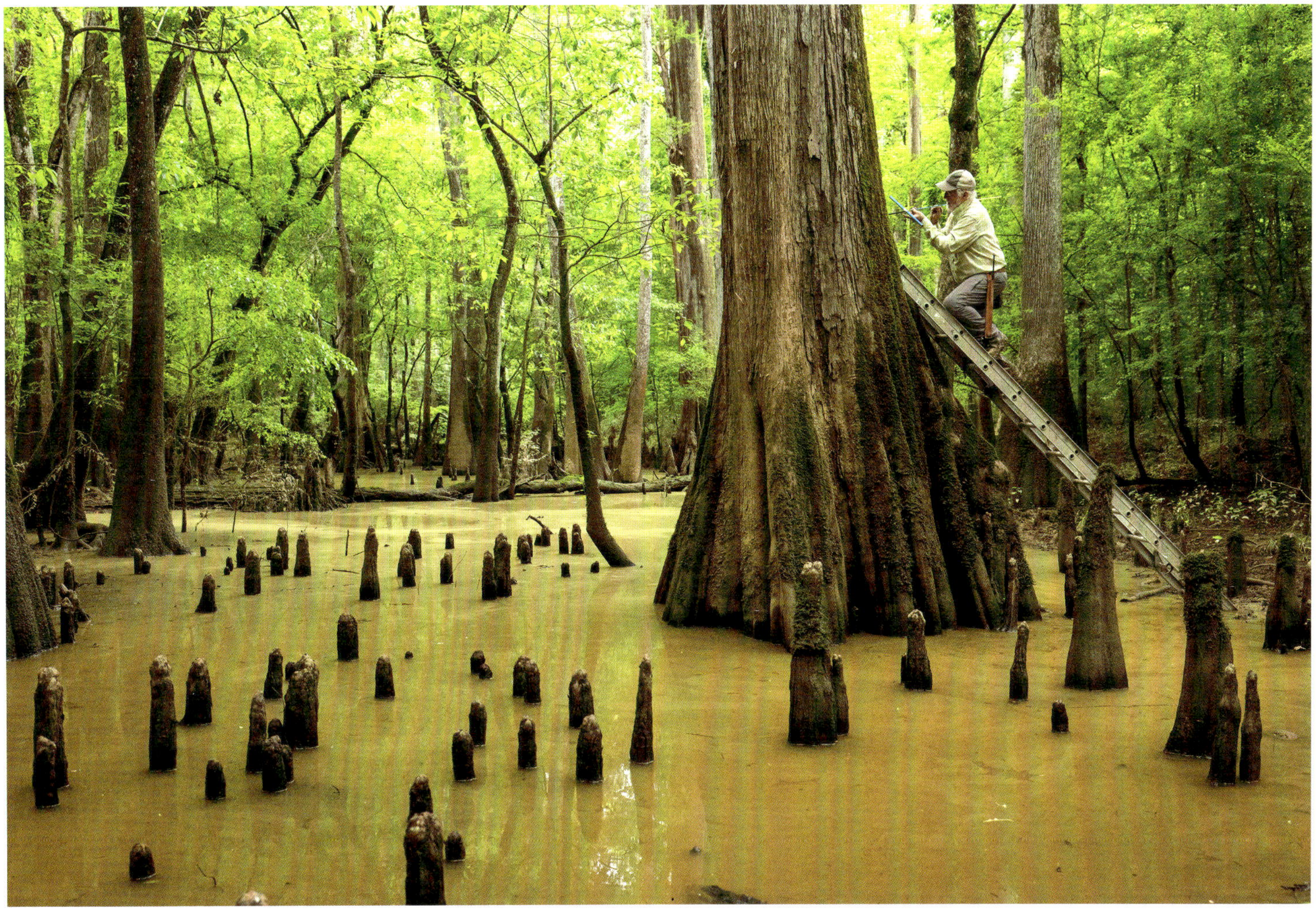

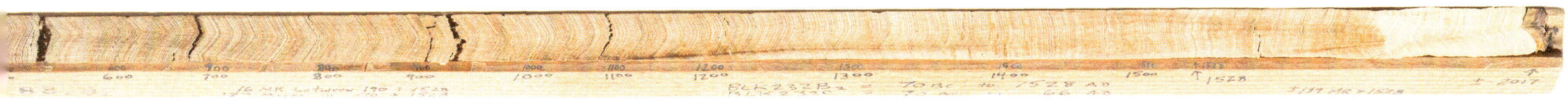
600 700 800 900 1000 1100 1200 1300 1400 1500 1528

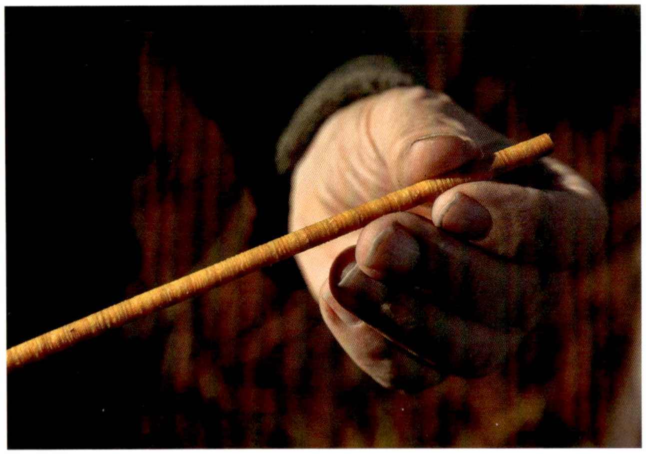

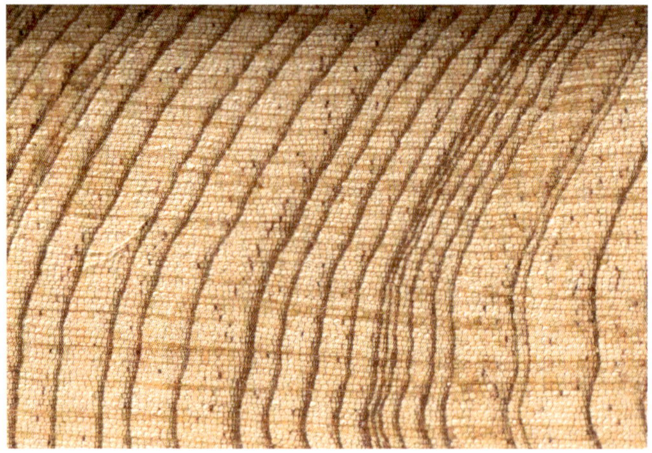

some that may have impacted the course of history and prehistory. Precipitation "reconstructions" from tree rings have revealed the Lost Colony and Jamestown Droughts during the first English settlements in the New World, and a twelfth-century drought in Mexico that coincided with the collapse of the Toltec civilization.

More than just providing long climate records, the Black River, Four Holes Swamp, Congaree, and Corkscrew forests are the best remaining examples of an ecosystem that once covered 40 million acres in the southern United States. These native bald cypress and bottomland hardwood forests were savagely logged, cleared, and drained. Just a handful of stands survive, including these four, but also a few others such as Blackwater River in Virginia, Bayou DeView in Arkansas, and Barranca de Amealco in Mexico. They are all small remnant stands, but they survive and can form the nucleus of a larger and long overdue ecosystem restoration effort to rehabilitate habitats and water quality in the Old South and ancient Mexico.

Ahuehuete is an old Nahuatl name for Montezuma bald cypress in Mexico meaning the "Old Man of the Water." Many rural people in semiarid Mexico believe that *ahuehuete* trees help to protect water supply and quality in the streams where they are found. These people have protected the trees and this sacred function for centuries. A precious few southern landowners have also protected their forested wetlands, including Francis Beidler at Four Holes Swamp and the visionaries of the National Audubon Society and The Nature Conservancy. A few more ancient cypress forests have managed to "protect themselves" by being so old, so decrepit, and so overmature as to be of limited lumber value. You can occasionally still find these old-growth survivors along southern bayous where they grow at streamside out over open water, harvesting sunlight, with asymmetrical branching and misshapen stems. They weren't worth the effort to cut, so some quiet southern waterways are still locally lined with ancient cypress trees. Look for their stout low-taper trunks, laterally twisted stems, heavy branches, hollow voids, and underfit canopies the next time you are out. They and the last old-growth swamps in this book deserve to be appreciated and protected so that some of what made the South beautiful and biodiverse can be that way again.

1. Cazzola Gatti, R., et al., 2022. The number of tree species on Earth. *Proceedings of the National Academy of Sciences,* 119, 6, https://doi.org/10.1073/pnas.2115329119

2. Brown, P. M., 2025. Rocky Mountain Tree-Ring Research, OLDLIST, A Database of Old Trees; http://rmtrr.org/oldlist.htm.

3. Crowther, T. W., et al., 2015. Mapping tree density at a global scale. *Nature,* 525, 202–205.

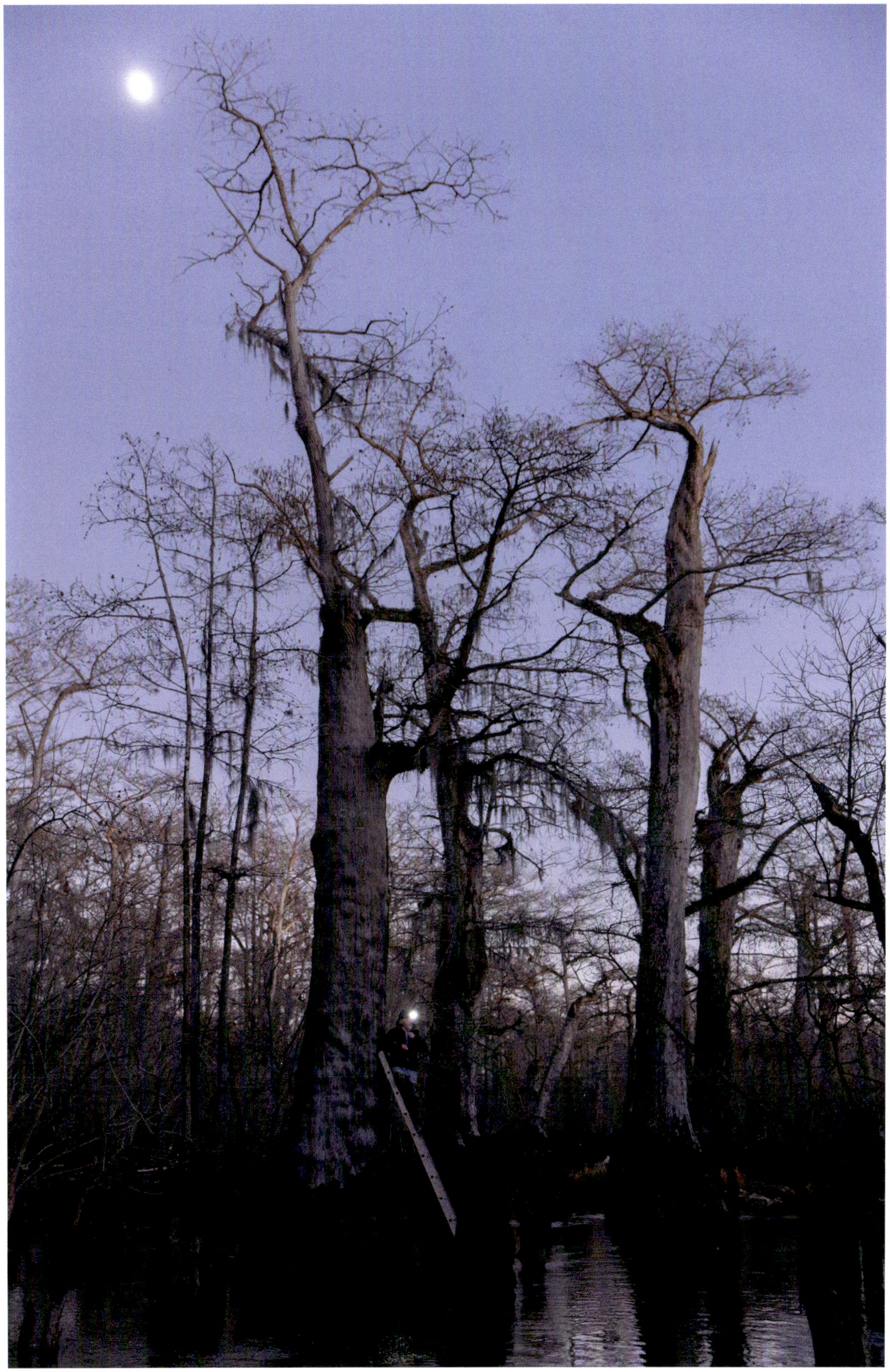

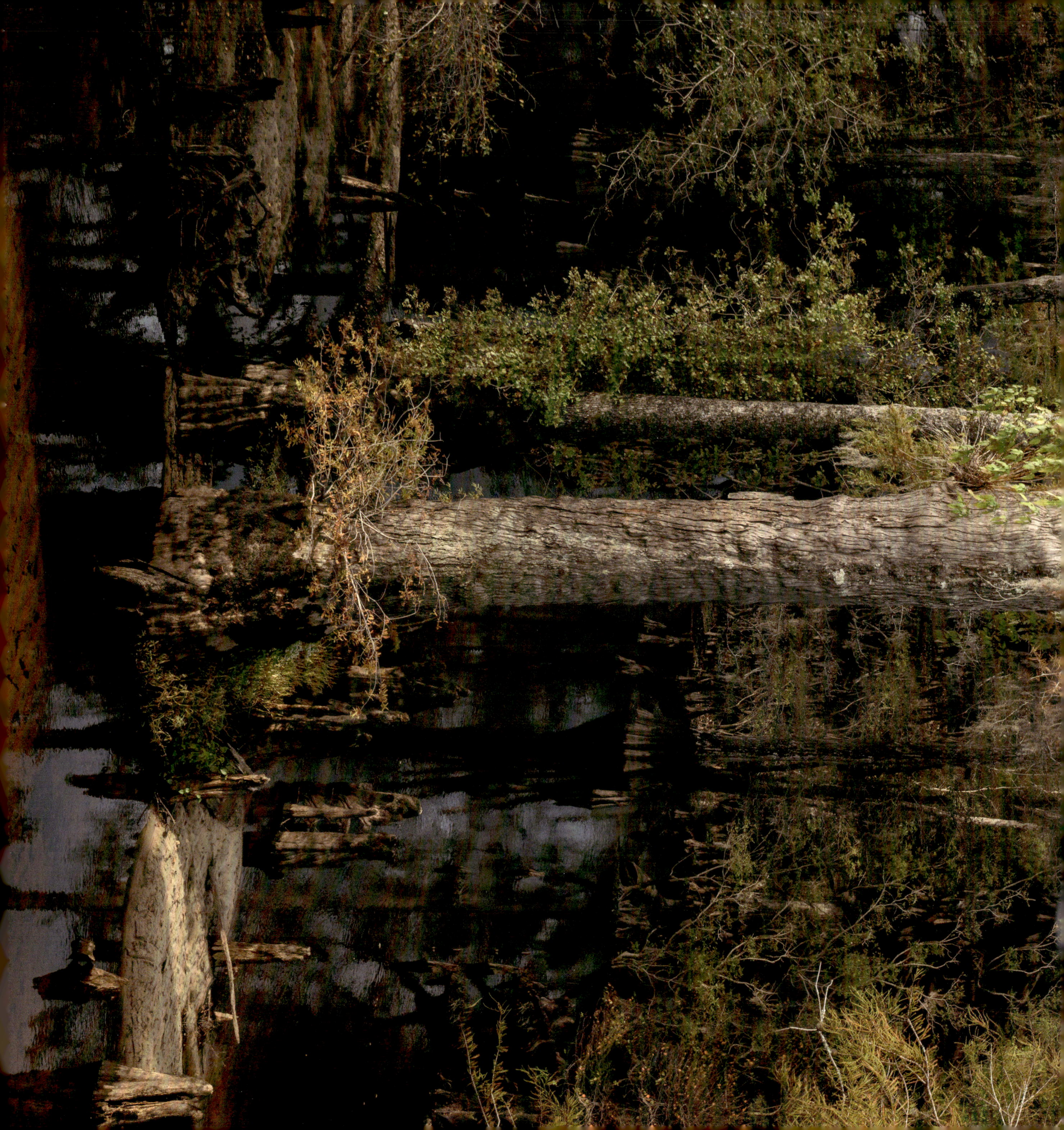

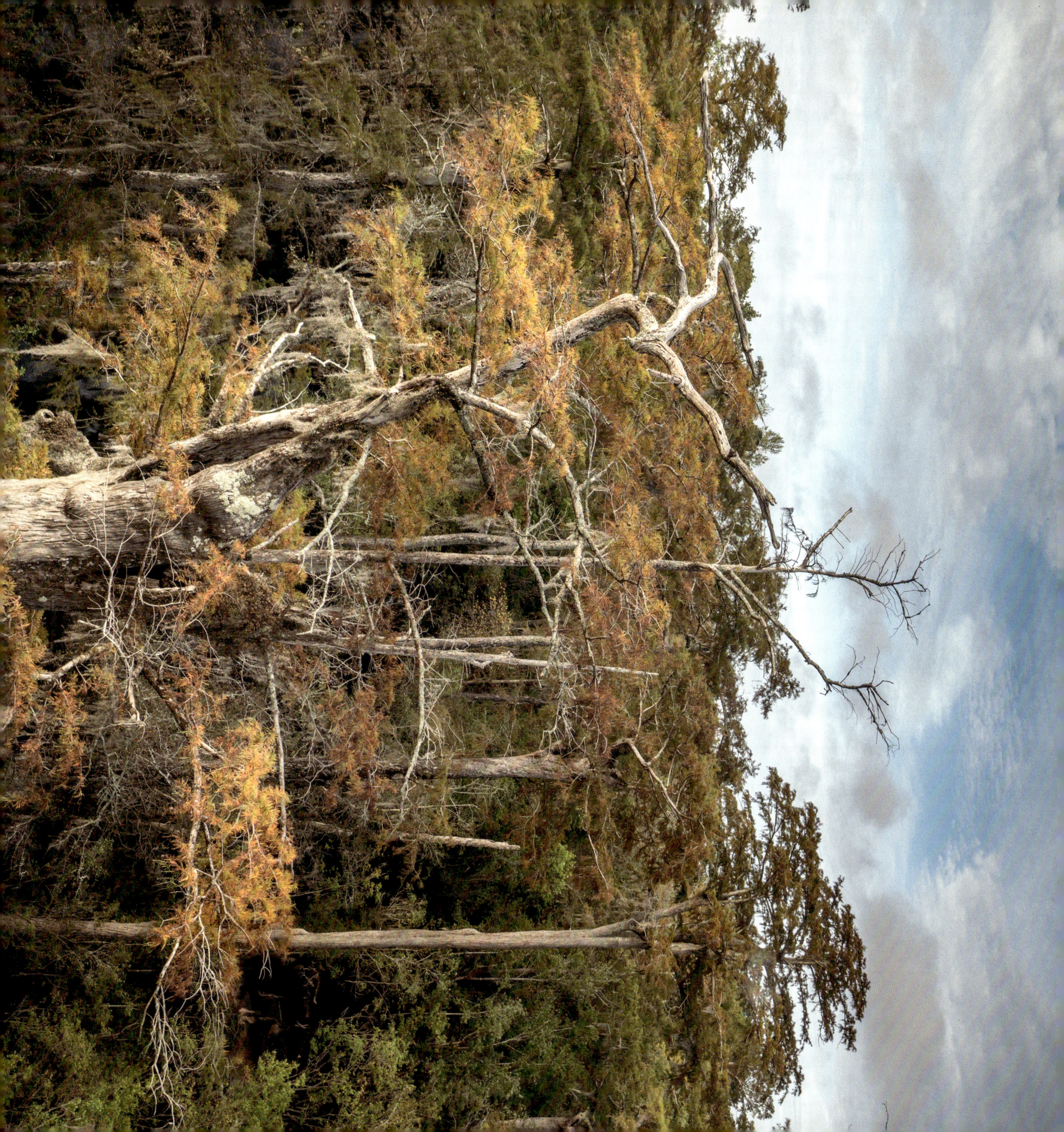

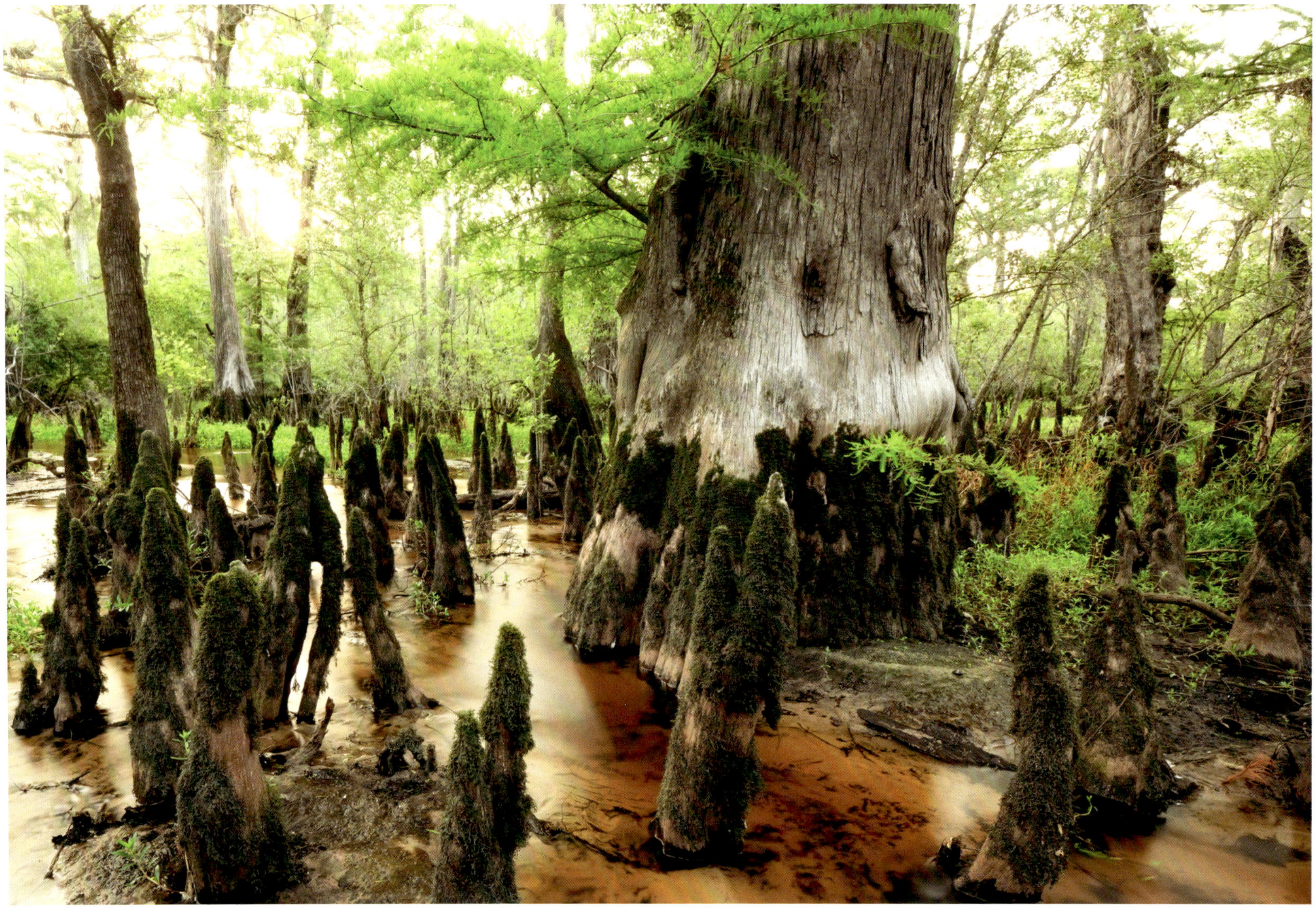

The swamp lives by a rhythm of rise and retreat, its waters surging and shrinking with the seasons—the ebb and flow carves tree rings, guides migrations, and determines breeding success of many animals.

PREVIOUS PAGE

BLK227 is the oldest known living bald cypress in the world. When Dr. Dave Stahle's team cored it in 2017, it was already 2,624 years old—taking root centuries before the rise of ancient Rome. This image is a panoramic stitch of 13 frames.

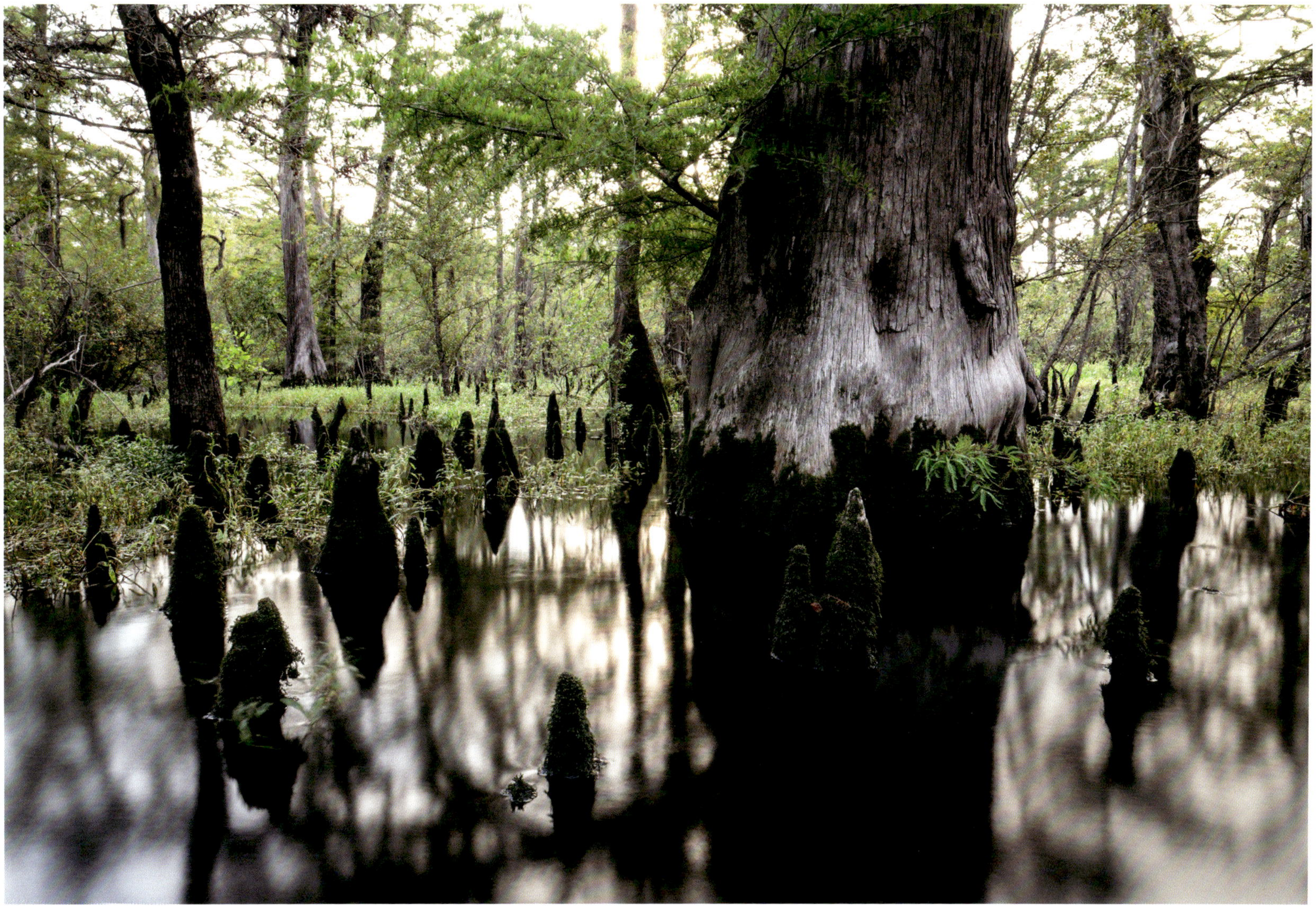

Once thought to function like snorkels for gas exchange, the true purpose of cypress knees remains unproven, though they most likely help absorb nutrients through fine root hairs along shifting gradients during high water.

FOLLOWING PAGE

Exhibiting an incredibly rare behavior among vascular plants, resurrection ferns can lose up to 95 percent of their water content during extended dry seasons, and yet spring to life within hours when the rains return.

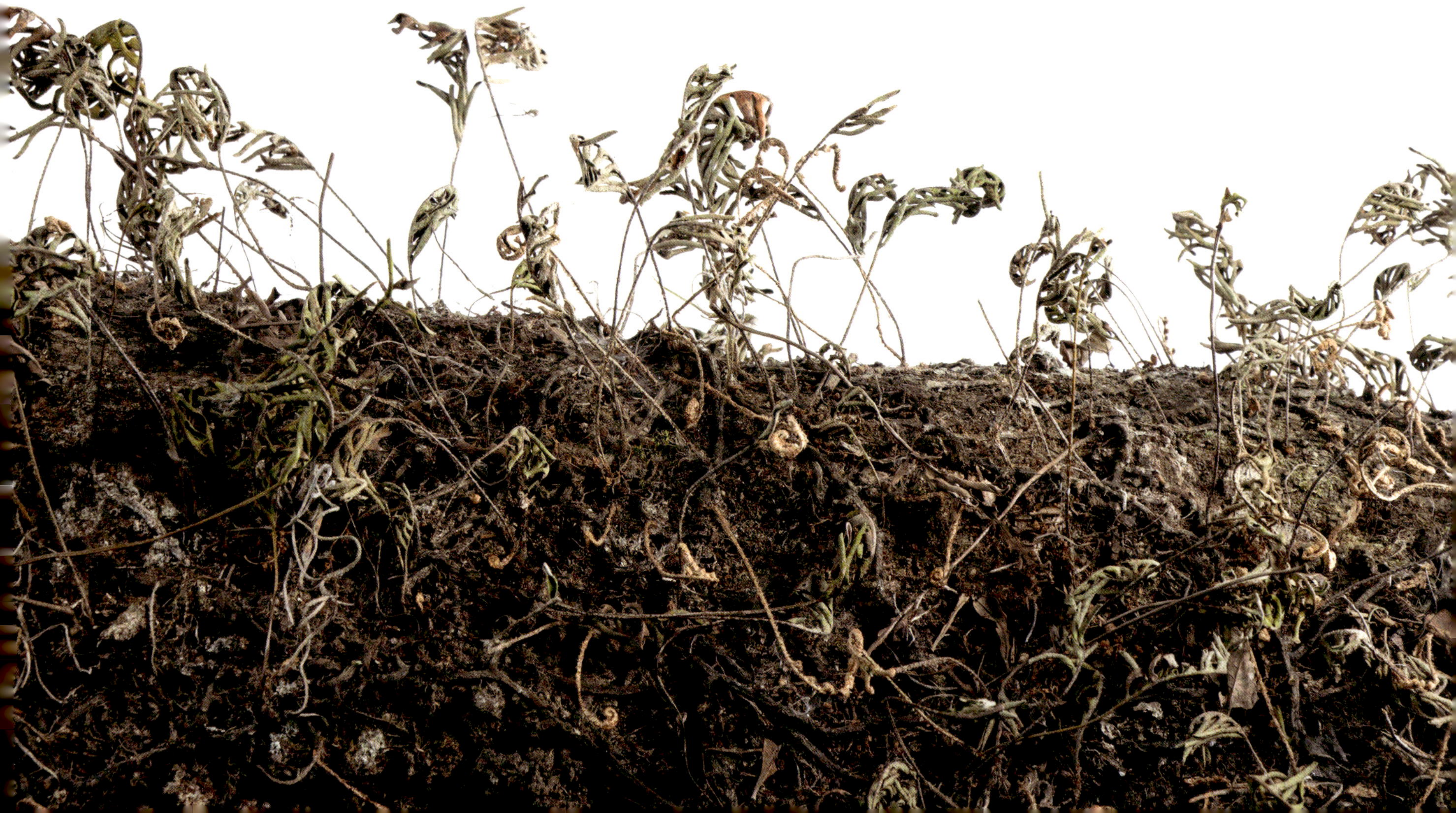

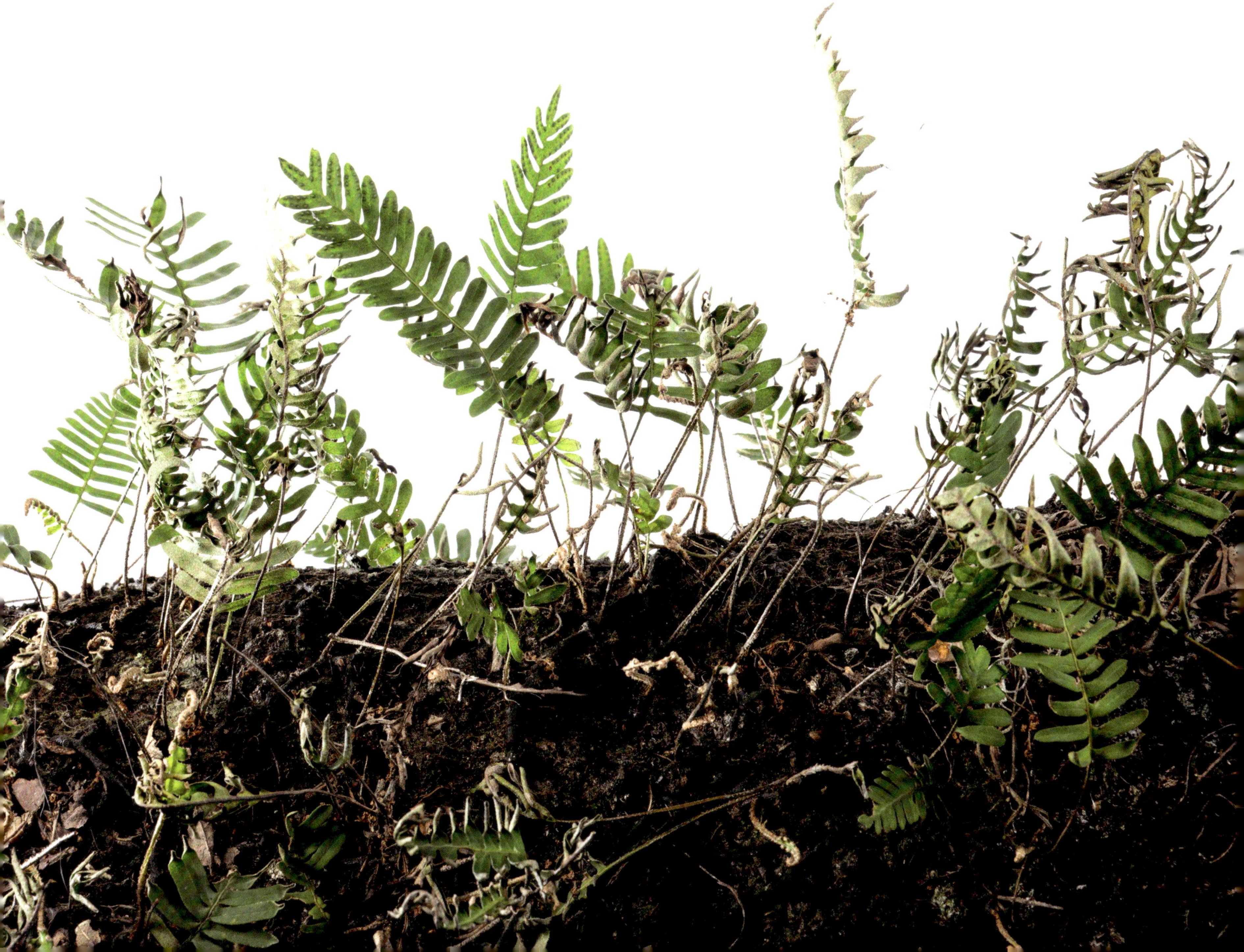

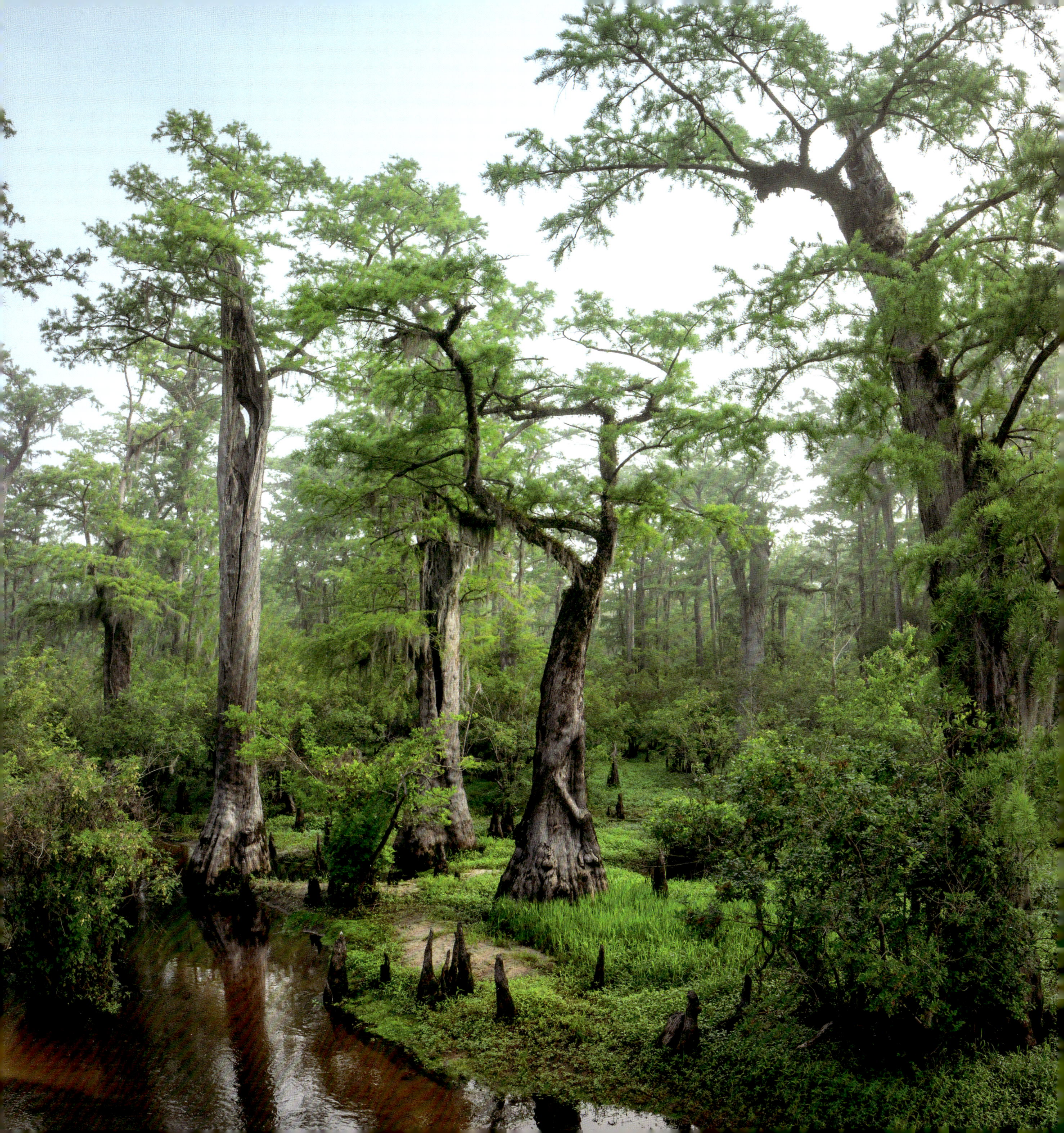

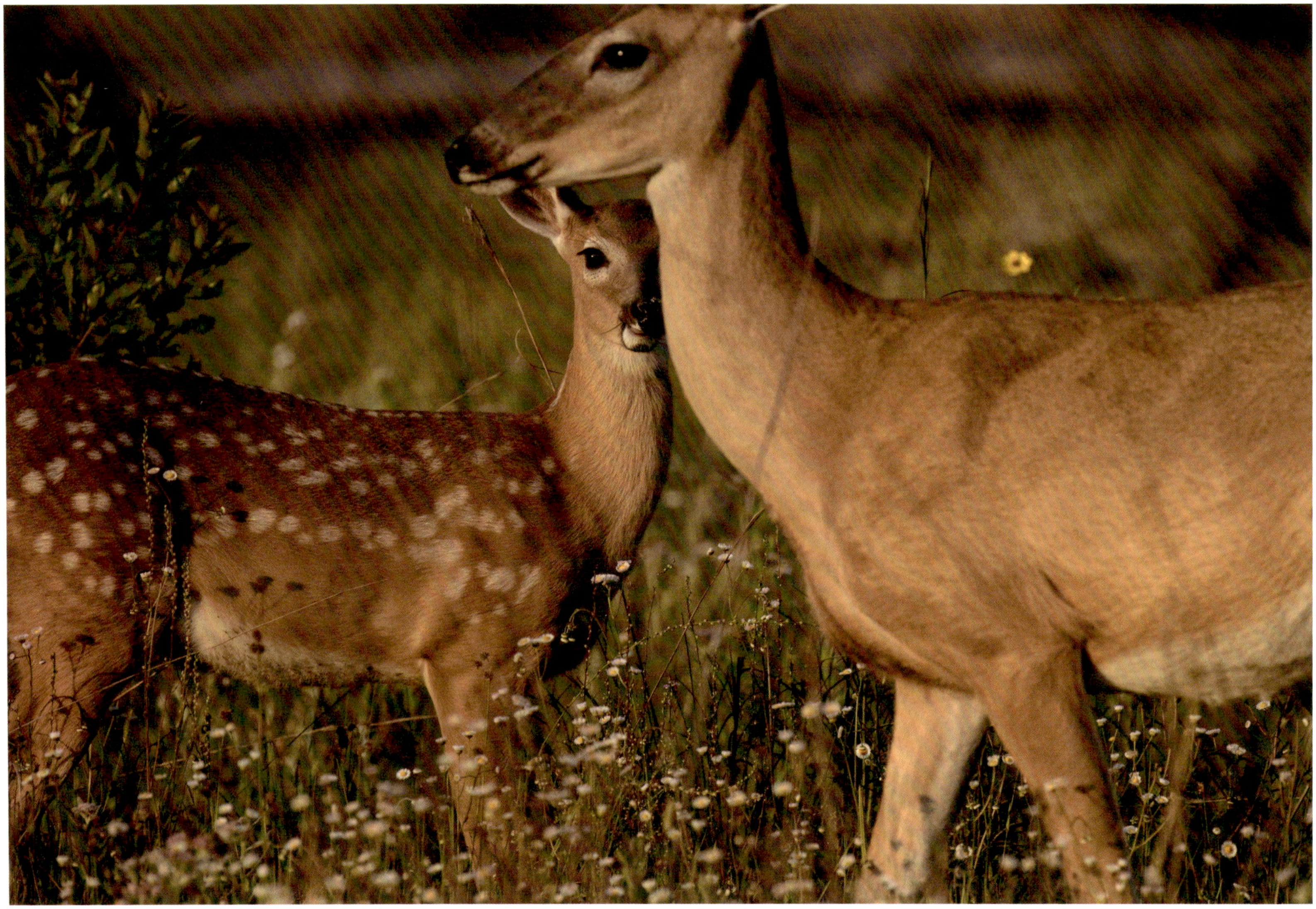

Whitetail deer fawns will accompany their mother for the first 10 months of their lives, after which they will go off on their own.

PREVIOUS PAGE

Unlike floodplains with rich alluvial soils, nutrient-poor blackwater swamps produce slow-growing trees—making age difficult to estimate by size alone.

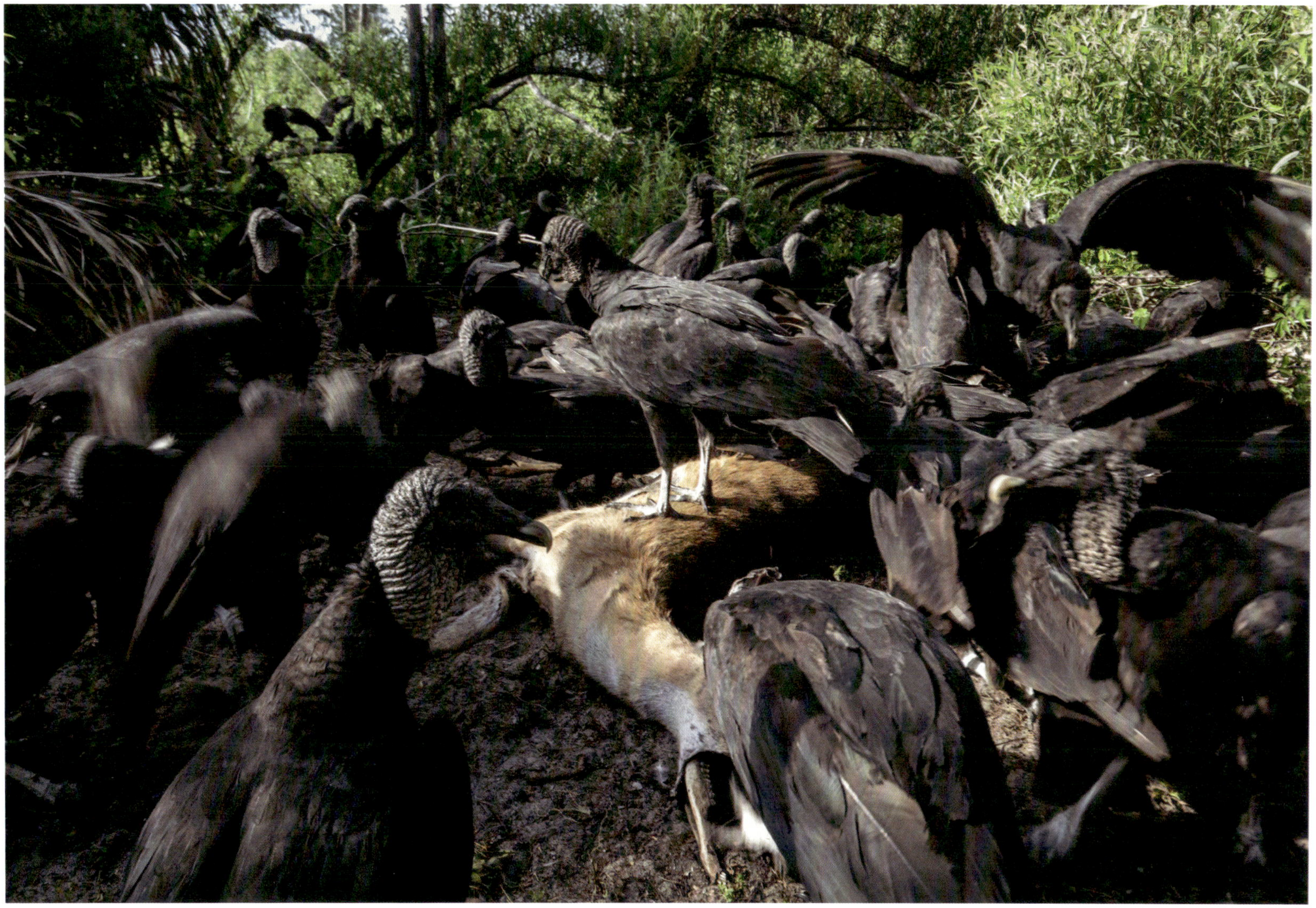

Important recyclers of the bottomland food chain, black vultures play a vital role in maintaining ecological balance.

FOLLOWING PAGE

Invasive Cuban tree frogs are advancing through Florida's swamps and outcompeting native species.

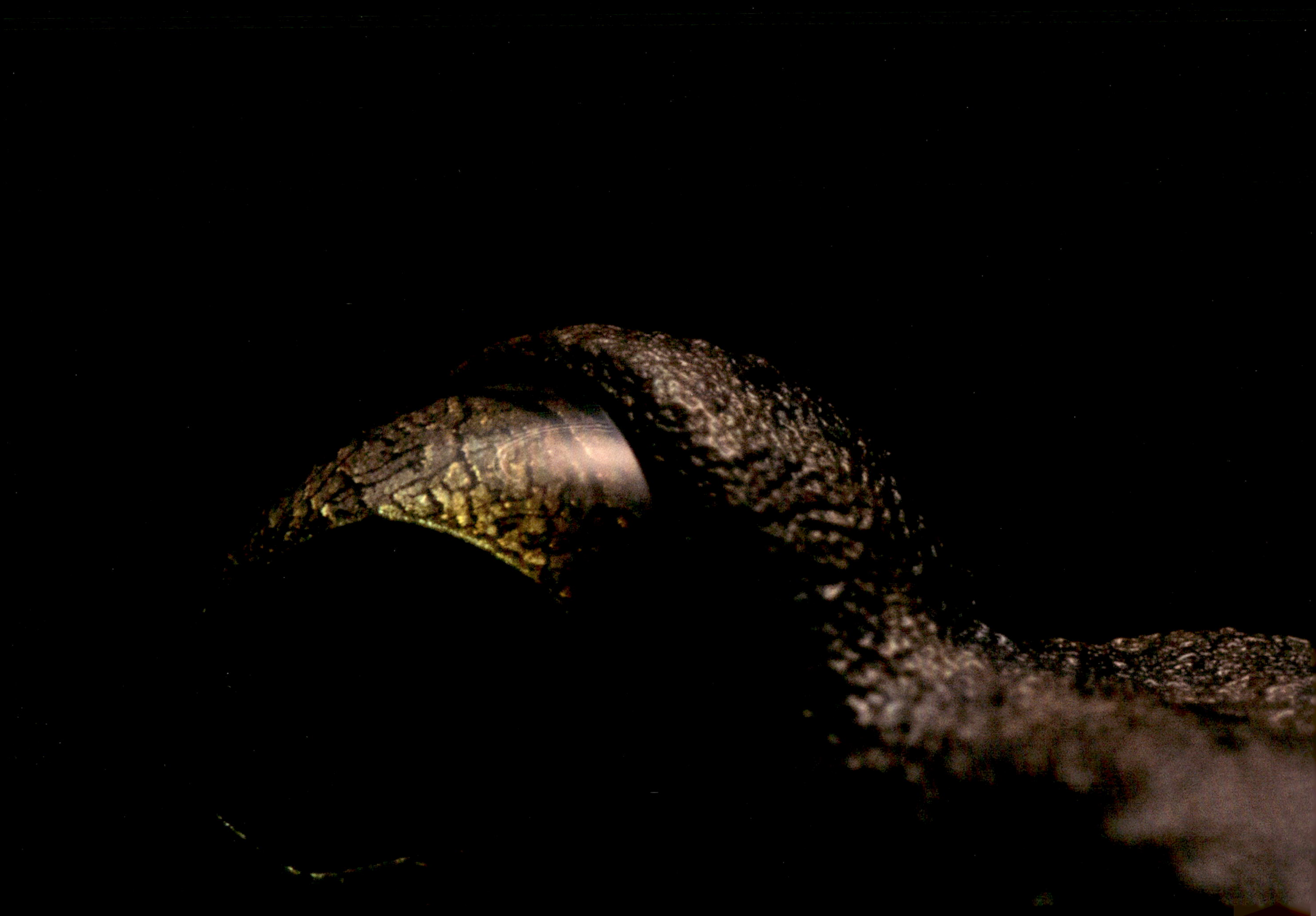

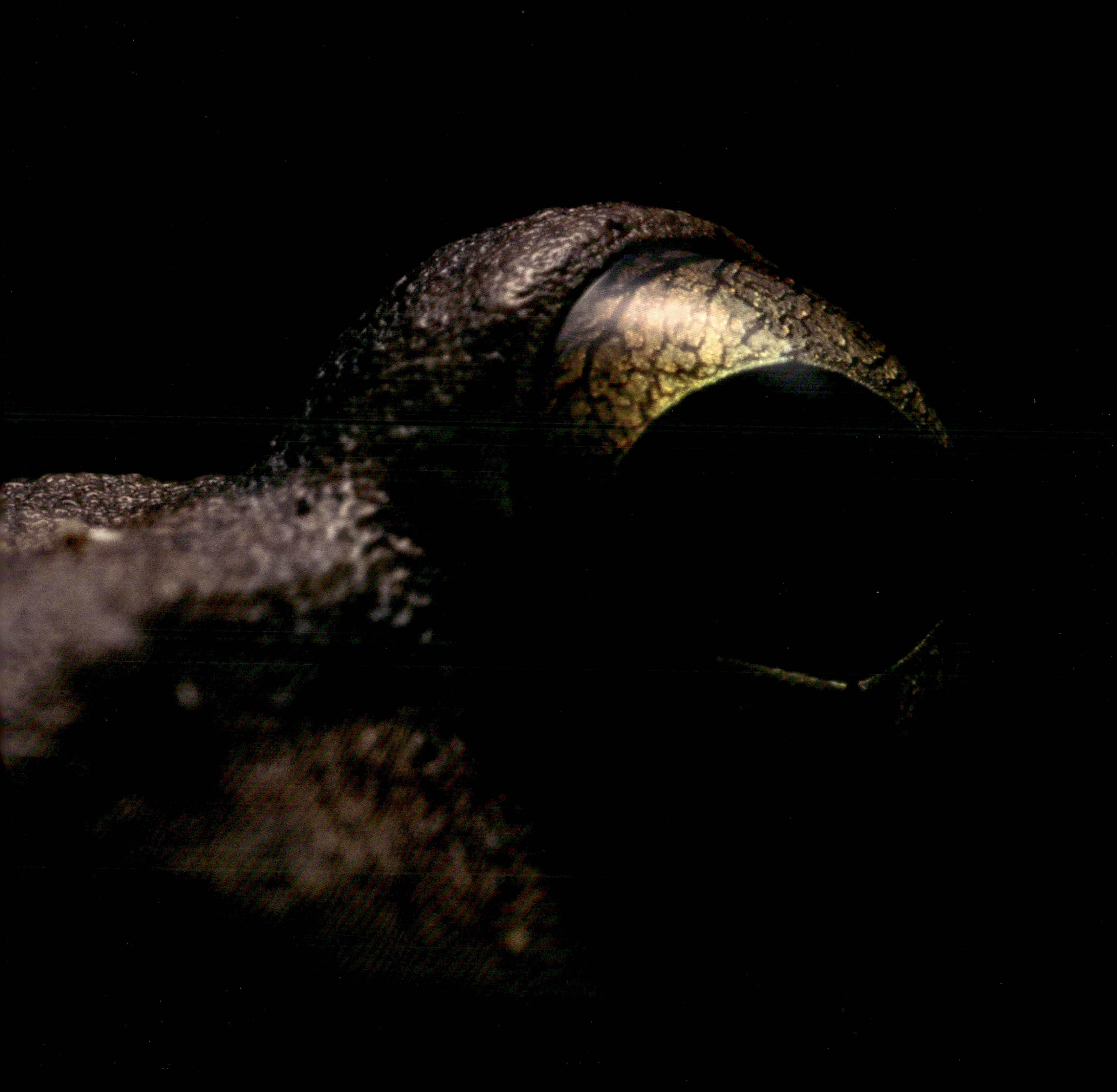

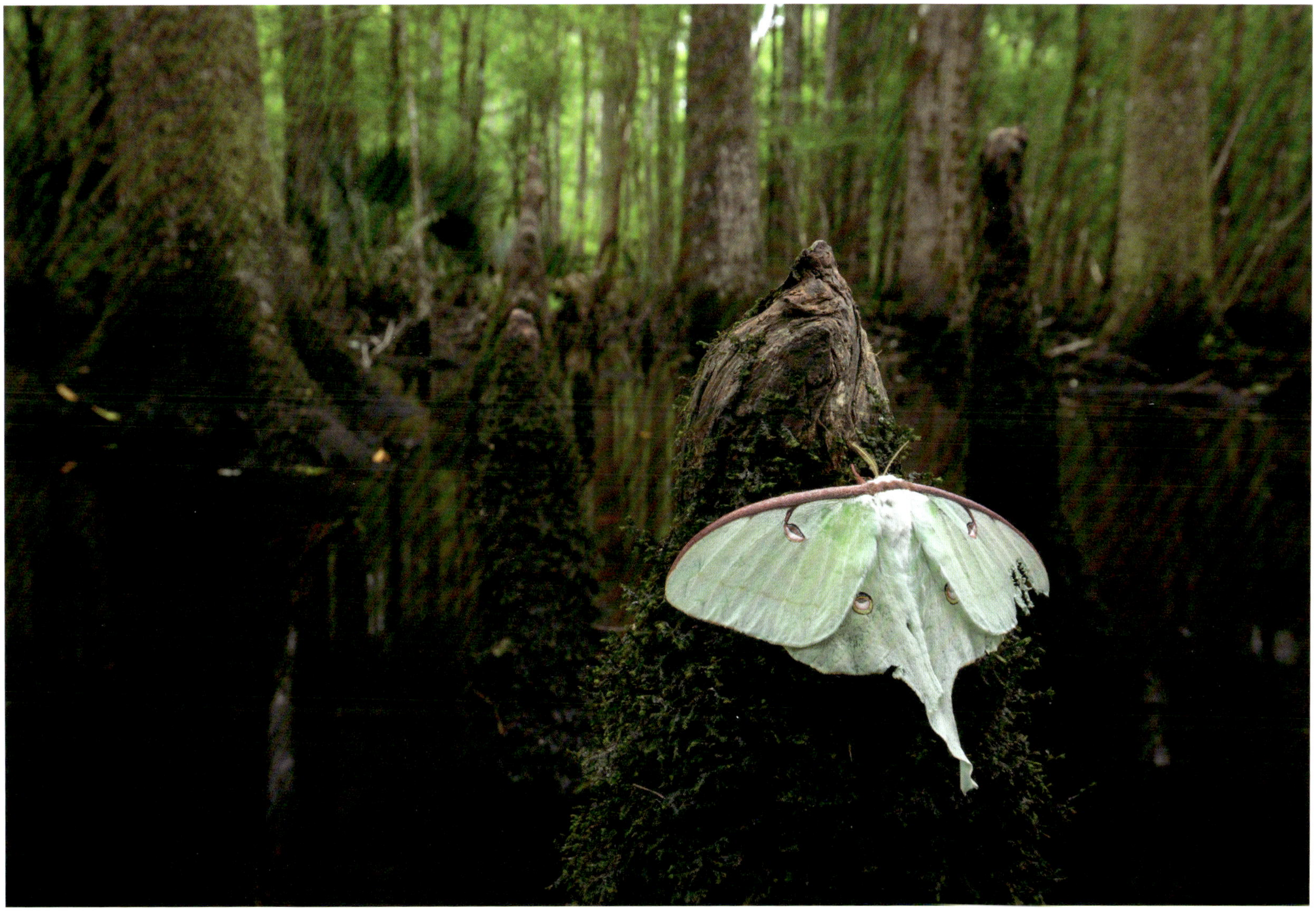

Luna moths have evolved long, trailing tails that deflect attacks from echolocating bats—
an adaptation that helps them survive their brief, week-long adult phase.

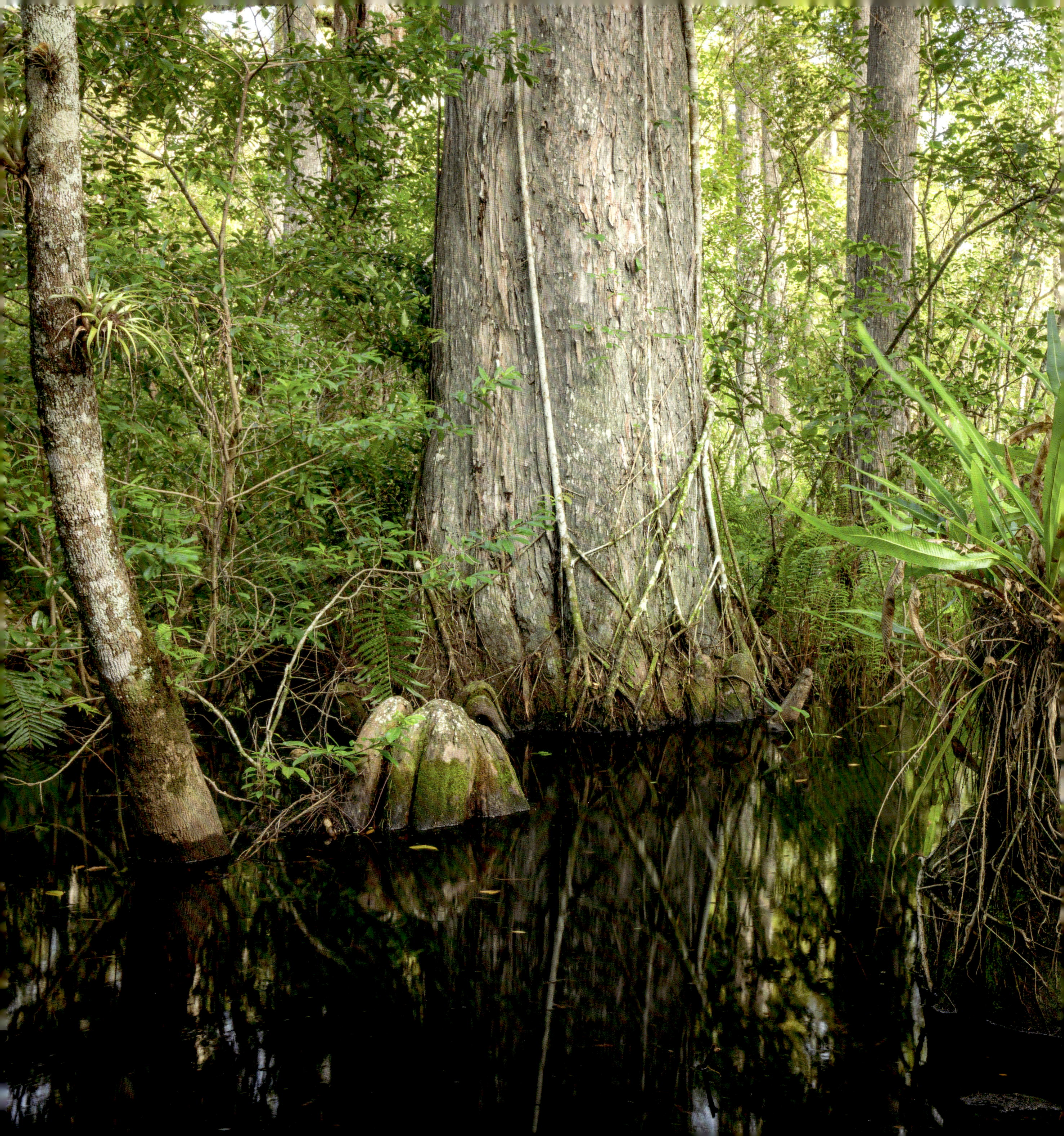

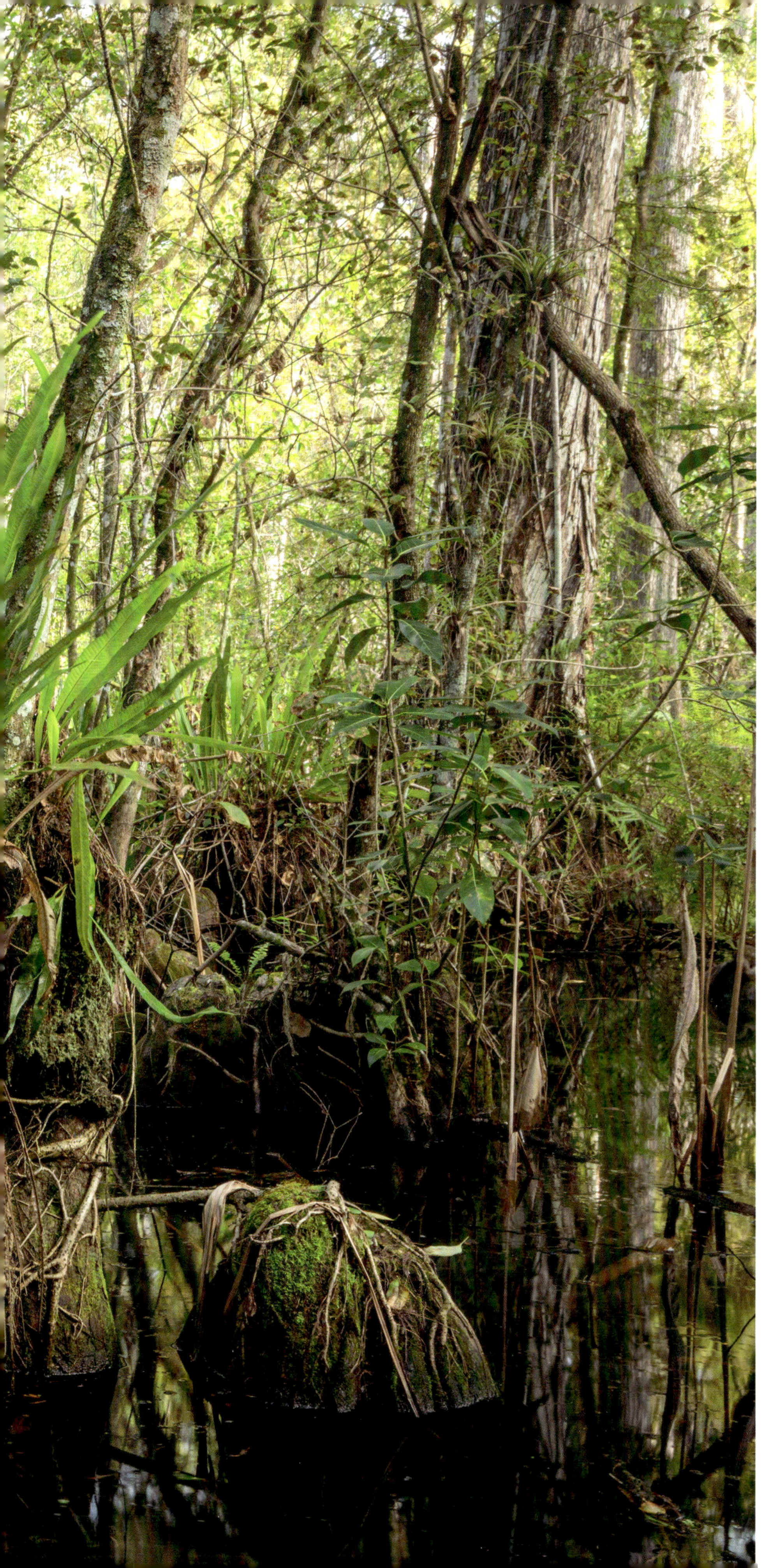

The peaty substrate of subtropical cypress forests retains moisture and creates the perfect conditions for a profusion of epiphytic life in the understory.

FOLLOWING PAGE

Thick mats of Virginia chain fern help wetlands hold onto precious moisture—cooling the soil, reducing evaporation, and creating humid microhabitats.

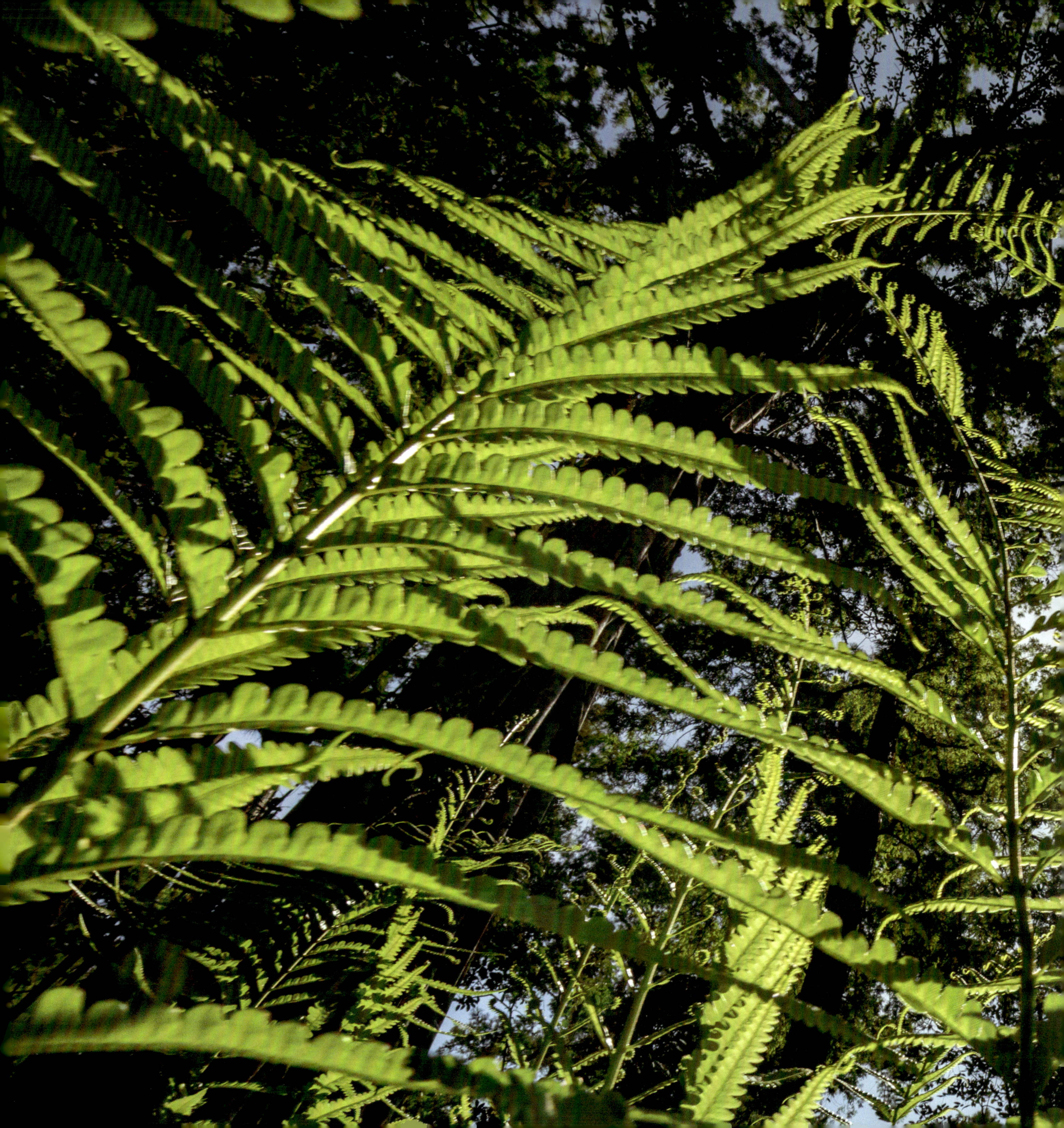

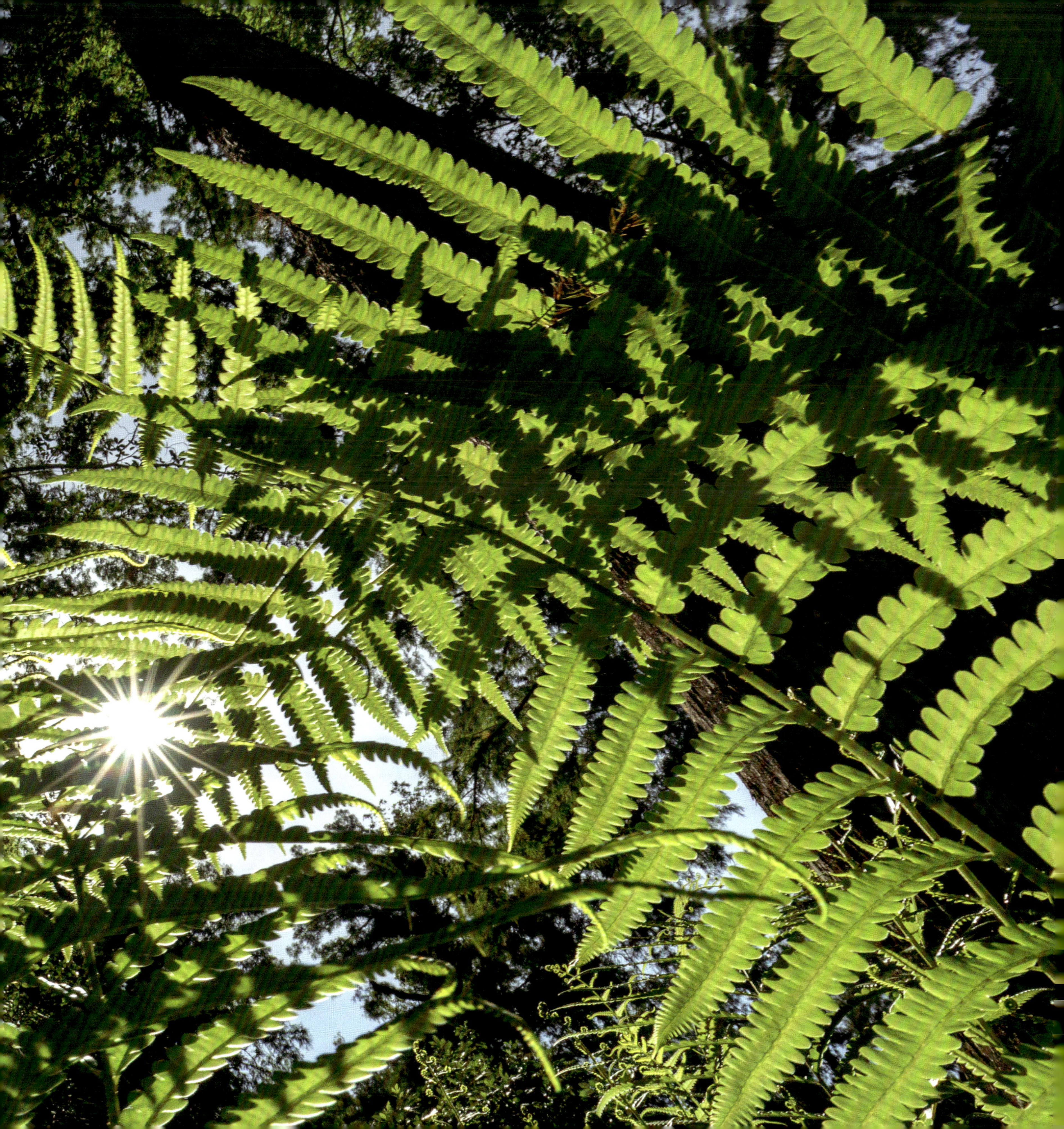

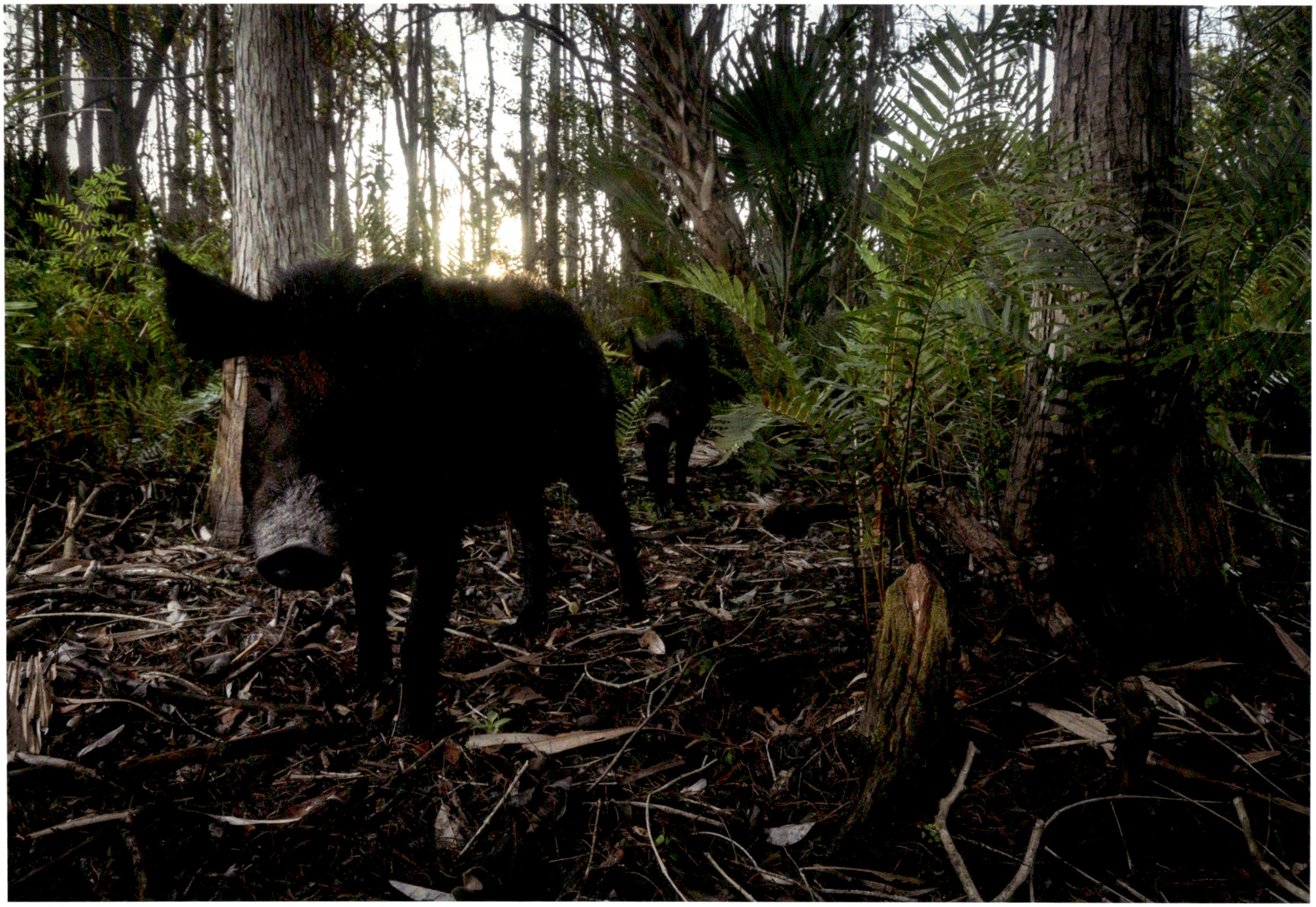

Known locally as “piney rooters,” feral hogs descend from a few dozen pigs brought by European explorers in the 1500s and have since exploded to six to nine million nationwide, wreaking havoc on native ecosystems.

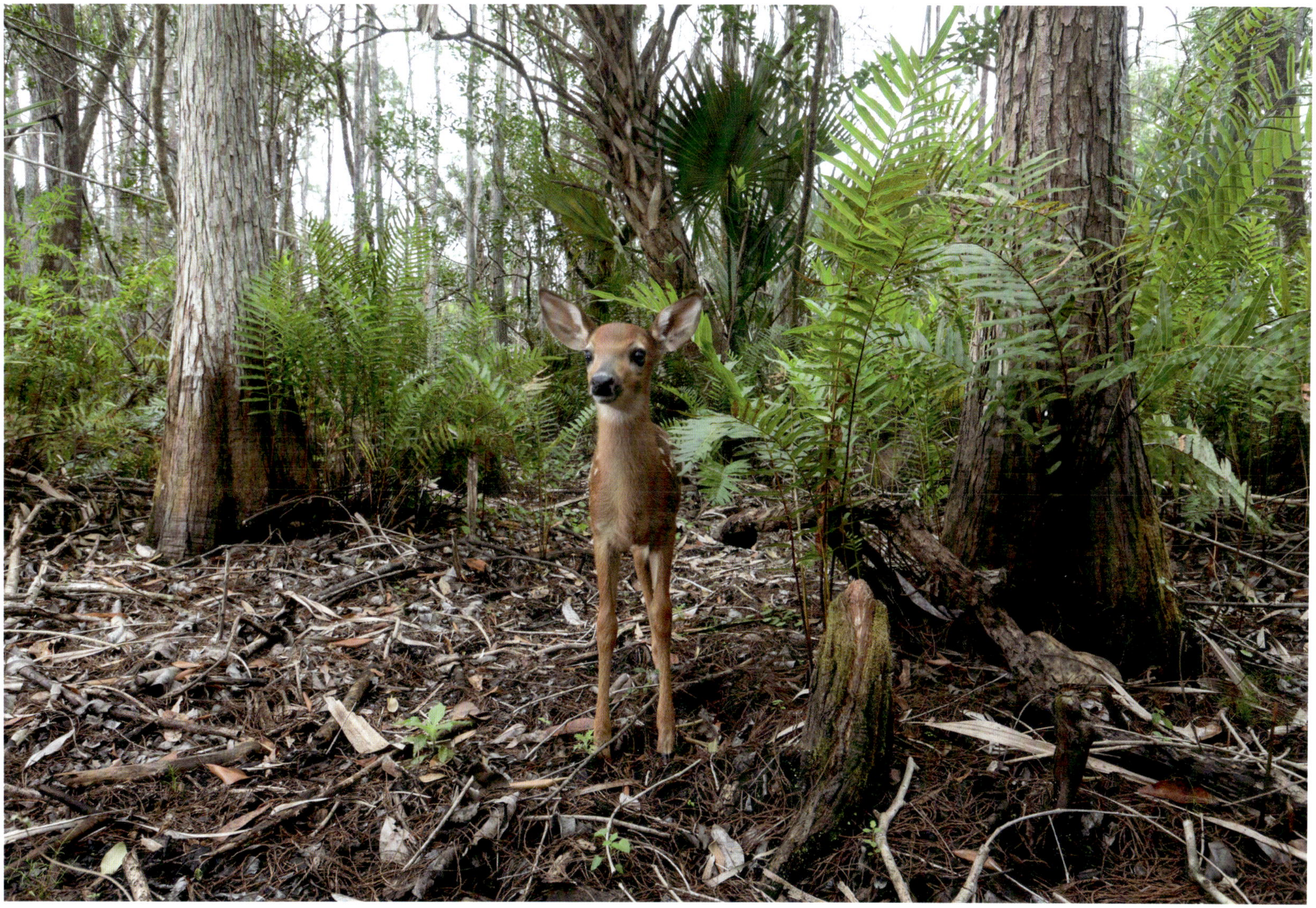

As waters recede during the dry season, cypress sloughs reveal hidden corridors, creating new opportunities for wildlife to roam and connect across the landscape.

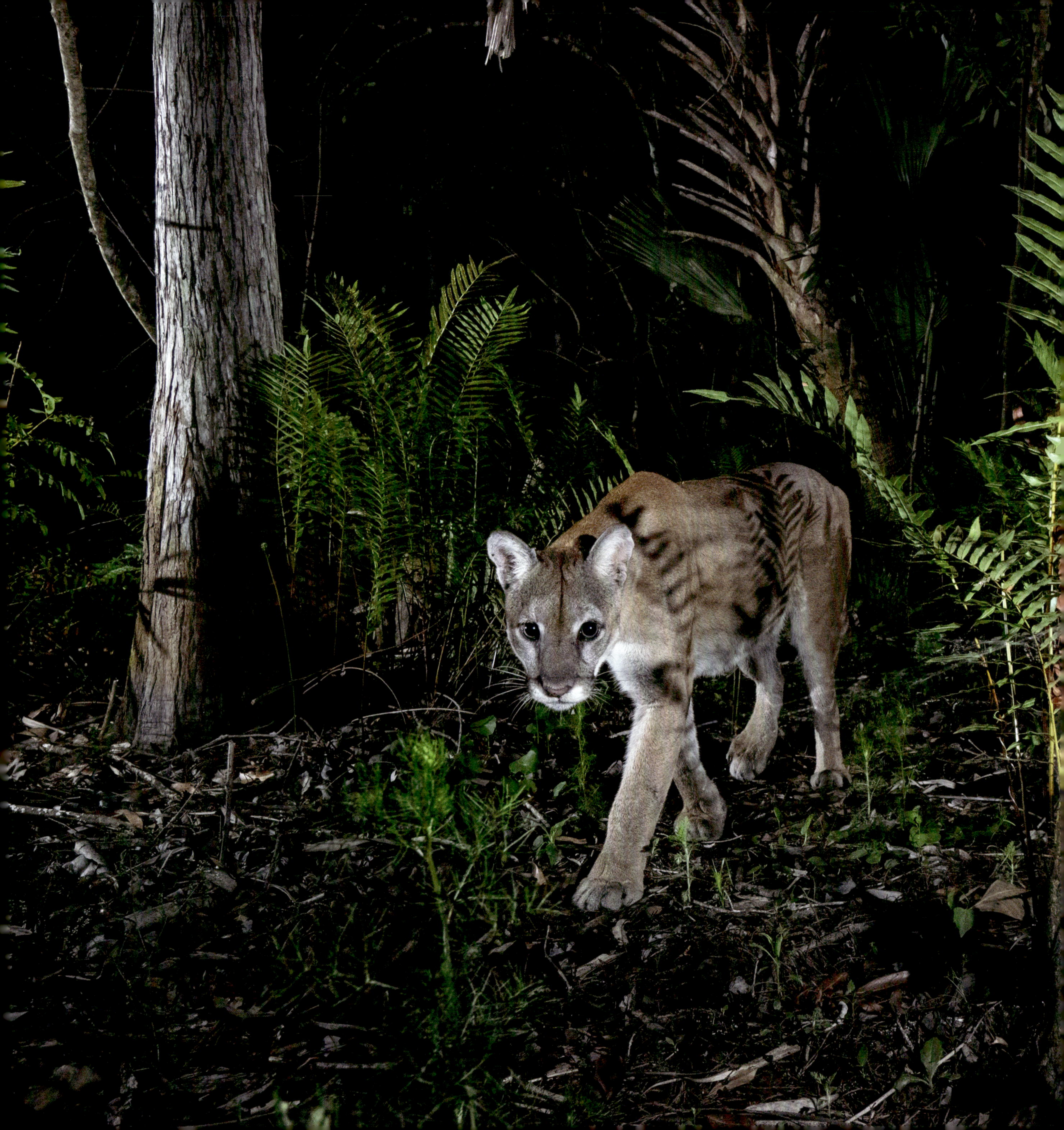

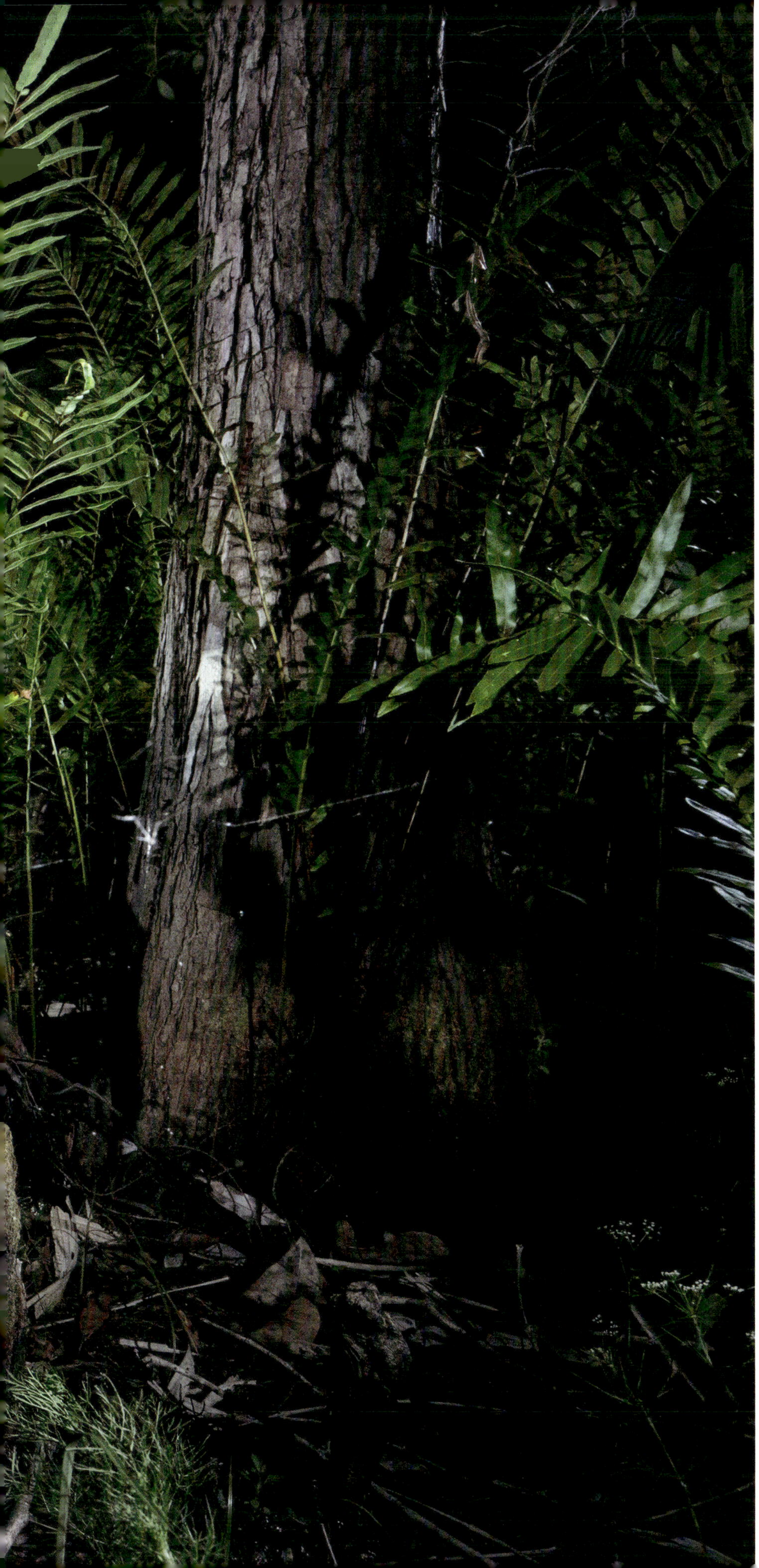

In a rapidly urbanizing state, the last stands of old-growth swamp provide sanctuary for endangered species like the Florida panther, now down to fewer than 200 in the wild.

FOLLOWING PAGE

Cottonmouths, also known as water moccasins, use potent venom to subdue prey, and when their eyes turn cloudy, it signals an imminent shed—a vulnerable phase marked by poor vision and heightened defensiveness.

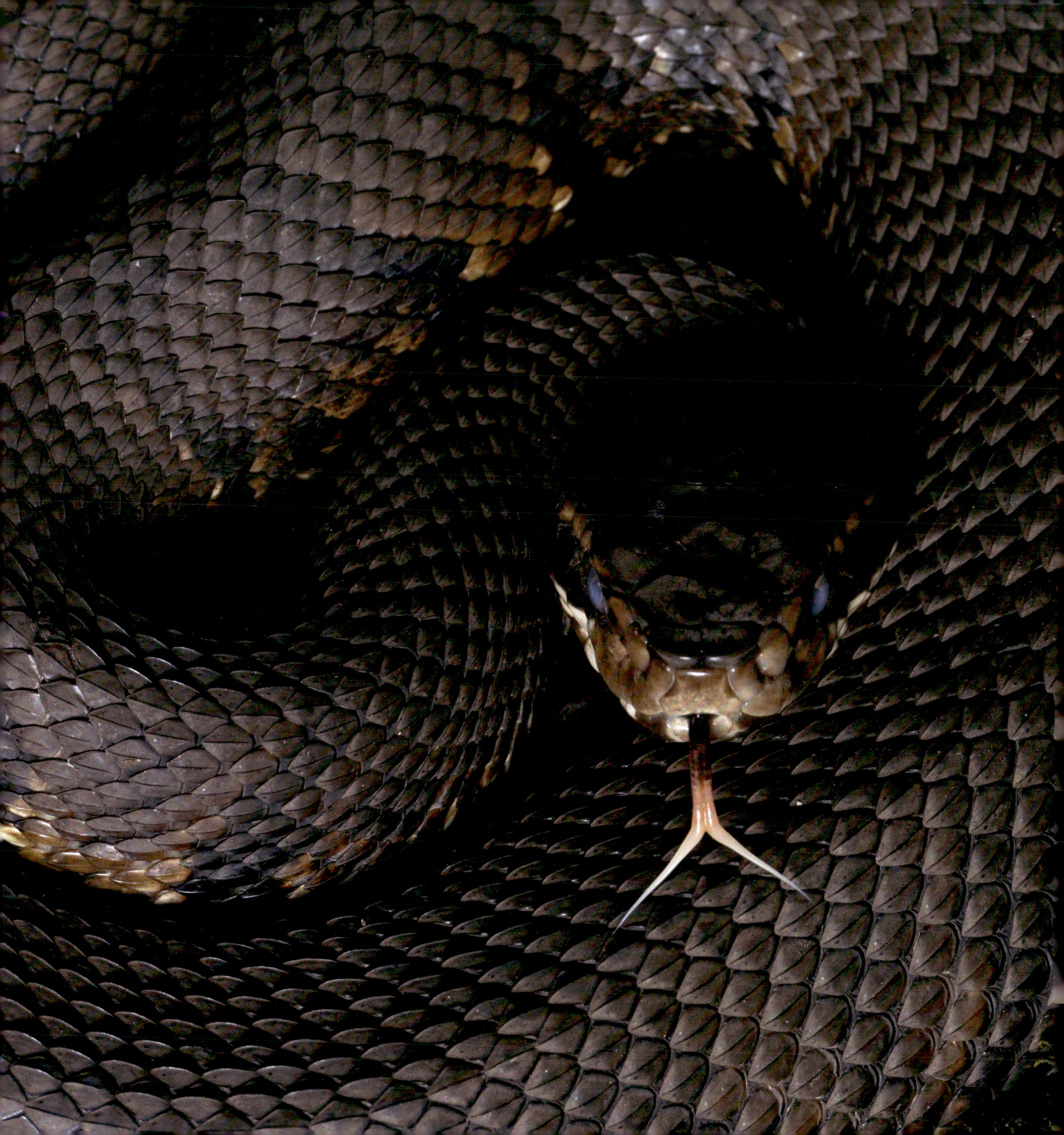

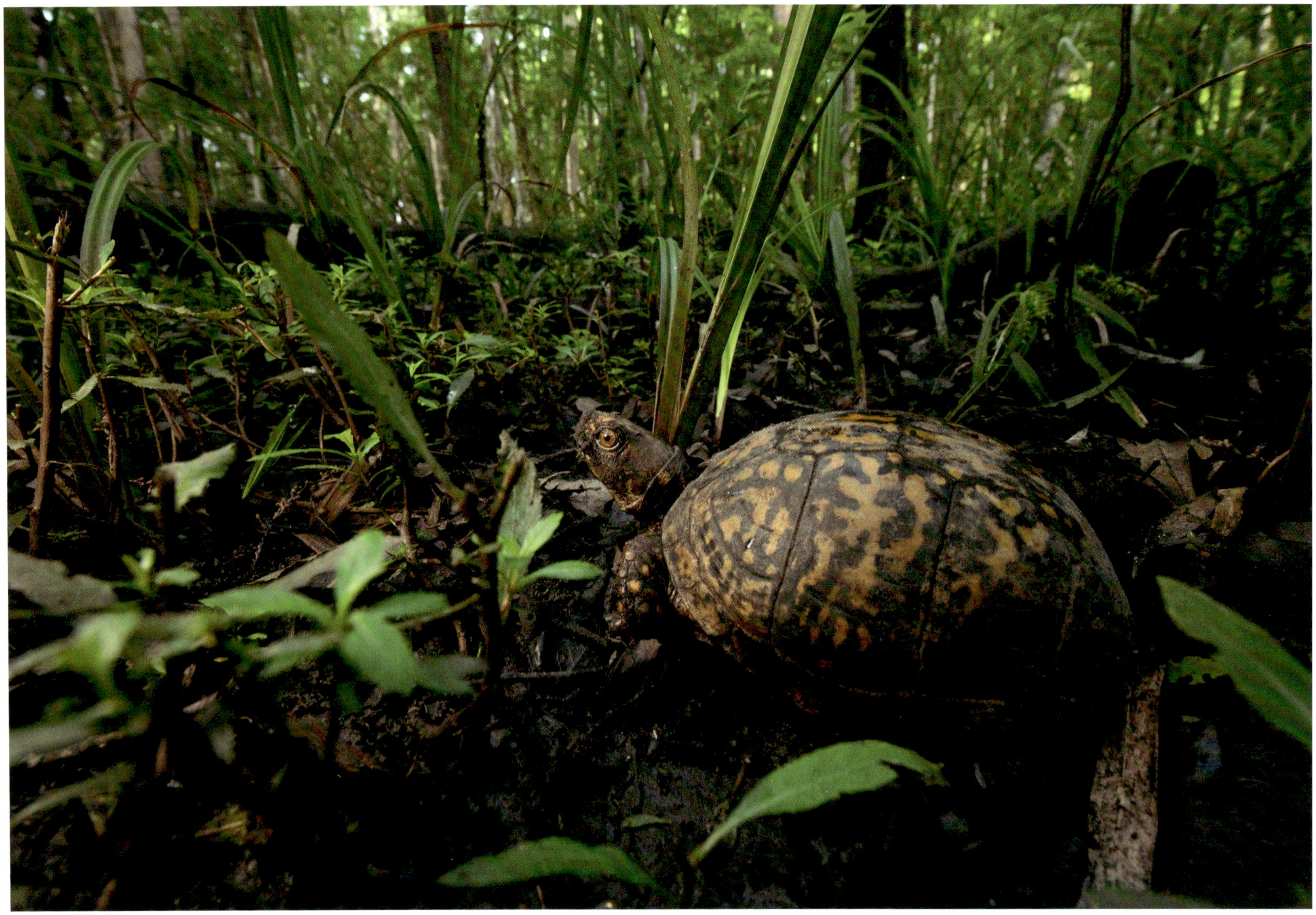

Eastern box turtles are long-lived and have a remarkable homing instinct that is so strong they often spend their entire lives within a few acres.

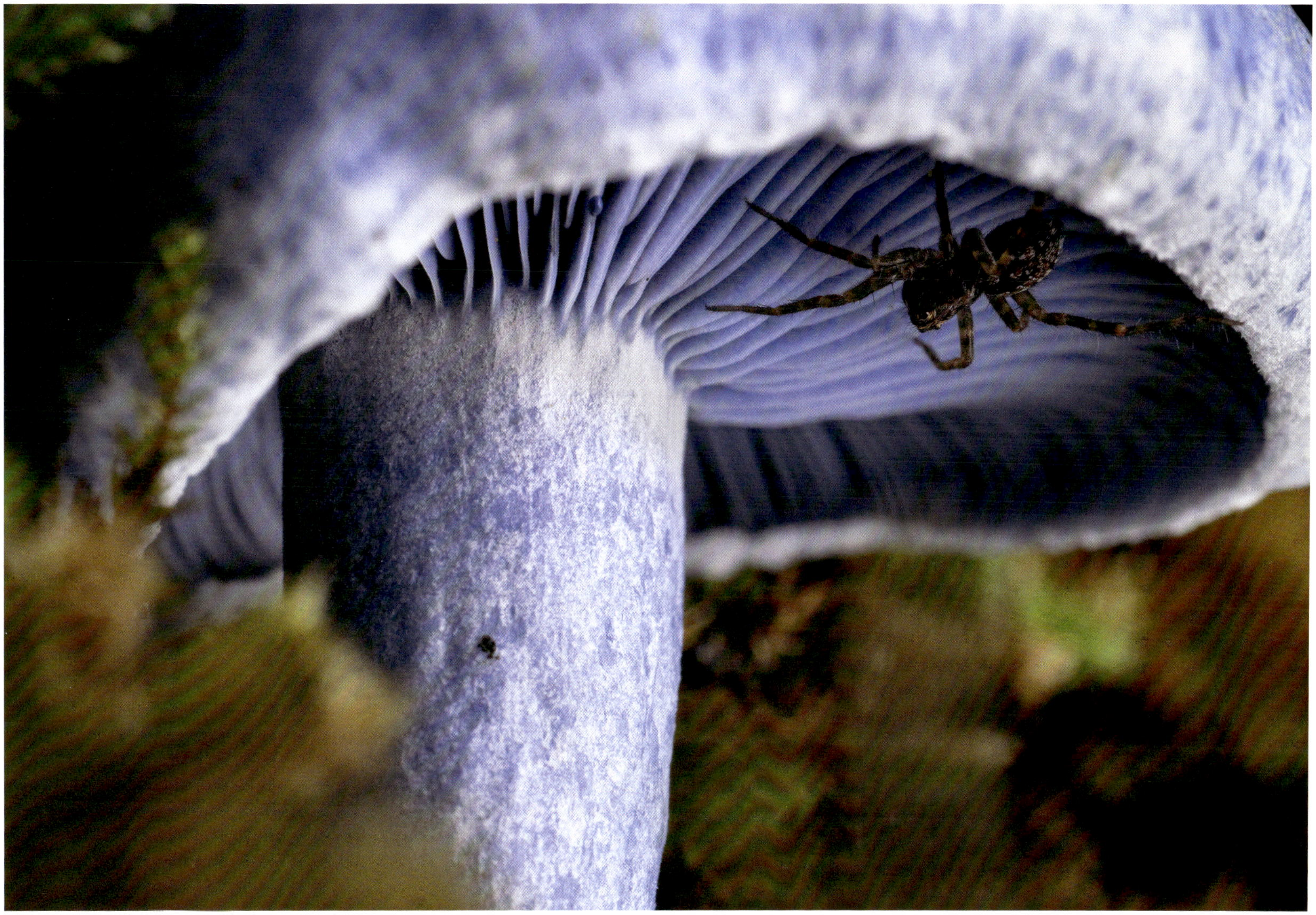

Interfacing within the roots of ancient forests, mushrooms are the fruiting bodies of vast mycorrhizal networks, an underground alliance that helps trees absorb water and nutrients and even exchange chemical signals.

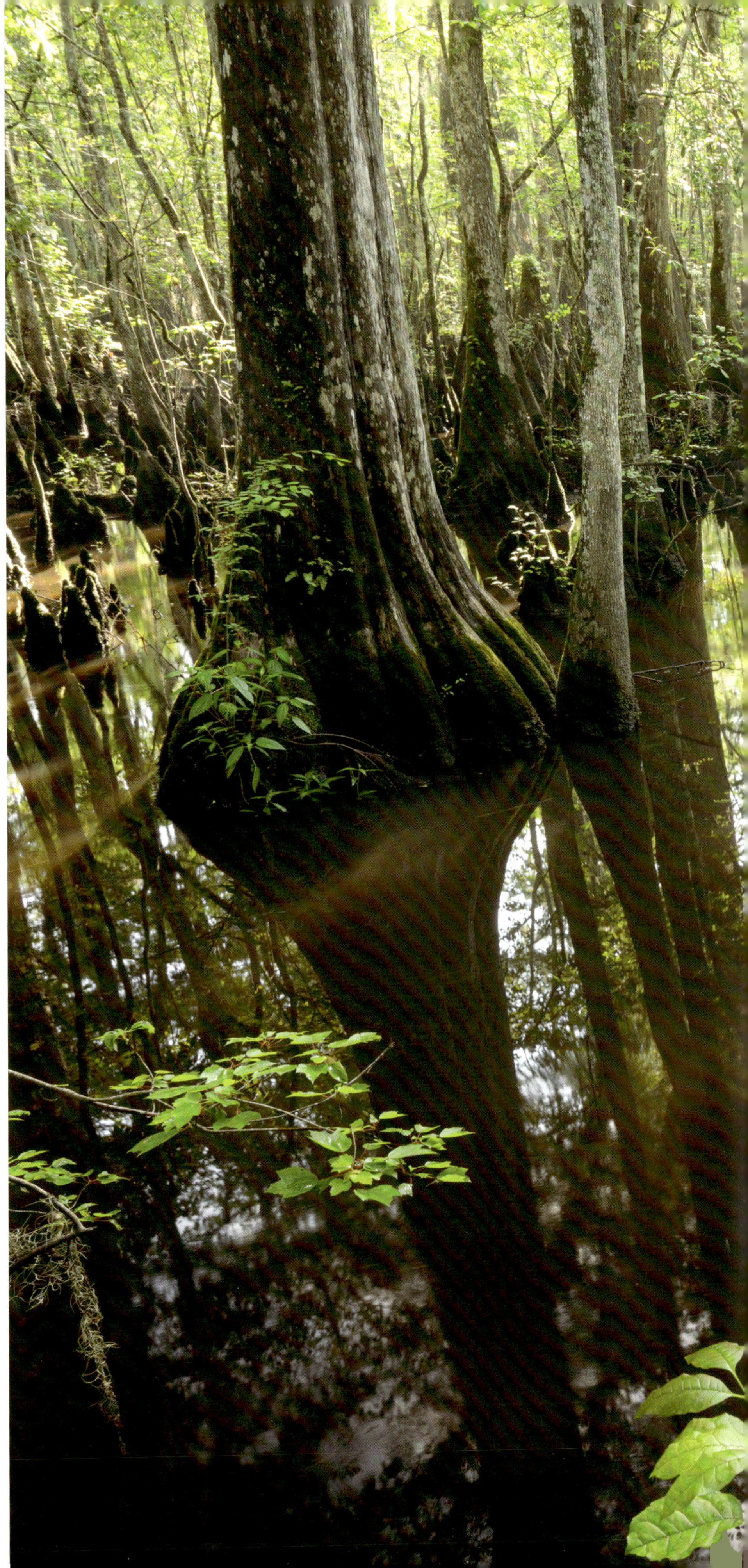

In perennial stream channels where germination is inhibited by continuous flow, cypress and tupelo line the banks.

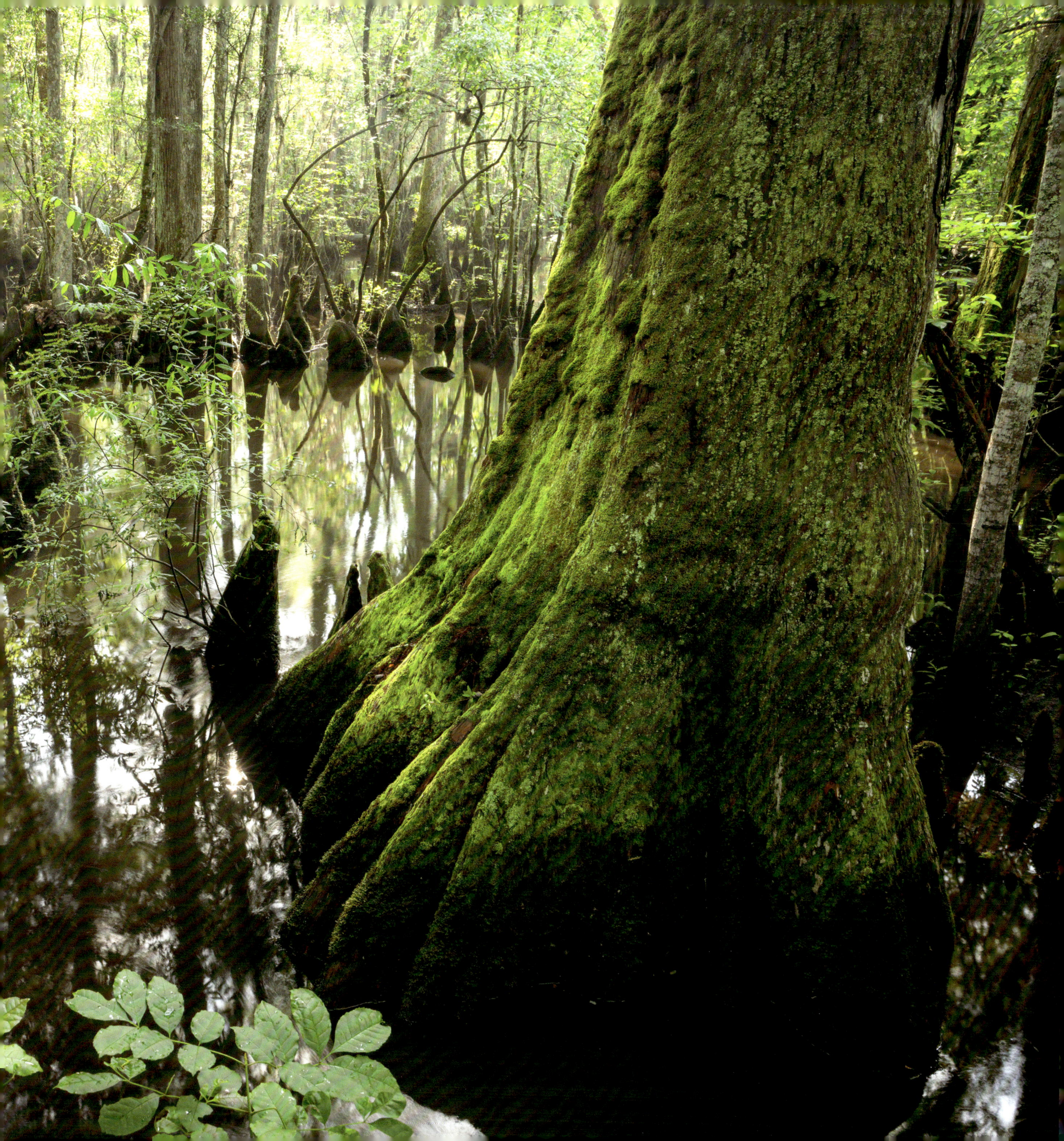

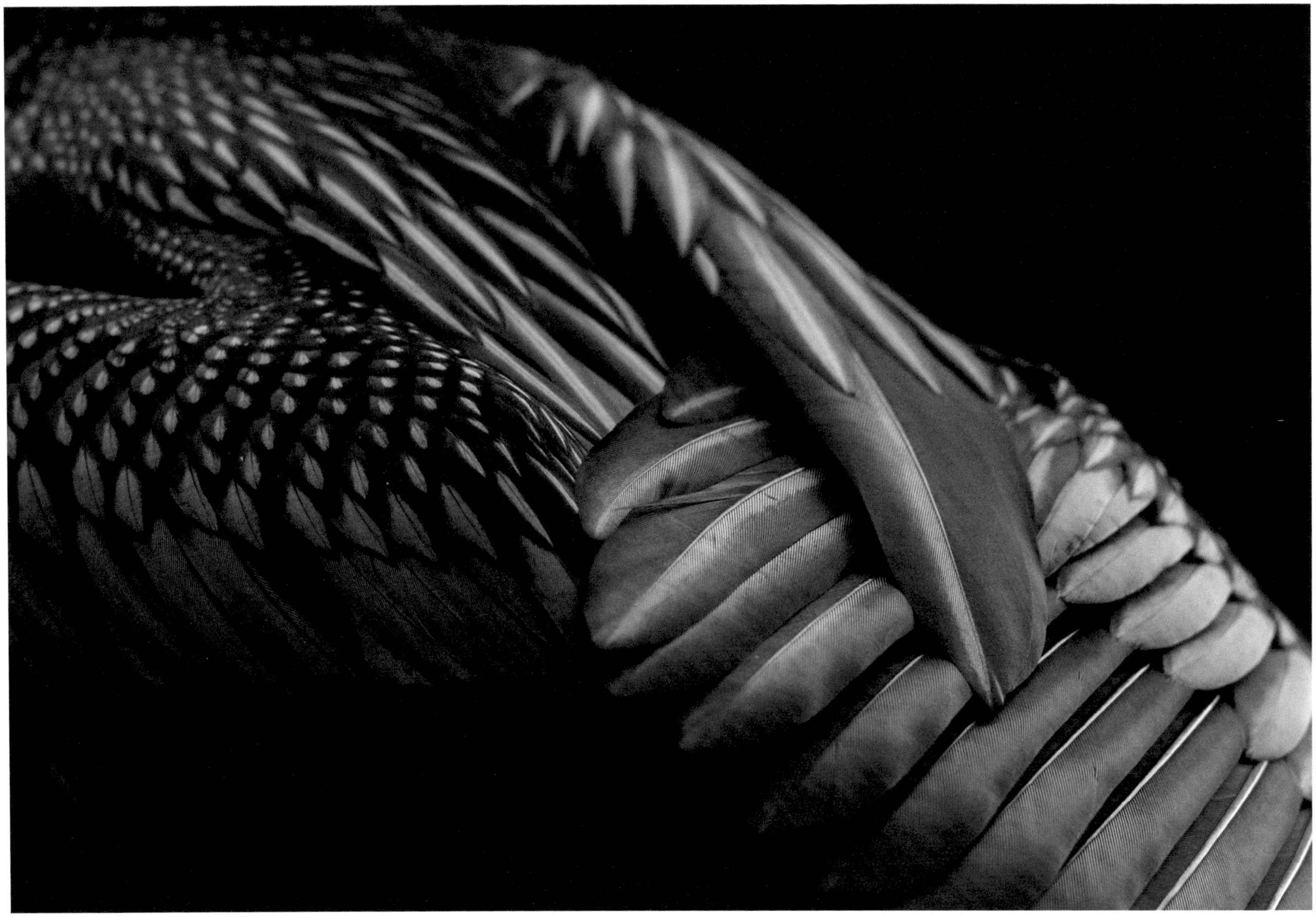

Unlike most waterbirds, anhingas have feathers that soak up water instead of repelling it—making them expert underwater hunters.

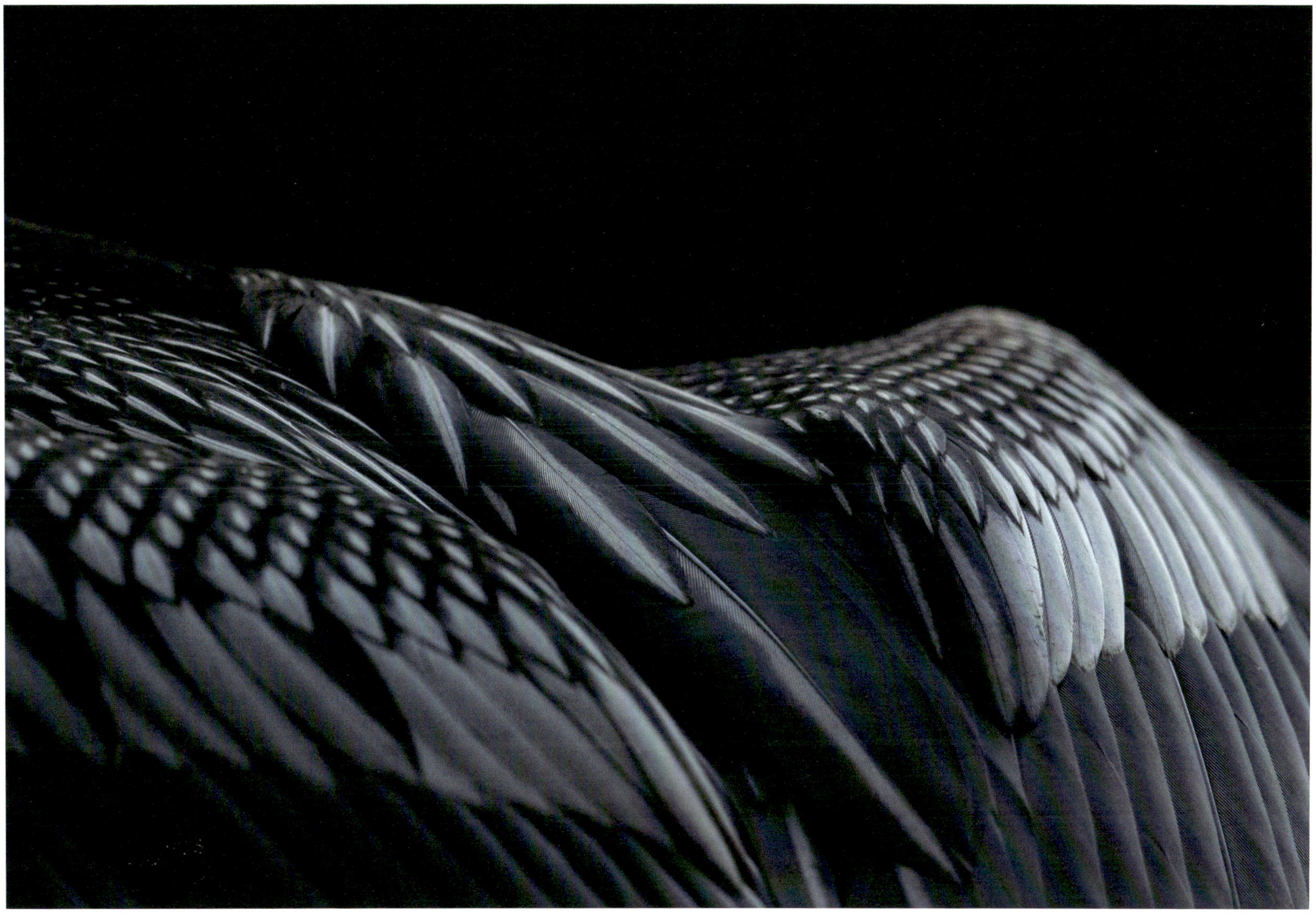

After a dive, they spread their wings to dry.

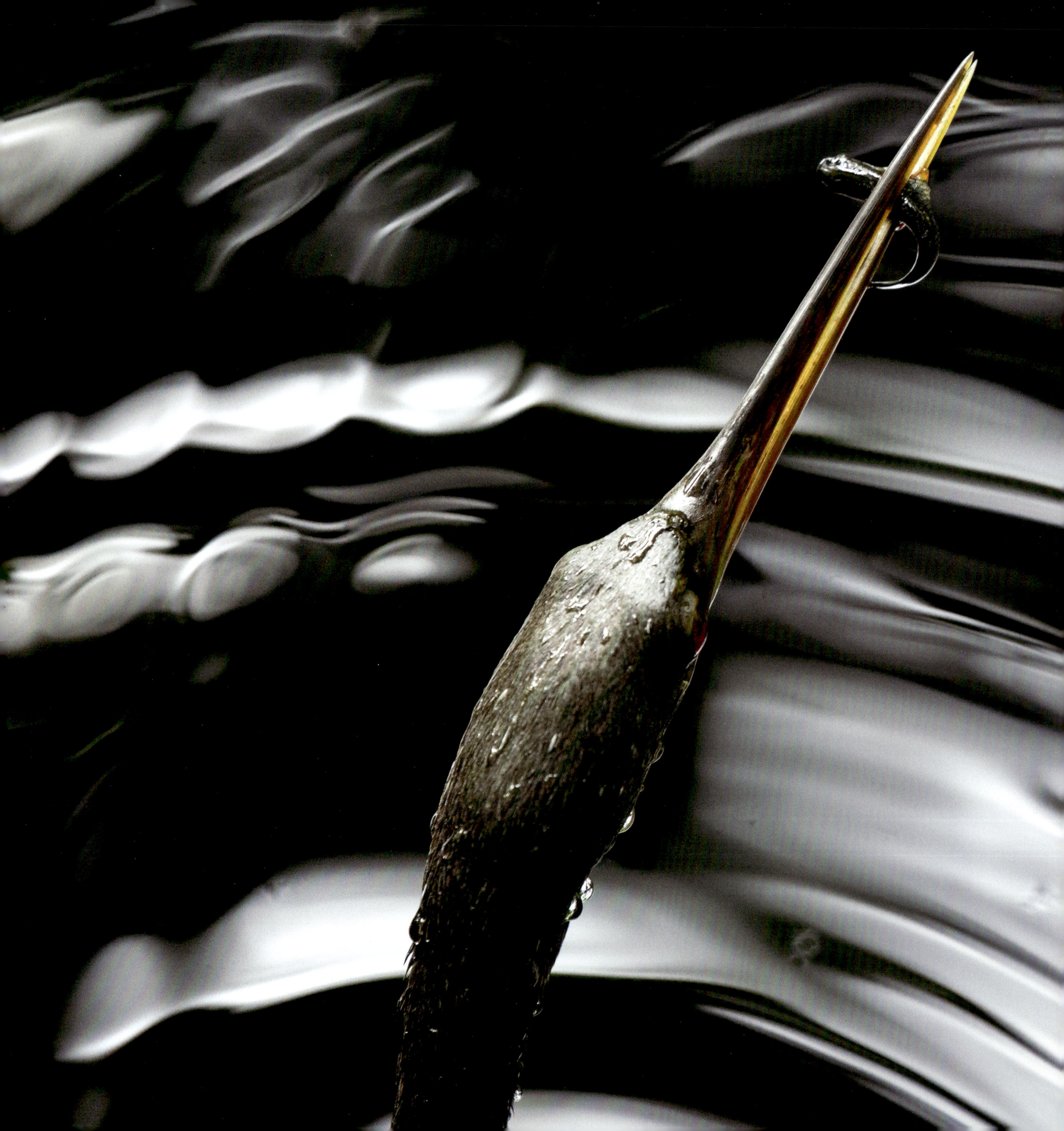

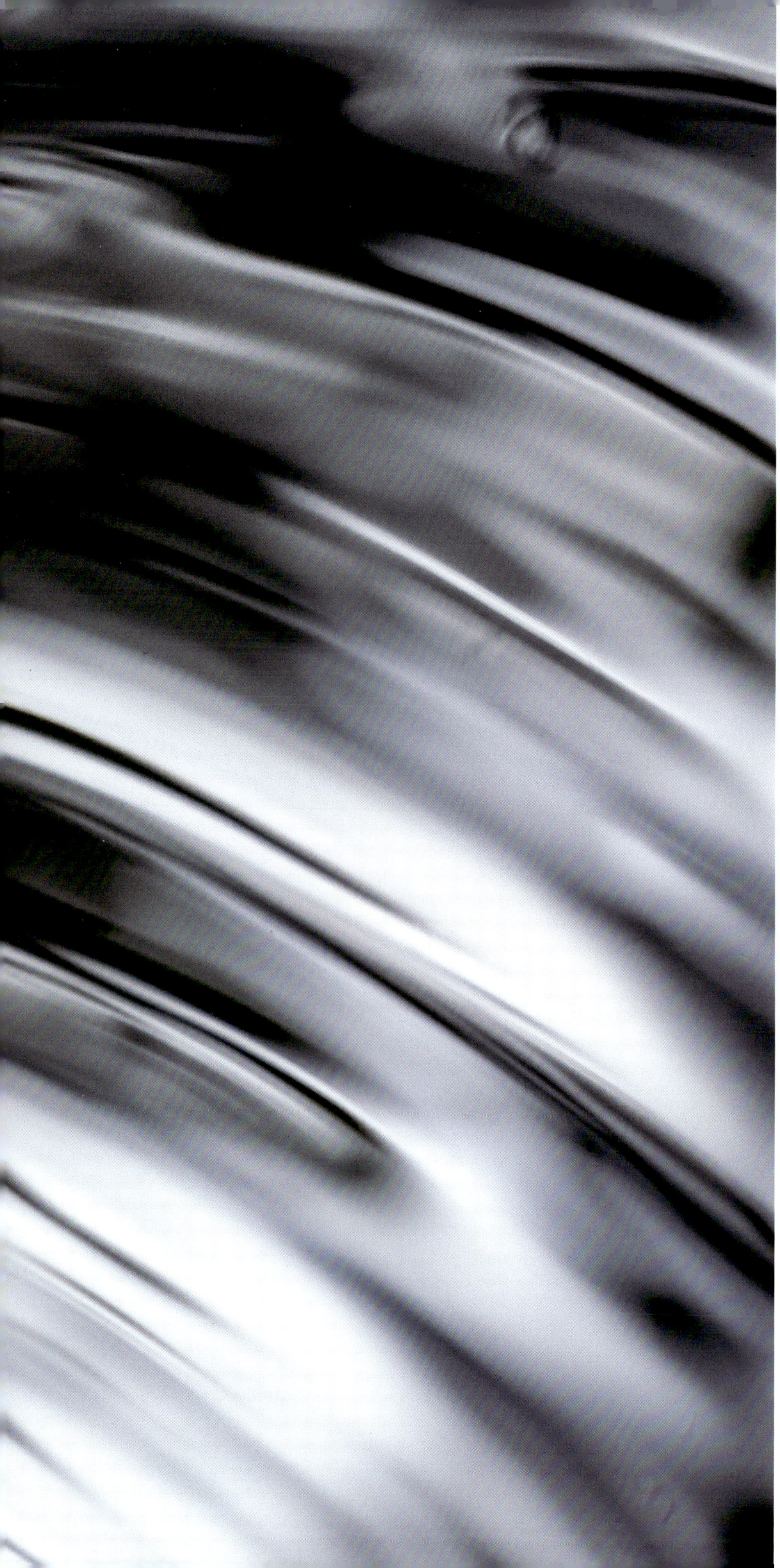

“Gambusia” originates from the derogatory Cuban word for “useless,” but gambusia, or mosquito fish as they’re commonly known, are vital to the ecosystem and are voracious mosquito larvae hunters.

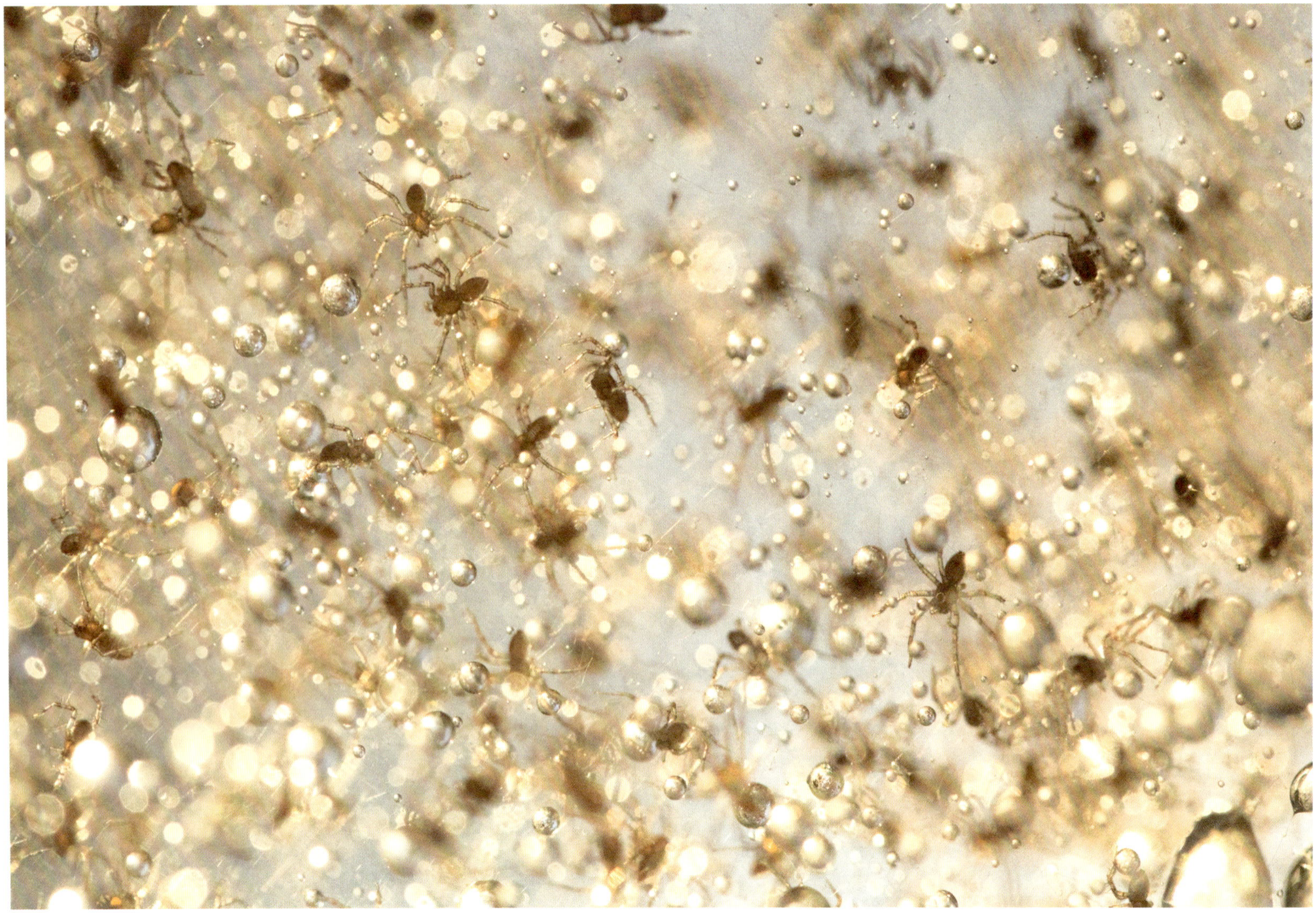

Like galaxies scattered across a celestial map, newly hatched spiders emerge beneath a dew-laced canopy.

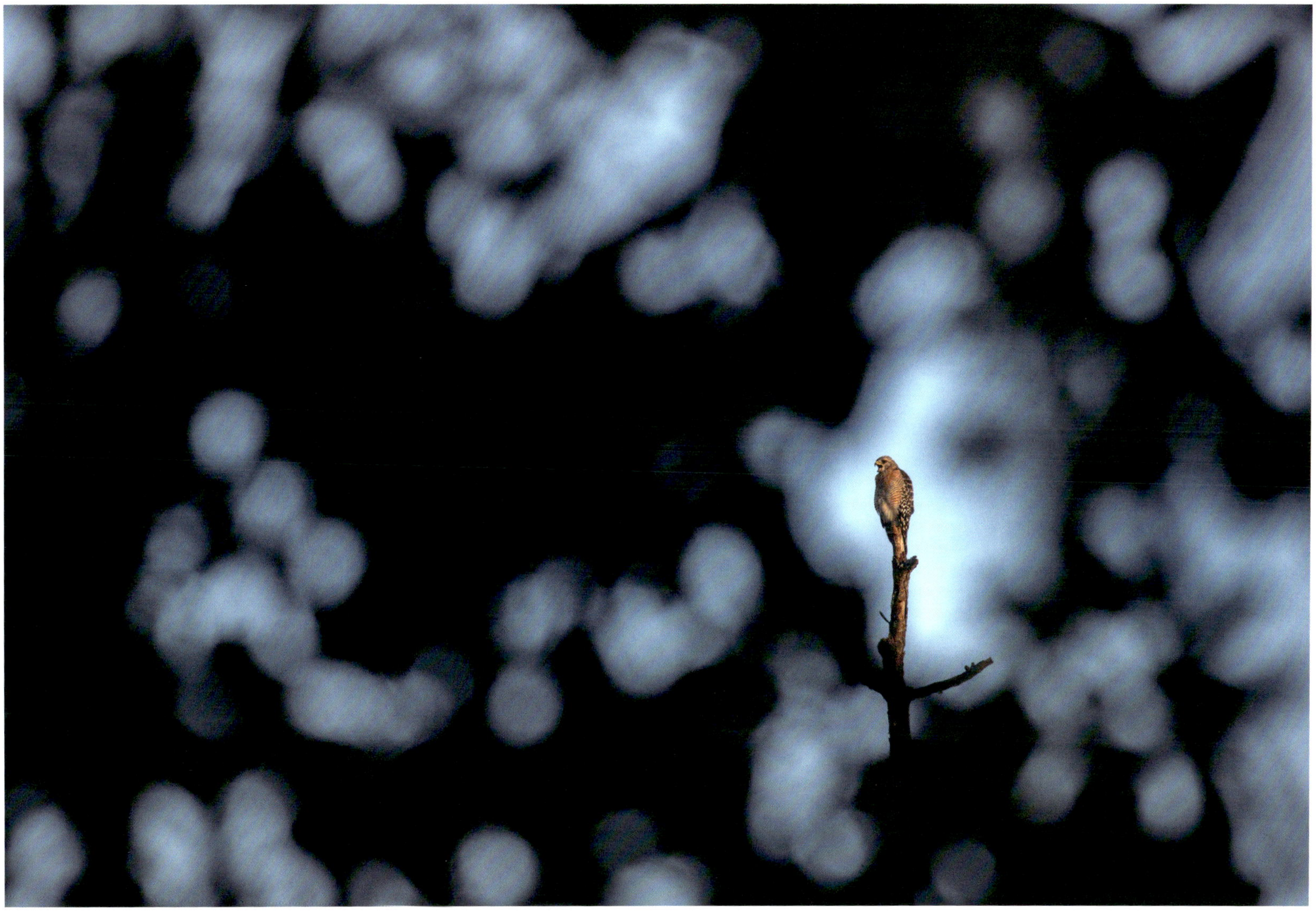

Nesting in pond cypress and maples, red-shouldered hawks skillfully navigate the understory to prey on snakes, rodents, and amphibians.

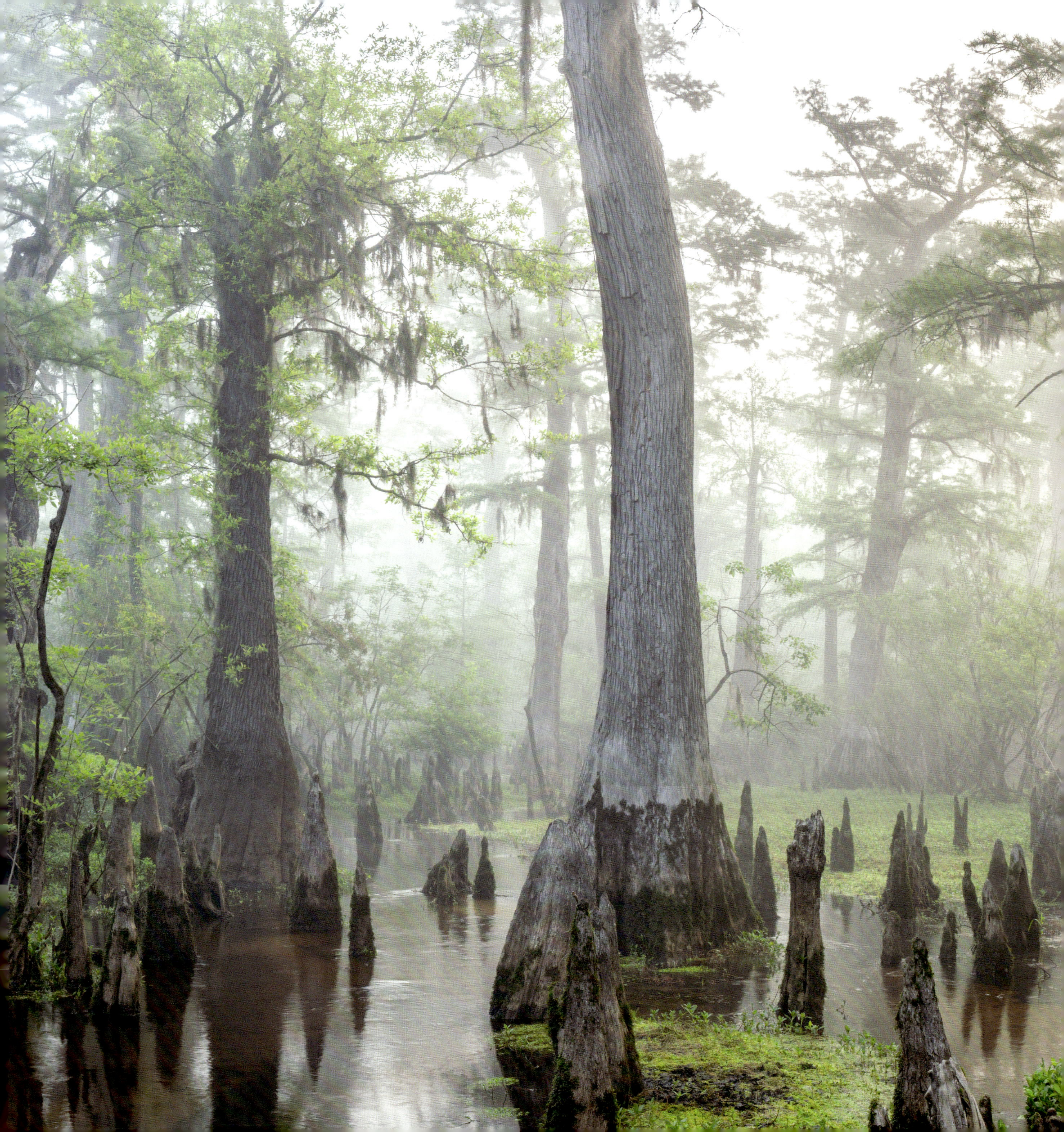

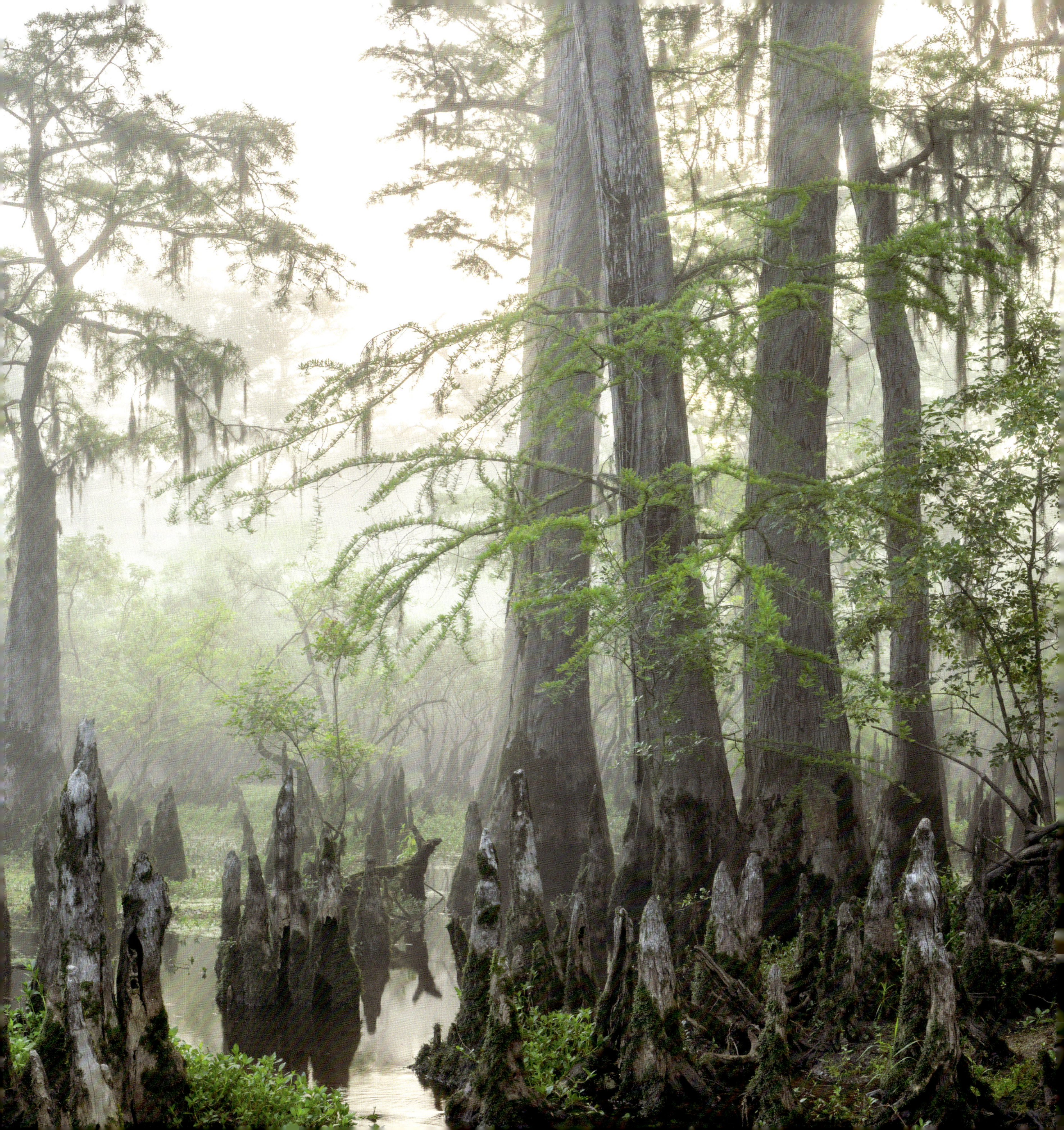

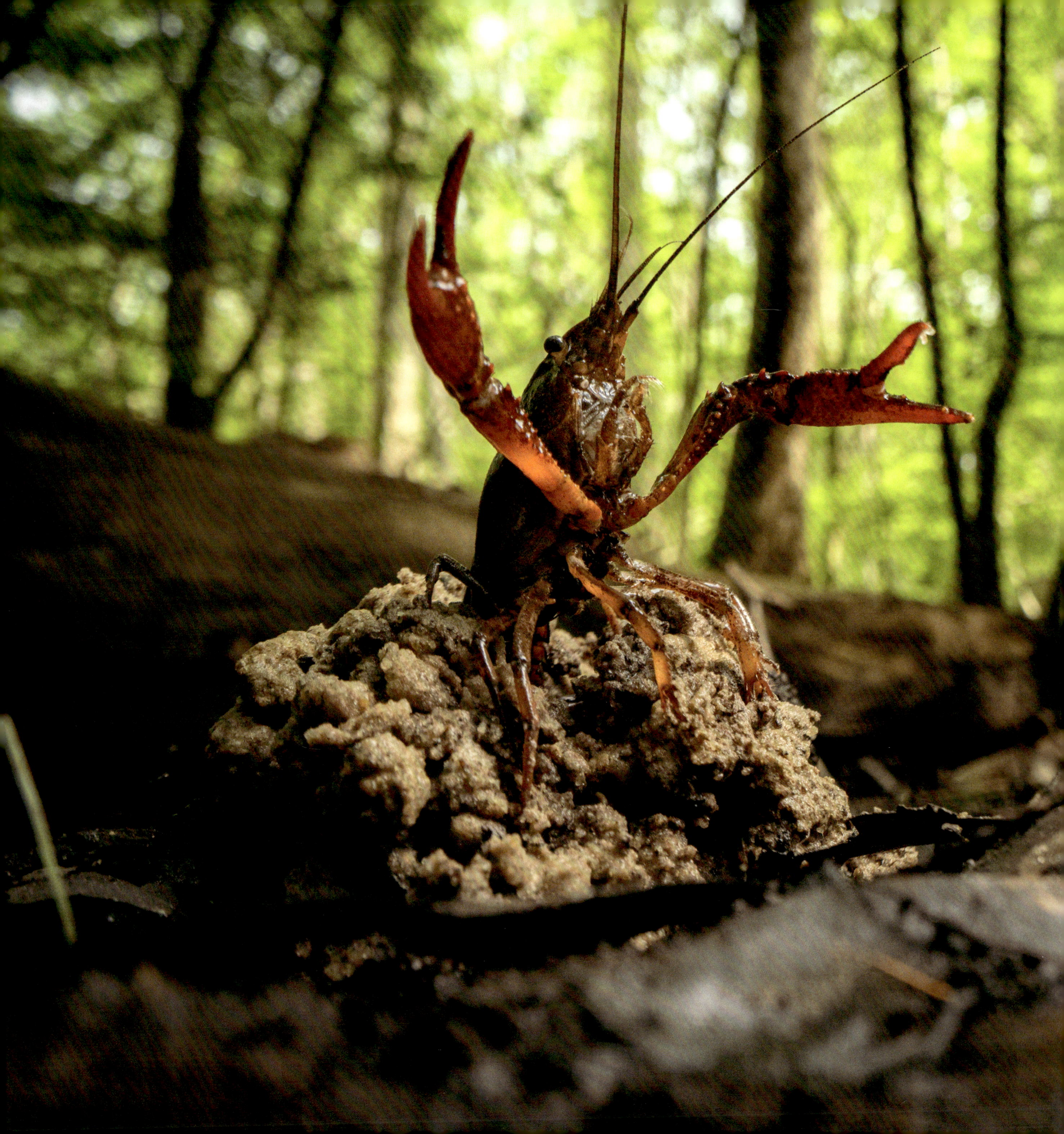

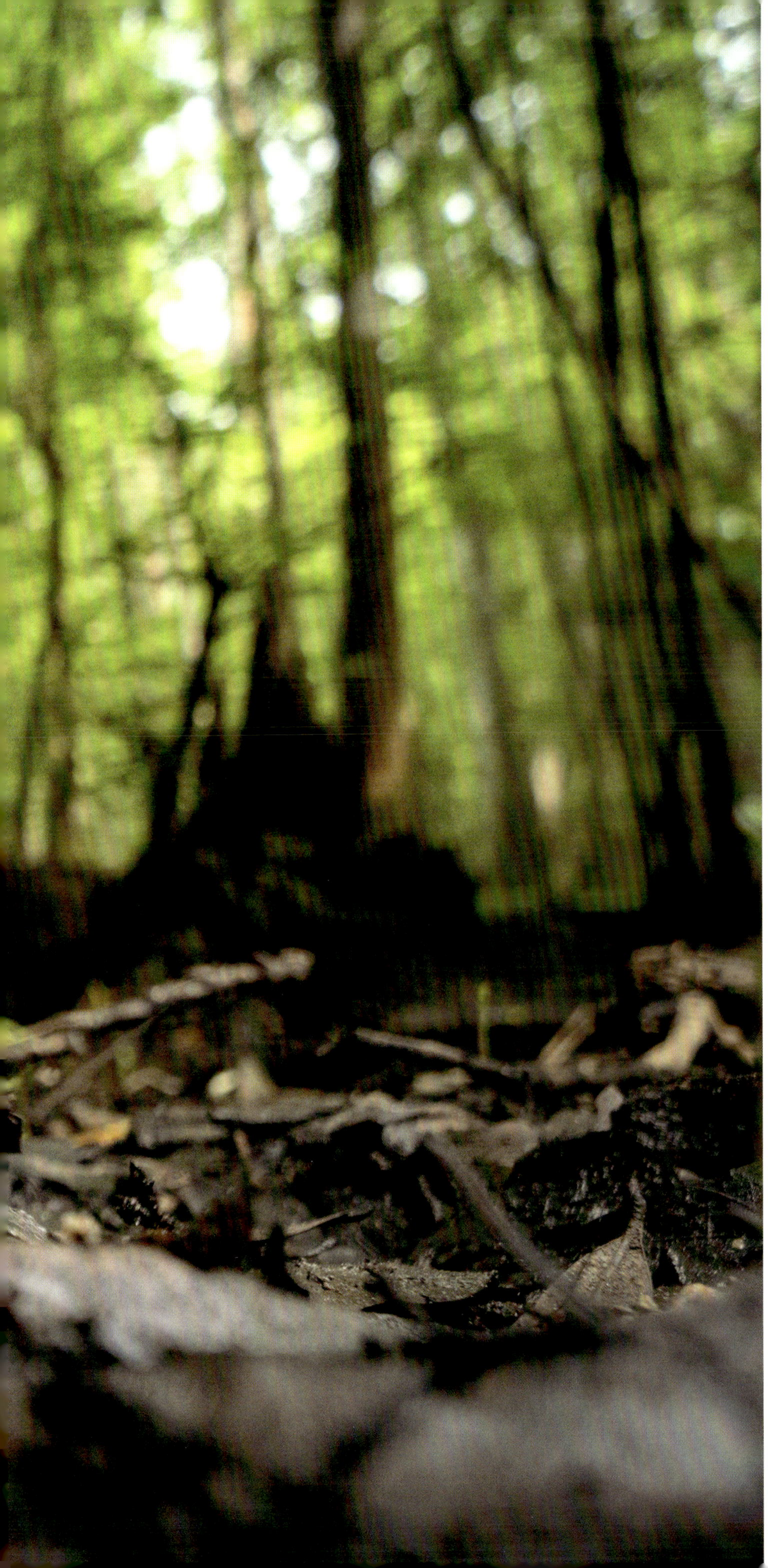

One of the many unsung heroes of the swamp, burrowing crayfish build elaborate mud towers to molt, to reach groundwater during droughts, and to escape predation underground.

PREVIOUS PAGE

With the arrival of spring, bald cypress awaken from dormancy, erupting in electric green needles that signal the start of the growing season—a striking transformation for the deciduous conifers that spend winter bare and skeletal.

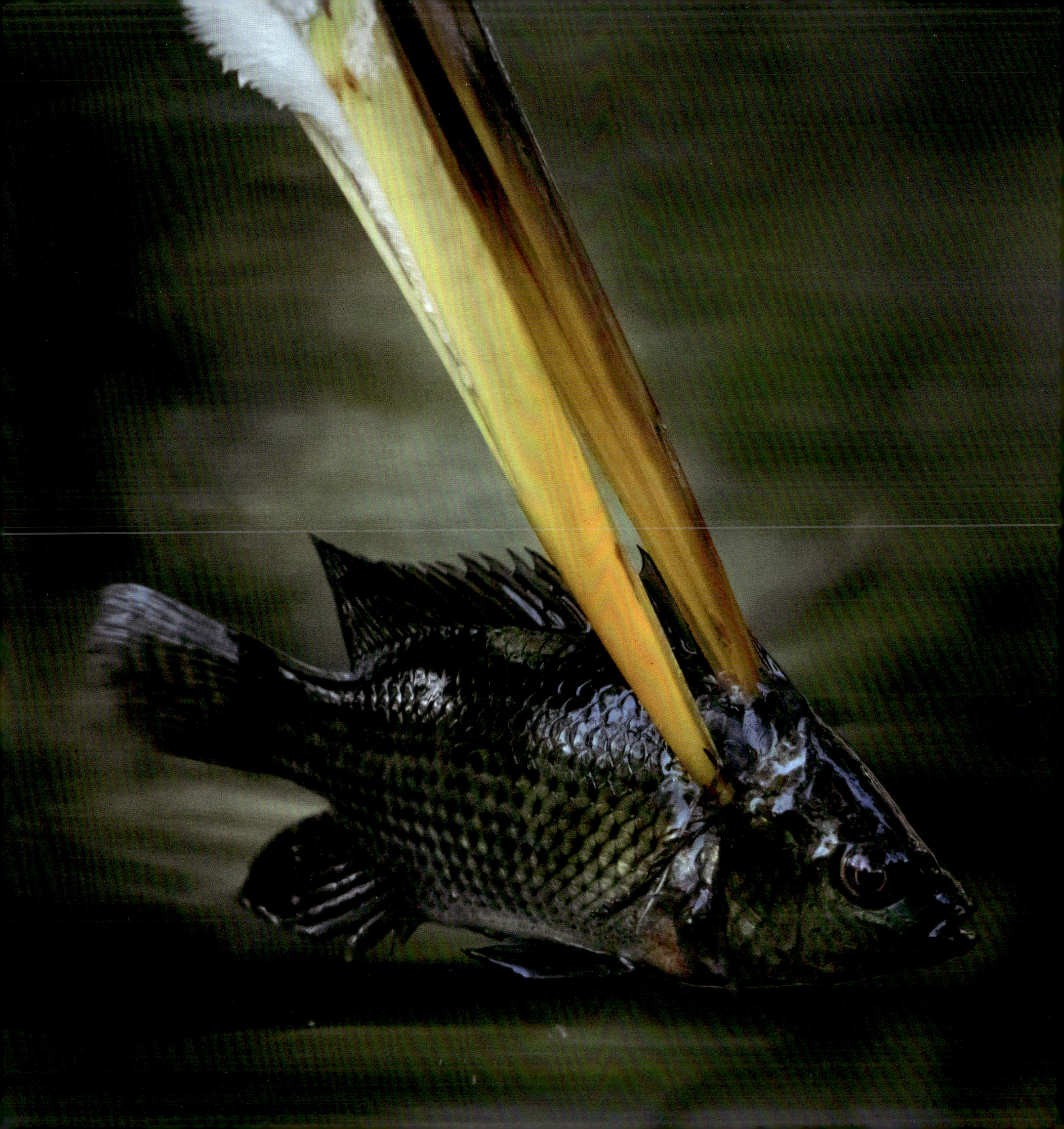

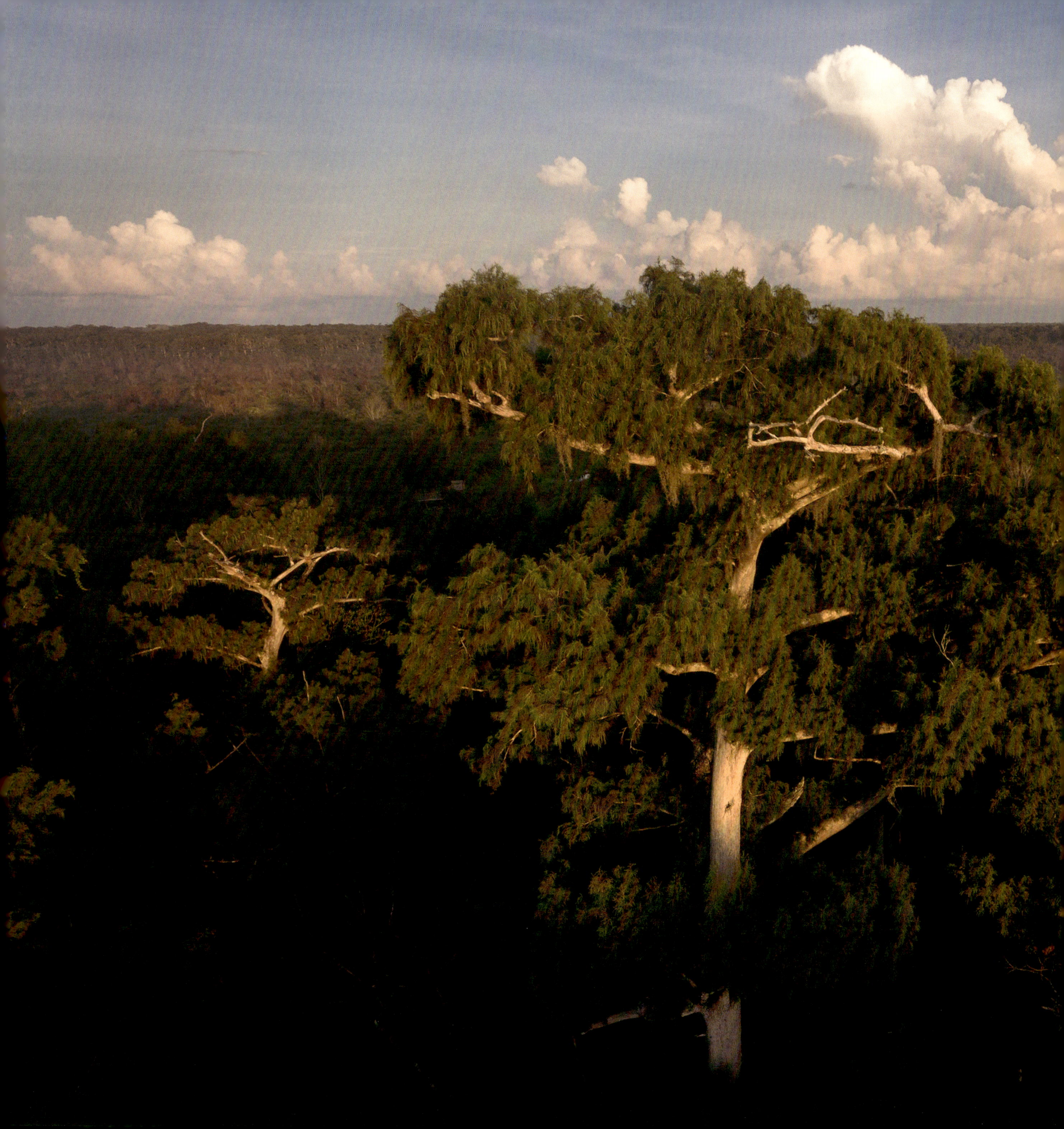

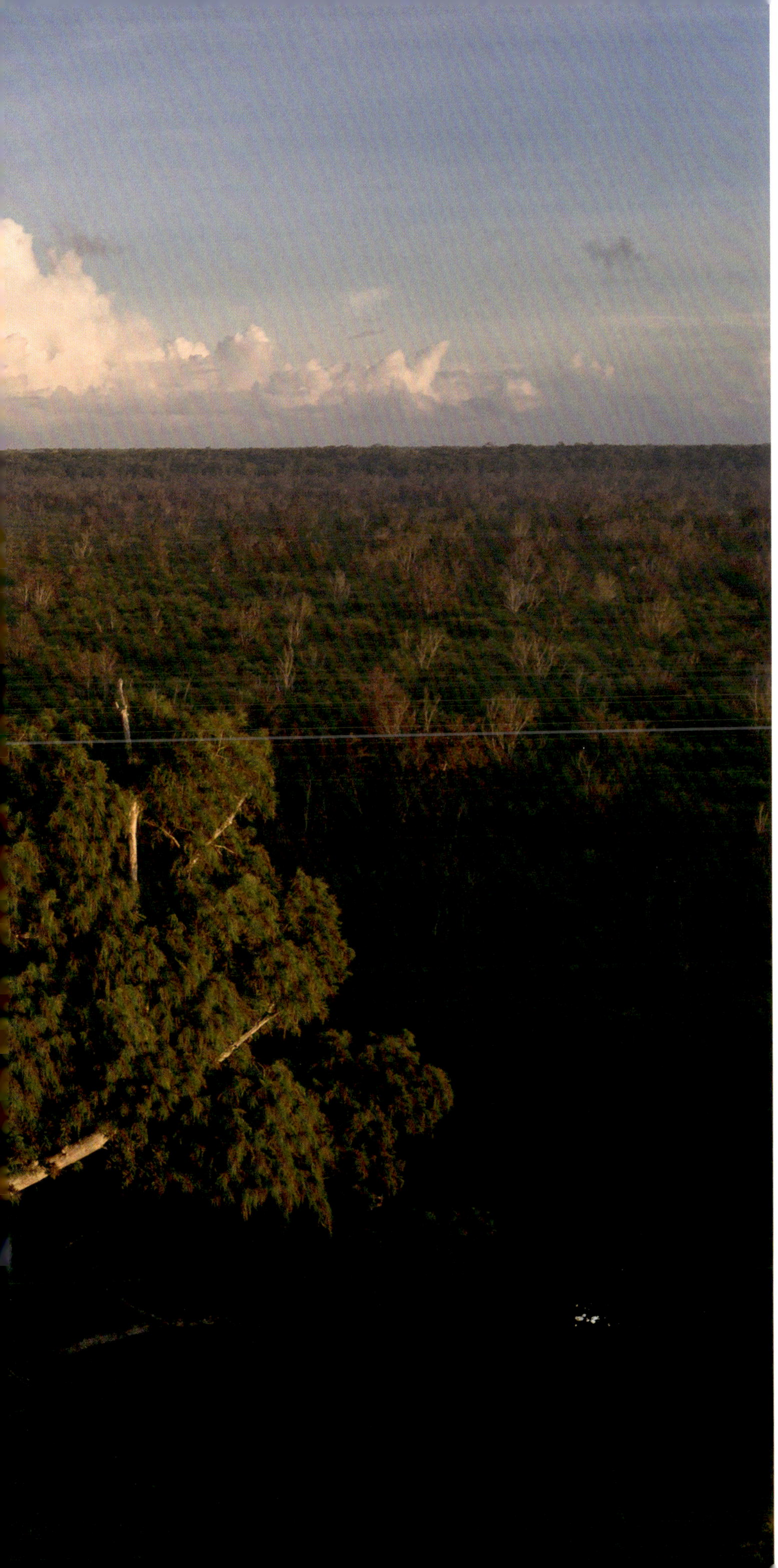

Hydroperiod and fire shape both species composition and the boundary between wet prairies and deeper sloughs, with flames halting where water remains too persistent to burn.

PREVIOUS PAGE

During the dry season in the Everglades, fish are concentrated into smaller pools, making them easy targets for wading birds like great blue herons.

The REAL ORCHID THIEF

In a state of 20 million people—webbed with highways and hemmed by sprawling metropolises like Miami, Orlando, Tampa, and Jacksonville—you'd think Florida would have surrendered all its secrets by now. But this peninsula remains stubbornly wild at its fringes. And paradoxically, those fringes are often found deep in the interior: swampy, primeval, and difficult to reach. In these sodden, seldom-visited corners, mysteries still cling to the trees.

One of the longest-standing puzzles in Florida's natural history lies in the strange life of the ghost orchid—an elusive, endangered flower with a mythic presence and an uncertain fate. For decades, biologists and botanists have puzzled over its pollination. How does it reproduce? Who visits it in the dead of night? No one could say with certainty, but the accepted theory was a single moth species as elusive and storied as the orchid itself.

The ghost orchid isn't just rare—it's otherworldly. Leafless, it survives by clinging to the trunks of pop ash, cypress, and pond apple trees, sending out photosynthetic roots that spider outward and fuse almost imperceptibly with the bark. When it blooms, typically in the rainy season of summer, it seems to levitate—a bright white blossom suspended over blackwater.

Its allure and scarcity have created its own ecosystem of devotees: scientists, writers, filmmakers, photographers, and poachers. Like the narwhal or the snow leopard, the ghost orchid enjoys cultural fame vastly disproportionate to how many people have actually seen one in the wild. My first encounter lit a fire that would smolder for years.

It began with a trek into Big Cypress National Preserve, led by two orchid bloodhounds—Chris Evans and Mario Cisneros. We slogged miles through knee- and waist-deep water, skirting thickets and gnarled roots. With only about 2,000 ghost orchids left in the Everglades, their locations are closely guarded. Even within our small group, I was asked to disable all GPS tracking before we stepped into the slough.

Somewhere among what felt like a cathedral of fern-covered limbs, Chris stopped me beside a pond apple. There it was. Suspended just above the ebony water, the flower floated like a phantom, impossibly delicate and quiet for all the hysteria and peripheral noise that it creates. Maybe it was the exhaustion, or the miles of effort that preceded it, but the orchid felt more profound than its biology could account for. The slightest breeze sent it dancing. Its pale white and sinuous petals contrasted completely with the chaos around it. I was hooked. As I composed my shots, Chris offered a detail that stopped me: only one in ten ghost orchids bloom in a season, and only one in ten of those are pollinated. And the job, as far as anyone knew, fell to just one insect—a giant sphinx moth with a seven-inch wingspan and a proboscis twice the length of its body—long enough to reach the reward buried deep in the flower's tail-like nectar tube.

That phrase—"as far as anyone knew"—sent my endorphins reeling. This was a globally famous flower, the focus of orchid fascination for more than a century, yet its basic biology remained a mystery—in a place I felt deeply connected to, and in a field I was uniquely suited to investigate. The challenge was irresistible.

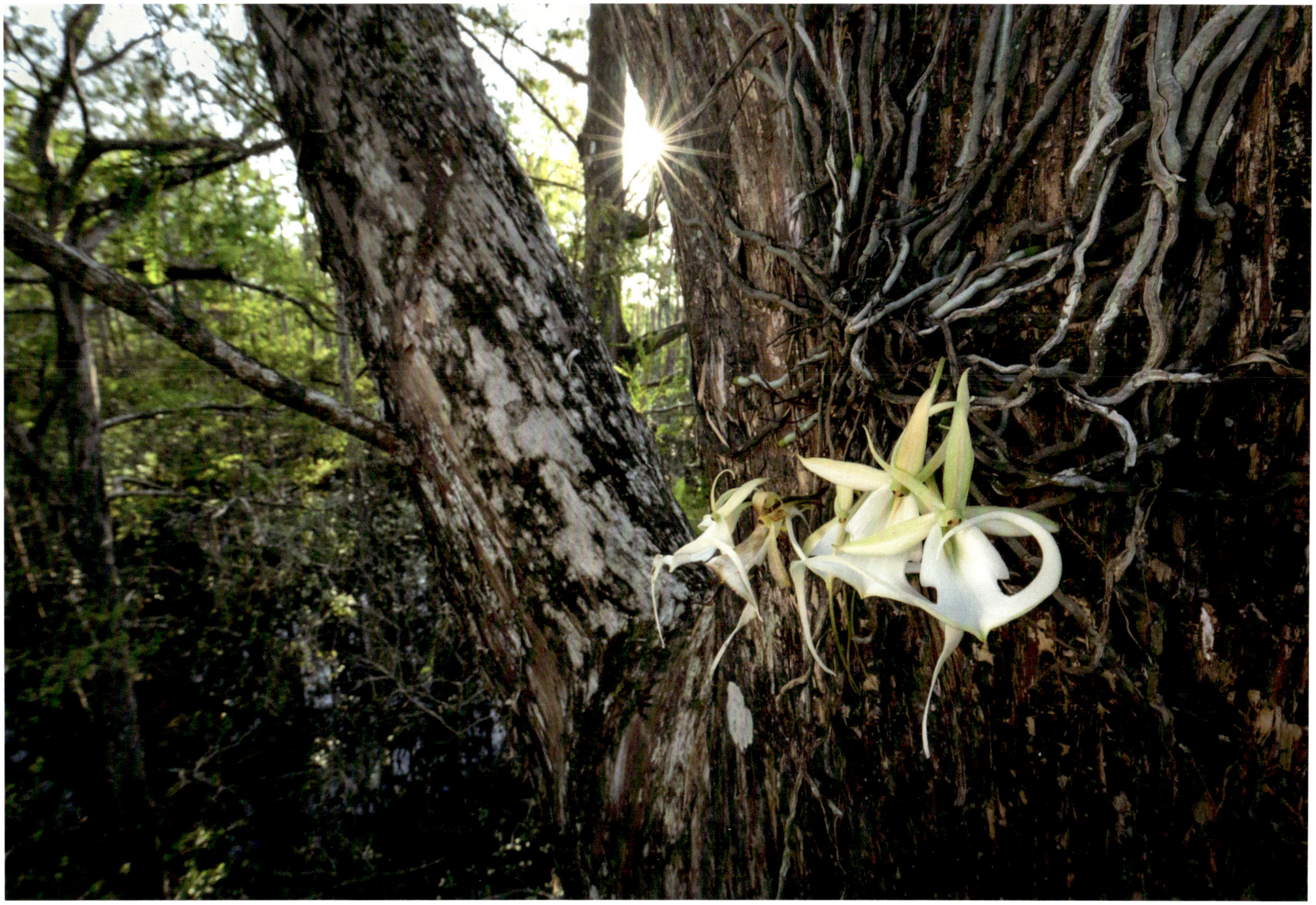

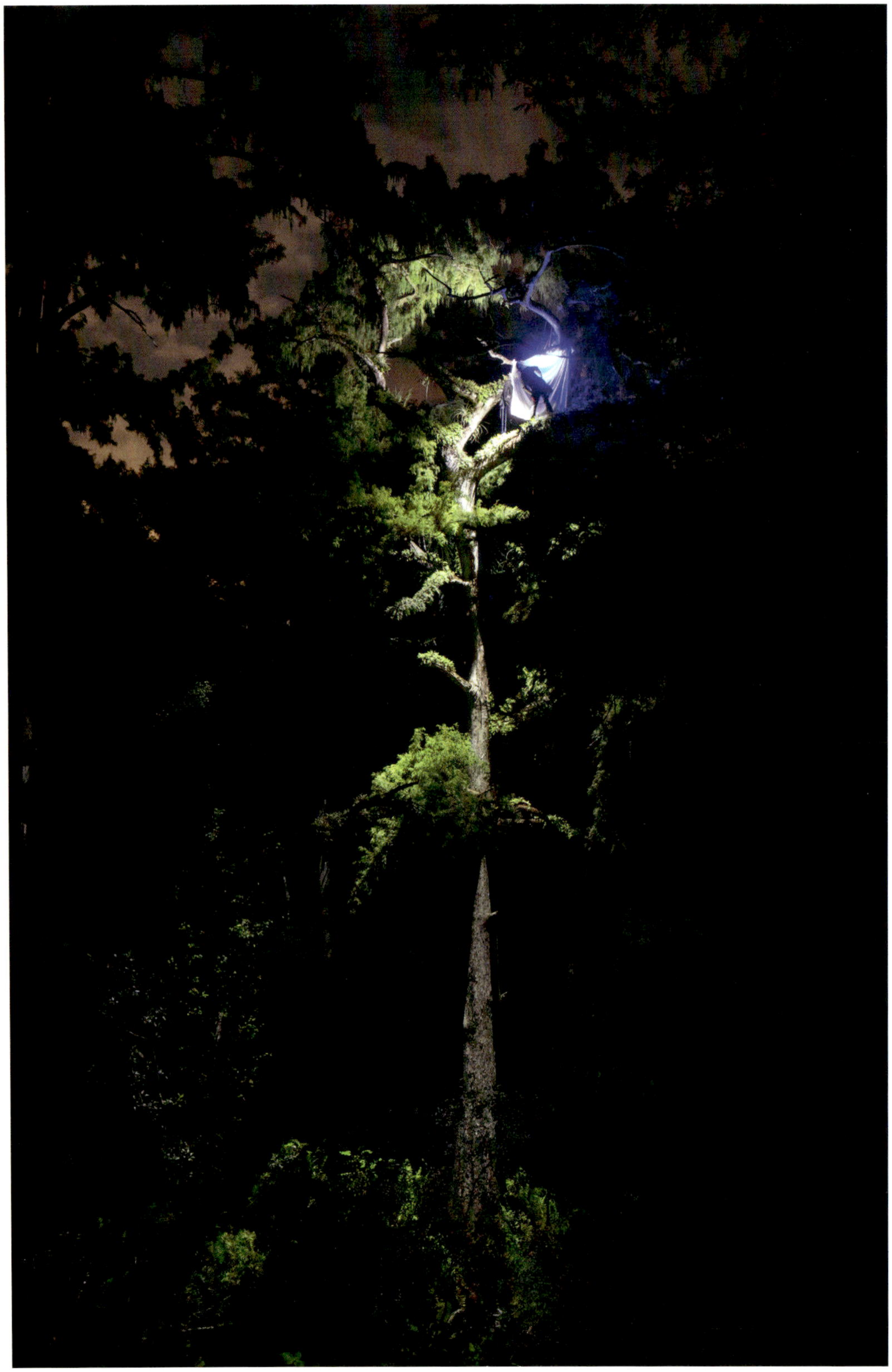

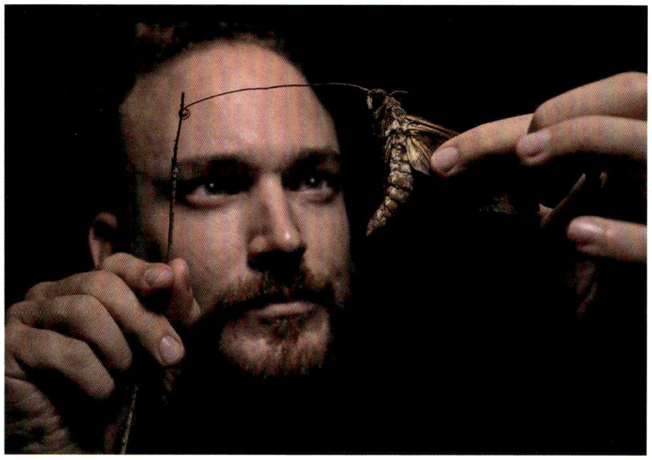

Peter Houlihan demonstrates the uncanny proboscis of a giant sphinx moth.

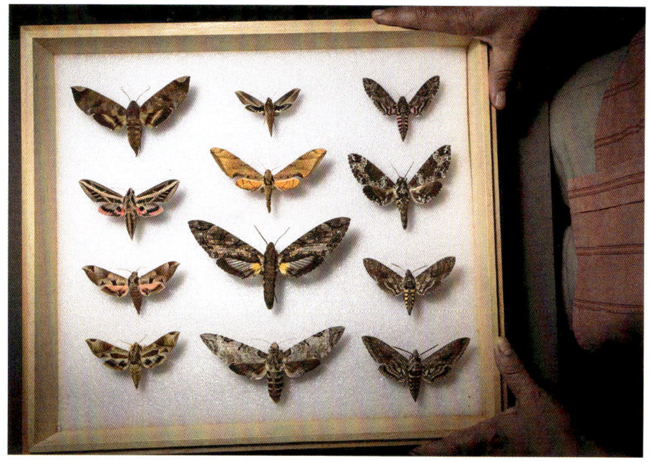

For years, Houlihan believed that several hawk moth species native to the area were capable of pollinating the ghost orchid.

Over the next few years, I set out to answer it.

I began by designing an unmanned camera system—an elaborate mix of custom housings, infrared sensors, and reinforced mounts—to document the holy grail: the moment of pollination at a ghost orchid. But not just any orchid. I chose the most prolific one known in the Everglades: a plant in Corkscrew Swamp Sanctuary that blooms up to 18 times in a season (most top out at two). They call it "the super ghost." It grows 50 feet up in a 500-year-old cypress, deep in the last remaining old-growth swamp in the state. My thought was that before the cypress trees were logged out of the Everglades, maybe ghost orchids were once common in the canopies. If any flower had a chance to attract the giant sphinx moth and complete the ancient ritual of nocturnal romance, it was this one.

I wasn't alone. Two fellow National Geographic explorers joined the effort: Peter Houlihan, a tropical ecologist, orchid expert, and skilled tree climber who had spent seven years trying to answer the same question; and photographer Carlton Ward Jr., who installed his own camera traps in the Florida Panther National Wildlife Refuge. Between us, we committed to months of slogging, adjusting gear, swapping batteries, wiping lenses, and praying the system would work when—and if—a moth finally came.

Like so many who fall under the ghost orchid's spell, I went headlong into obsession. When I was at the sanctuary, I'd schlep my equipment out into the swamp every morning, haul myself up the fixed rope, and check the camera, breath held, hoping the night had delivered something—a visitor, a clue. Most days, there was nothing. On others, near-daily downpours would trigger the sensor thousands of times, filling my memory cards with empty frames and draining the speedlights. Spider webs, fogged lenses, dead batteries: it was a never-ending ritual of tweaking sensor sensitivity, rebalancing lights, and clearing obstructions while suspended over the forest floor.

I was so neurotic I eventually became convinced that even my scent—sweat-drenched, human—might discourage a moth from approaching the bloom. I began staggering my visits, trying to minimize my presence. But every day away gnawed at me. It was the same uneasy panic as leaving the oven on—only the oven was 50 feet up in a tree, in the middle of a flooded tropical forest, three states away.

Back in Greenville, South Carolina, I'd lie awake at night, replaying the setup in my head. Did I turn the strobes on? Did I put a memory card in the camera? On more than one occasion, the anxiety won. I'd book a last-minute flight, rent a car, drive straight to the sanctuary, climb the tree, and confirm what I already feared: everything was working fine. It was madness. But it was also purpose. I was chasing a ghost—and like any good ghost story, it demanded belief.

Then, on July 17th, Peter and I climbed the tree together to check the camera. Like every visit, we were hopeful, but not expectant. Dangling in the canopy, we reviewed the images from the night before. After hundreds of empty frames, my thumb numbly scrolling the image advance, my heart skipped a beat at the flash of color. Like a magic trick, a massive hawk-moth appeared out of the ether, hovering in front of the fragrant bloom with the tell-tale orange stripes on its abdomen. Eureka. For Peter, it was the closure he had sought for nearly a decade. For me, it was confirmation that I wasn't crazy. We had captured the first ever photograph of a giant sphinx moth at a ghost orchid.

By summer's end, I had logged more than 1,800 camera-trap hours and made 7,938 images, only 23 of which had moths in the frame. And buried in that 0.2 percent batting average, another revelation emerged.

Not one, but two different species of moths appeared to be pollinating the ghost orchid in Corkscrew Swamp—including the long-suspected giant sphinx. But something stood out when I pored over the images, zooming in, scrutinizing every detail. The sphinx moth's proboscis was so long, it seemed to drink the nectar without ever touching the orchid's pollinia—the pollen sacs required for reproduction. On its head was the dusting of pollen from another flower, most likely a moonvine. Here it was at the ghost orchid, taking the reward without offering anything in return: a nectar thief, not a pollinator.

Just five days later, a fig sphinx moth hovered in front of the ghost orchid, clearly carrying and depositing pollinia. Carlton's camera traps confirmed the pattern, documenting three additional moth species visiting orchids in the Panther National Wildlife Refuge.

The discovery rewrote the narrative. For decades, the giant sphinx had been cast as the orchid's evolutionary soulmate, its singular partner in survival. But our cameras told a more complicated story—one in which the supposed savior might actually be a parasite, and survival may lie not in monogamy, but in a quiet, diverse network of nocturnal visitors.

In some ways, this was good news. The ghost orchid was made more resilient because it wasn't wholly dependent on the fate of one rare moth. But its future is still uncertain. Corkscrew Swamp has seen its hydroperiod—the duration the swamp stays flooded—shrink by nearly 30 percent over the past half-century. That's not just bad news for ghost orchids and other epiphytes who rely on specific microclimates. It's a crisis for everything that depends on the slow, pulsing heartbeat of Everglades water: fish, birds, panthers, gators, trees, estuaries—and the nine million people who depend on its watershed when they turn on the tap.

We went looking for answers in the canopy of a cypress tree and found a story far bigger than a flower. We also found a warning. A reminder that beauty is not a shield, and rarity offers no refuge. The most extraordinary things don't always disappear in silence. Sometimes, they vanish while we're still trying to understand the question.

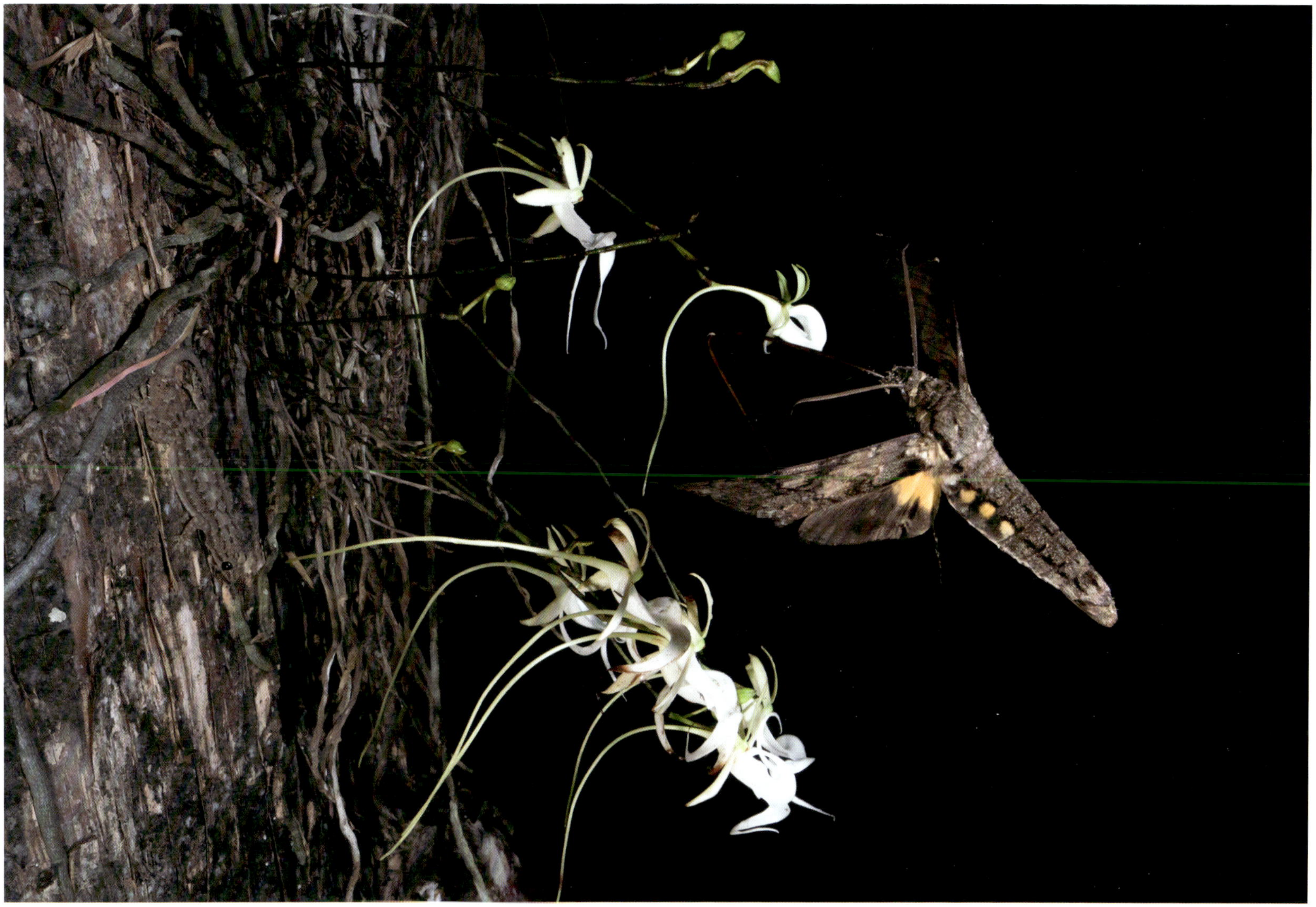

A giant sphinx moth dwarfs the large orchid blooms and a gecko (*left*) waiting in ambush for an easy meal.

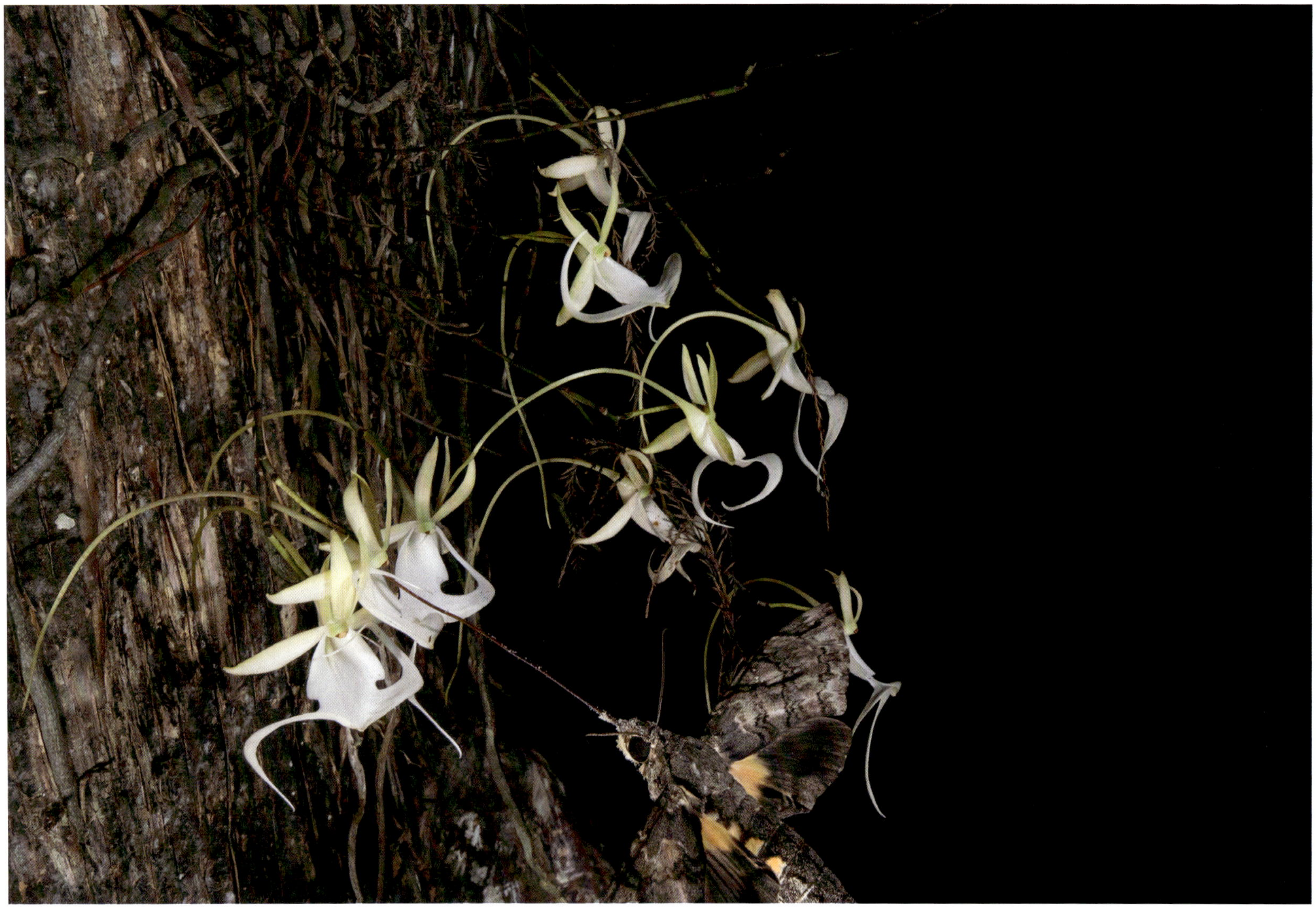

Drinking nectar from the ghost orchid, the giant sphinx moth is dusted with pollen from another flower—but this image suggests its proboscis may be too long to pollinate the ghost orchid effectively, never bringing the moth close enough to pick up its pollinia.

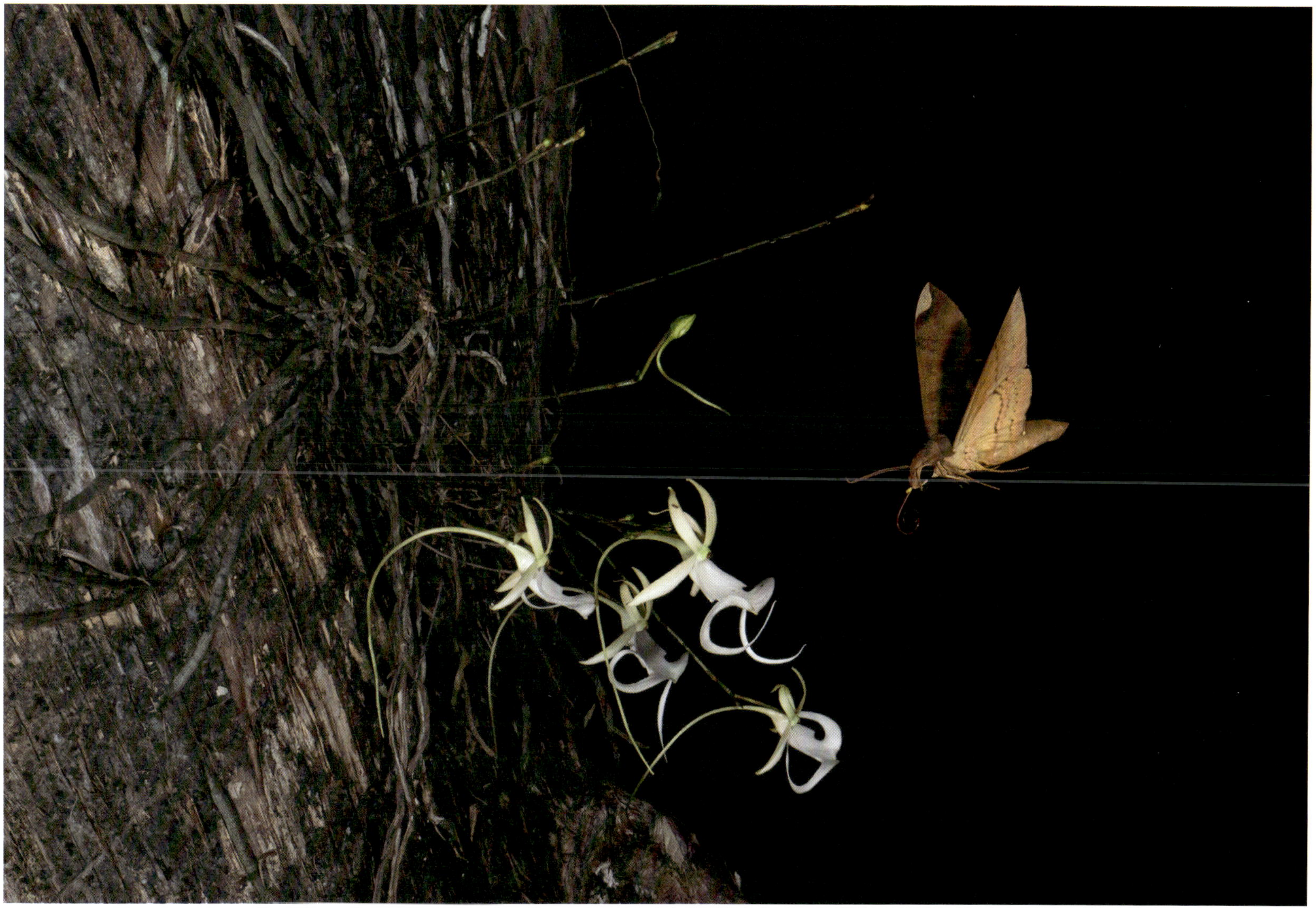

With pollinia from a ghost orchid on its frons, a fig sphinx moth visits various flowers at the super ghost in Corkscrew Swamp.

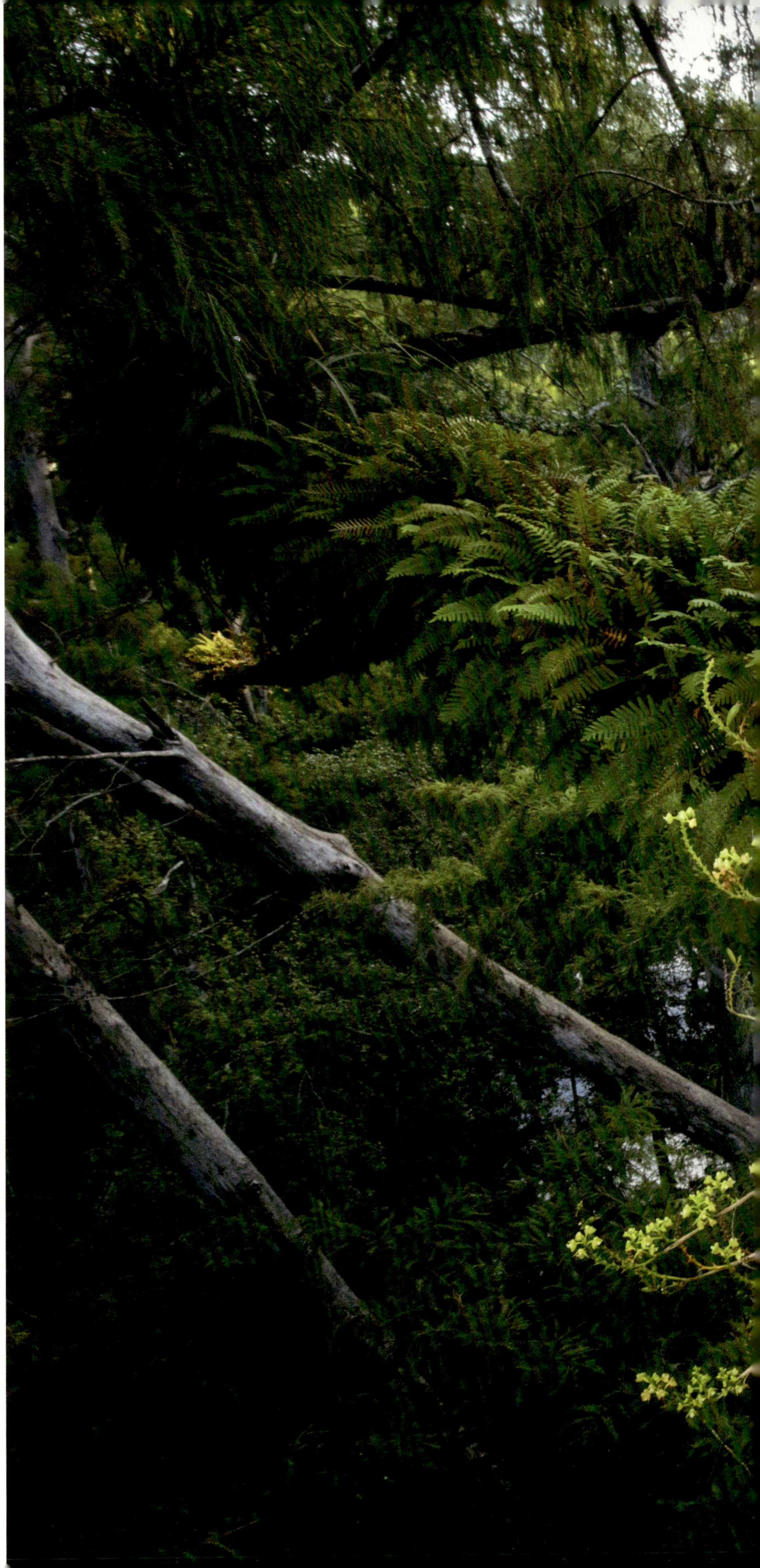

Growing 90 feet above the forest floor, a yellow helmet orchid blooms among a carpet of resurrection fern and tillandsia.

FOLLOWING PAGE

Spore packets appear as half-open clamshells on the back of a Christmas fern.

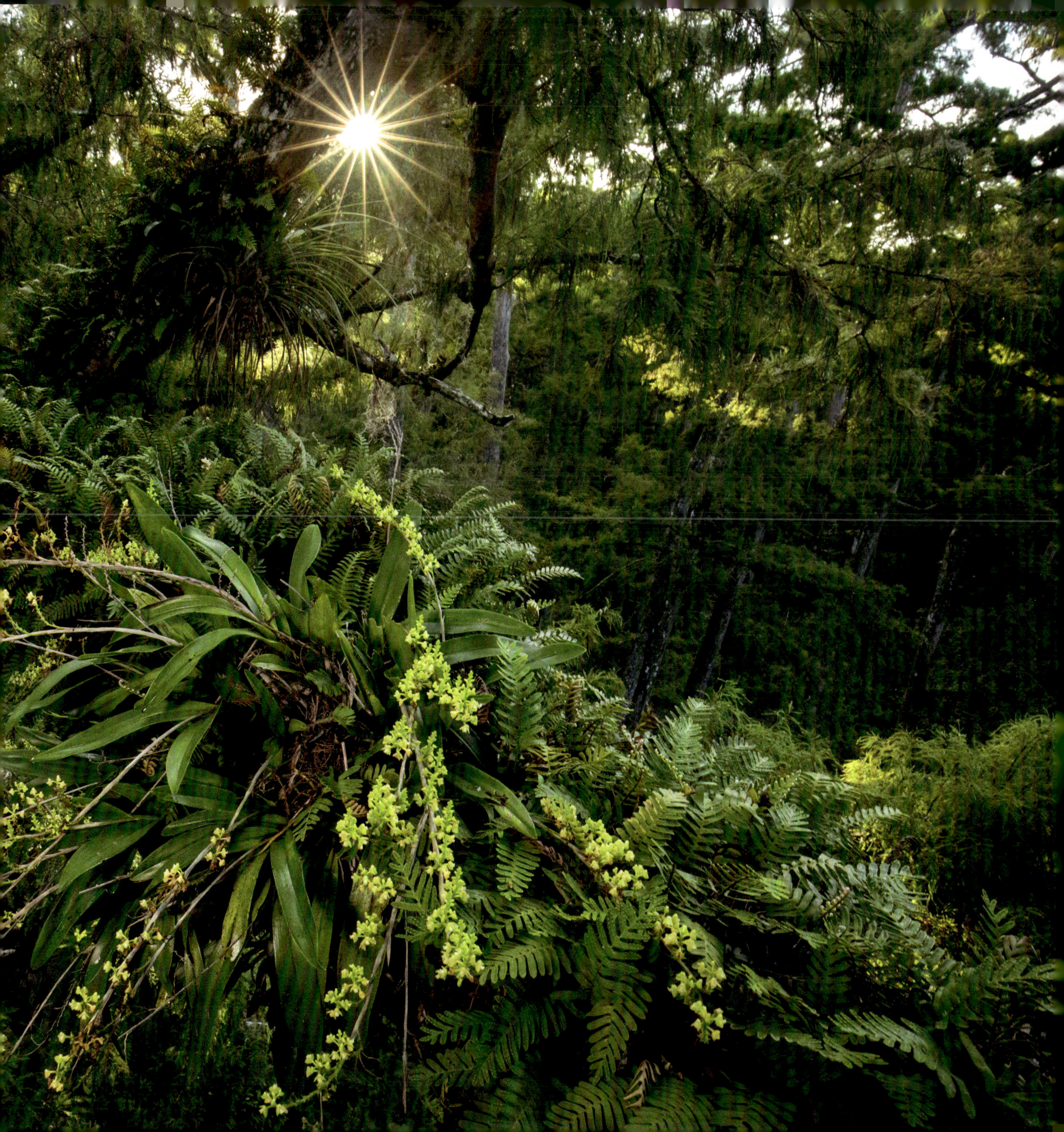

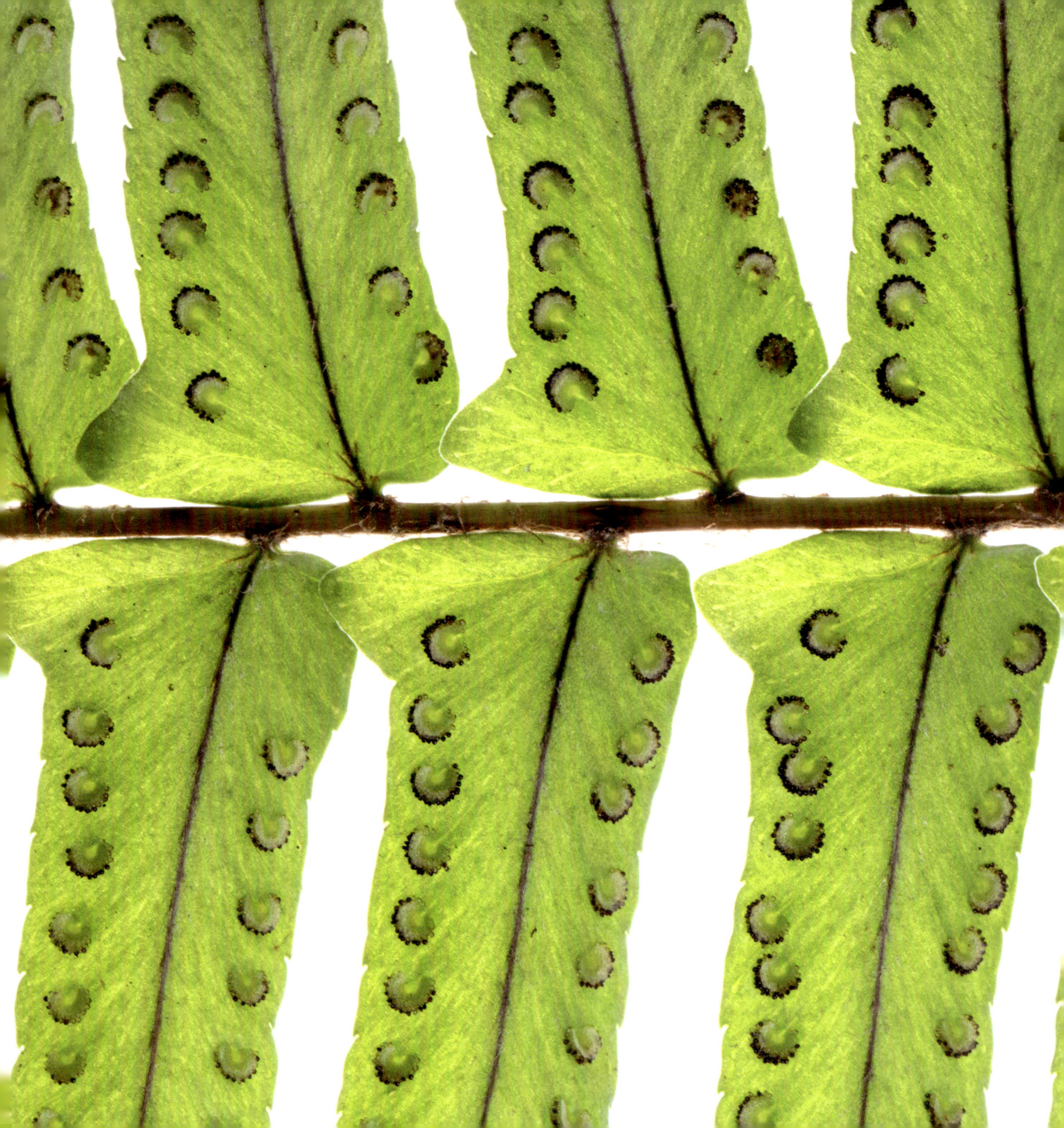

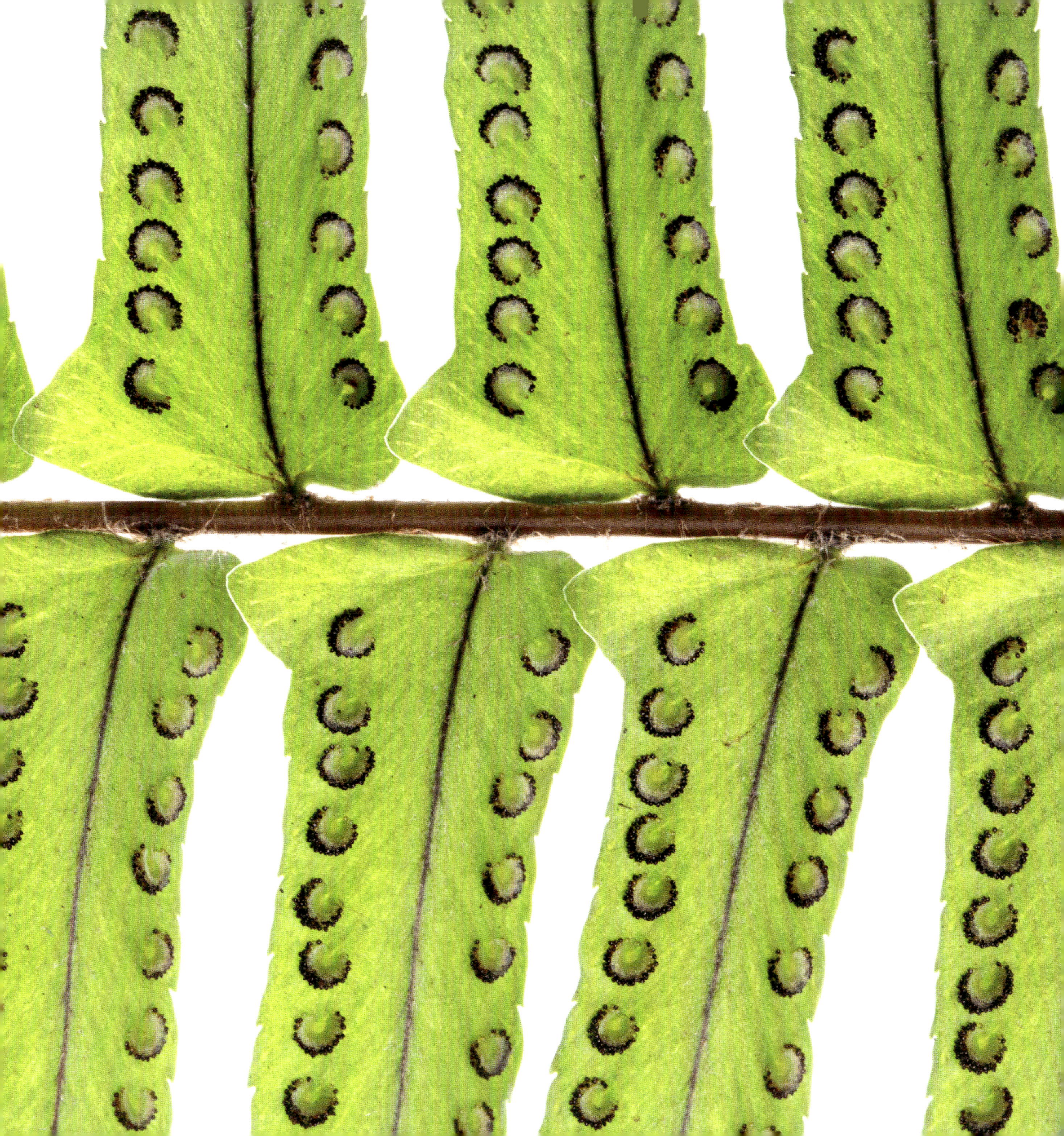

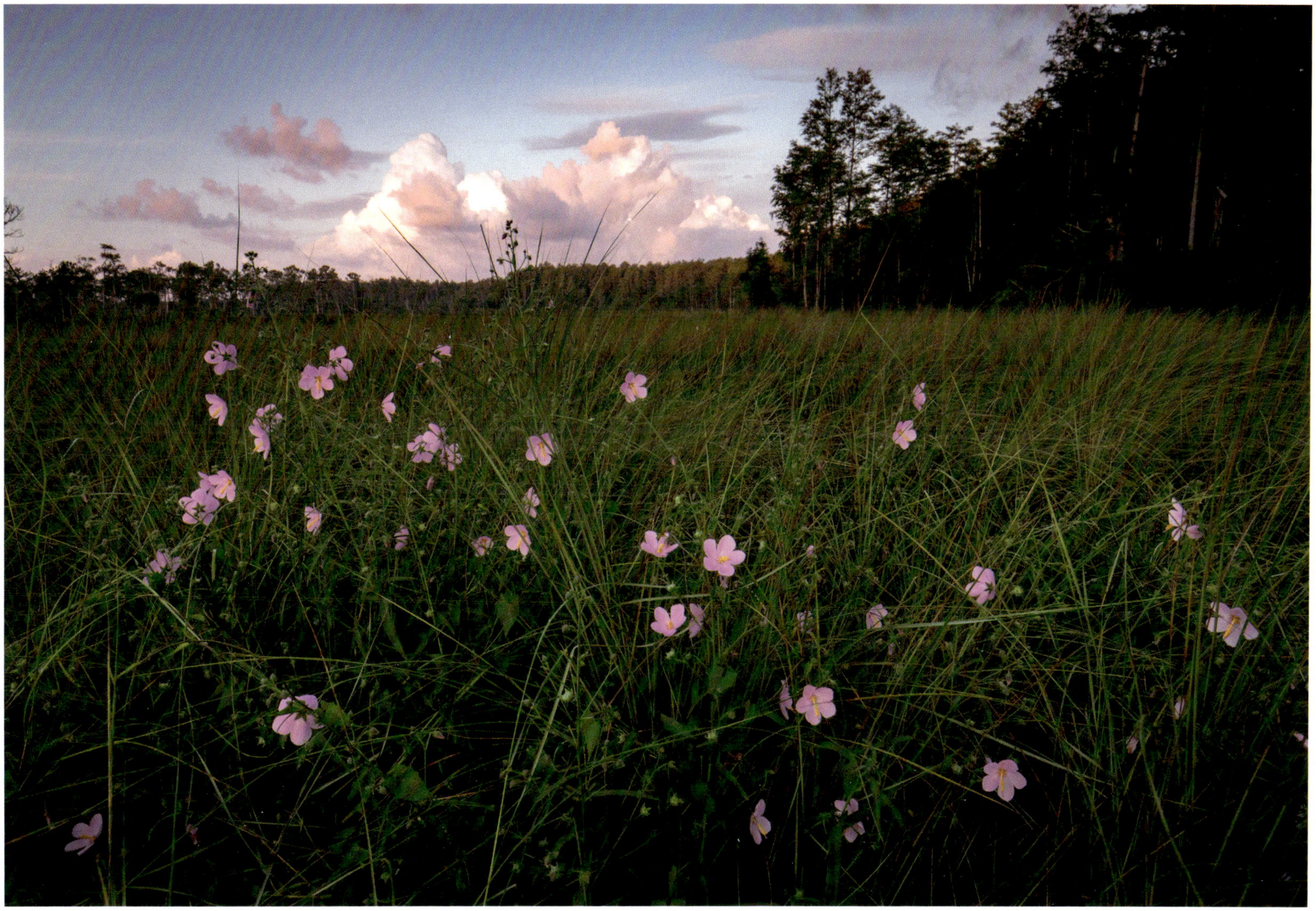

Wet prairies dry out for part of the year and after
a fire, they blossom with stunning flowers and native grasses.

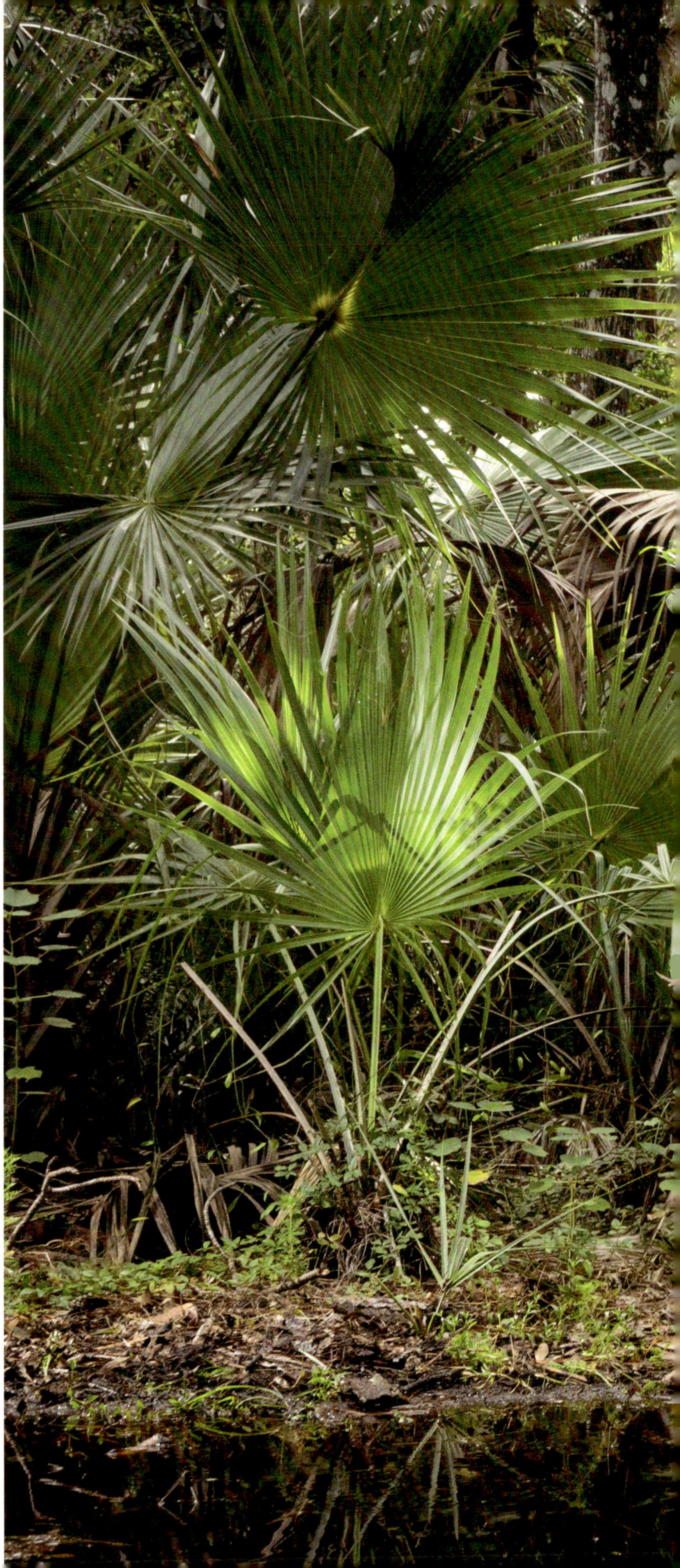

A motion-triggered camera trap illuminated by speedlights reveals a “rub tree”—a key scent-marking hub for Florida black bears to avoid potential conflict between males.

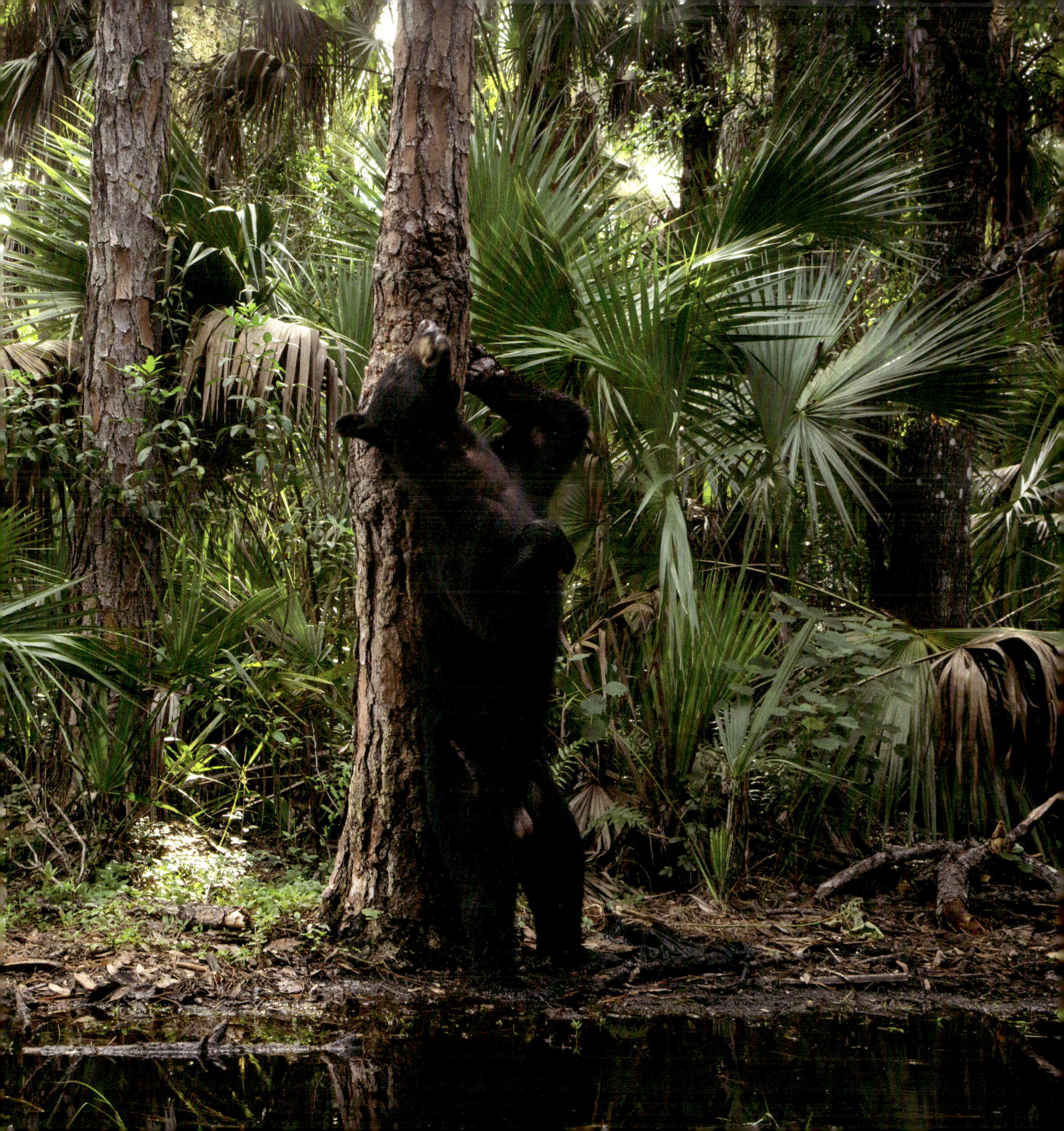

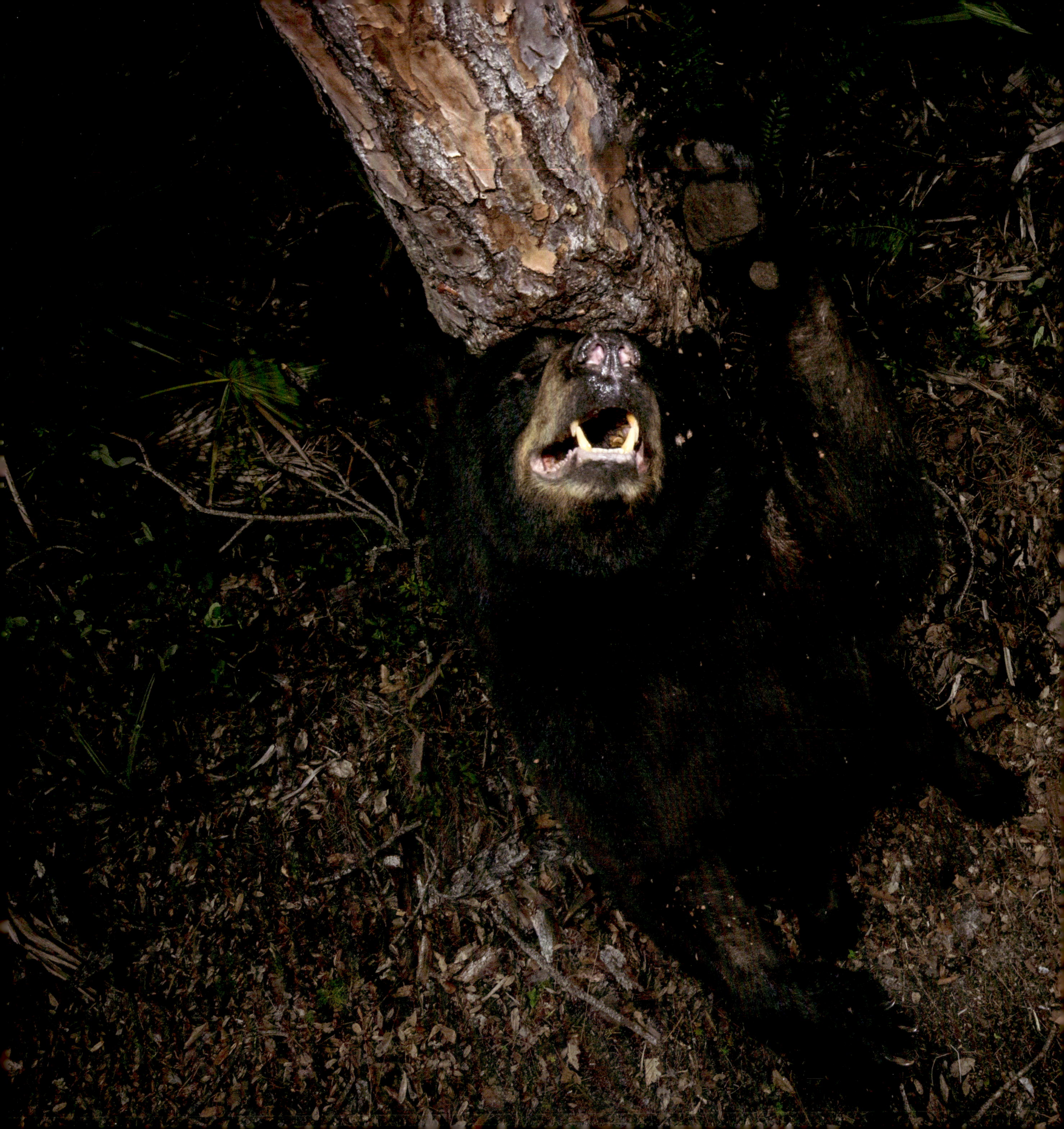

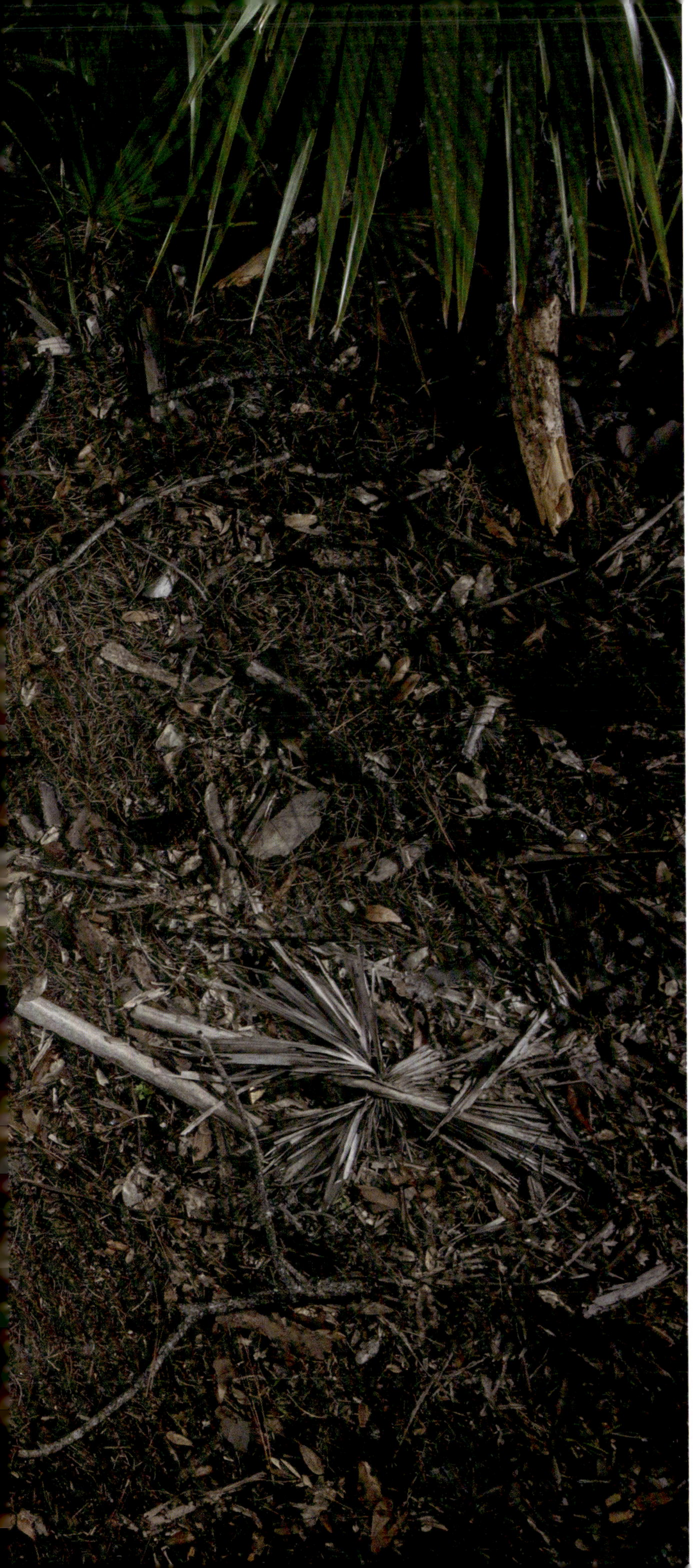

On well-traveled game trails, “rub trees” stand out—etched with claw marks and polished by years of head-rubbing.

FOLLOWING PAGE

Some tracts, like many along North Carolina’s Black River, escaped the saw because their ancient, weathered trees held little commercial value.

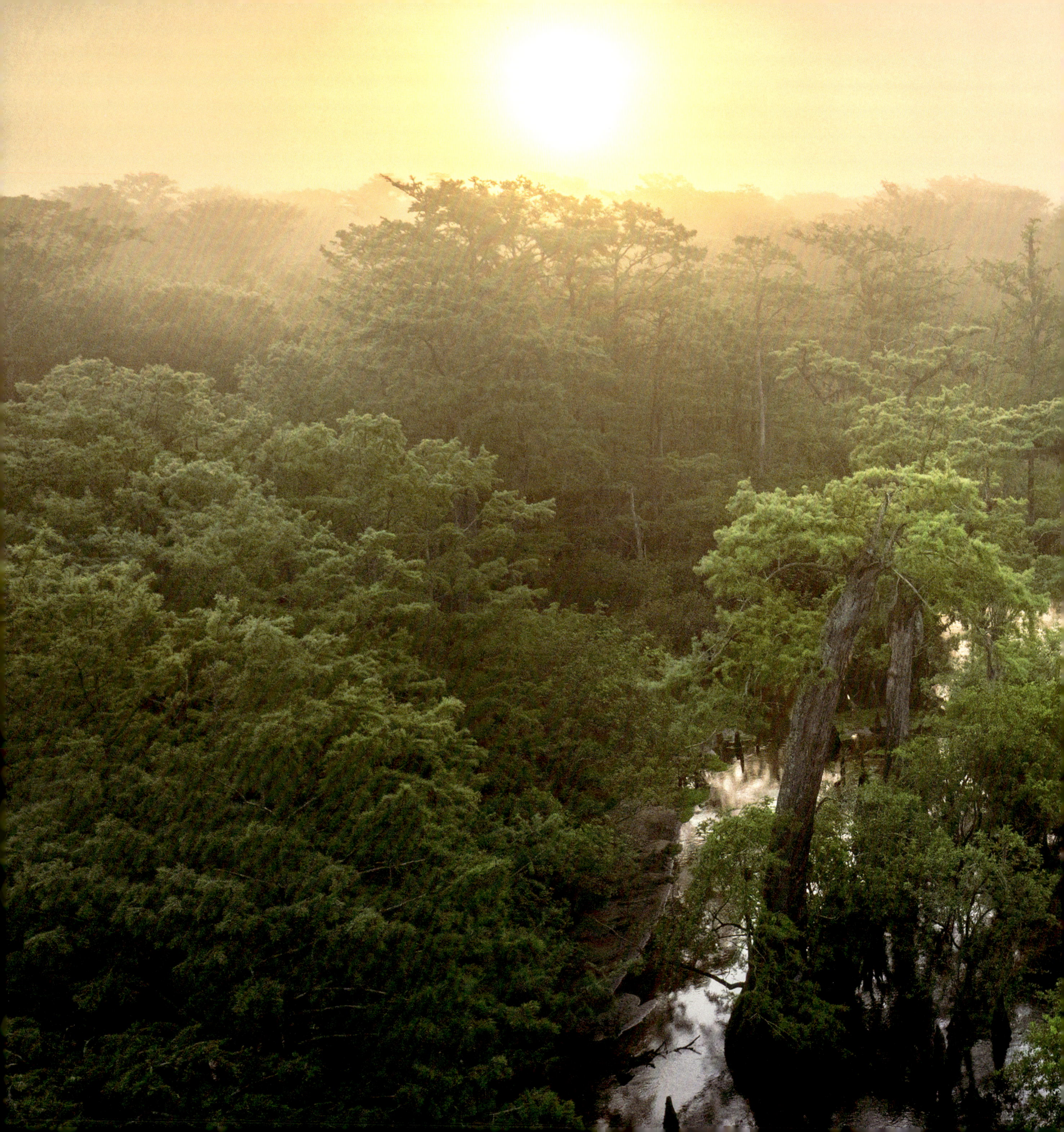

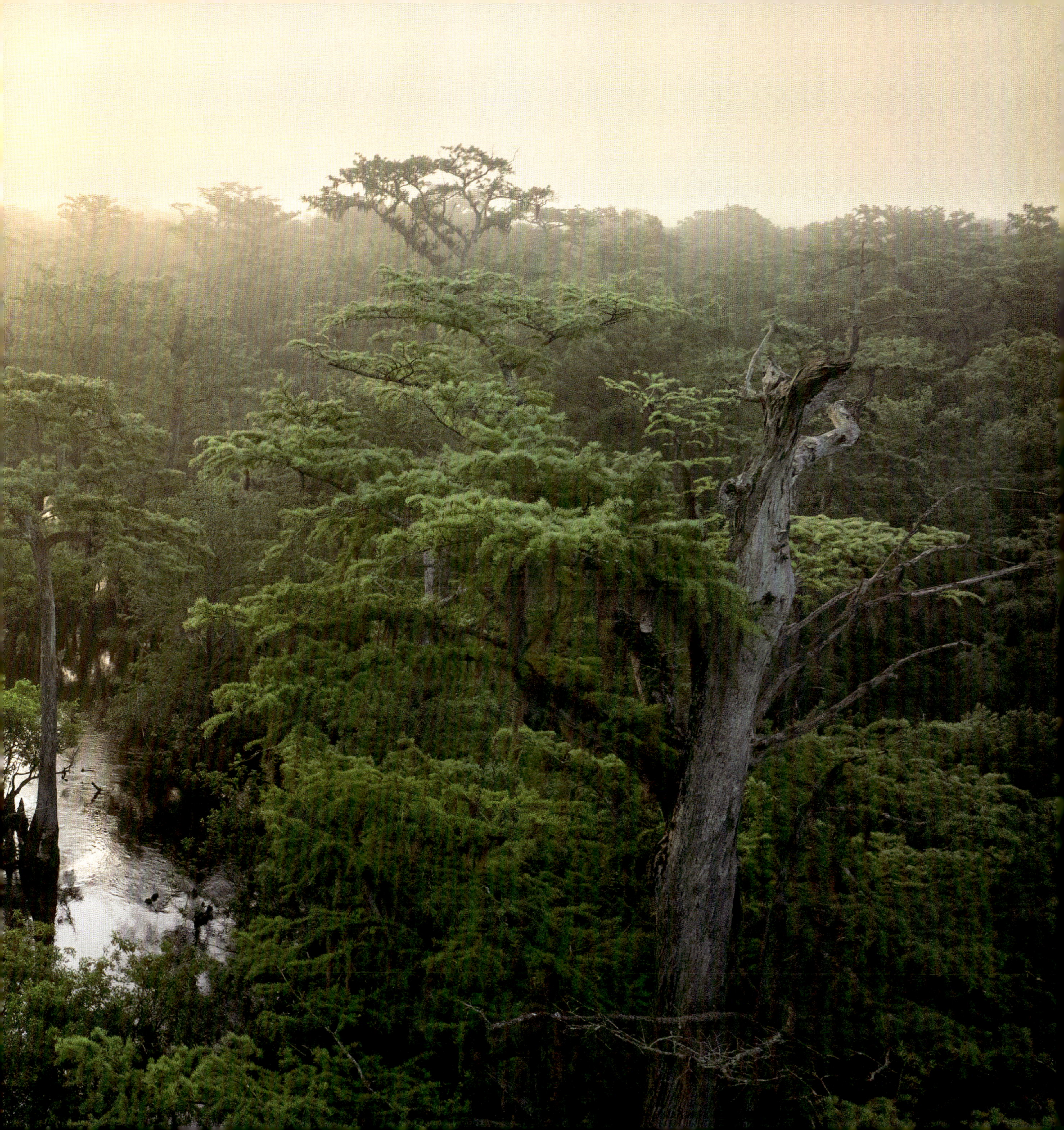

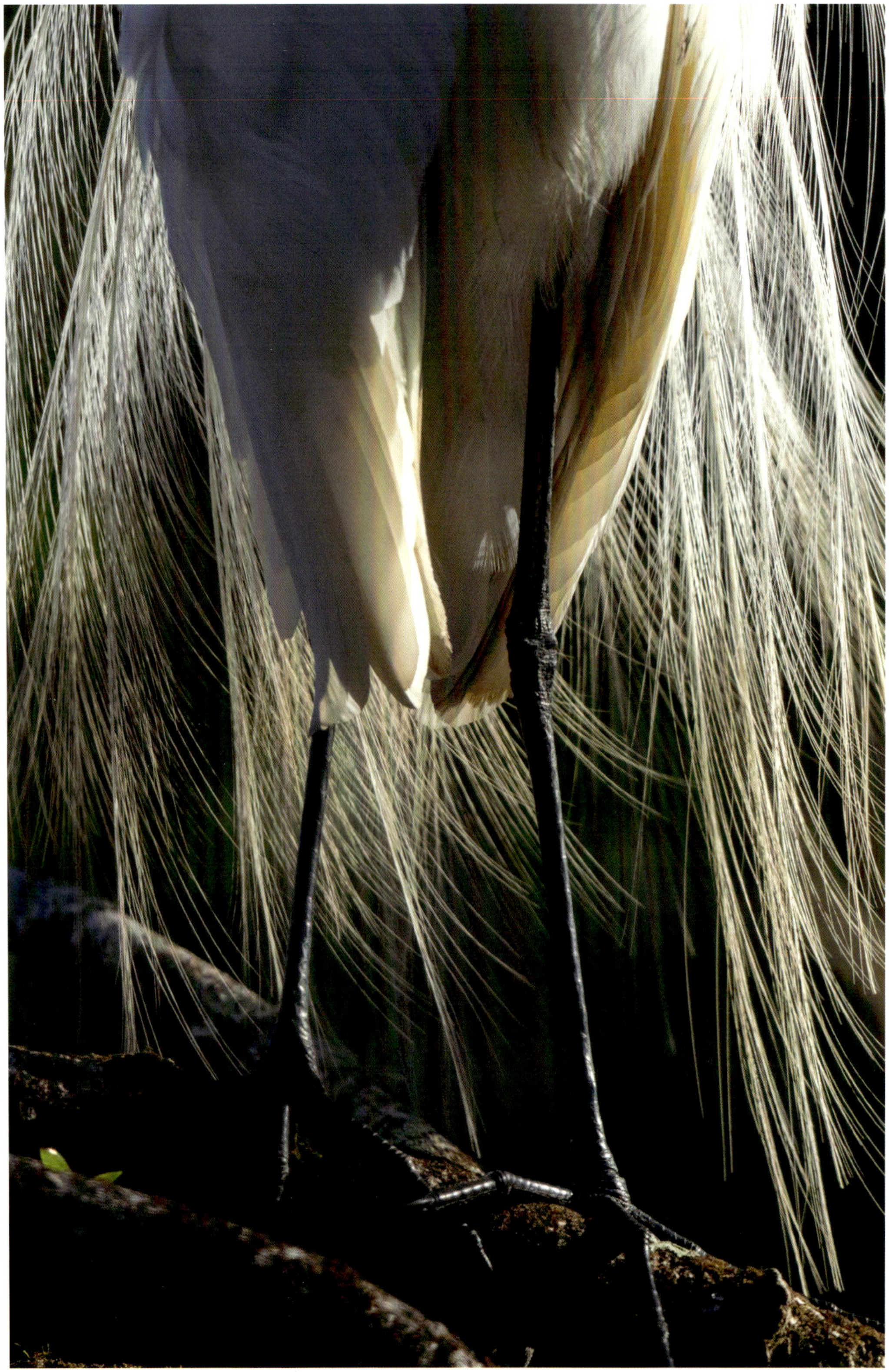

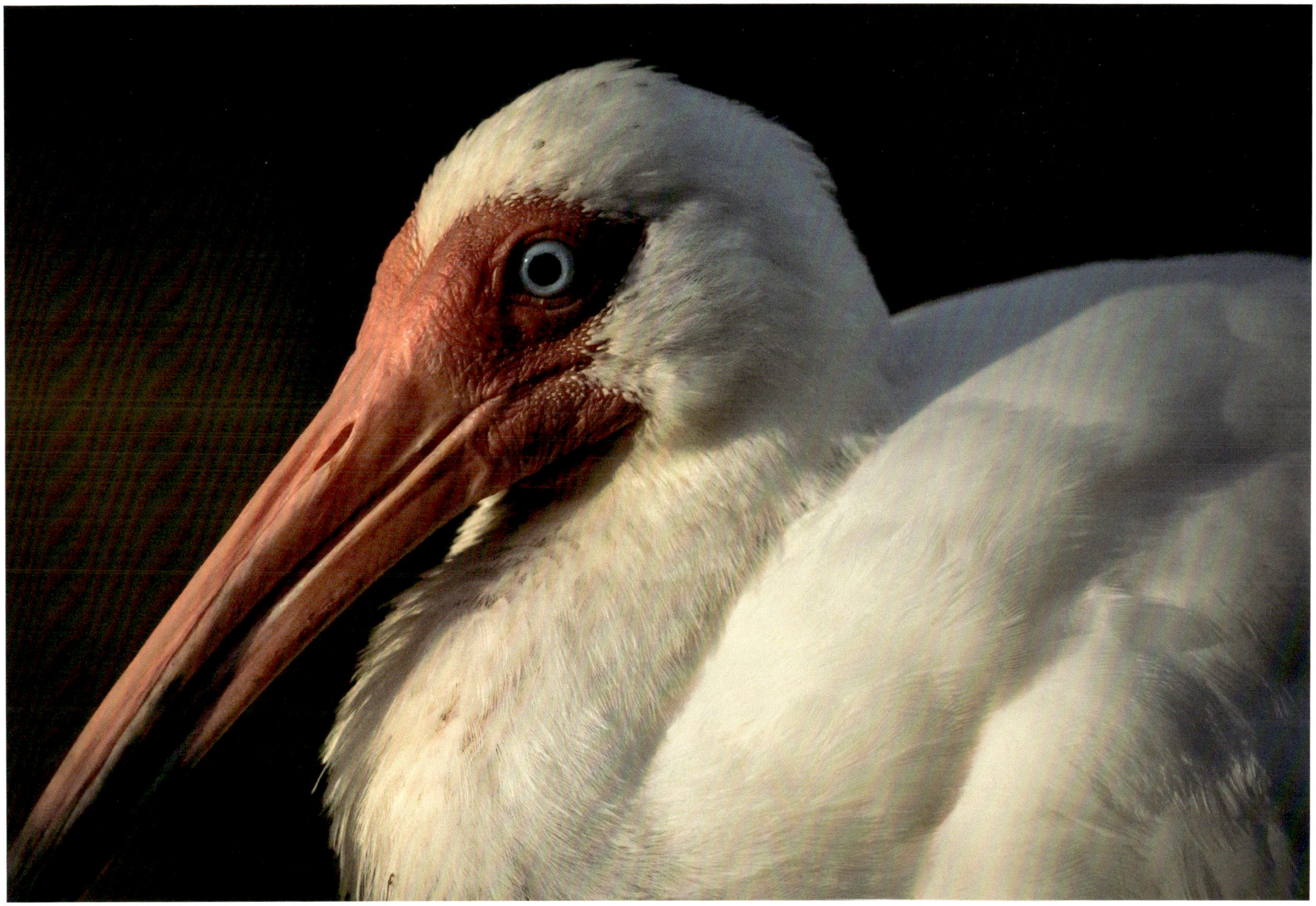

White ibis are tactile feeders, using their long, curved bills to probe for prey in shallow water—and during breeding season, their red lores and pale blue eyes signal readiness to mate

PREVIOUS PAGE

In the late nineteenth century, great egrets were hunted to near-extinction for their delicate breeding plumes—called aigrettes—which were highly prized as adornments on women's hats in high society.

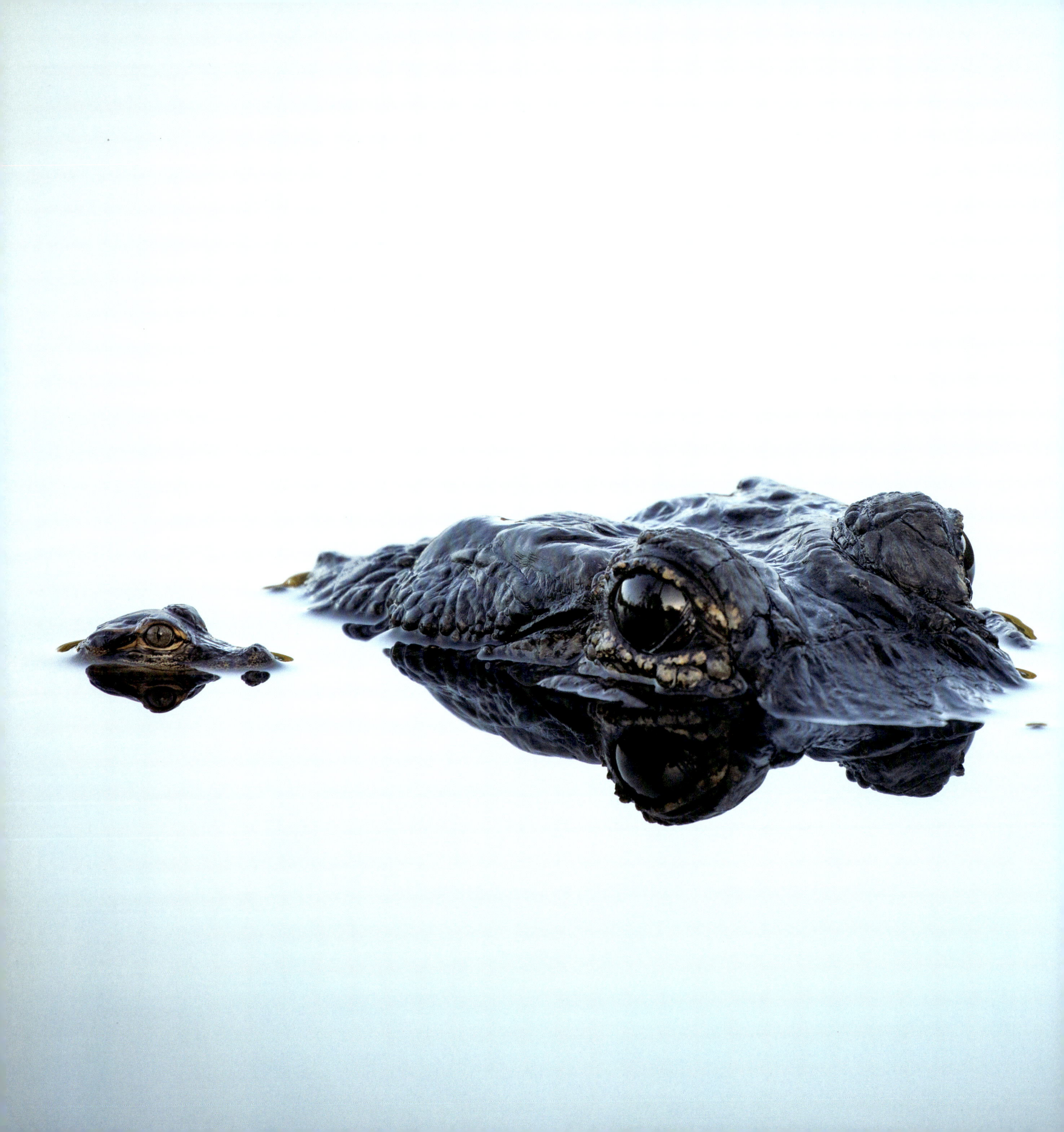

Alligator hatchlings will immediately begin foraging on their own, but will stay close to their mother and under her care for up to two years.

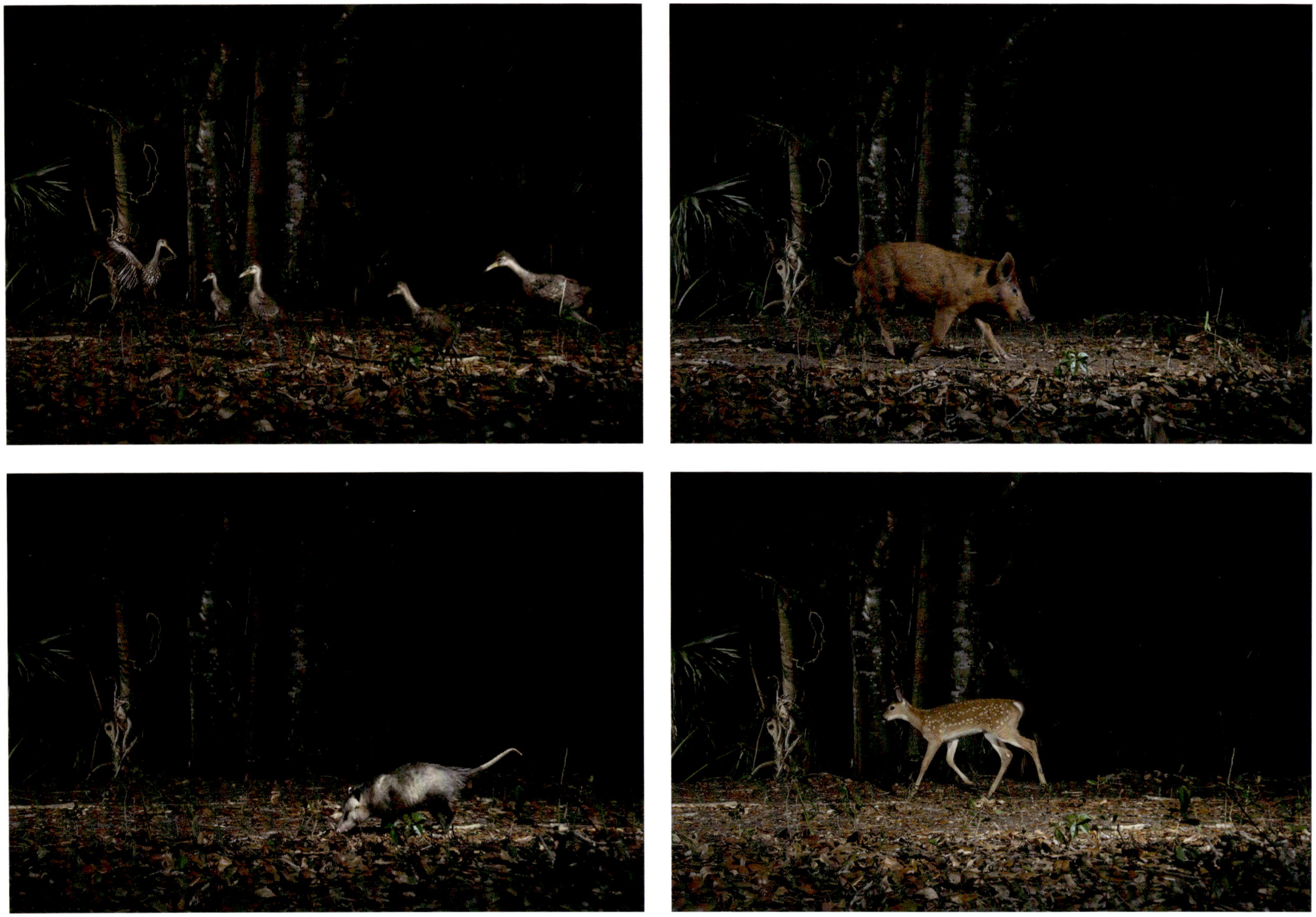

Upland trails that connect wetlands and forests are important wildlife corridors for numerous animals.

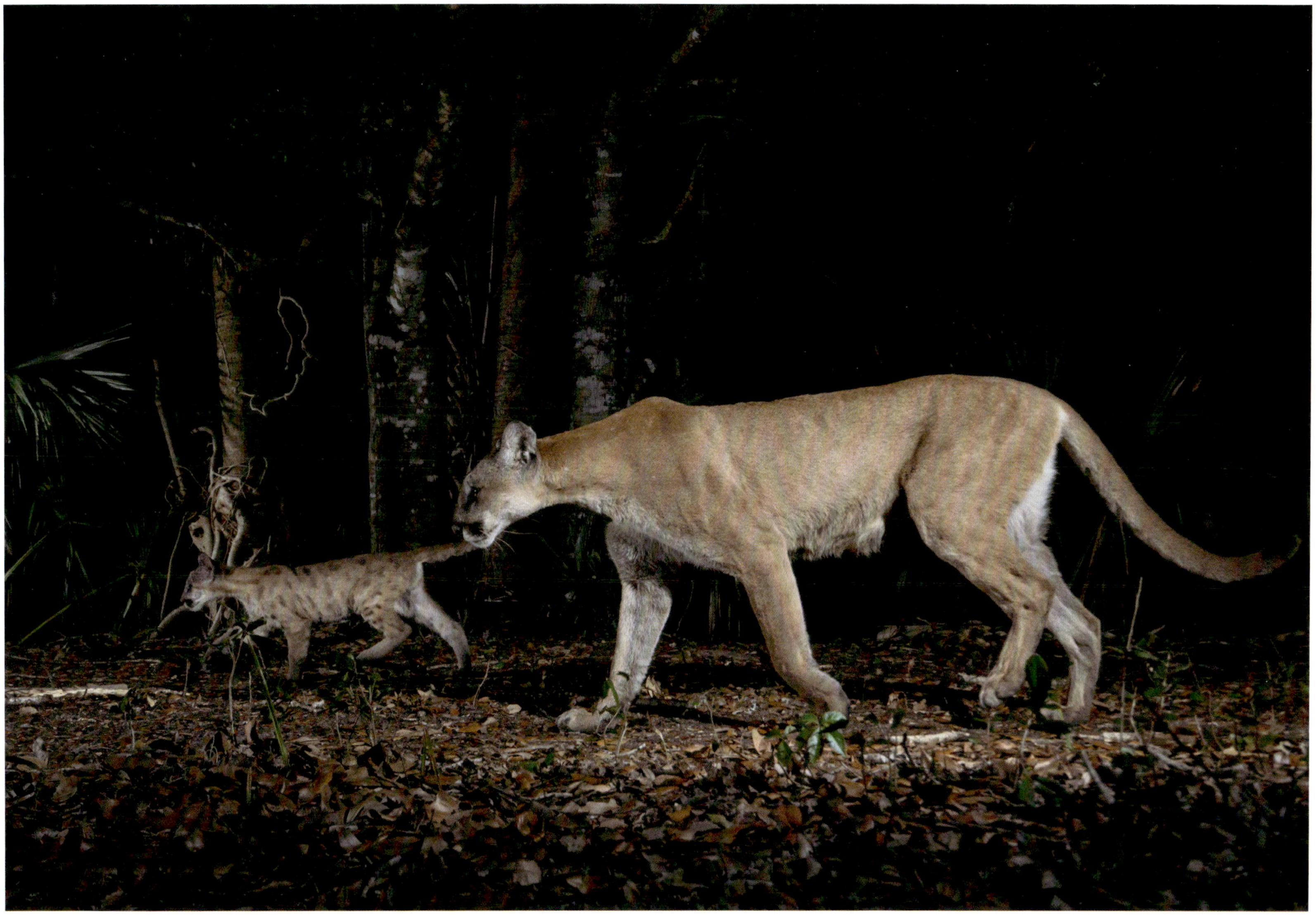

Florida hosts the only breeding population of panthers or puma east of the Mississippi, and they rely on vast territories of connected rural lands and diverse habitats to raise the next generation.

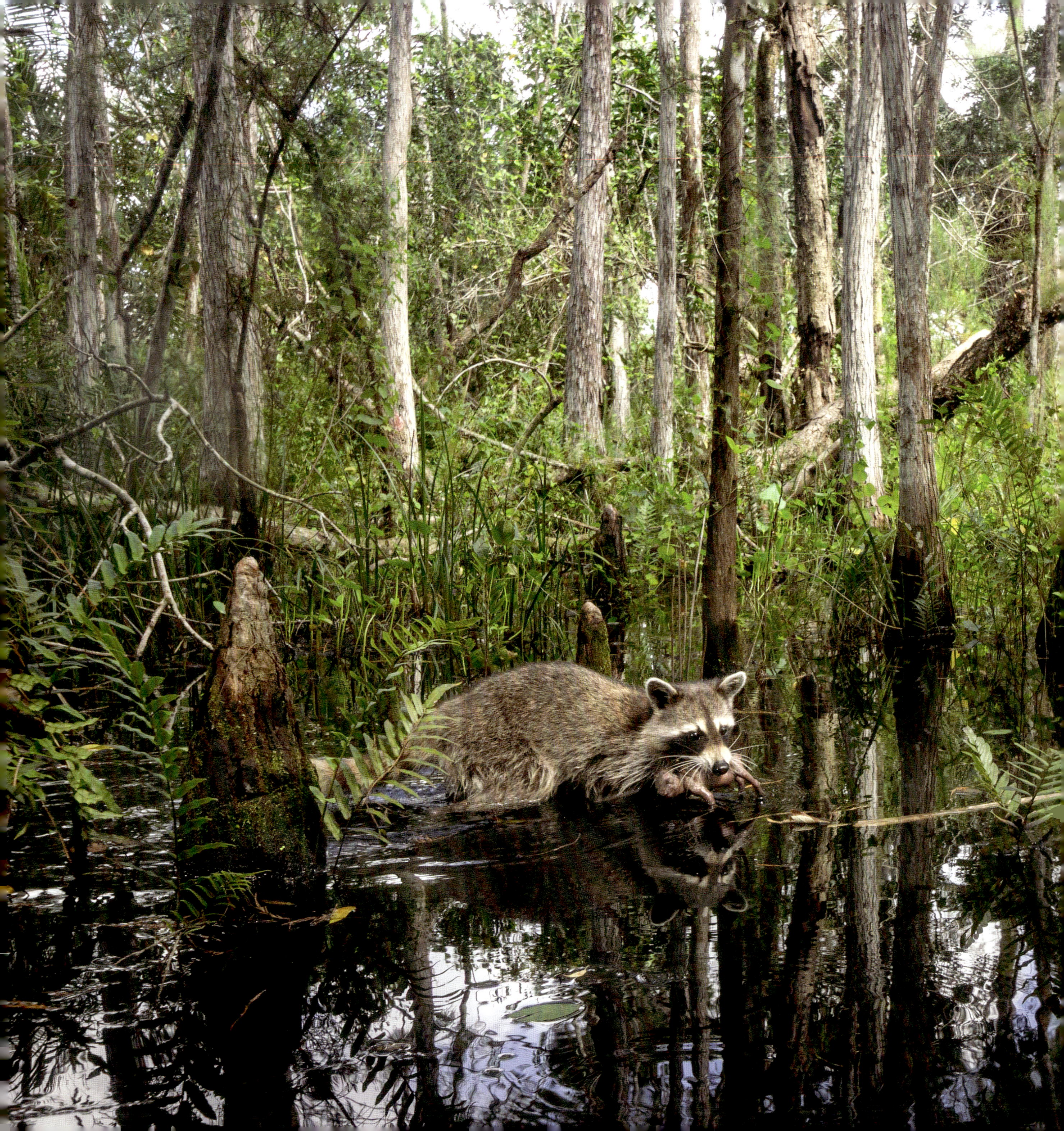

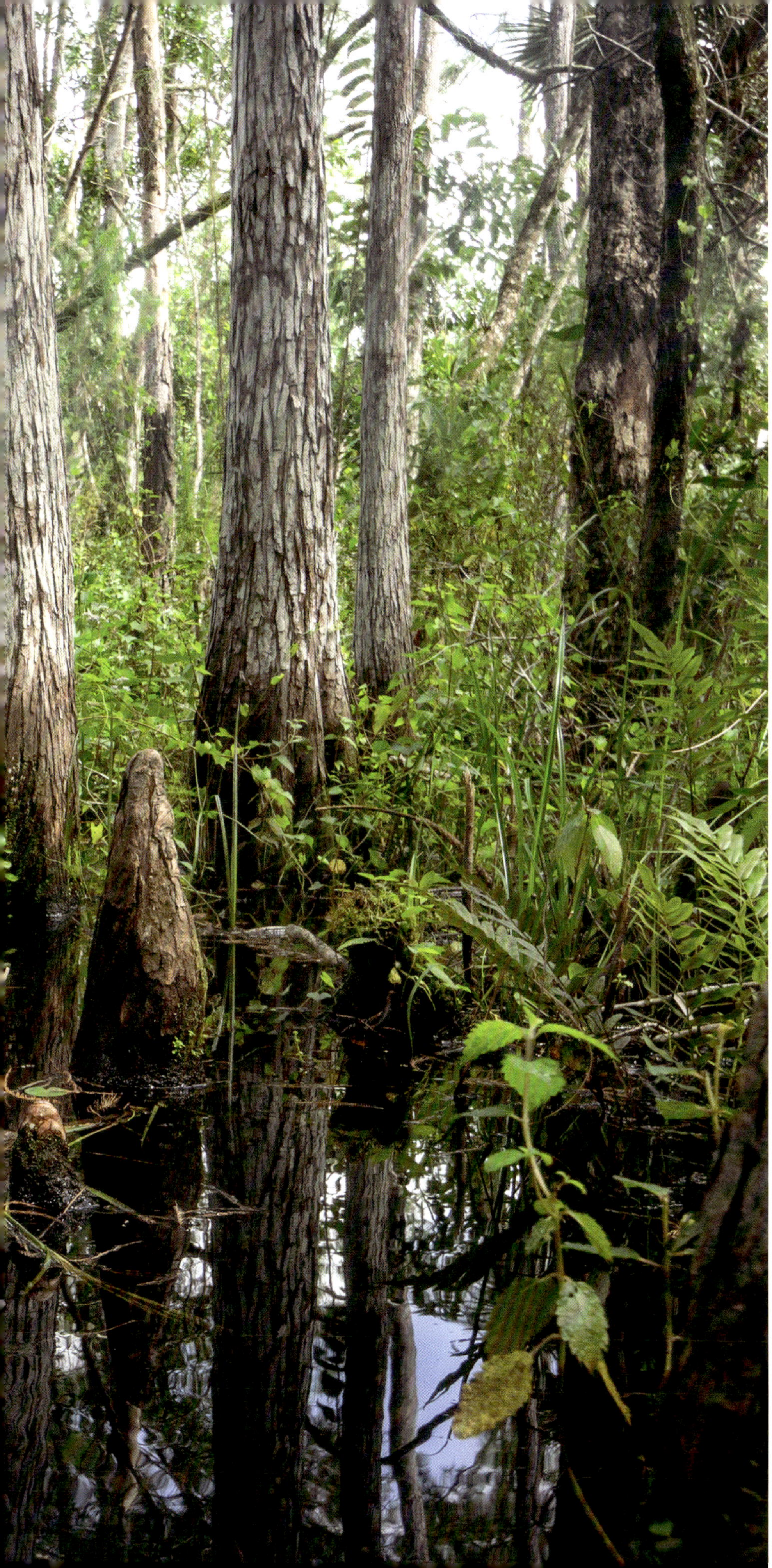

A mother raccoon rescues her newborn kit and brings it to safety after unseasonal rains suddenly brought water levels up.

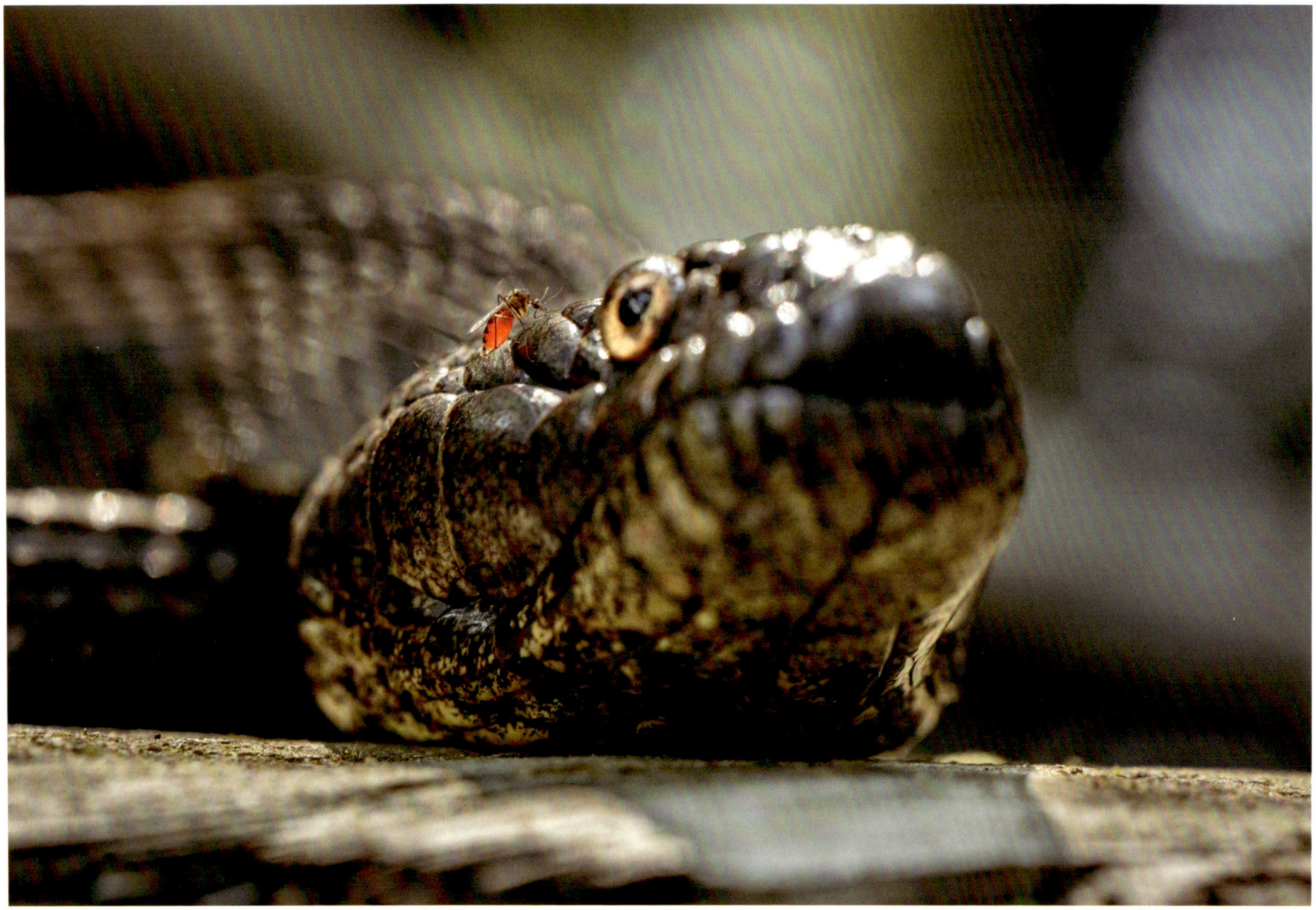

Through small chinks in the armor of a brown watersnake, female mosquitoes—drawn by the need for blood to nourish their eggs—find an easy meal.

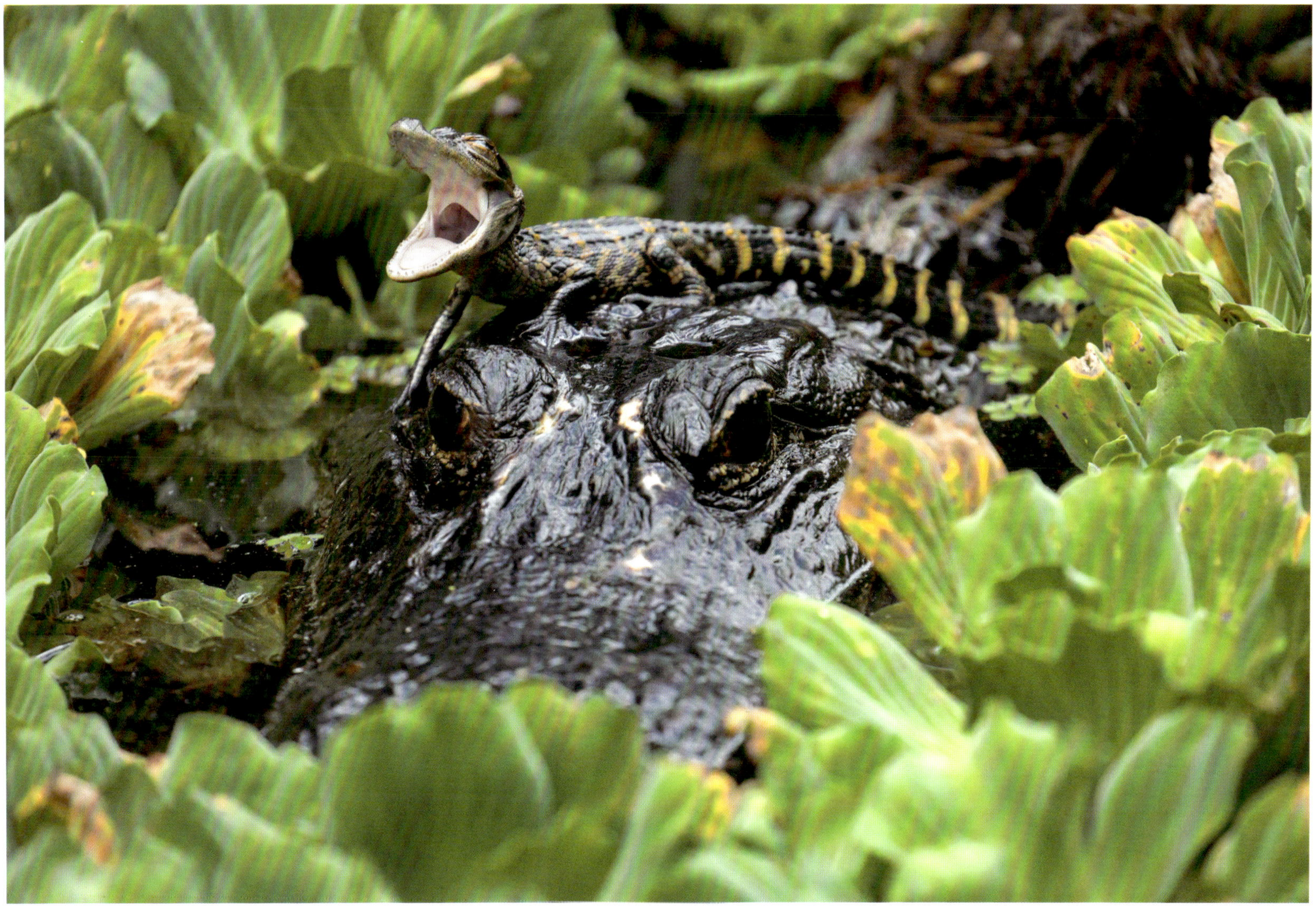

When basking sites are limited and with predators all around, hatchling alligators will often seek the safety of their mother's head to soak up afternoon sun.

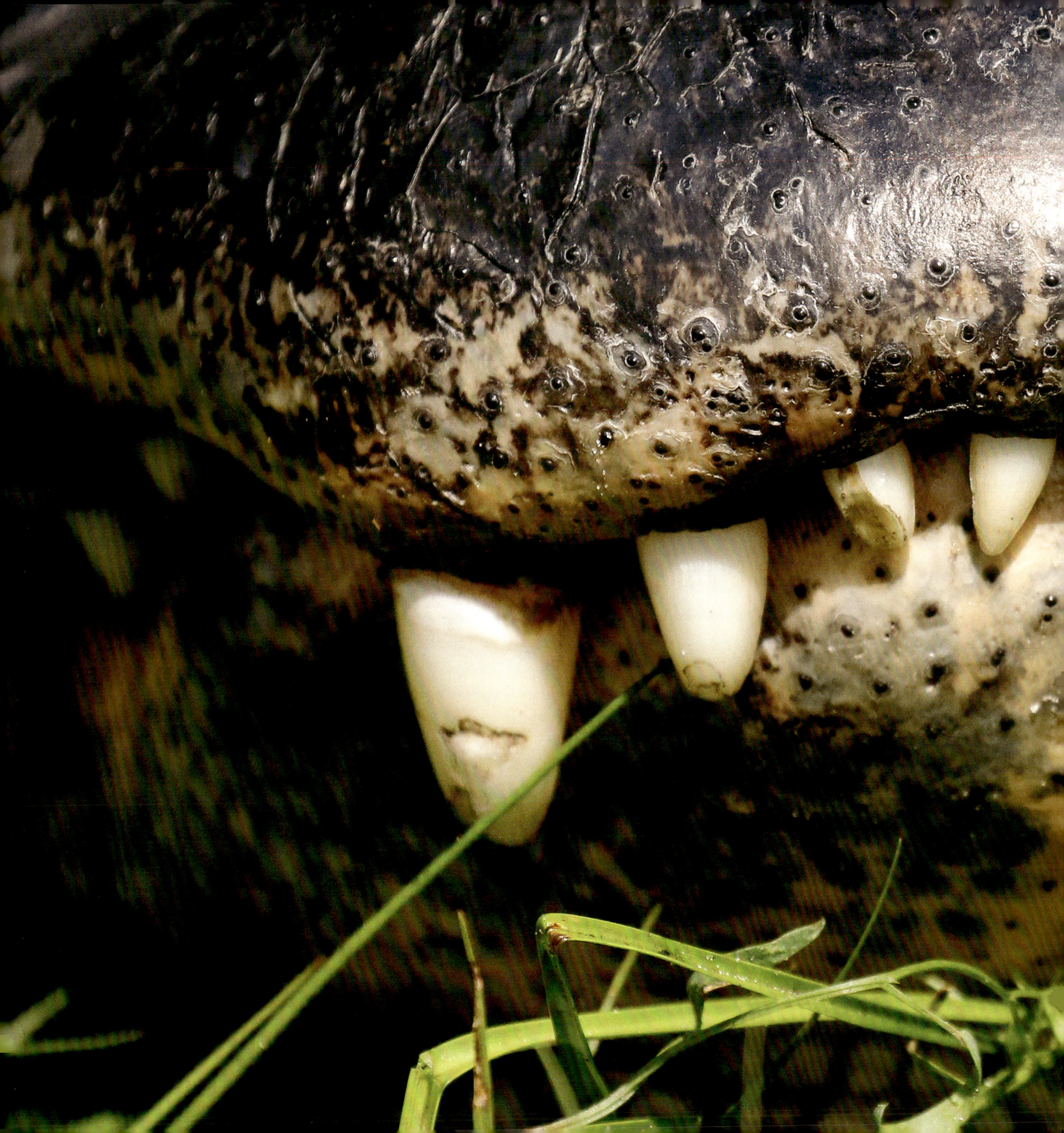

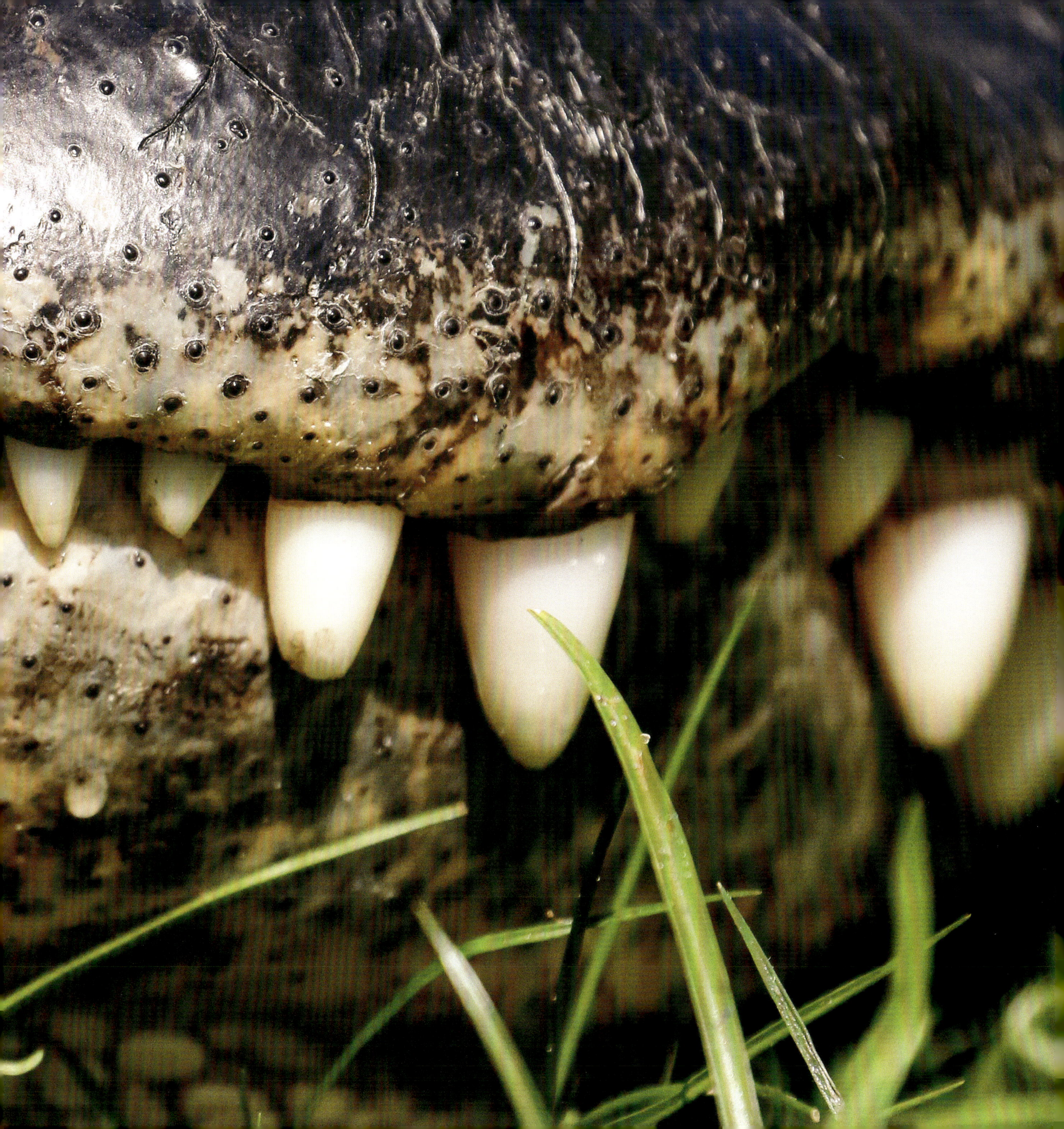

Perfectly adapted to the aquatic and arboreal life of the swamp, a yellow rat snake climbs up a pond cypress in search of food. When it gets to the top, with or without its quarry, it will fall to the ground because it cannot climb down.

PREVIOUS PAGE

Called integumentary sensory organs, the small raised dots on an alligator's snout are highly sensitive receptors that detect the faintest movements in the water, allowing them to ambush prey, even in total darkness.

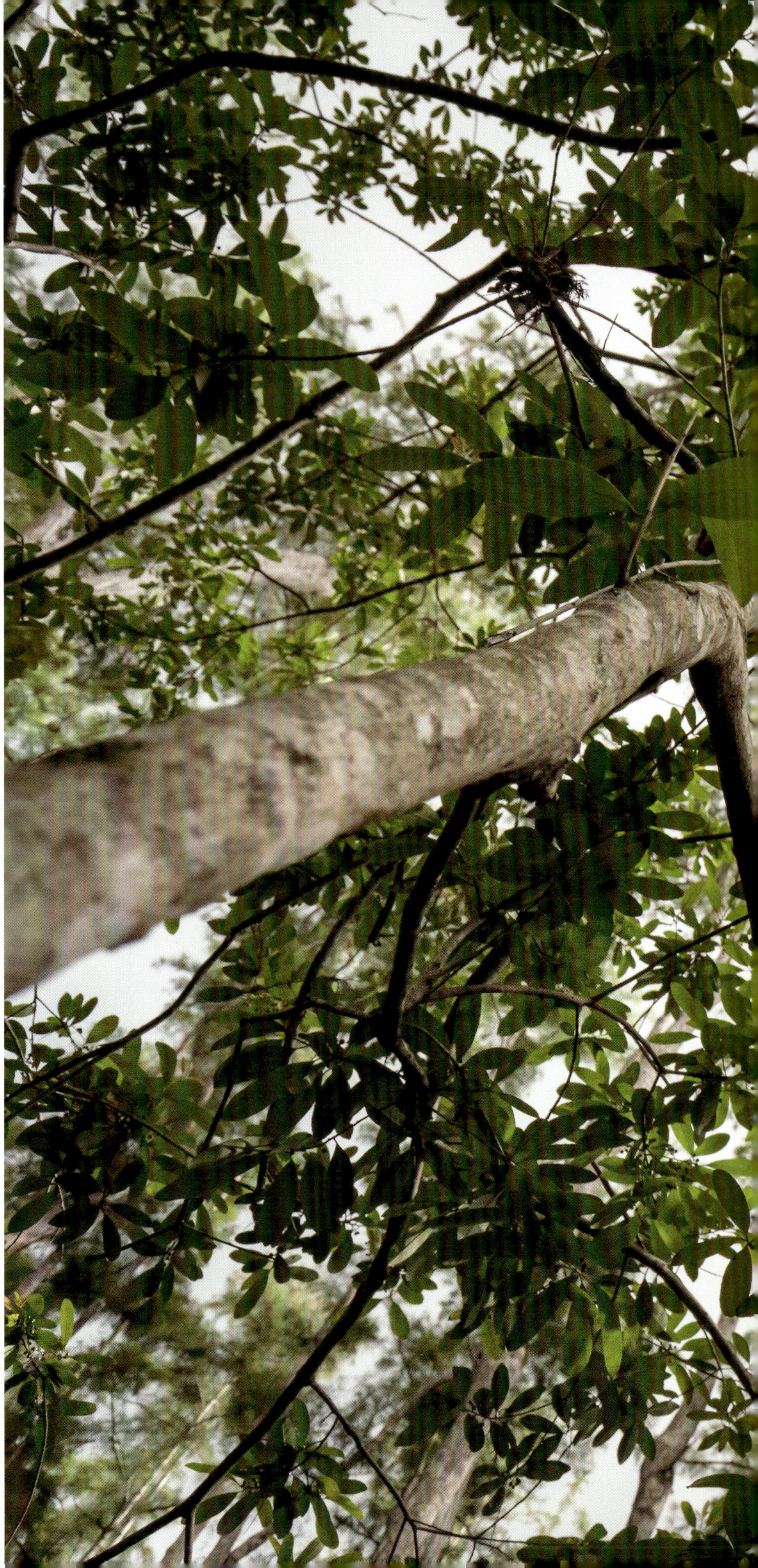

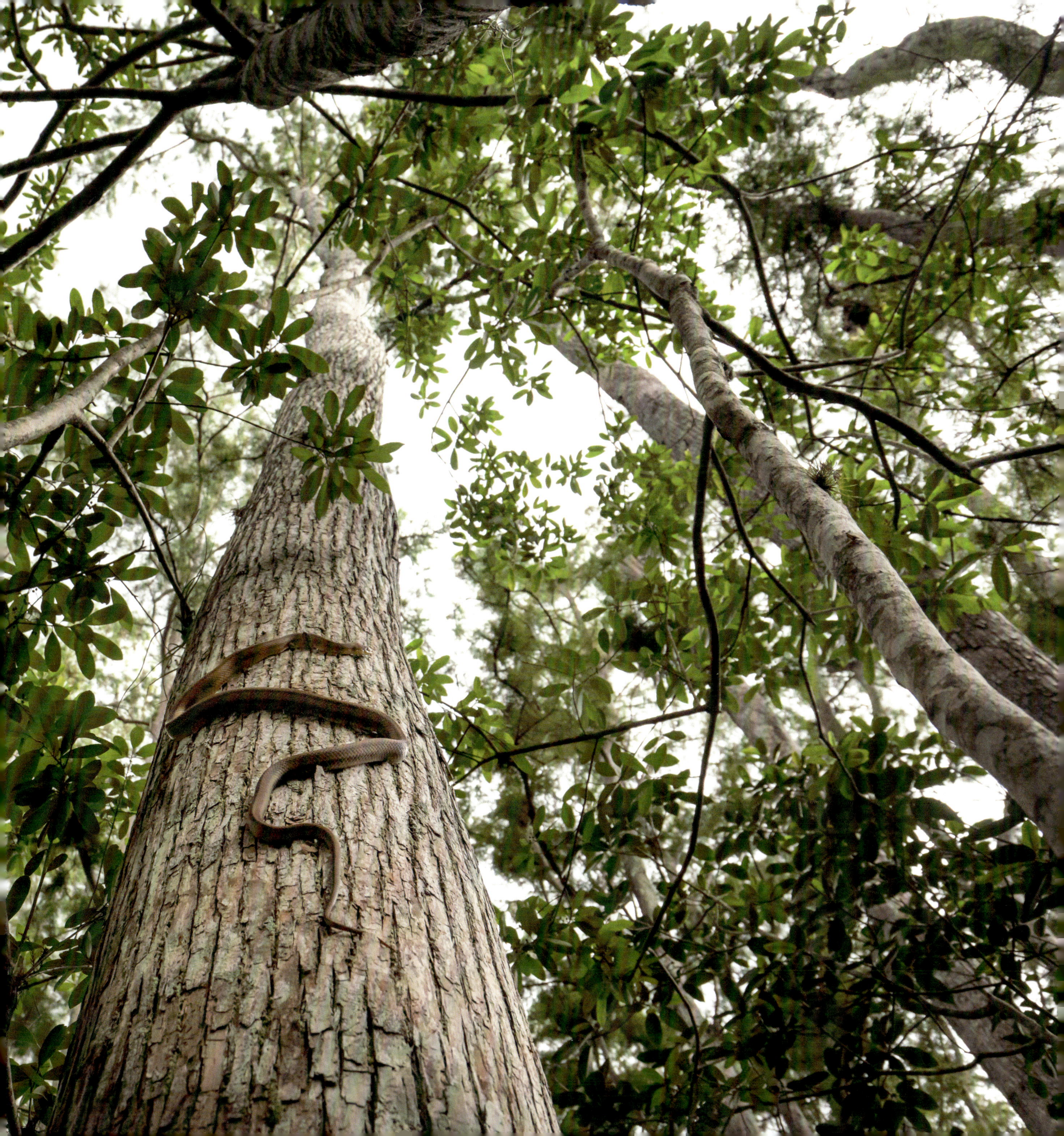

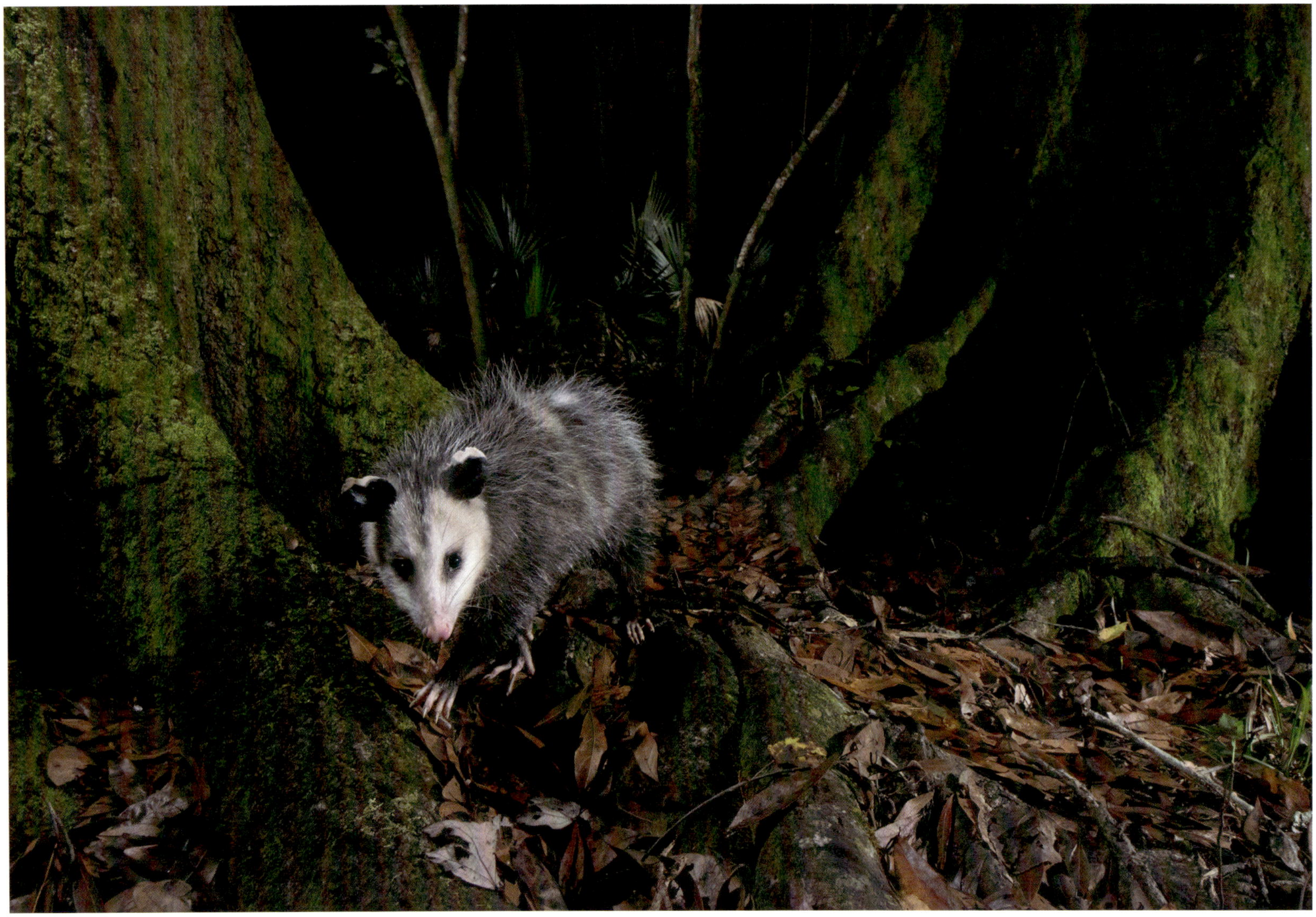

North America's only marsupial, the opossum is a nocturnal scavenger with a taste for ticks, making it one of the swamp's most underrated cleanup crews.

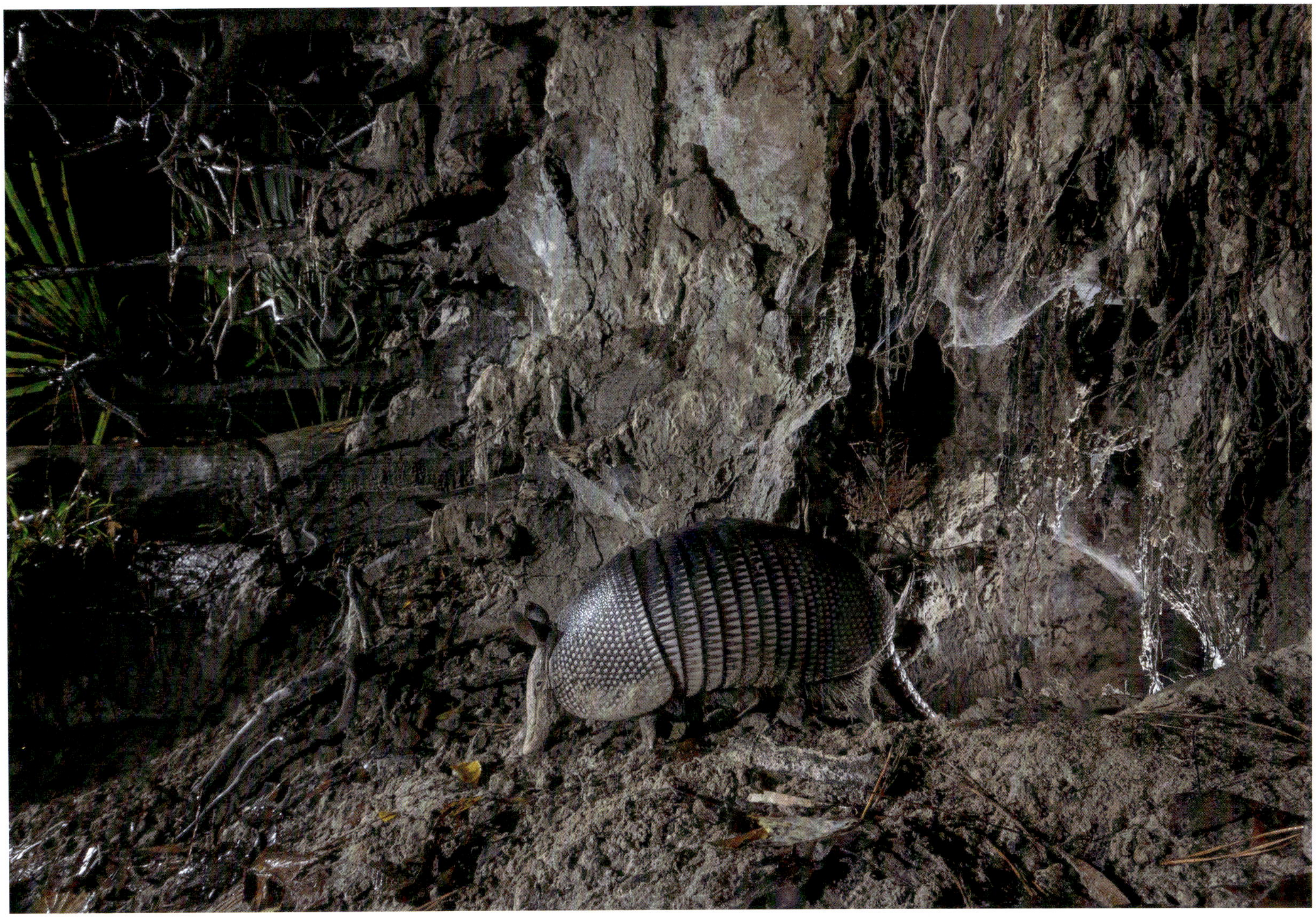

Tip mounds, formed by uprooted, decomposing trees, create microhabitats rich in invertebrates, making them prime foraging sites for insectivores like nine-banded armadillos.

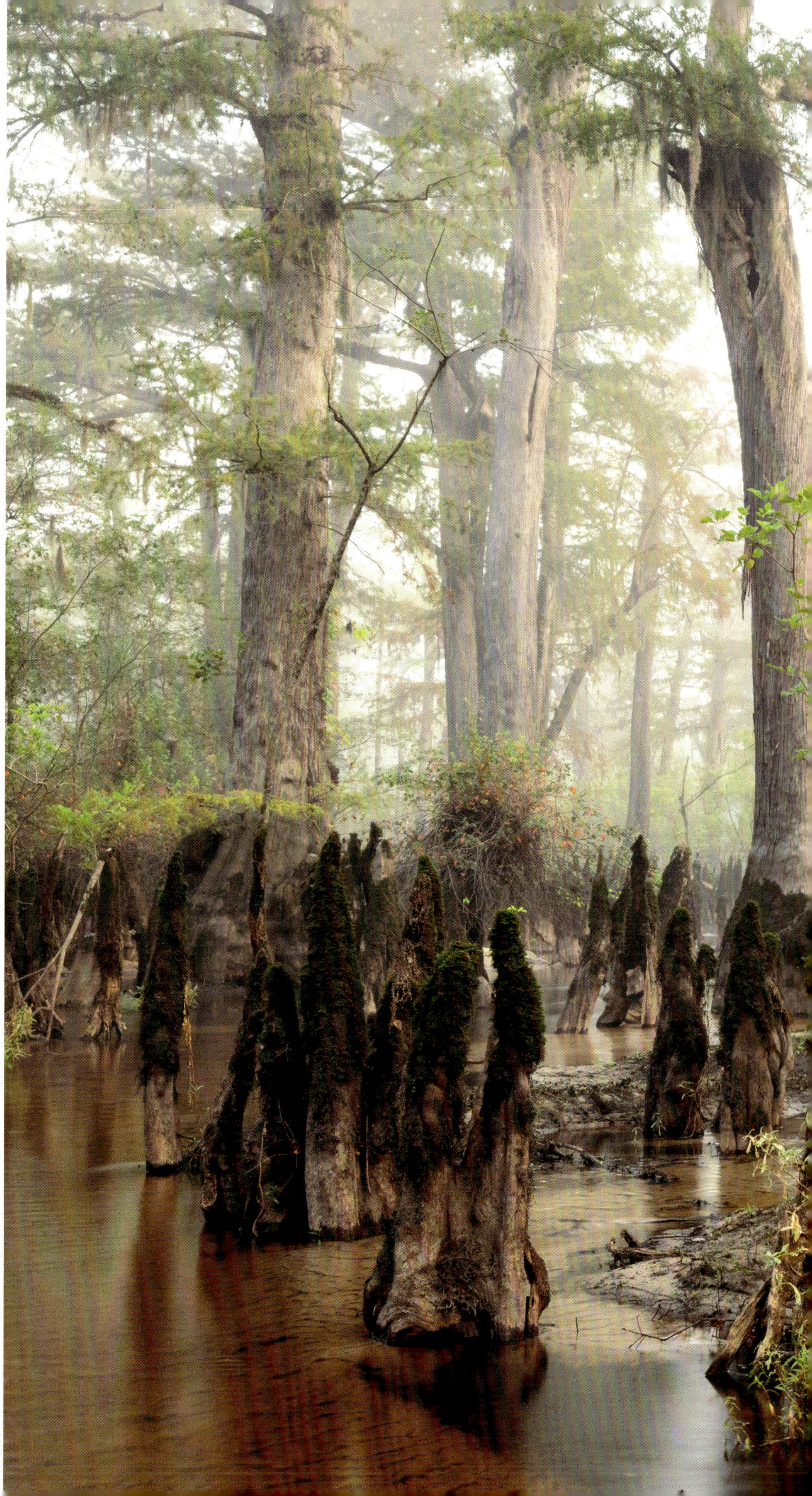

A starvation diet of low nutrients in sandy soils is one reason cypress trees in North Carolina's Black River live so long—their slow growth, driven by scarcity, is key to their longevity.

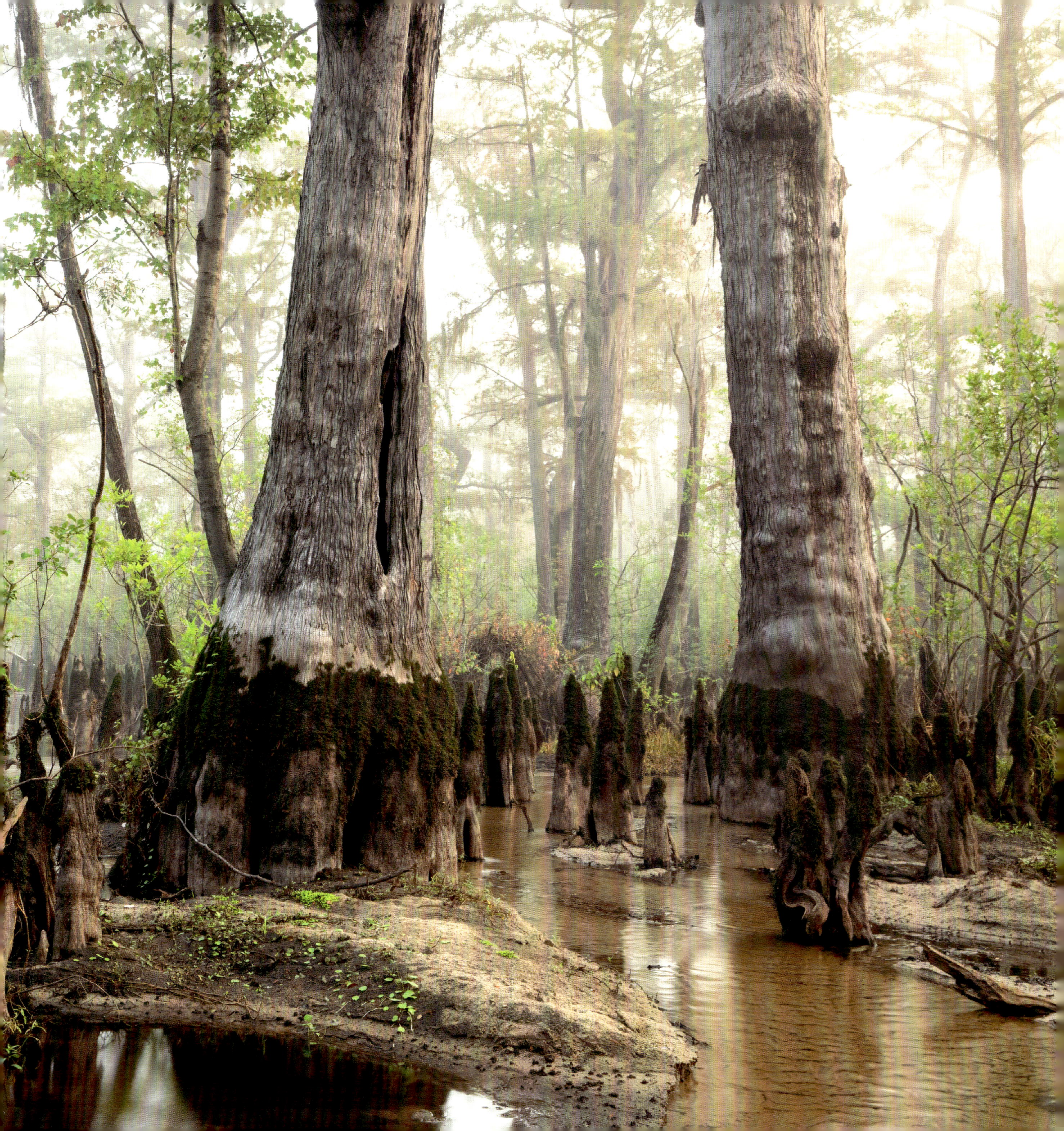

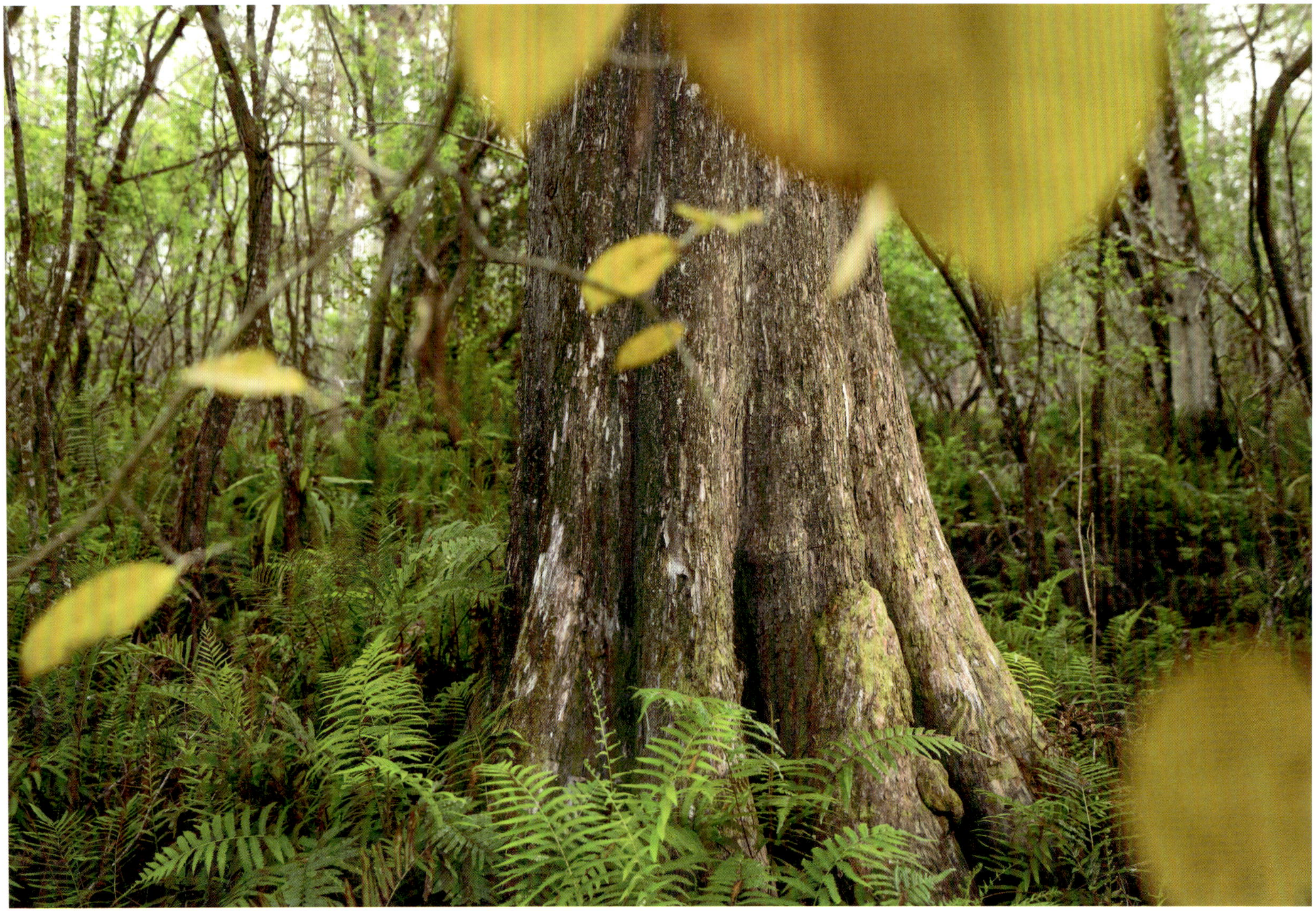

A strangler fig, an arboreal parasite, inches toward one of Corkscrew Swamp's ancient cypress trees.

FOLLOWING PAGE

Sprouting from seeds dropped by birds high in the canopy, strangler figs send roots downward that wrap around host trees, slowly squeezing the life from them until they claim the crown for themselves.

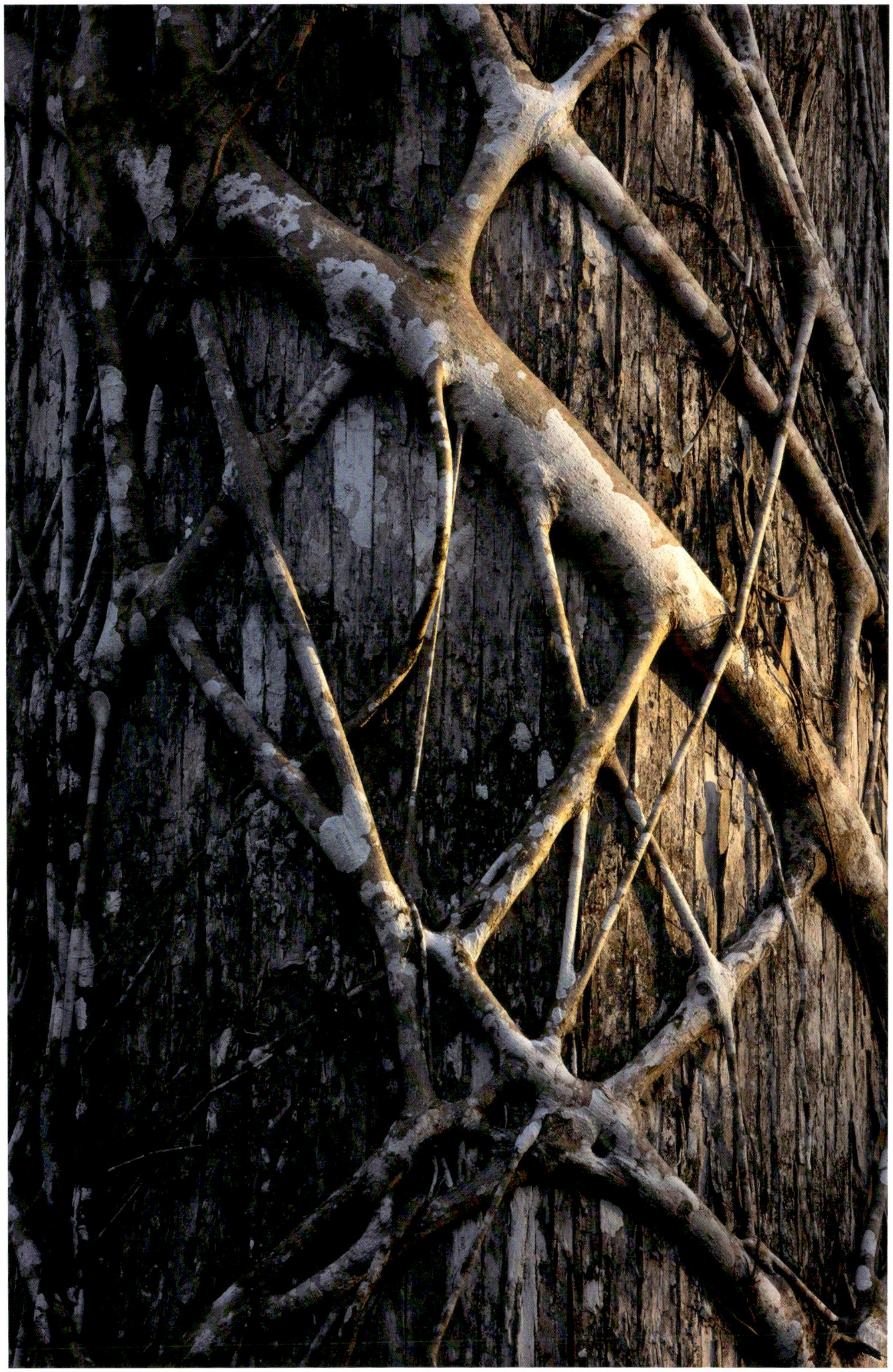

HIGH FIDELITY

As I drive the 200 miles from my home to the Audubon Center & Sanctuary at Francis Beidler Forest in Harleyville, South Carolina, a soft but confident female voice guides me along. "In half a mile, turn right, then a slight left." The omniscient mandate is rarely wrong, and I have come to place complete trust in my digital copilot. I even programmed my navigation to dictate in a British accent—it just sounds more authoritative. I've made this trip more than a dozen times, yet the last few miles of unremarkable pavement stubbornly refuse to map themselves into my memory. Perhaps my reliance on the device hinders more than it helps. But I am also not the sort of person who boasts about an innate sense of direction.

This small personal failing stings more when I consider that a bird the size of a tennis ball, less than a year old, can travel 25 times this distance unaided—over forests, oceans, and islands, through high winds and rain—and not only arrive at Beidler Forest but also land in the very tree from which it departed. The miracle of migration is still at work here, in this outpost of primordial wilderness where life persists much as it did thousands of years ago.

In the late 1960s, residents of a small South Carolina town halfway between Columbia and Charleston noticed something peculiar. Logging trucks trundled along back roads, hauling away enormous bald cypress. The locals, many of them Audubon members, watched in disbelief as trees with buttresses the size of Volkswagen Beetles disappeared to the sawmill. No one had thought old-growth forest still existed in the region, let alone that it could be harvested. Yet nestled deep in Four Holes Swamp, untouched giants had stood for centuries, anchoring the blackwater ecosystem.

Alarmed, conservationists moved quickly. Working with the Beidler family estate, the National Audubon Society and The Nature Conservancy pooled their resources and secured 3,400 acres, including 1,800 acres of old-growth cypress and tupelo swamp that had, by sheer luck or oversight, evaded the blade.

Beyond their towering grandeur, these ancient trees provide something even more essential: decay. The ecosystem's vitality is found not just in the living but in the dead—the fallen giants, the rotting husks, the tangled detritus that supports an intricate web of decomposers, fungi, and foraging animals. Here, the natural order remains unpruned, unmanicured. It is a complete system, a cathedral of life operating as it was meant to. Perhaps that is why, per acre, Beidler Forest boasts one of the highest nesting songbird densities in the country. Chief among them is the prothonotary warbler.

Certainly, a more amiable ambassador for the bottomlands than the swamp's other residents—alligators, snakes, and mosquitoes—the golden-hued warbler offers a gentler introduction. It is familiar, charismatic, and striking enough for even the most amateur birdwatcher to identify on sight. Audubon South Carolina has embraced it as the swamp's warm public handshake. More importantly, the prothonotary is a keystone species: what is good for this bird is good for an entire swath of biodiversity, from swallow-tailed kites to otters and even armadillos.

Their name, a mouthful at first encounter—"PRO-THON-O-TARY"—harkens back to Roman Catholic clerks who donned golden robes. Their color, however, comes not from divine ordination but from a steady diet of aquatic macroinvertebrates, grubs, and spiders. And if the birds are thriving, it means the swamp is, too.

One of only two cavity-nesting warblers, prothonotaries require hollow trees and cypress knees to raise their young. Over an average lifespan of three to five years, a single adult

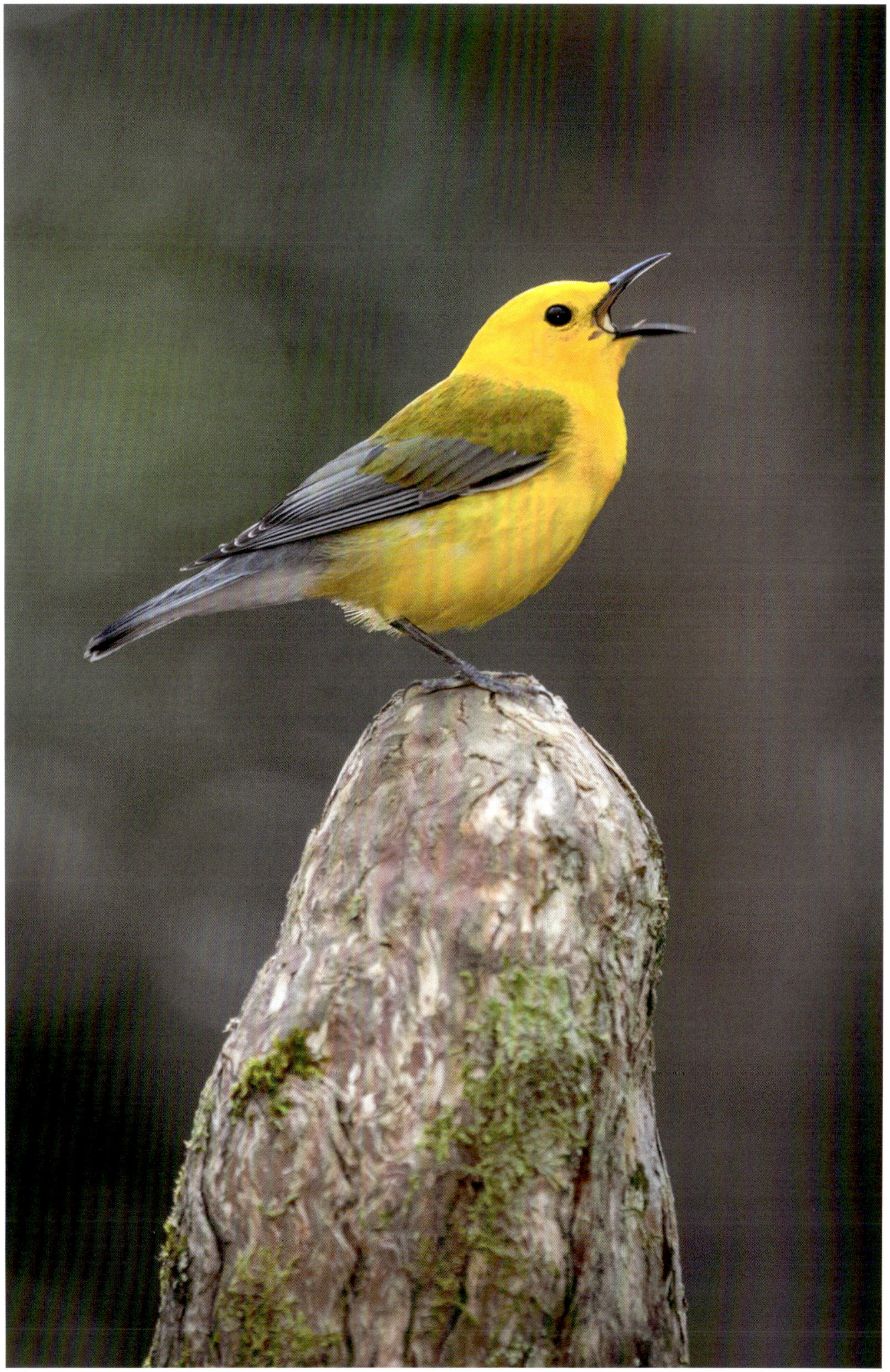

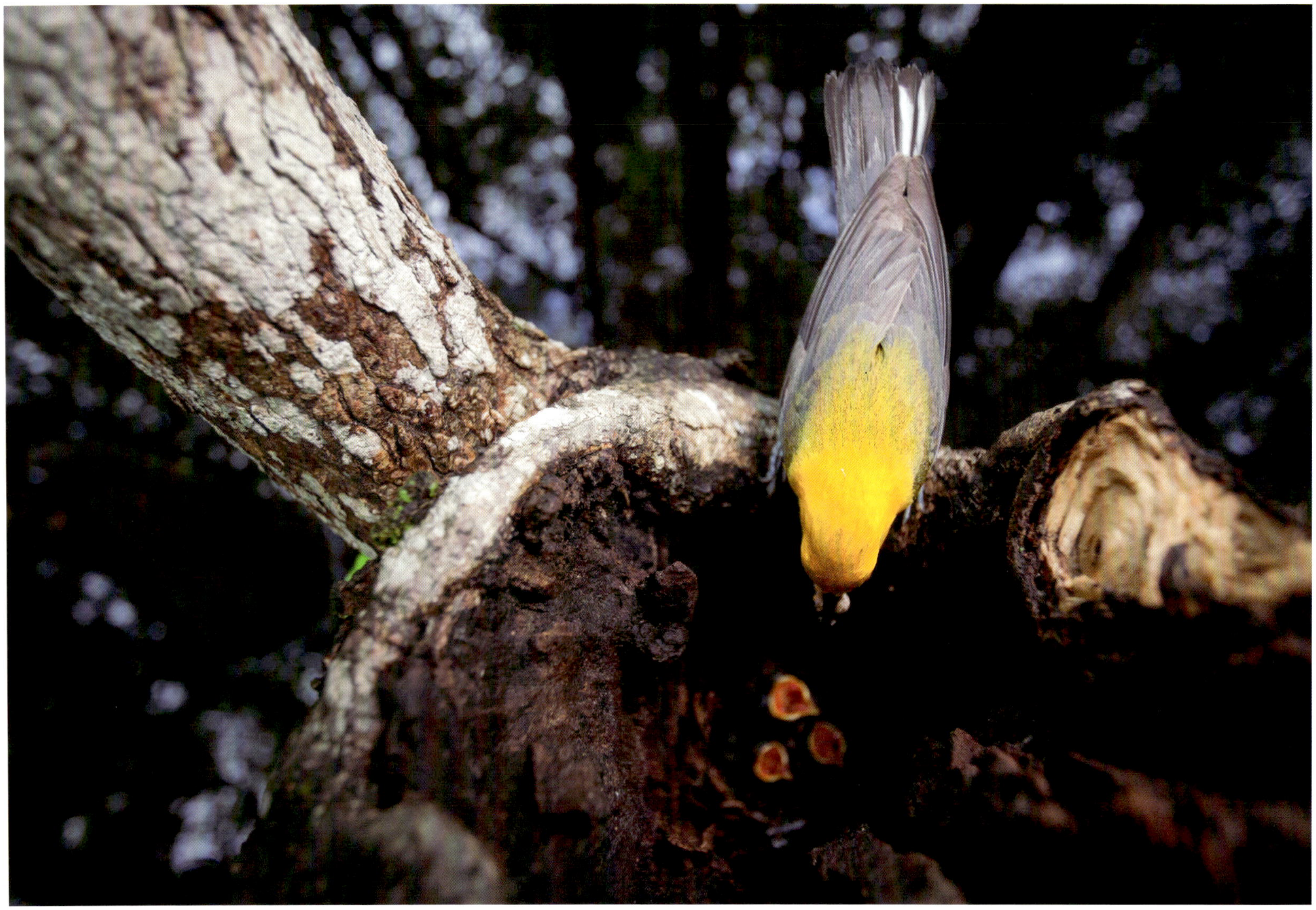

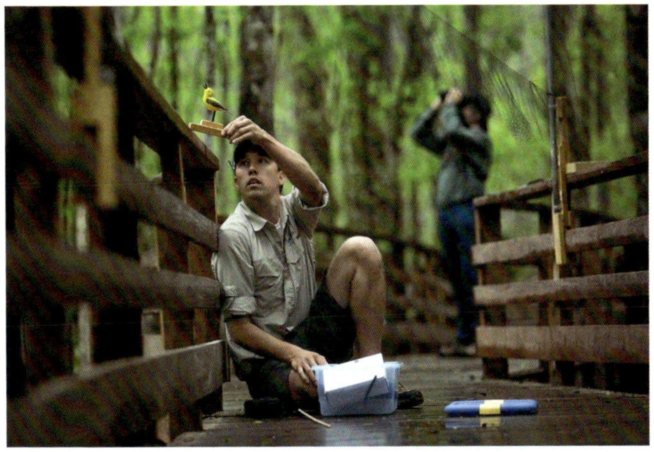

Matt Johnson, the center director of Audubon's Francis Beidler Forest, places a decoy to attract warblers to his mist net for study.

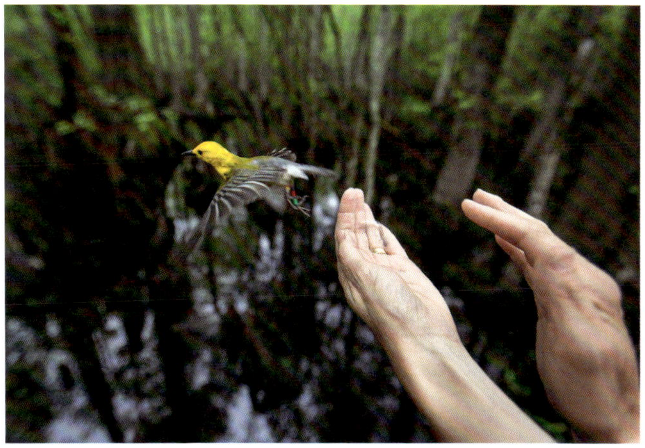

Equipped with unique identification bands, a prothonotary is released back into the swamp.

may rear some 20 chicks. While Beidler Forest remains a stronghold, their range stretches across the southeastern United States through the upper Midwest and into New York along the Atlantic flyway, with population hubs from southern Virginia to the lower Mississippi River basin. Come March, the bottomland forests shimmer with streaks of yellow as their unmistakable "sweet, sweet, sweet" song rings through the understory.

It is during this nesting season that biologists set up mist nets to gently capture the birds and affix tiny, colored leg bands. Year after year, adorned with these avian ID tags, the prothonotaries return, exhibiting an astonishing fidelity to their breeding grounds. Research has shown that some will return to the same 20-foot by 20-foot patch of swamp, often reusing the same nesting cavity.

Yet even with pristine breeding grounds in the United States, prothonotary populations have been in steady decline throughout the last half-century. The limiting factor, biologists believe, lies in the degradation of their wintering habitat—the disappearing coastal forests of Central and South America. By tracking more birds, scientists hope to guide conservation efforts that transcend borders.

While international preservation may seem an insurmountable challenge, local conservationists are tackling what they can. Only about 20 percent of the species' historic breeding habitat remains, and it will take centuries to make more old-growth swamp. To counteract this, biologists are installing artificial nesting boxes in key locations, from James River in Virginia to Louisiana, hoping to bolster breeding success.

Until recently, the details of their winter migrations remained a mystery. The development of smaller geolocators has greatly expanded our knowledge of migratory paths, especially for small songbirds like the prothonotary. At the tail end of the breeding season in Beidler Forest, Audubon biologist Matt Johnson placed a geolocator on an adult male warbler. With a knowing nod to the odds, he named the bird "Long Shot." Johnson released him and waited, hopeful but realistic.

Nine months later, as the swamp stirred with the first warblers of spring, Johnson paced the boardwalk, scanning the trees. At the far end of the path, where the slough spills into a deeper lake, he froze. From the very spot where Long Shot had been captured, a familiar and confident song rang out. Raising his binoculars, Johnson caught the unmistakable flash of green and black leg bands. Against all odds, the bird had returned, singing as boldly as ever. Johnson recaptured the warbler and downloaded the information stored in its data logger, revealing a staggering itinerary: over the course of two months, the bird had traveled 2,500 miles across six countries to winter in southwestern Colombia. He crossed four major bodies of water and, remarkably, made the return trip to Beidler Forest in just a few weeks.

Its uncanny ability to fly over millions of acres of secondary growth swamp and bottomlands to land precisely where it took off six months prior is still a mystery. Perhaps the magic that guides the bird is paralleled by uniqueness of the old growth.

From the moment they hatch, prothonotaries face a gauntlet of challenges: dodging predators in a landscape teeming with snakes, raptors, and raccoons; learning to forage and fly; undergoing a full molt before embarking on a transcontinental journey. The odds are staggering, but the little yellow warbler proves, time and again, that it is up to the task.

Perhaps not everyone will overcome their fear of snakes or mosquitoes to embrace the swamp in all its damp, primeval beauty. But even the most reluctant nature lover can find something to admire in the underdog. And if nothing else, we can all root for the long shot.

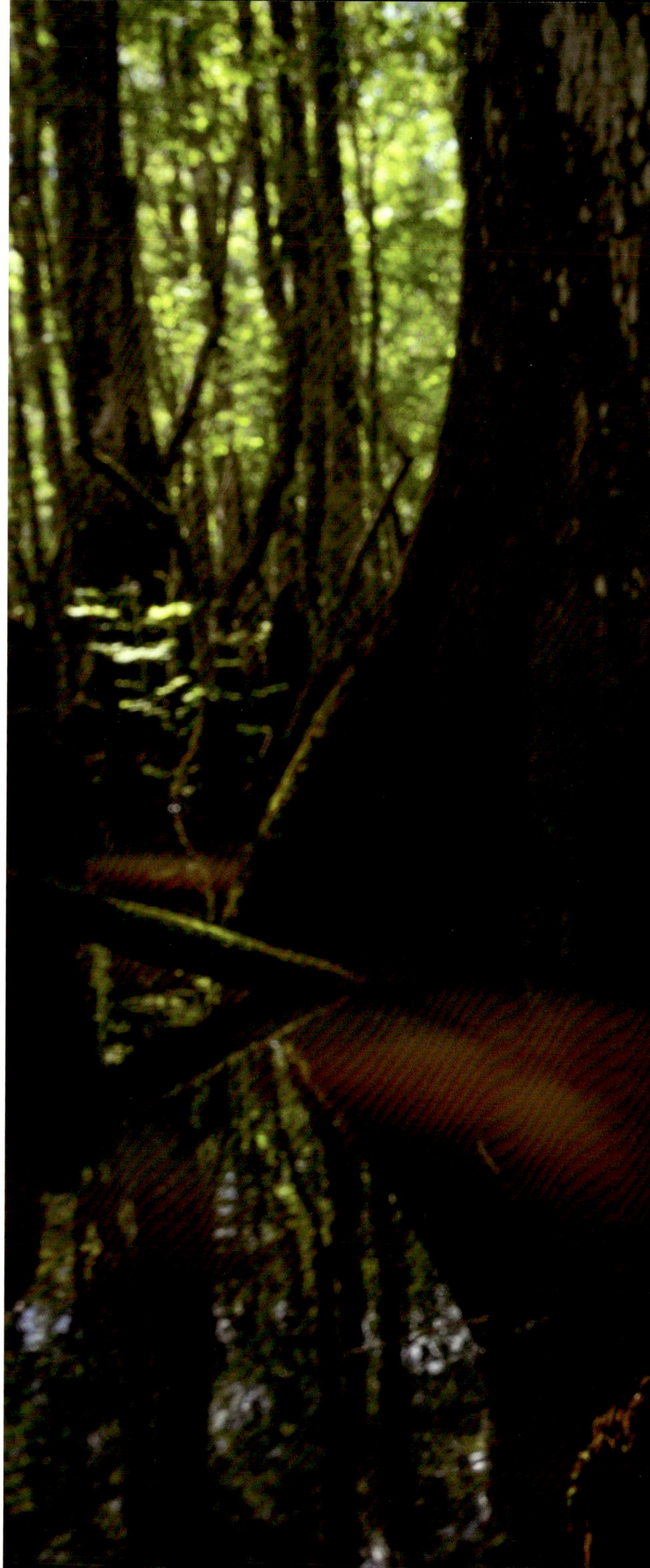

An expert hunter, a female prothonotary warbler returns to the nest with forest tent caterpillars for her growing chicks, which will fledge in just 10 to 11 days.

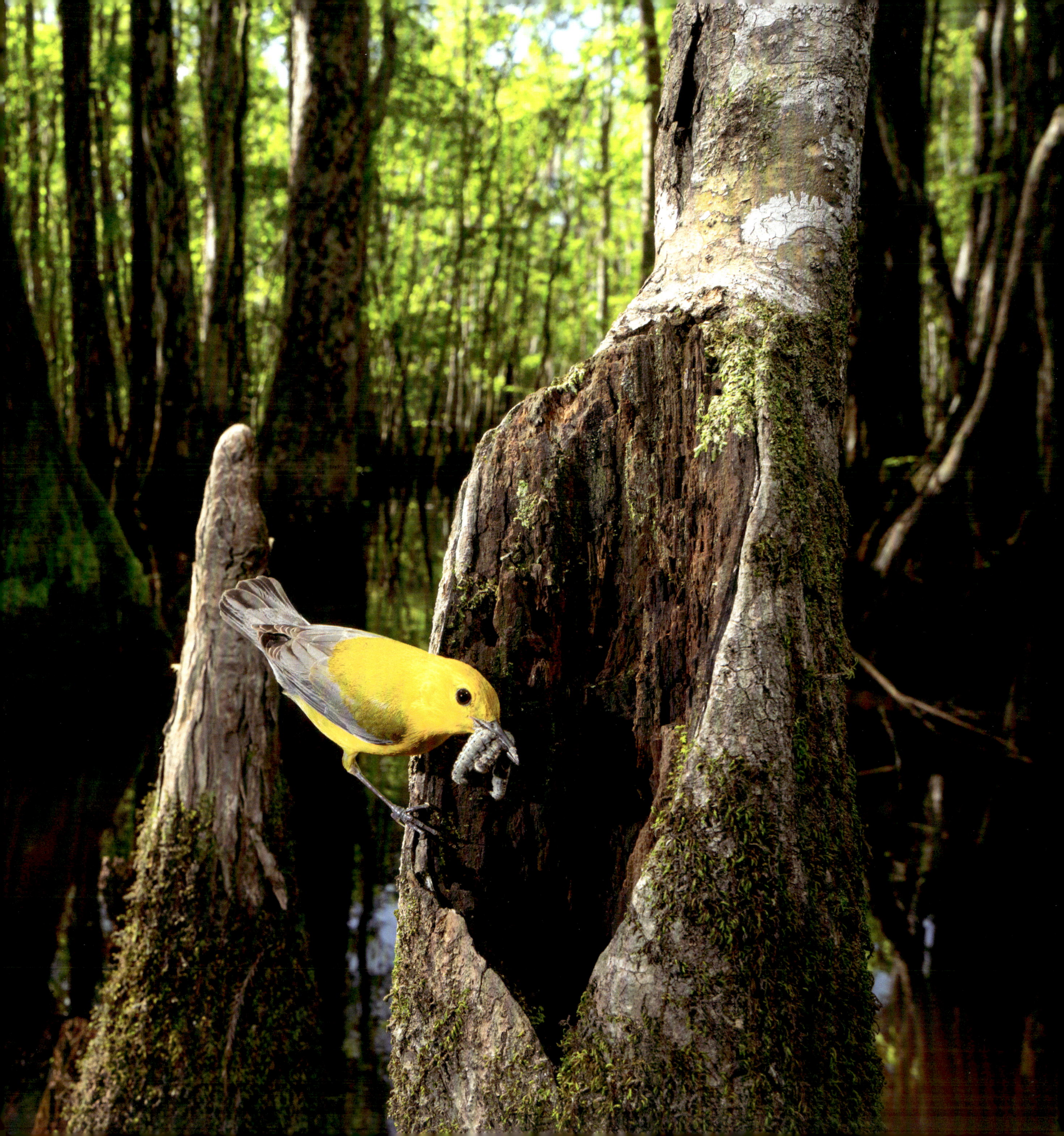

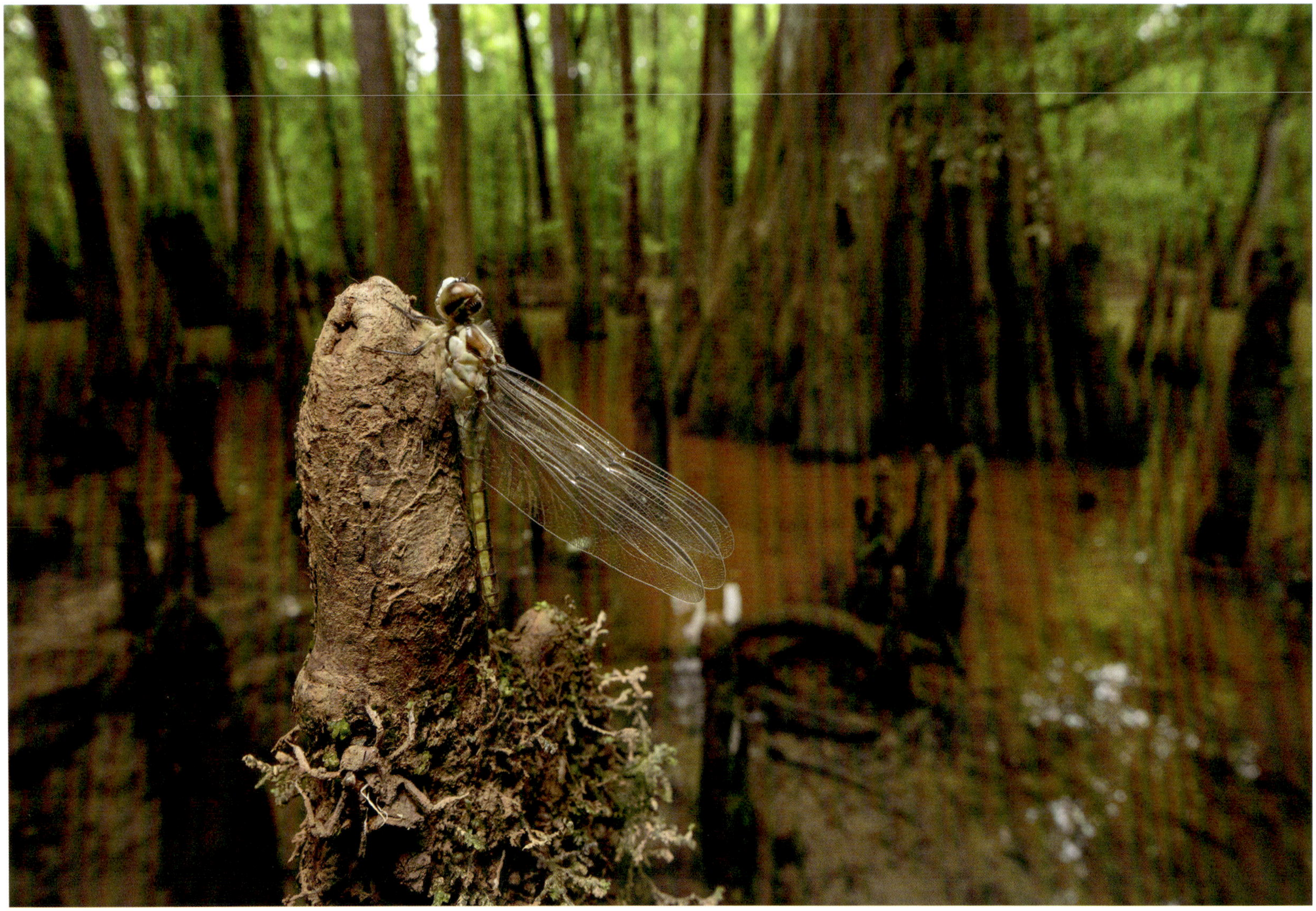

Dragonflies spend months—even years—underwater as nymphs before rising in a single night to shed their skins and take flight.

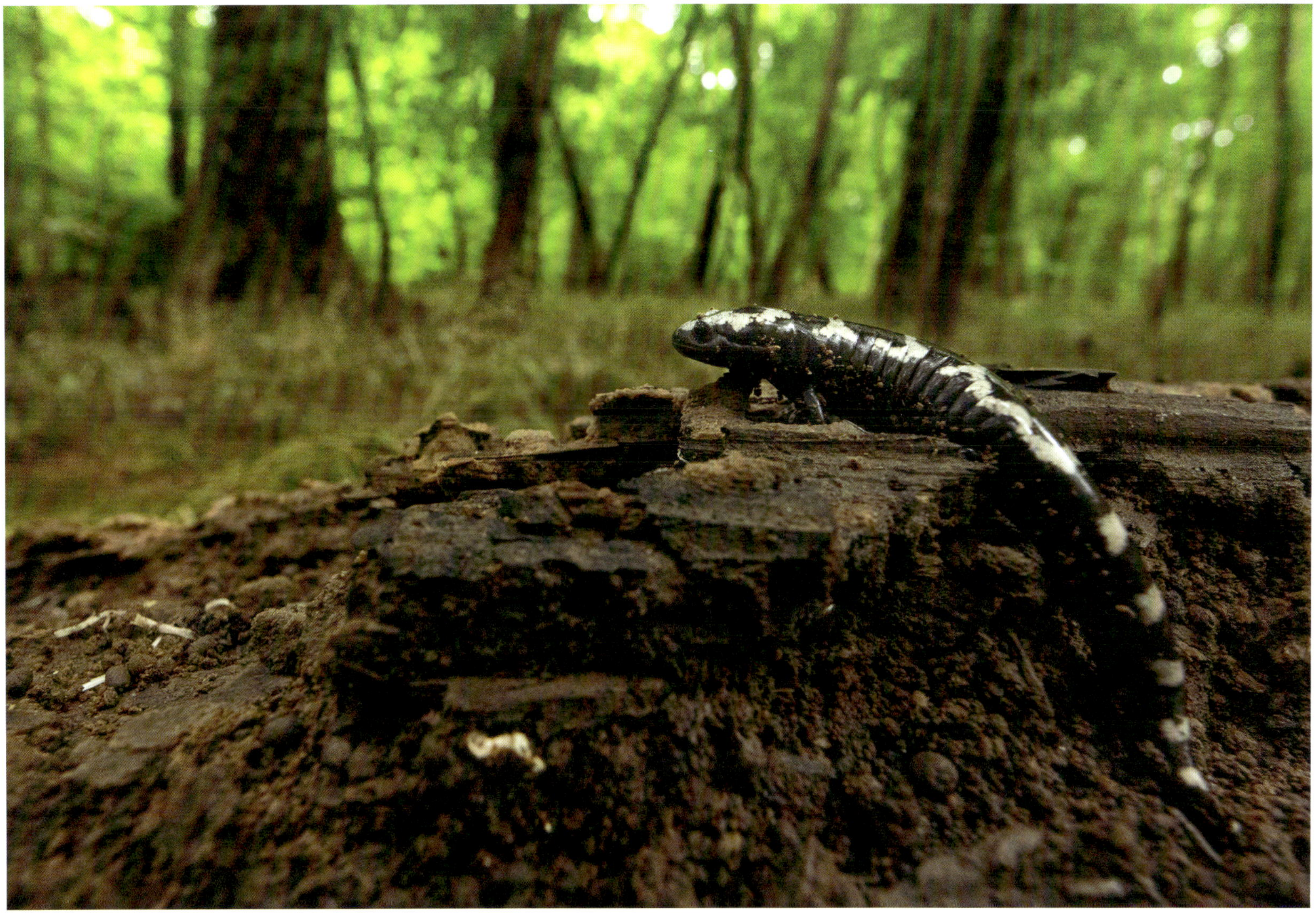

Marbled salamanders thrive in the damp, hidden world beneath rotting logs and fallen trees—where decay creates the moisture, shelter, and prey base these secretive amphibians need to survive.

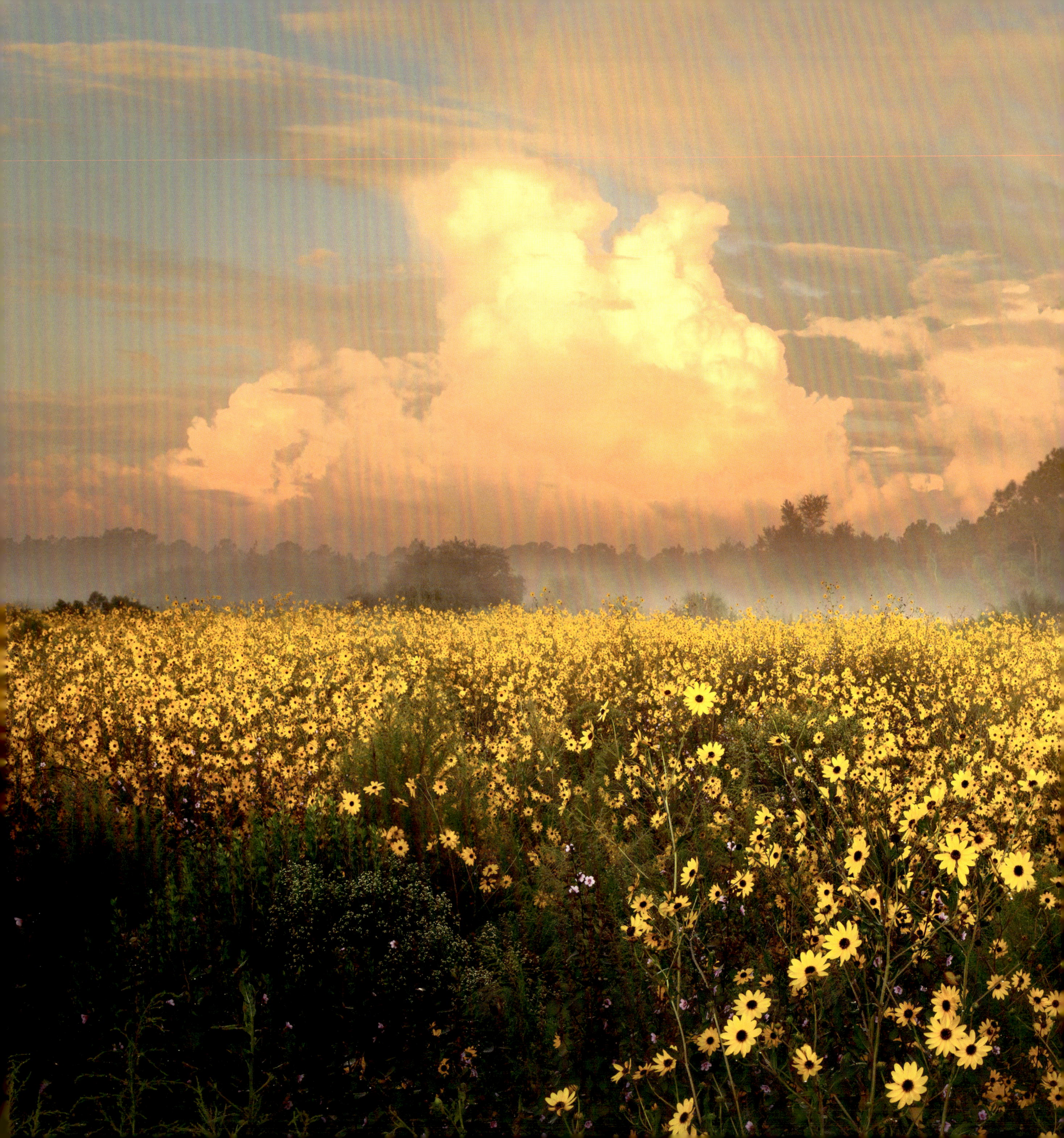

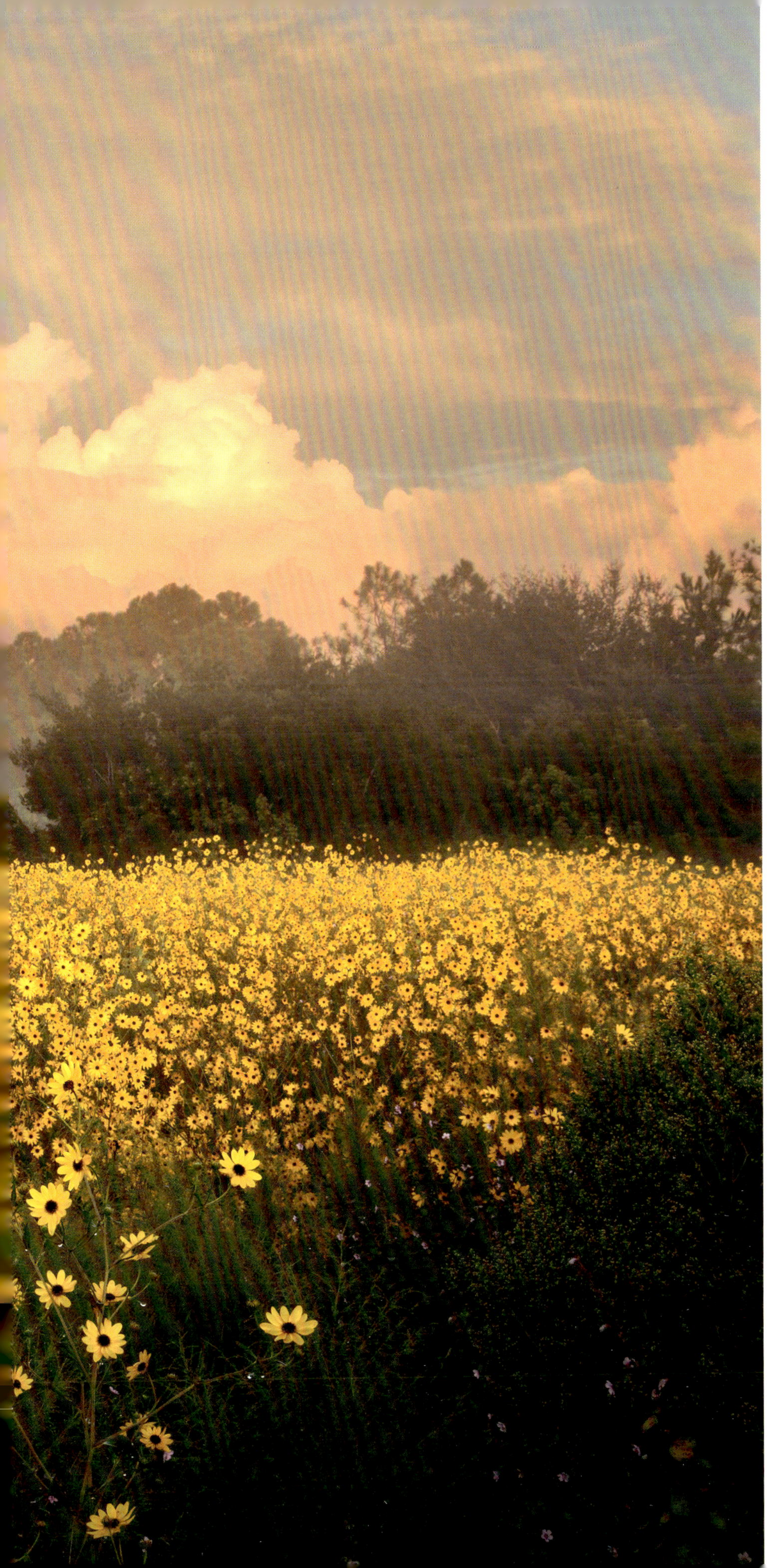

In October, the wet prairies explode with color as helianthus blooms stretch 10 feet tall and as far as the eye can see, providing a critical late-season nectar source for pollinators.

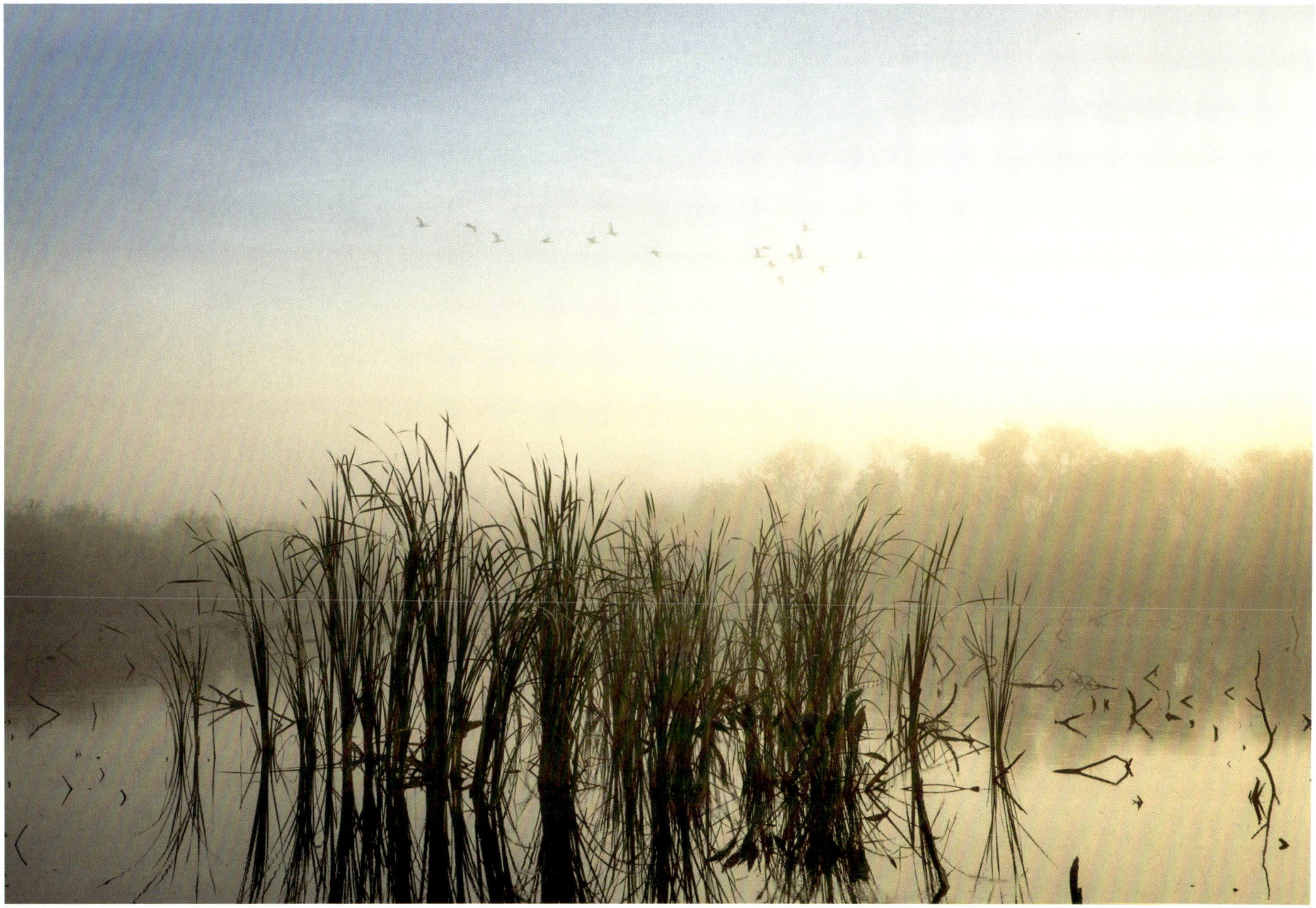

A restored wetland, once crowded out by willow, now
offers foraging habitat for myriad wading birds.

Barred owls mate for life, and they have very high site fidelity, rarely leaving their local woods.

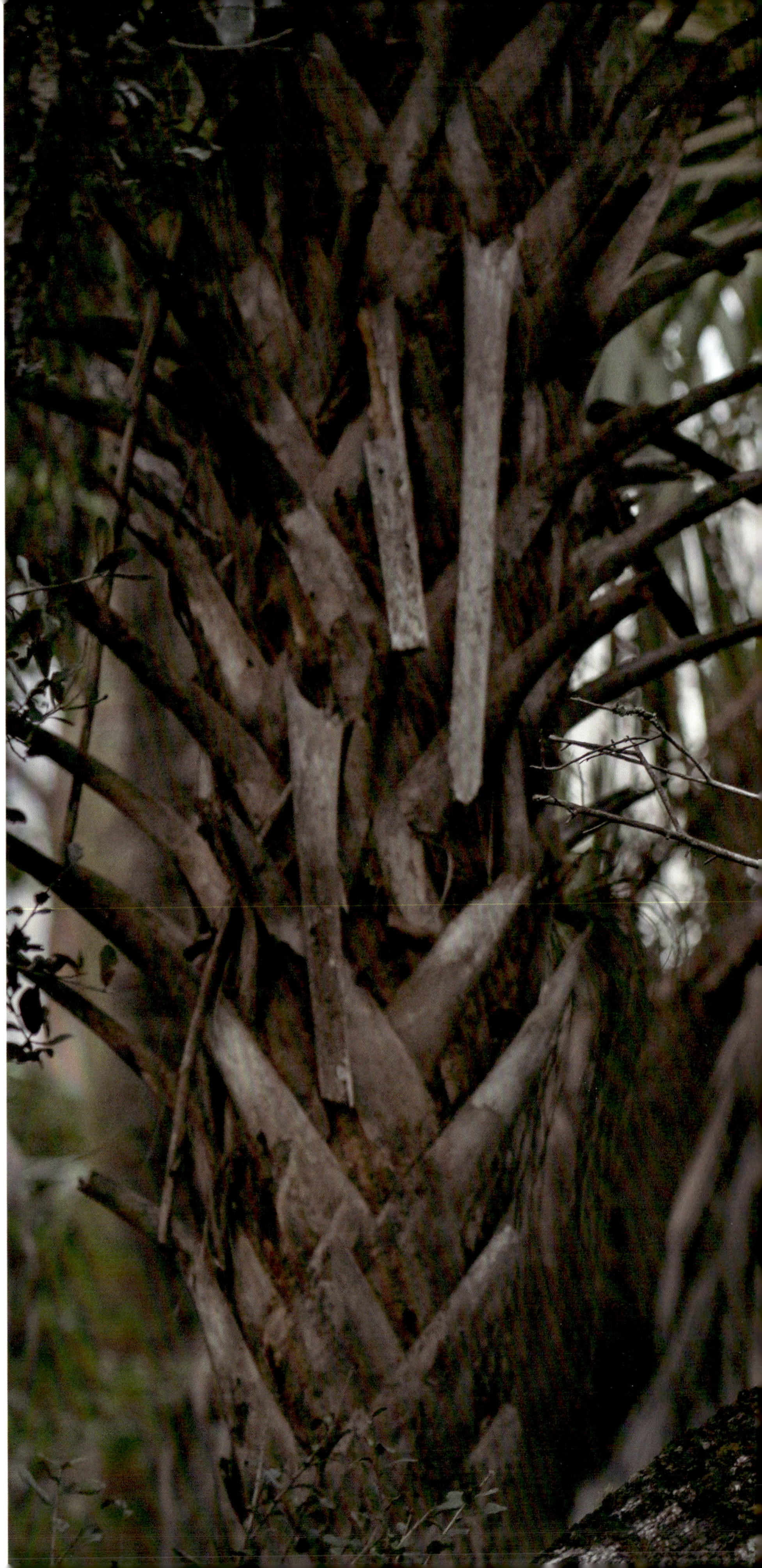

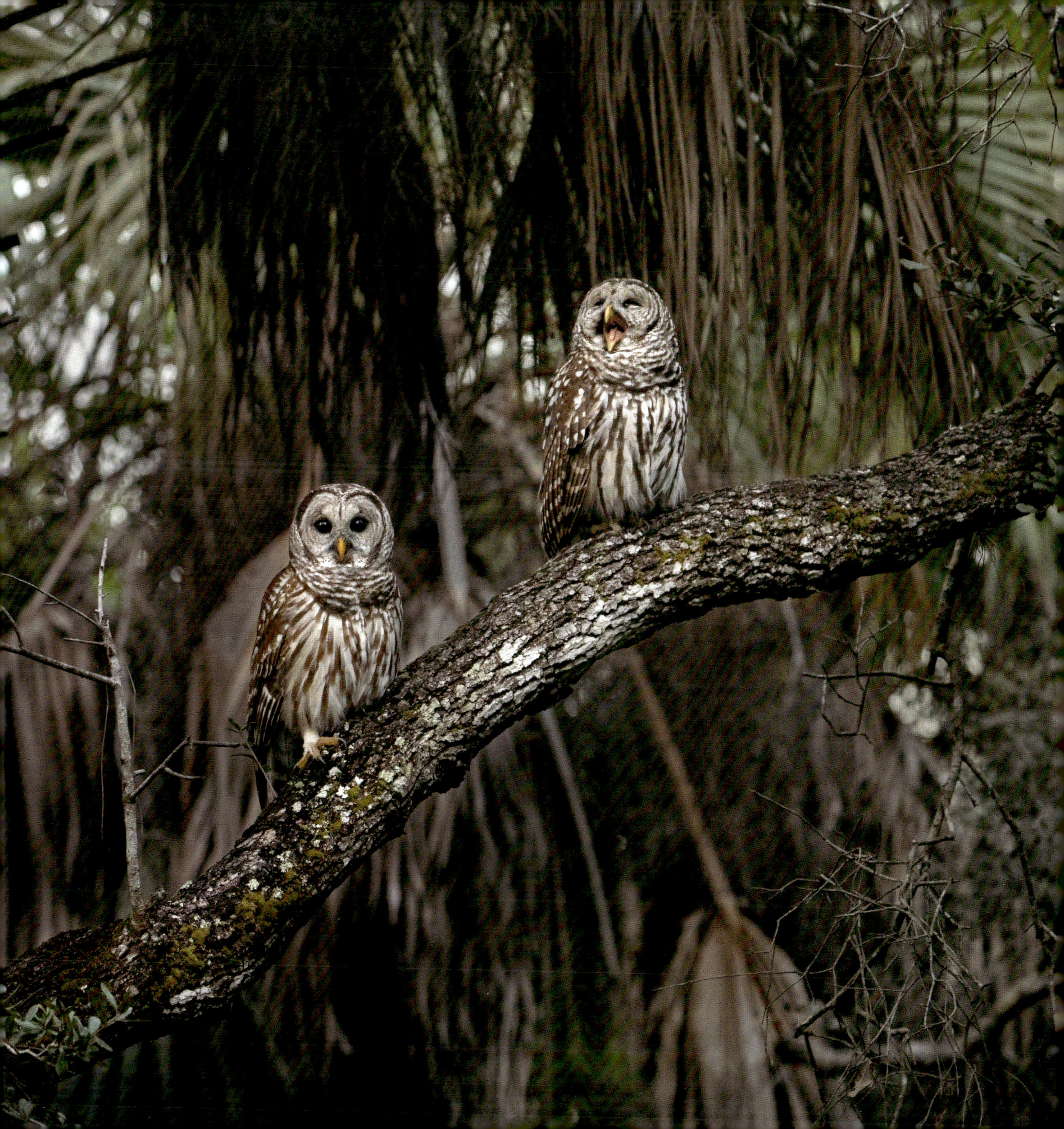

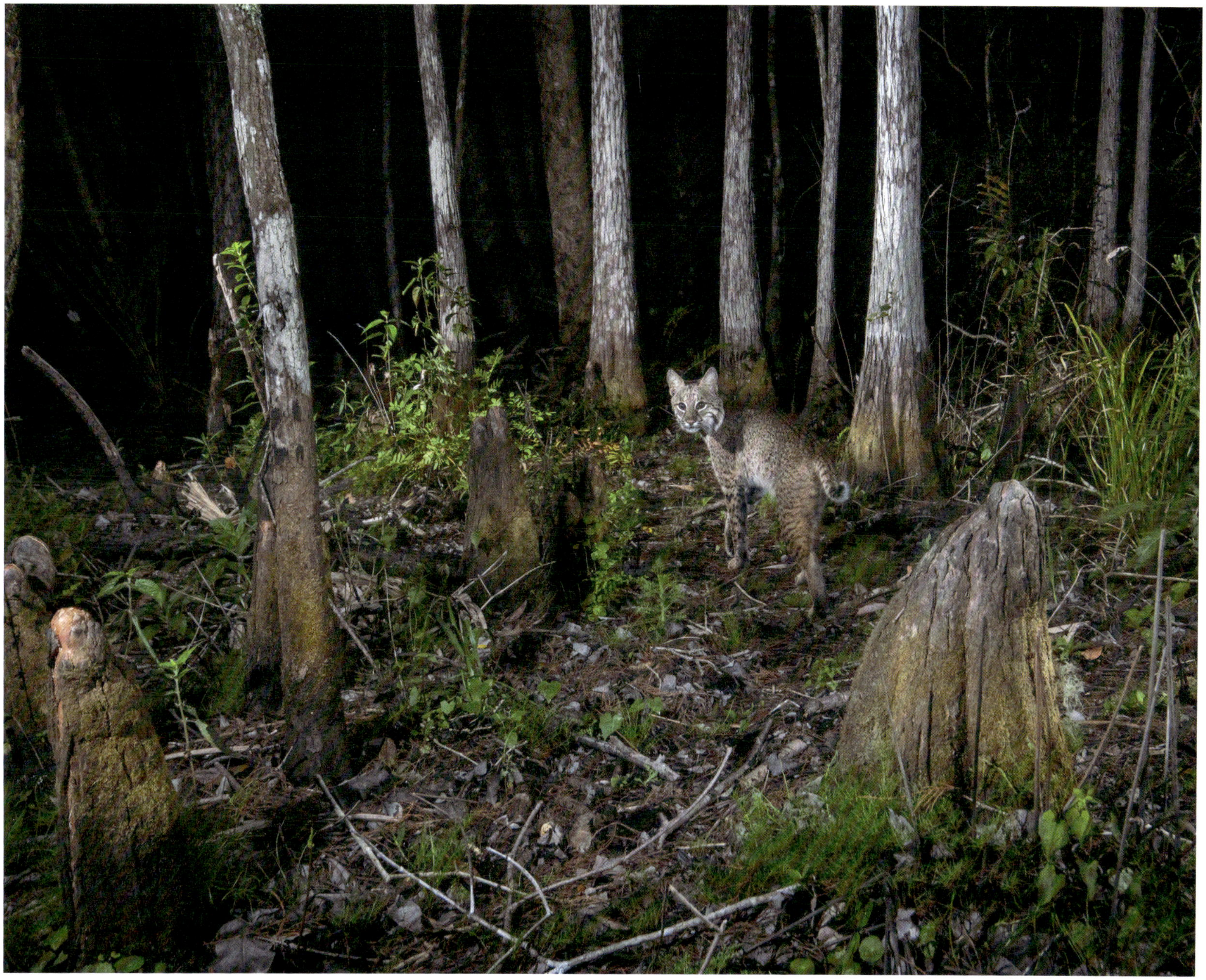

In wetlands and flooded forests, bobcats use elevated logs, game trails, and even alligator paths to navigate flooded areas while staying dry and undetected.

FOLLOWING PAGE

In early spring, a kaleidoscope of color erupts in the understory, as hardwoods leaf out first, racing to soak up sunlight before the towering cypress trees cast their shade.

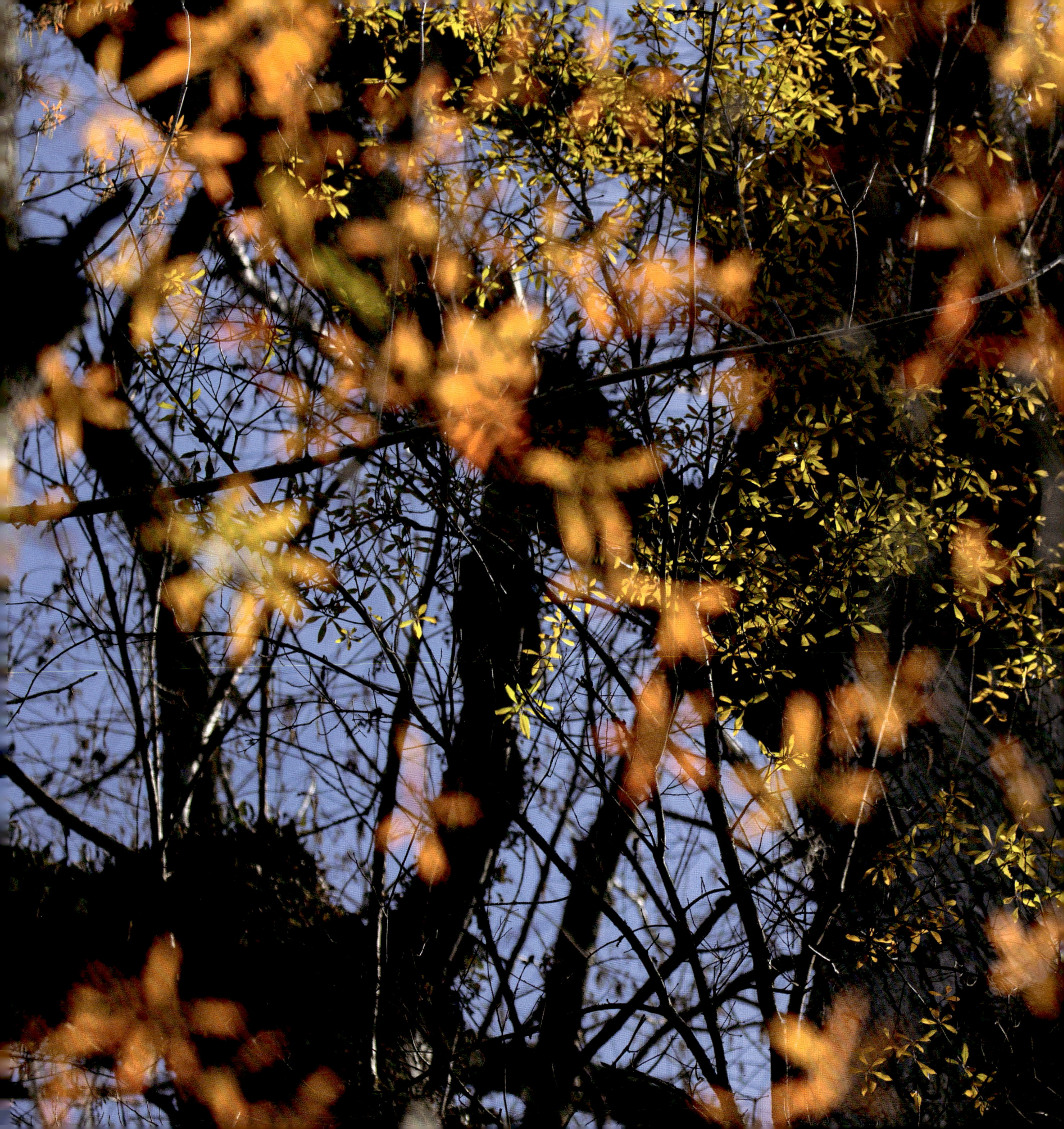

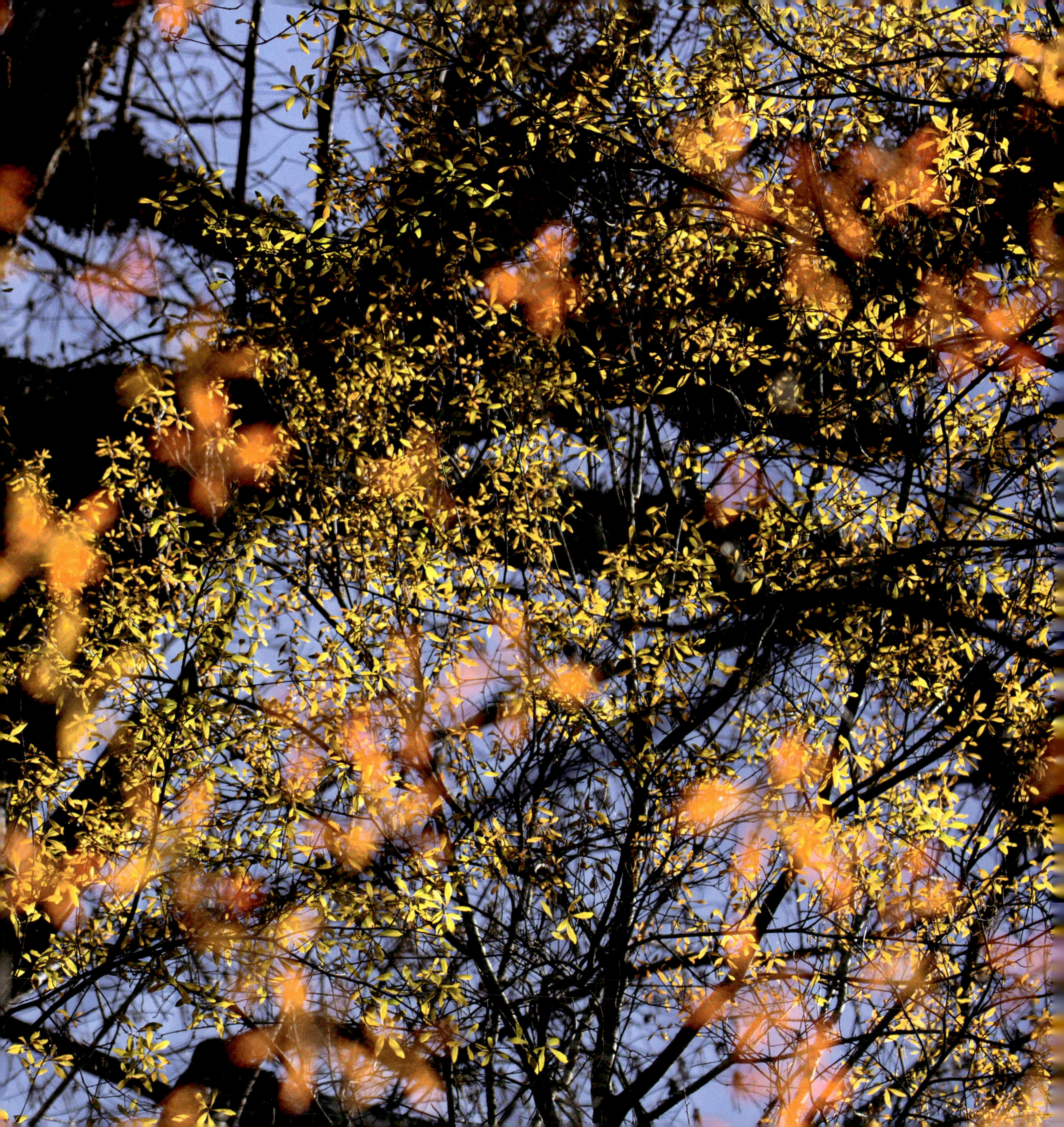

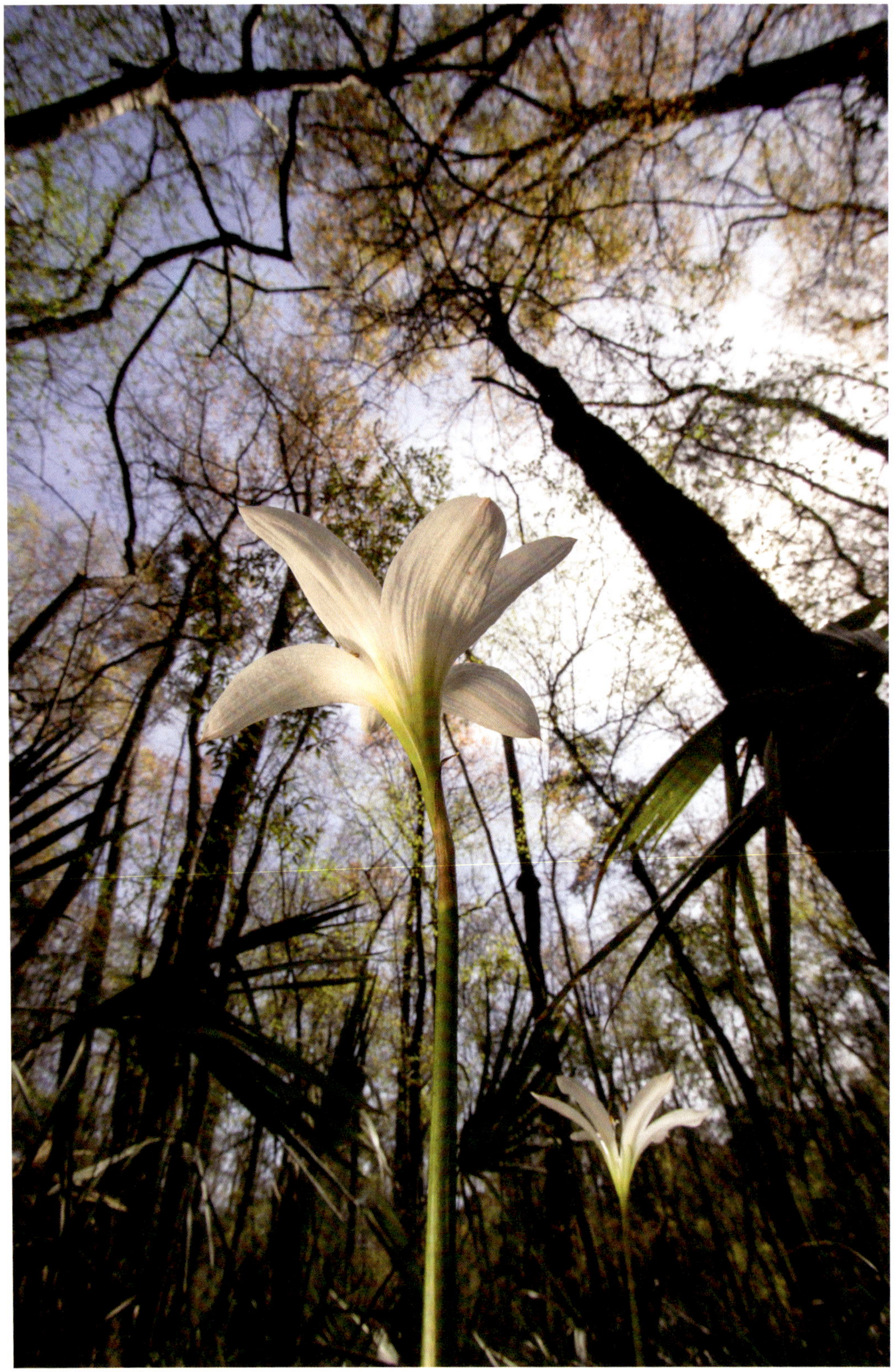

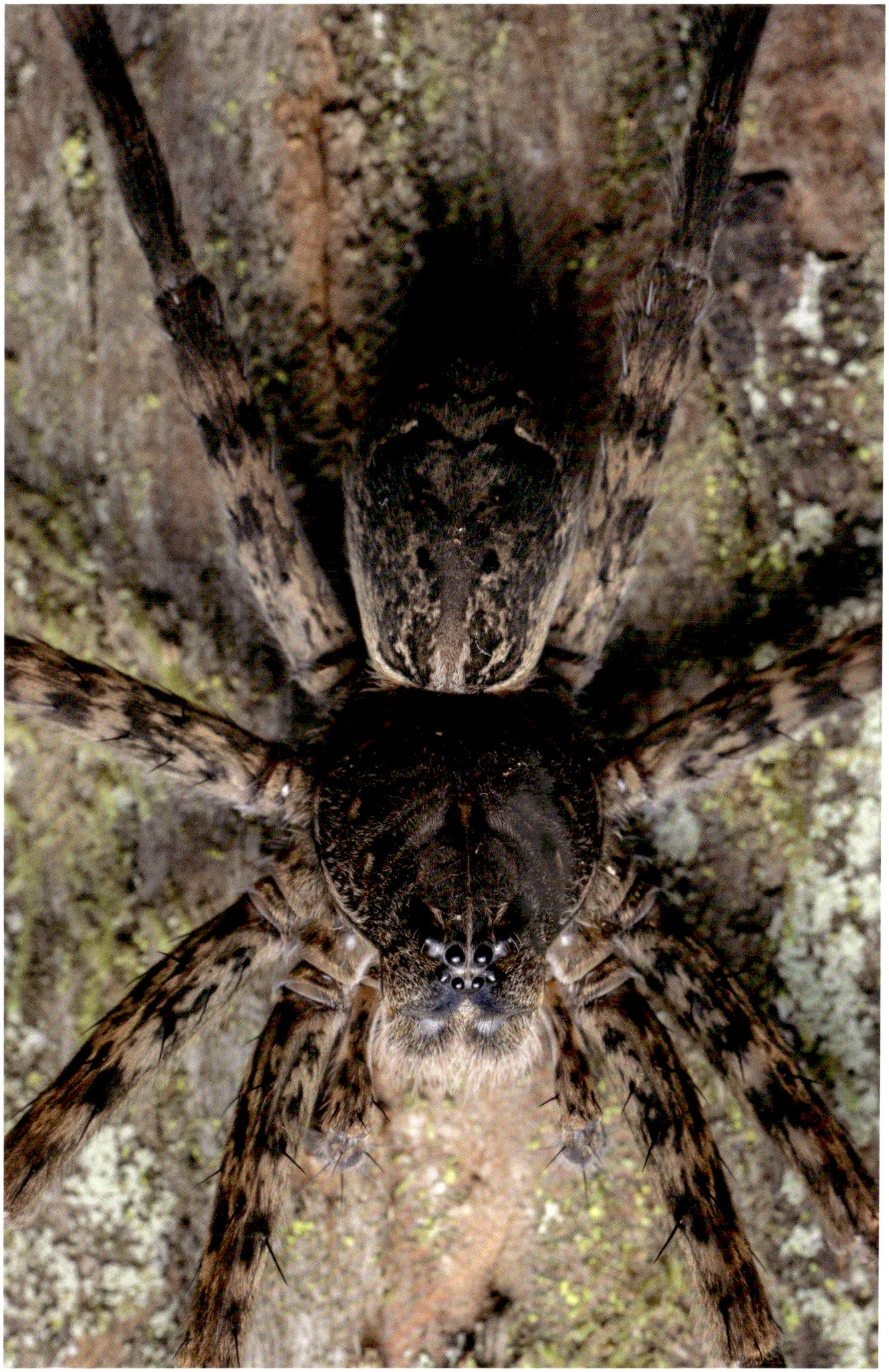

Unlike major river systems, Four Holes Swamp is defined by braided sloughs where water moves gently across a wide floodplain through upland palmetto islands and stands of hardwoods.

PREVIOUS PAGES

Triggered by spring rains, atamasco lilies emerge briefly from saturated soils, their short-lived blooms marking a narrow window of wetland renewal in the southeastern United States.

With leg spans stretching four inches, fishing spiders stalk the water's edge, diving below the surface or skimming across it to ambush insects, tadpoles, and even small fish.

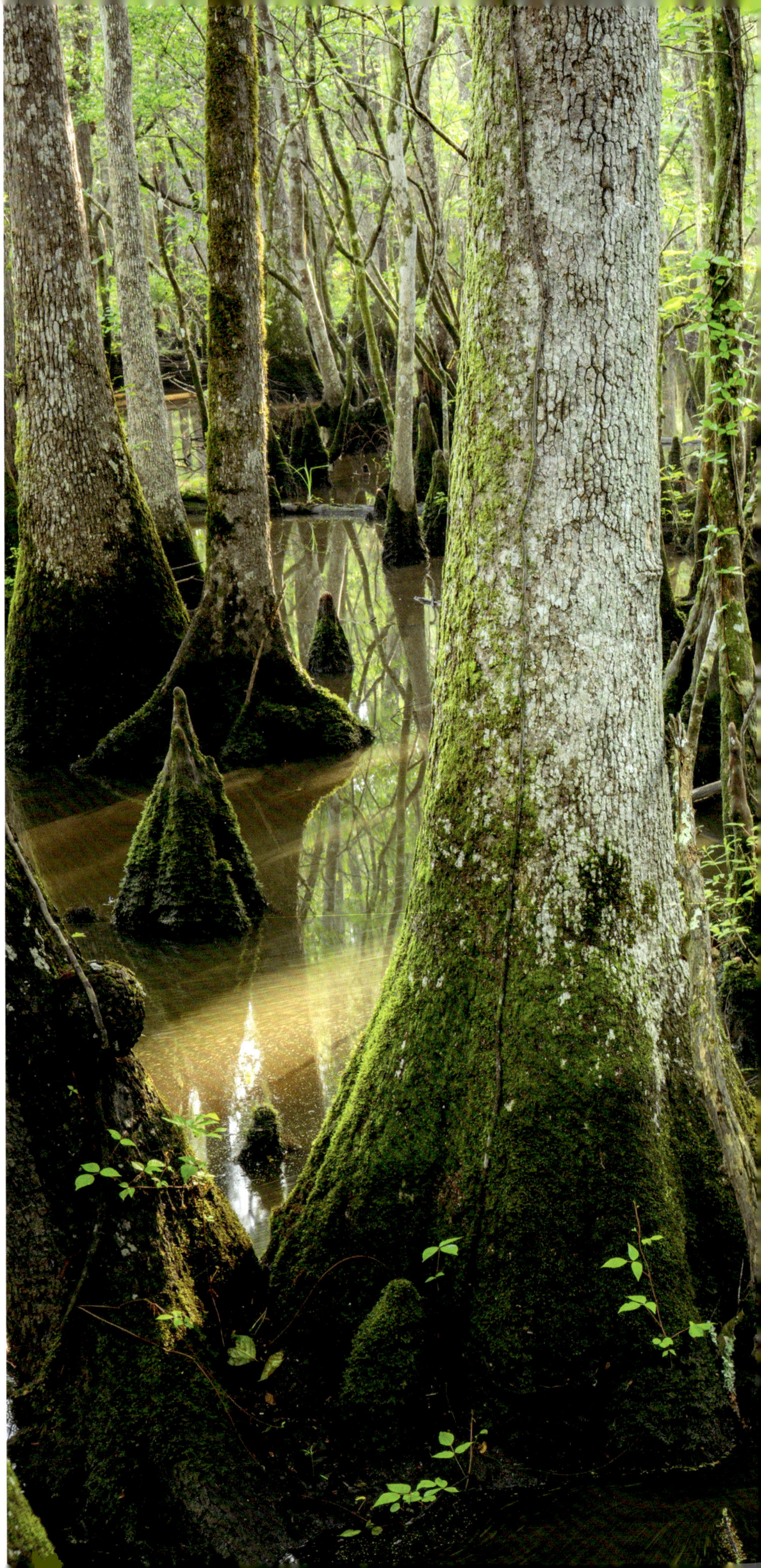

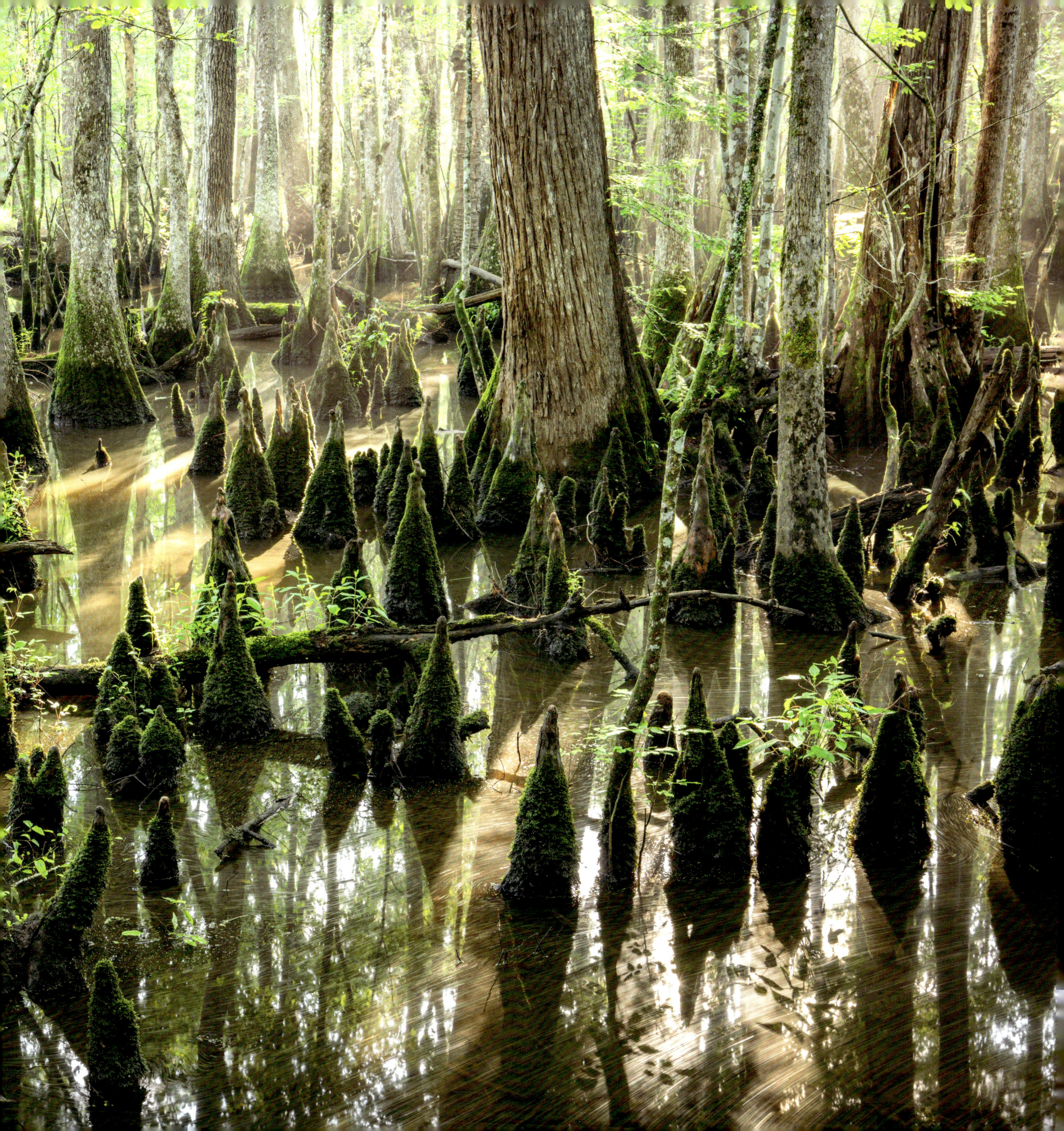

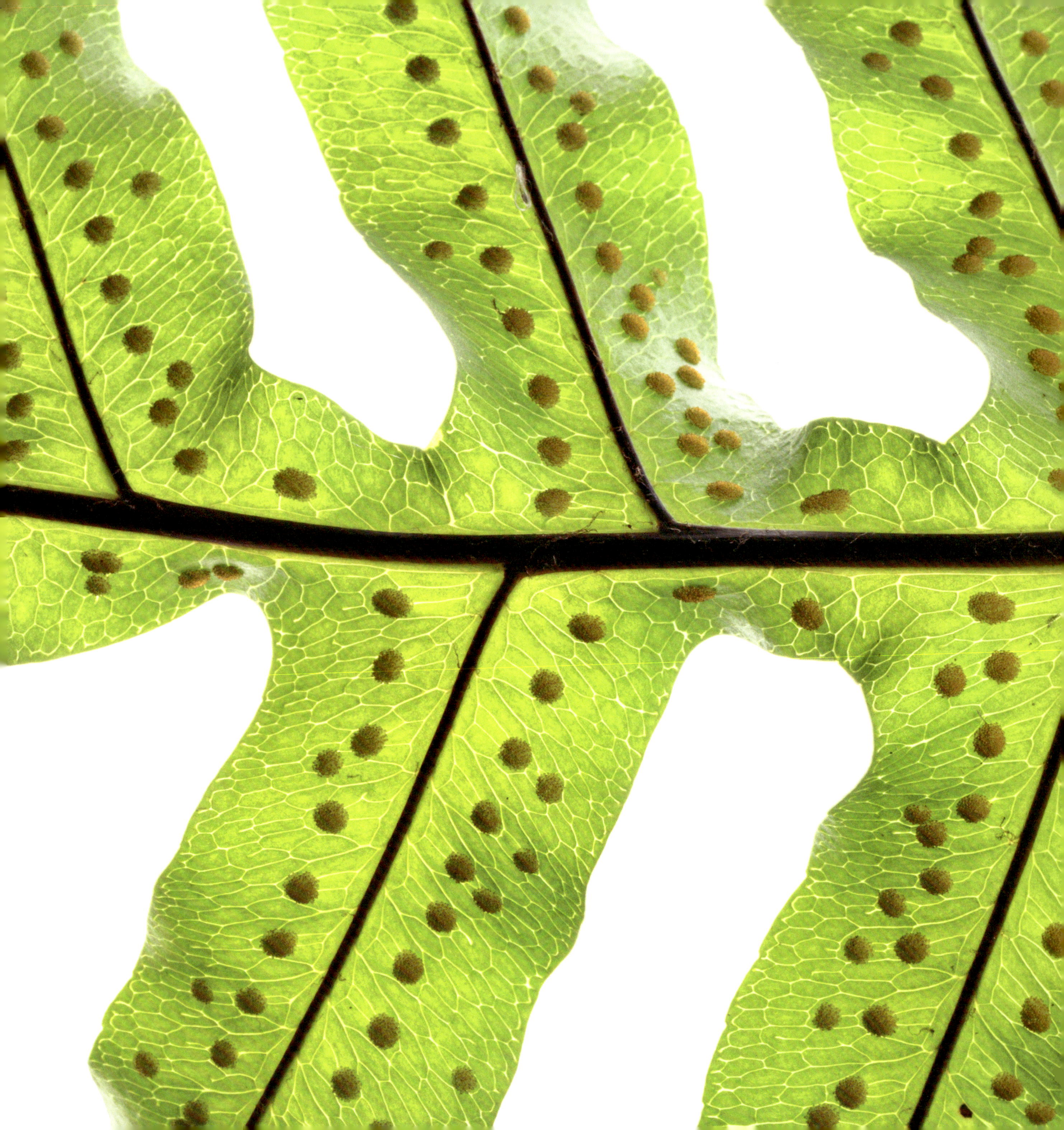

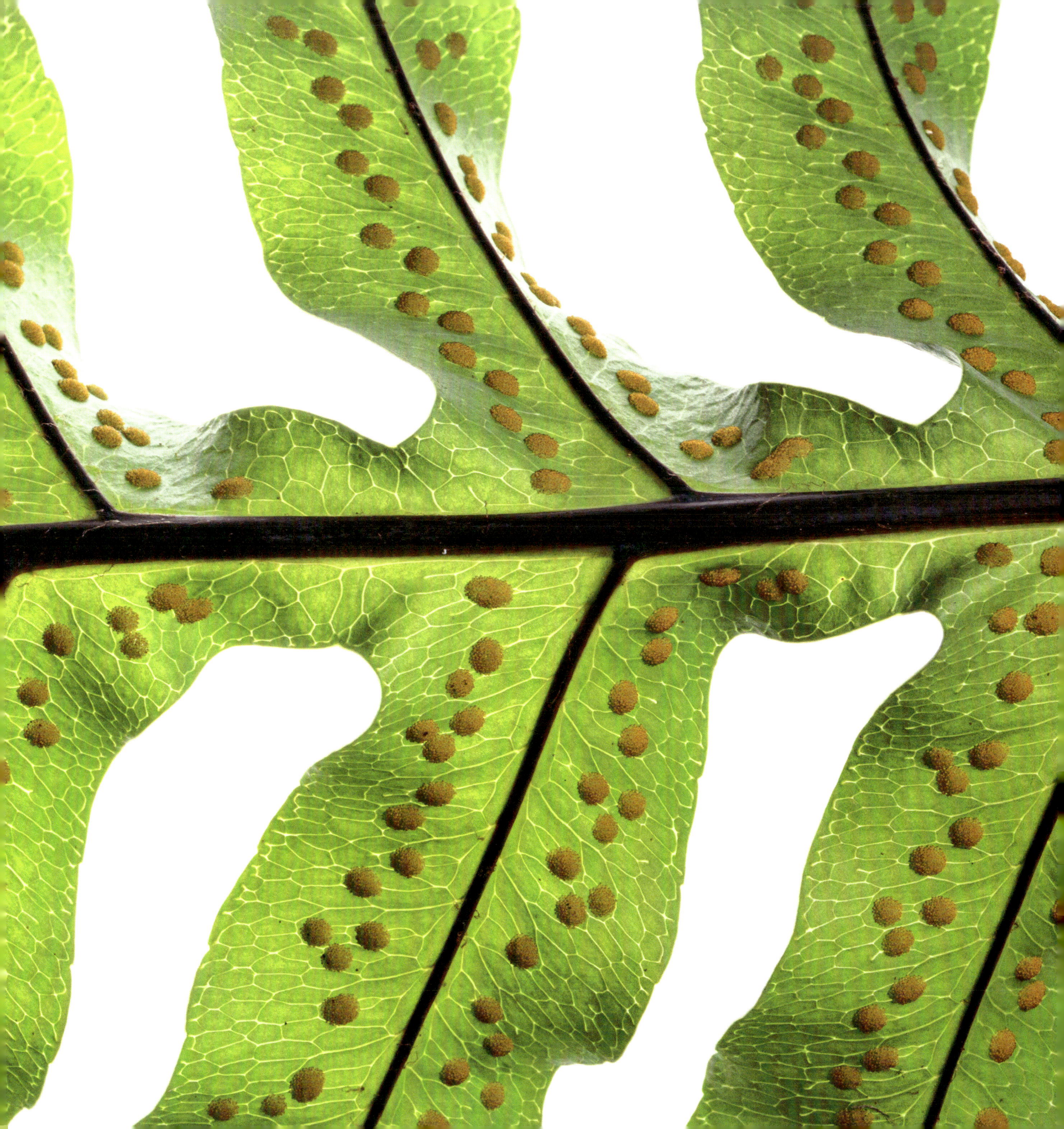

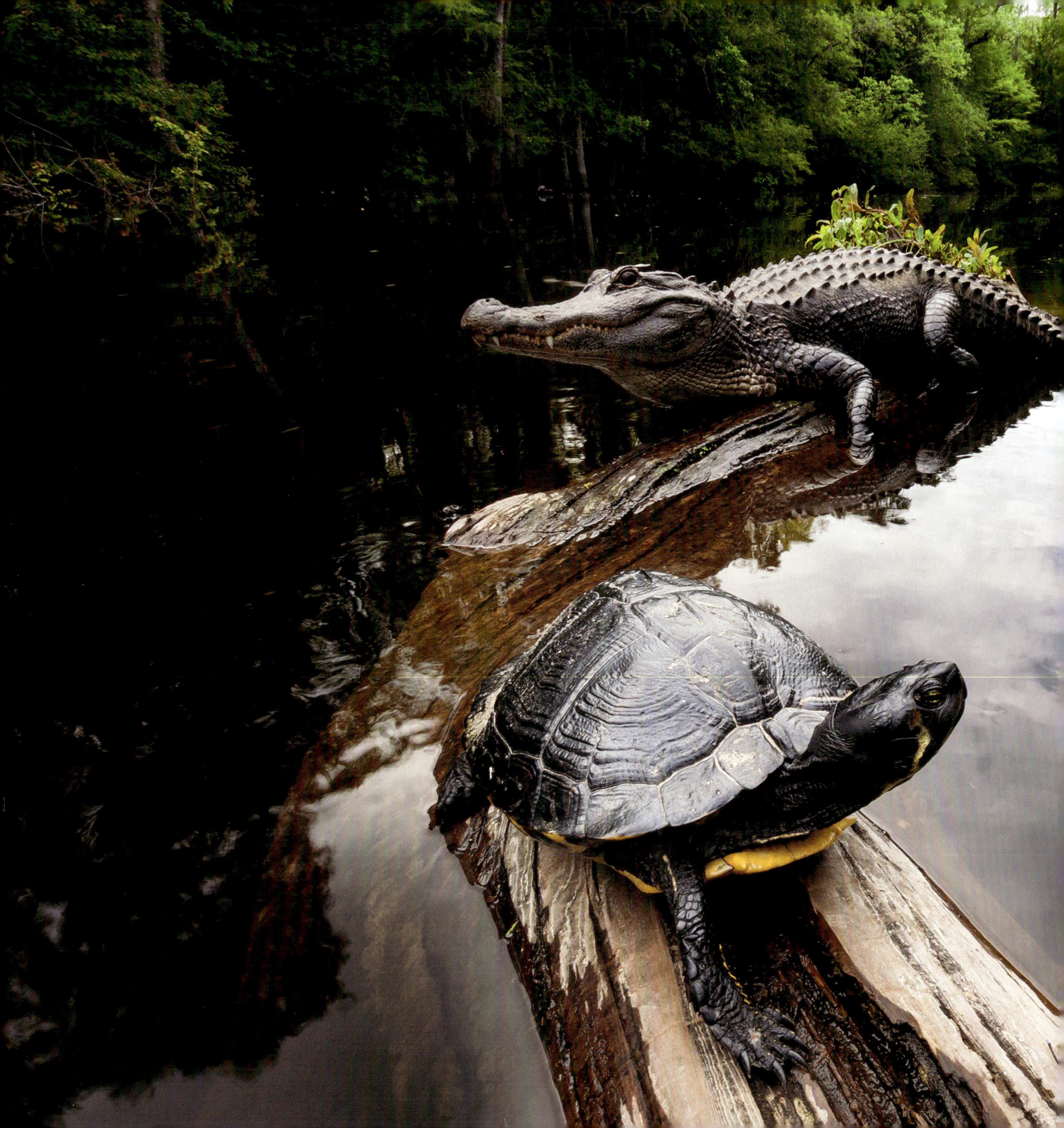

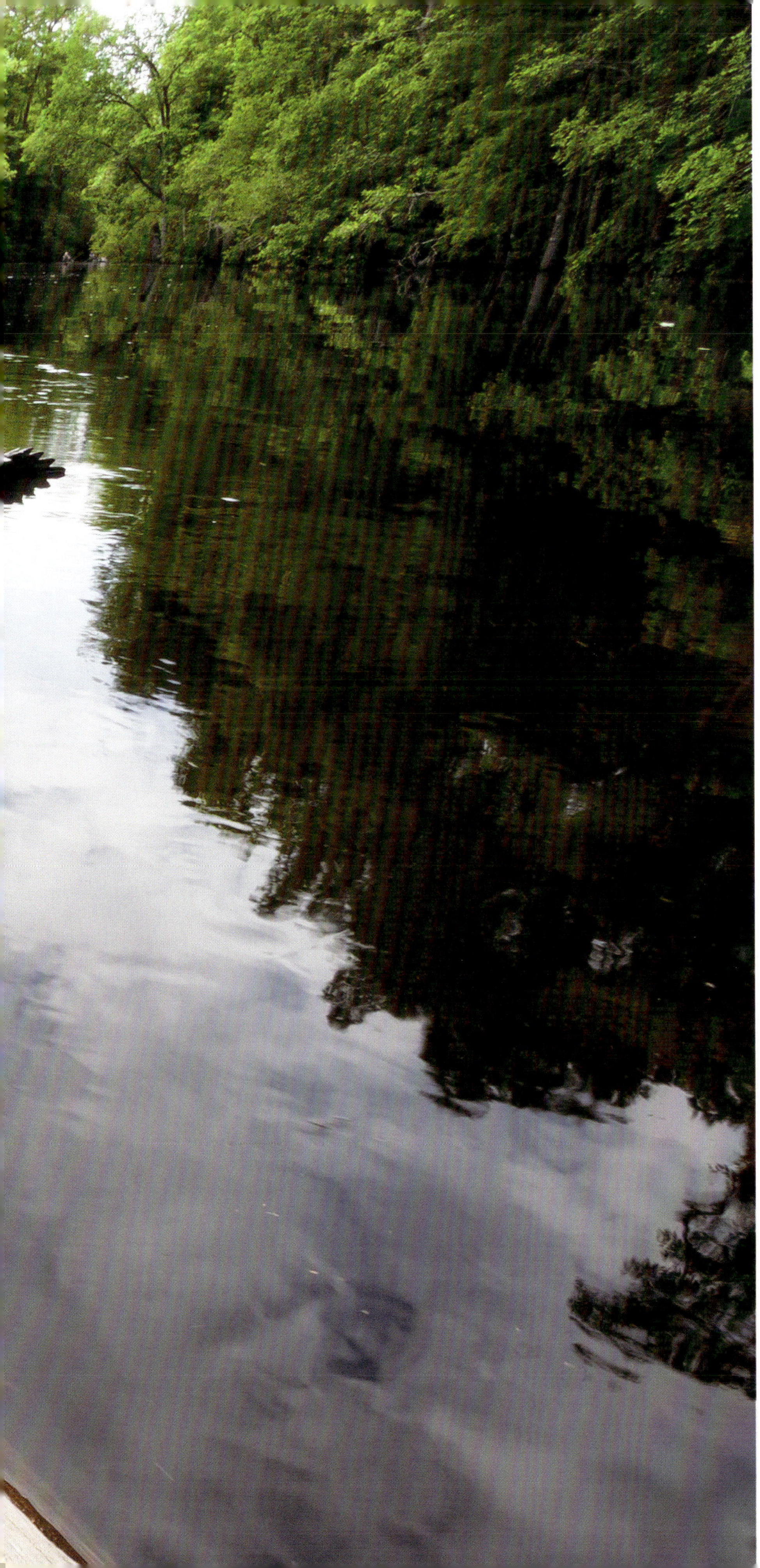

With limited options, predator and prey often share prime real estate for sunbathing in the swamp.

PREVIOUS PAGE

Spore packets pepper the underside of a blue star fern.

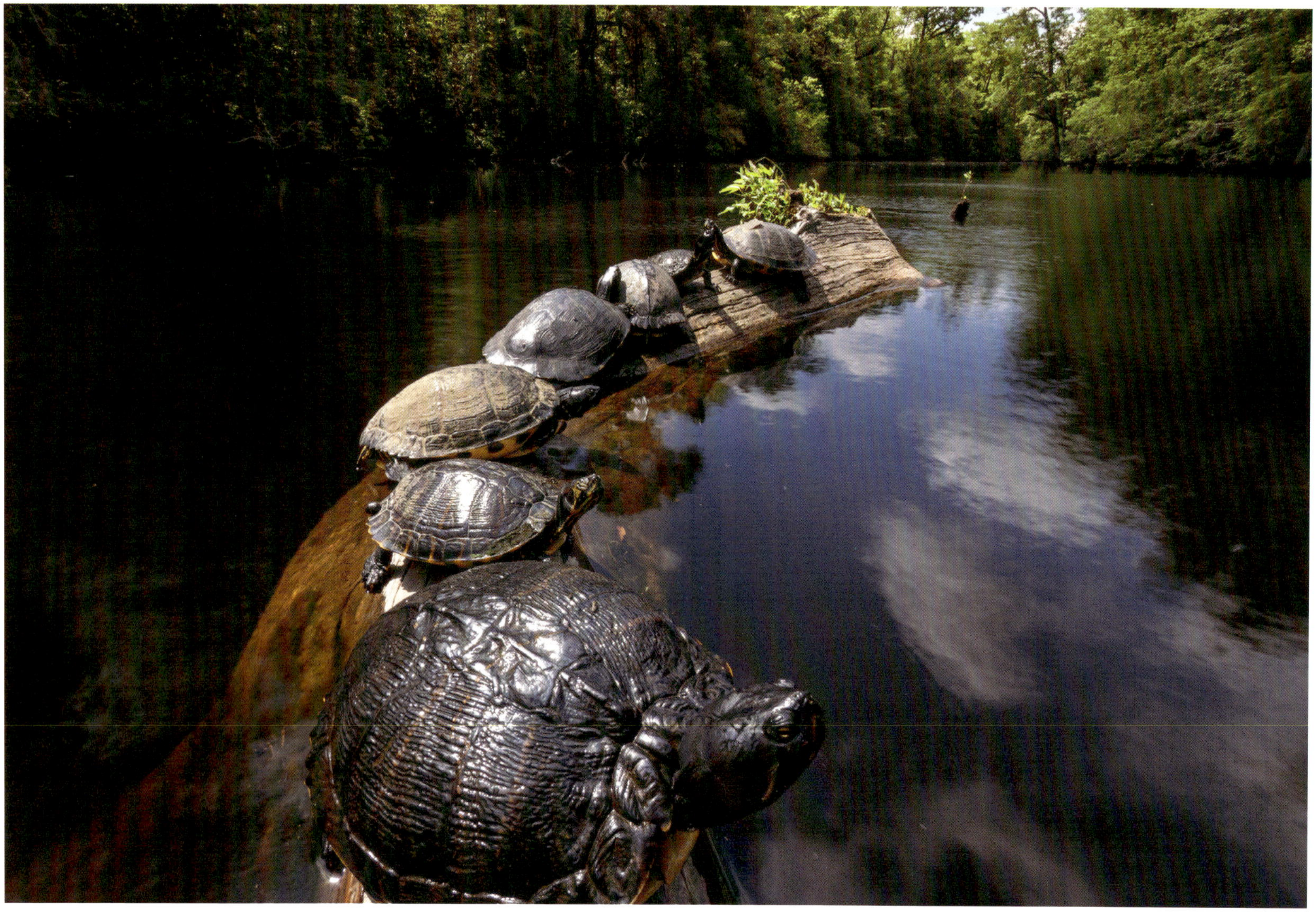

Yellow-bellied sliders need between 30 and 60 minutes of direct sun in the morning to maintain an active body temperature.

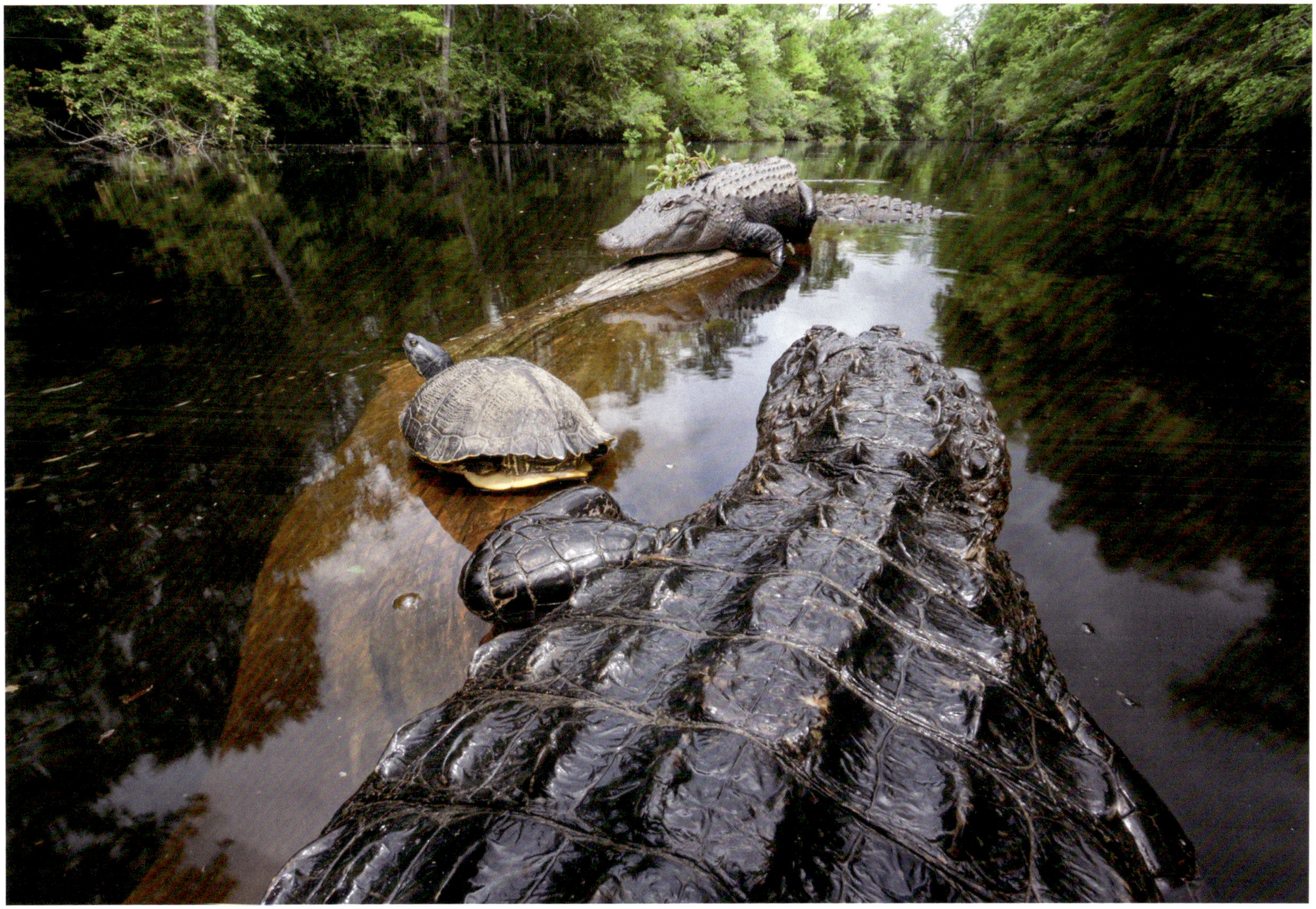

Between an alligator and a hard place, a yellow-bellied slider tucks its legs into its shell at a popular basking log.

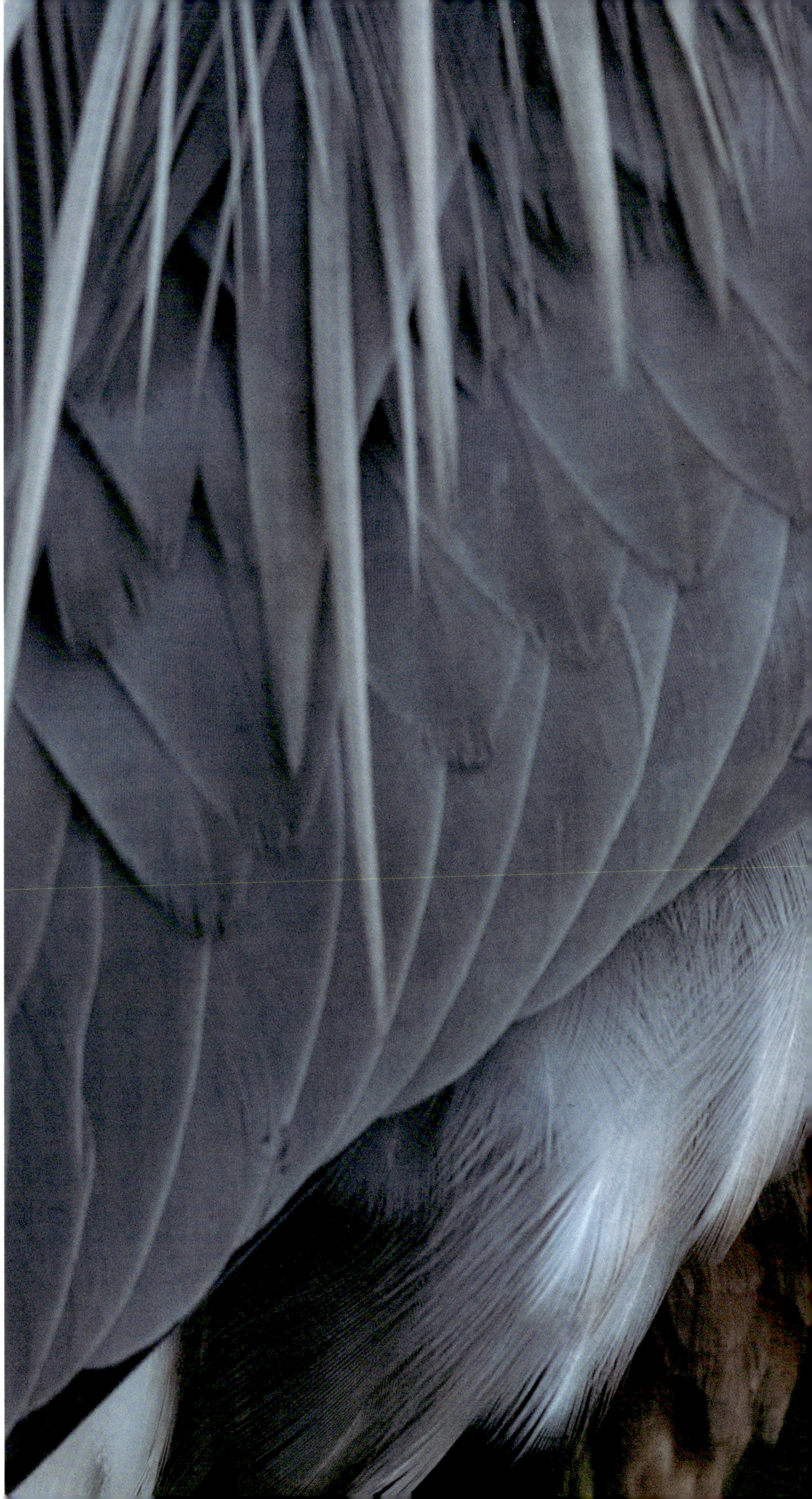

With prehistoric poise and a six-foot wingspan, the great blue heron can strike fish, frogs, and reptiles at speeds of 100 milliseconds with its spear-like bill.

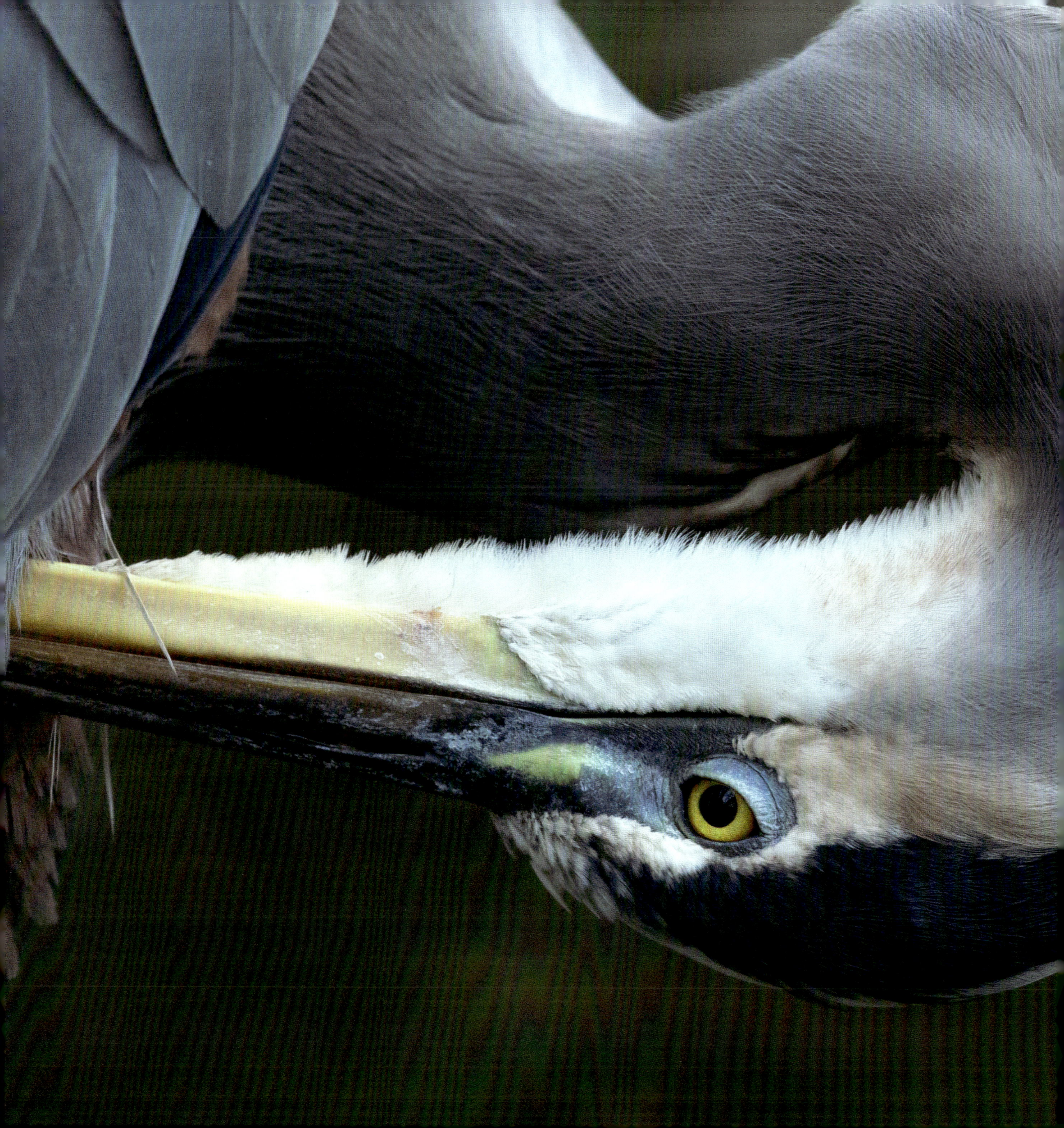

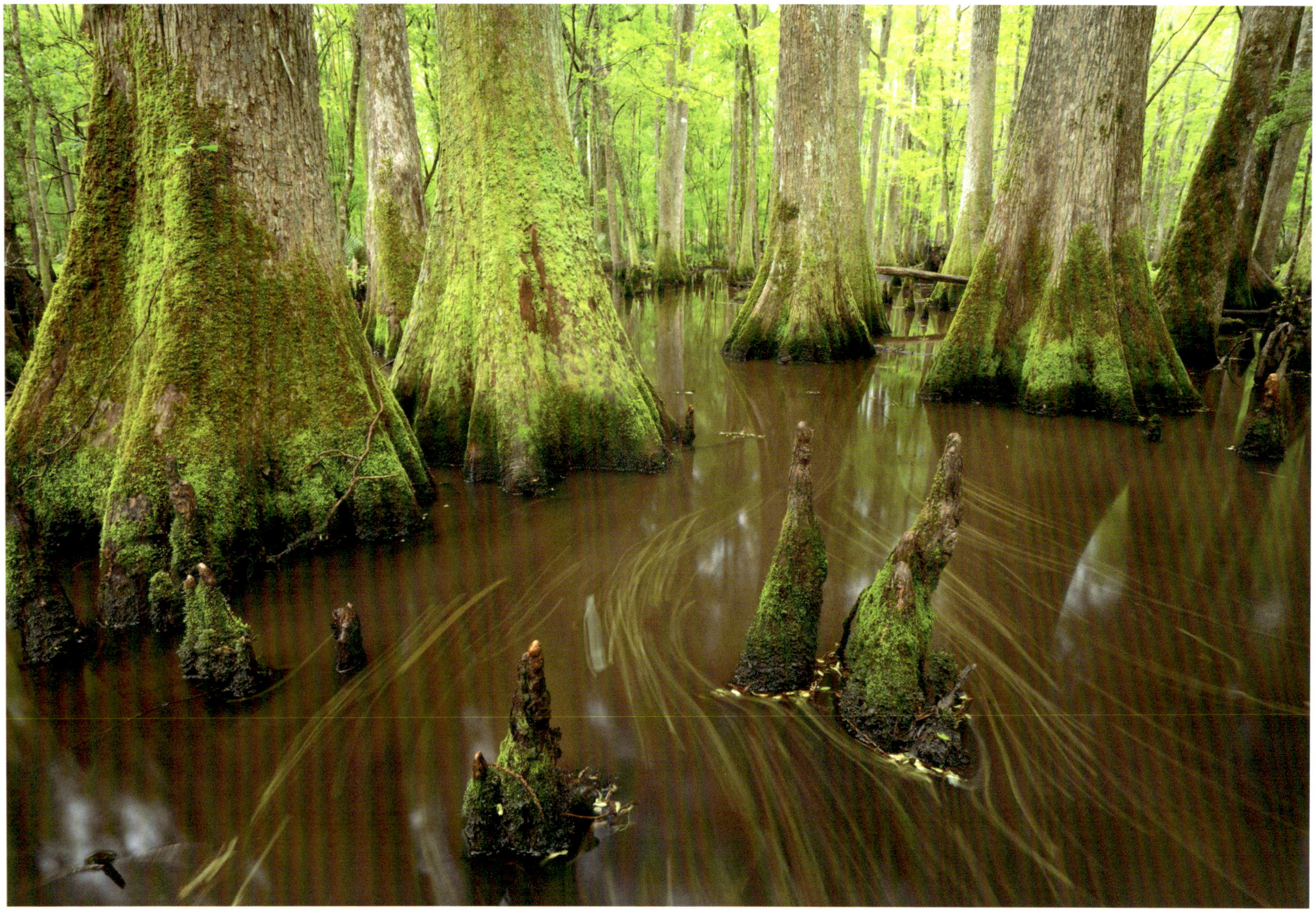

Spring rains carry flower petals down the sloughs,
winding through tupelo gum and cypress.

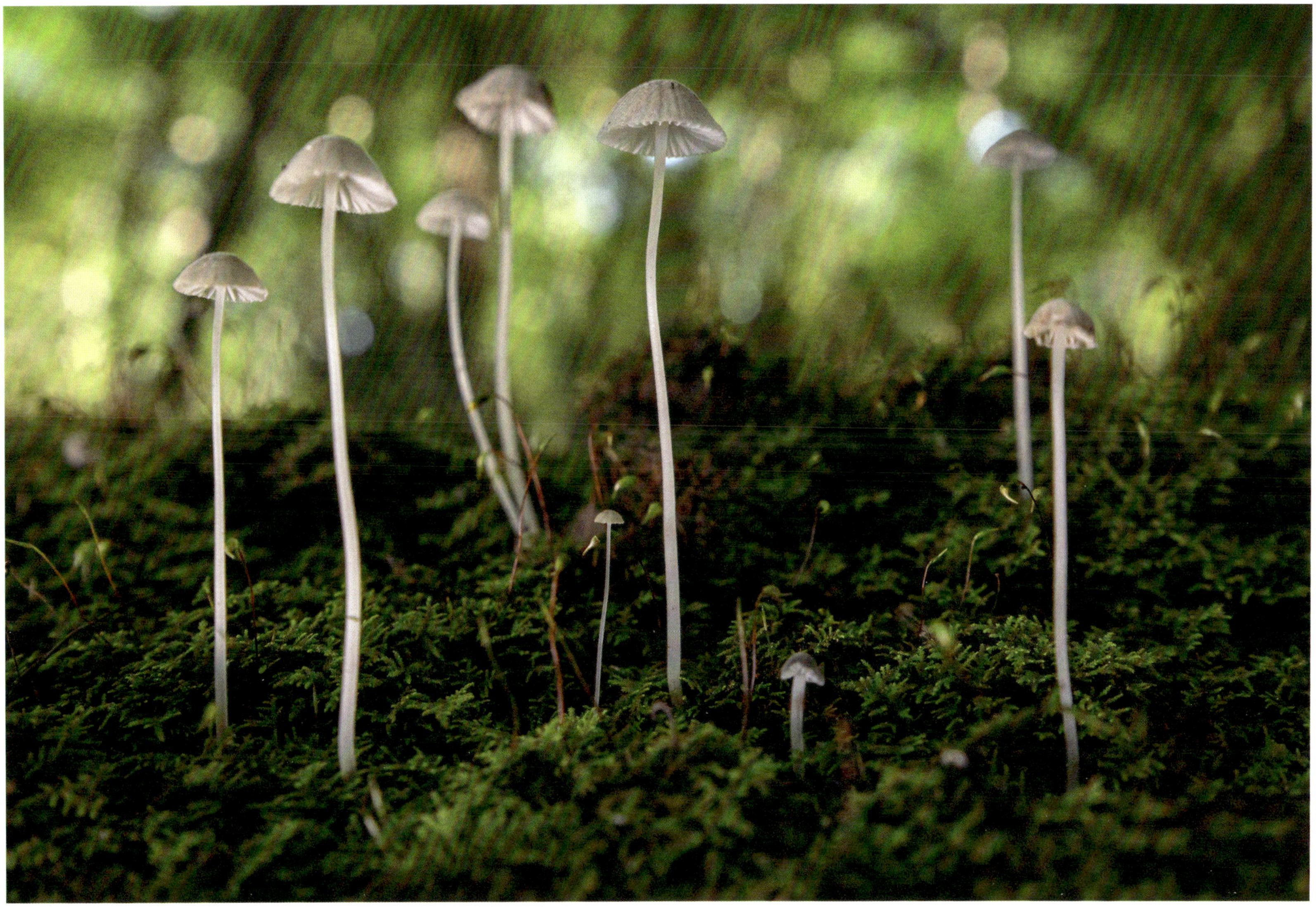

Fallen trees—called nurse logs—litter the ground in old-growth forests, providing habitat and nutrients for mosses, fungi, and detritivores.

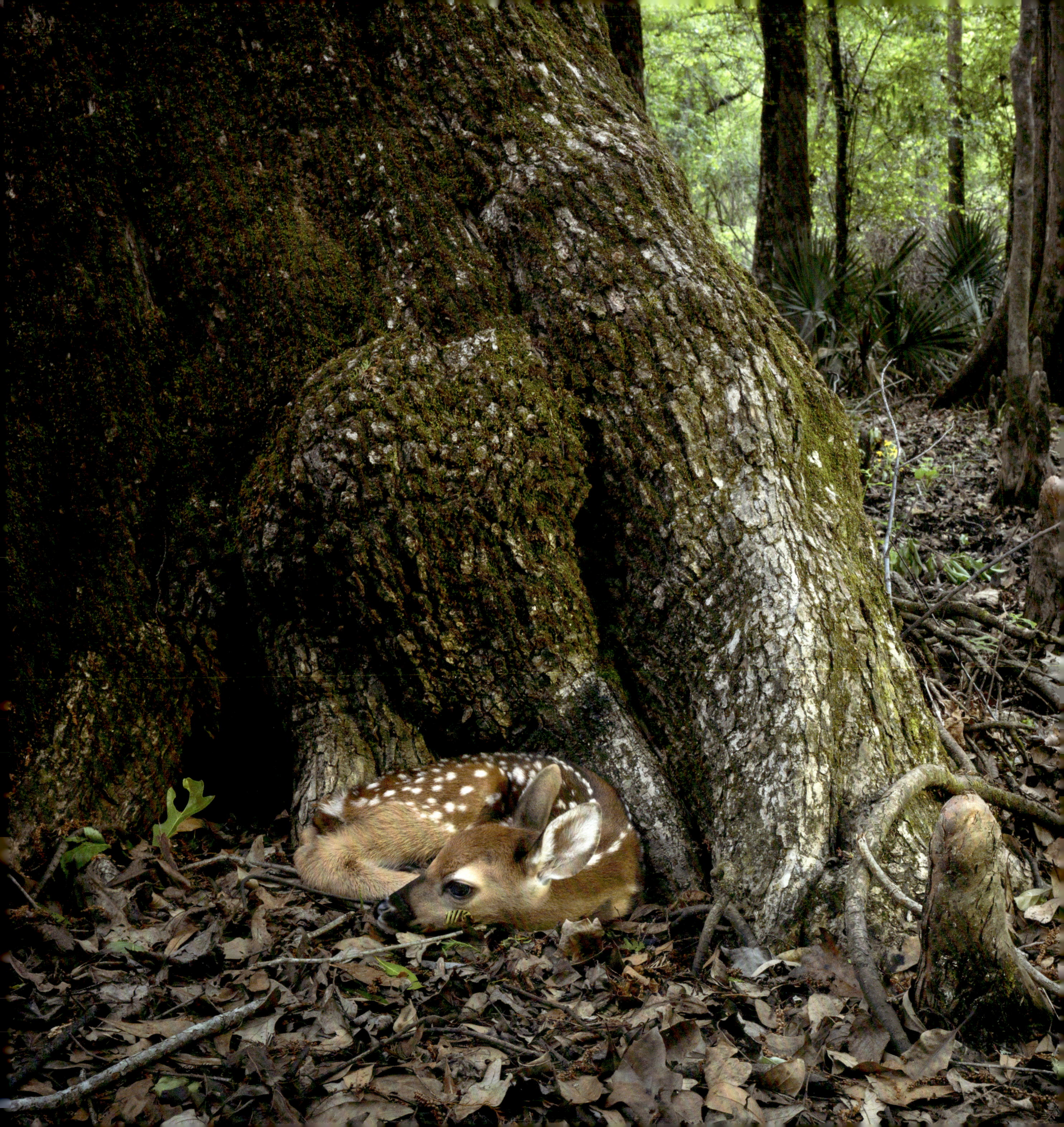

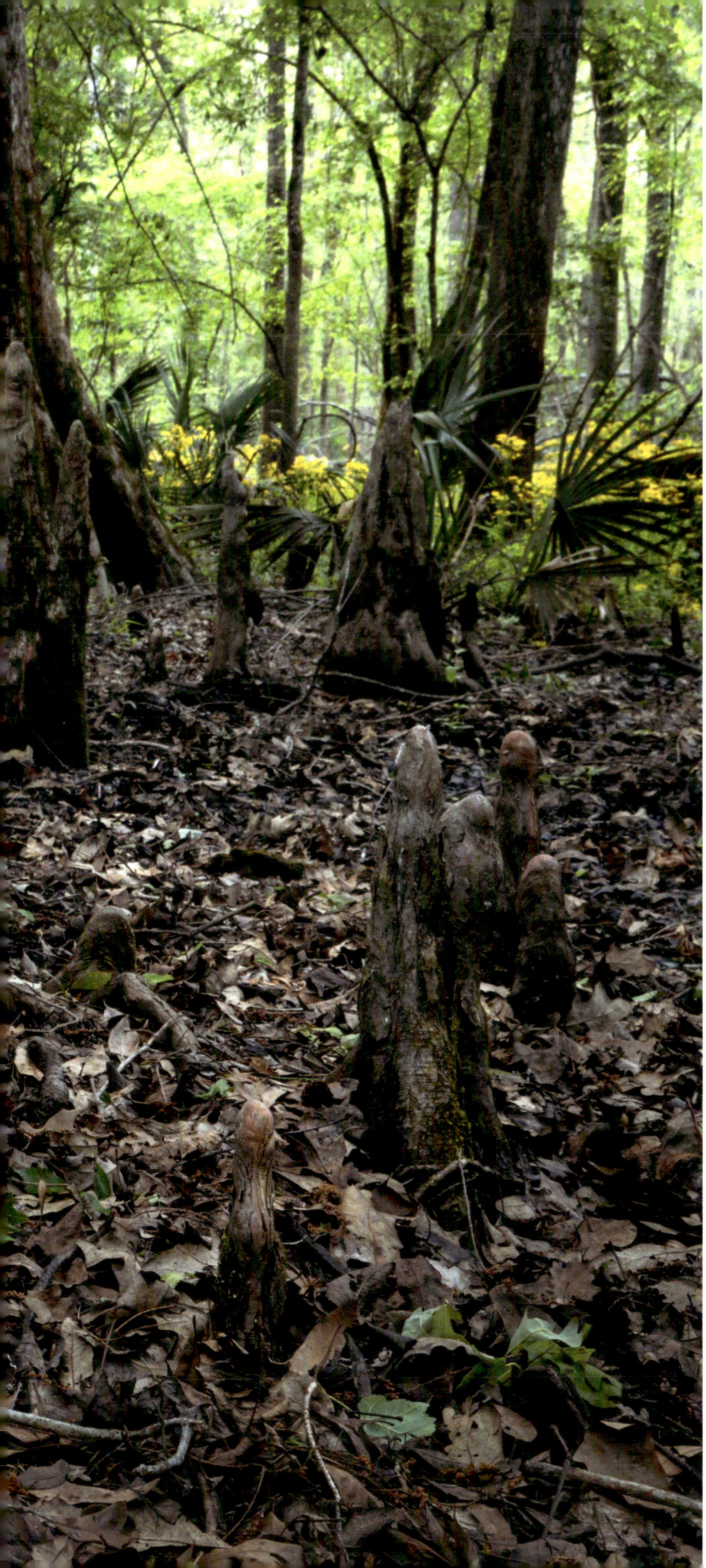

Curled at the base of an oak, a whitetail deer fawn instinctually lies motionless for hours until its mother returns from foraging.

HEARTBEAT *of the* SWAMP

"But how do you deal with the mosquitoes?" is the most frequent question I get when speaking to audiences. They want a pro tip—a field-tested way to keep the swamp angels at bay. I can see them deflate, their faces transforming with disapproval, when I confess I haven't worn bug spray in 20 years. The secret? Long sleeves.

In nearly every place I've lived, mosquitoes were part of the summer landscape. In fact, as I write this, my two children have just barged inside to show off a collection of cicada husks—their arms and legs peppered with pale welts from dozens of bites. They should probably come to one of my talks.

My dad once told me that when he was young, his family would camp at Myrtle Beach, South Carolina. He and his four siblings would join the other kids playing in the DDT mist trailing behind evening fumigation trucks. The 1950s were wild. Smoking on planes, asbestos insulation, and lead-based paints are now relics of the past. Yet today, I still get weekly mailers tucked into our storm door offering mosquito control services.

In suburban yards, technicians spray trees, grass, and shrubs—places mosquitoes like to land—with chemicals that disrupt insect nervous systems. But these plants also shelter bees, caterpillars, moths, butterflies, spiders, ladybugs, and dragonflies (voracious mosquito-hunters, by the way). The insecticides don't discriminate.

Globally, scientists are sounding alarms about the catastrophic loss of insect biomass over the last half-century, warning of inevitable cascading effects up the food chain. A save-the-spiders campaign may be a tough sell, but the crisis of the "smaller majority" has led many researchers to believe that this could be the last generation of children to regularly see fireflies—once a bedrock of southern adolescence.

It turns out those tiny bioluminescent beetles not only require dark skies, they also share similar habitats with mosquitoes. Seeking refuge from light and chemicals, both find sanctuary in Congaree National Park in Hopkins, South Carolina.

At the visitor center in late May, a wooden semicircular oracle—the Mosquito Meter—is mounted on the wall. Its lone hand teeters between 1 ("All Clear") and 6 ("War Zone"). This time of year, it usually hovers around 4 ("Severe") or 5 ("Ruthless"), depending on rainfall. The Mosquito Meter serves as a kind of implied waiver; visitors must pass it and tacitly "Accept All Terms" before entering. Park rangers also use it as a reliable predictor of weekly attendance.

All bets are off, however, in late spring during a brief three-week window when an ancient ritual unfolds, drawing visitors from around the globe. As nights grow warmer and more humid, no swarm of bloodthirsty insects can deter the masses from witnessing the swamp's most enchanting and ephemeral spectacle.

For a few short weeks, male *Photuris frontalis* fireflies emerge from the leaf litter, take flight an hour after sunset, and begin a remarkable courtship. Like a silent disco playing Marco Polo, the males blink their patterned calls in hopes of attracting a female hidden on the forest floor or low vegetation. What sets this species apart is the synchrony of their bioluminescence.

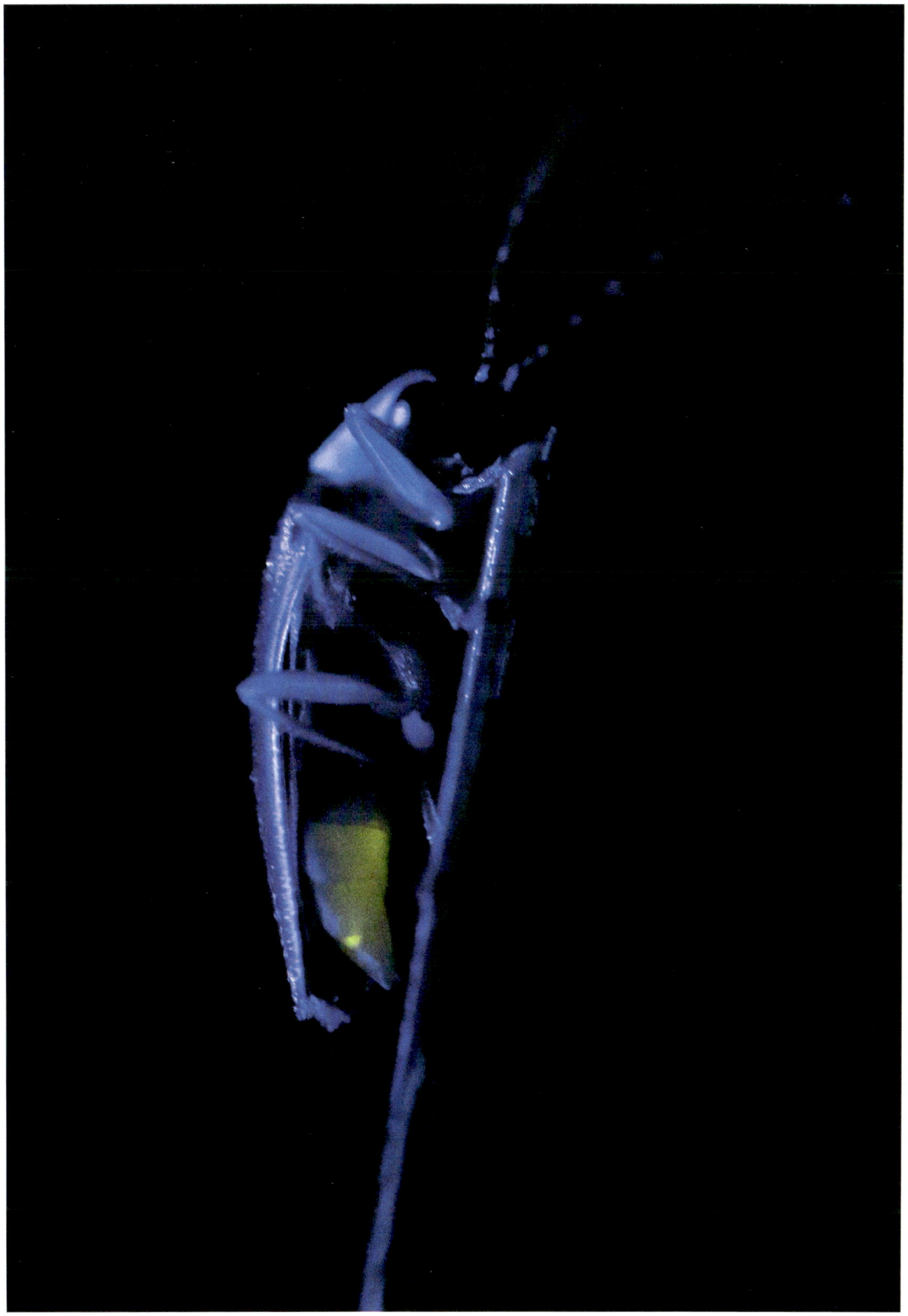

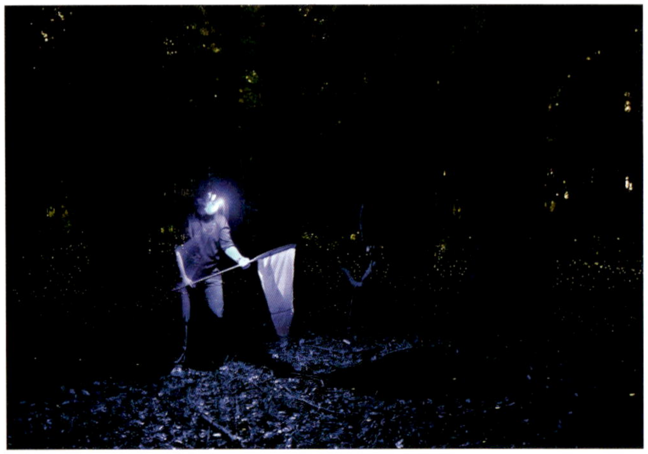

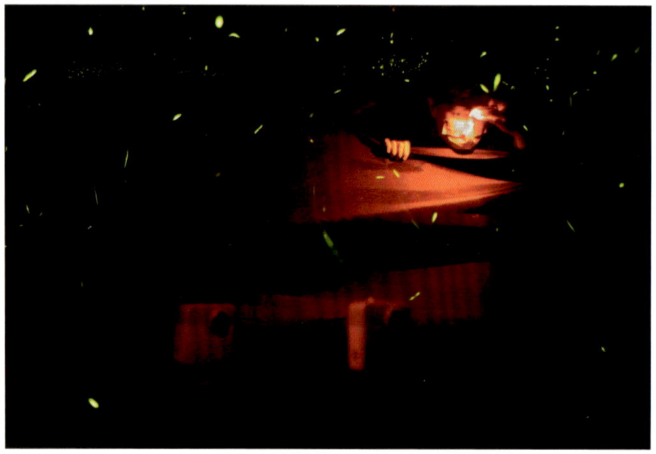

Of the approximately 170 species of fireflies in the United States, only a handful—at least three—blink in unison.

Although *Photuris frontalis* is found throughout the Southeast, Congaree harbors an exceptionally dense population. Spanning more than 26,000 acres, the park protects the largest remaining stand of virgin bottomland hardwood forest in the country. Often called the "Redwoods of the East," its towering loblolly pines, swamp chestnut oaks, water hickories, American elms, cherrybark oaks, and laurel oaks are among the tallest and oldest in the nation. The absence of logging not only preserved these giants, but also safeguarded the vast fungal networks and soil biomes that sustain them.

Beneath the decaying leaf litter and fallen timber, a hidden world thrives—where the larval stages of beetles, cicadas, ants, walking sticks, and fireflies burrow into a subterranean mix of roots, mycorrhizae, microbes, and detritus. Far from city lights, under a centuries-old canopy, fireflies emerge in astonishing numbers when conditions are just right.

From the deepest shadows of the forest floor, the first flickers appear—hesitant, scattered, barely lifting above the tangled undergrowth. Like musicians in a darkened orchestra pit, each tests their abdominal instrument with erratic, staccato pulses, warming up before the grand performance. Within 30 minutes, hundreds of golden-green lights drift like embers. Then, without discernible cue, it seems as if an invisible conductor taps a baton. Suddenly, they flash in unison. Hundreds of perfectly synchronized lights surround you with a rhythmic precision that feels both impossible and ancient. It is the heartbeat of the swamp.

How they achieve this synchronicity has long puzzled scientists. During the COVID-19 pandemic, when many parks were closed, I joined a research team from Dr. Orit Peleg's lab at the University of Colorado Boulder to study fireflies in Congaree. With no visitors and no errant flashlights, we experienced the forest in its full nocturnal glory. It was easy to imagine how singular and mesmerizing the display would have seemed to Indigenous tribes who once hunted and traversed these forests.

The team brought LED lights to trigger synchrony, 360-degree cameras to map firefly patterns, and blackout tents to film captive insects. I watched scientist Julie Hayes

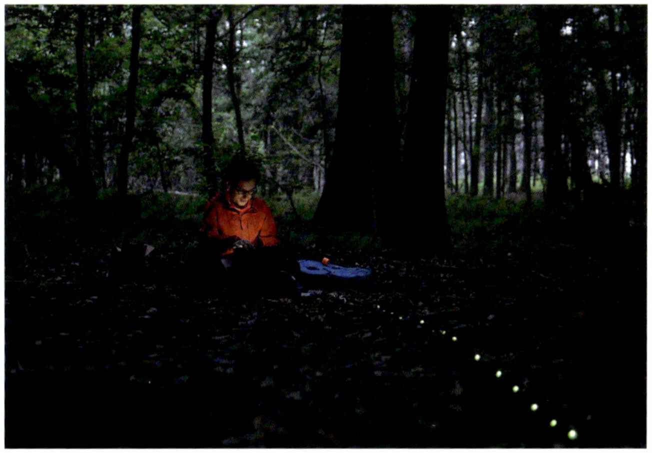 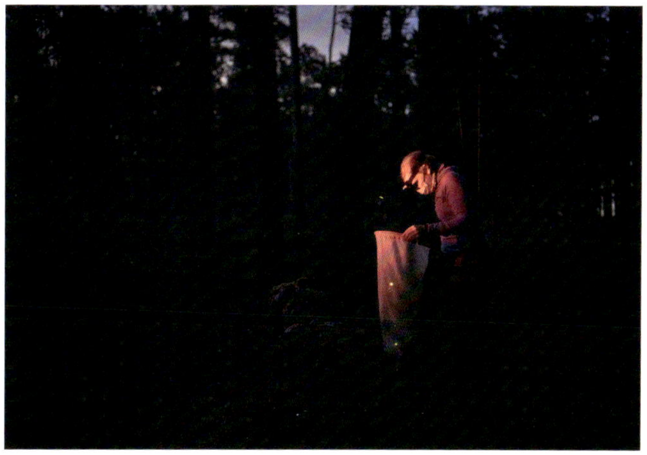

weave through swarms of fireflies, deftly dodging limbs and sinkholes, and emerging triumphant with a glowing net. Thousands of rural kids would trade their siblings for a job like that.

Much like a total eclipse, the only thing that tarnishes the experience is trying to capture its magic in a single exposure. Photographing fireflies is a nightmare. The ambient light is so low and fleeting that focus, composition, and exposure must be either instinctive or perfectly pre-planned. During the brief three-day peak, there's a 15-minute window each night when just enough light spills into the bottomland to show the fireflies dancing among the trees.

Every firefly species has a unique flash pattern, all believed to evolve through sexual selection. For *Photuris frontalis* males, synchrony must have conferred some evolutionary advantage. But the females remain elusive. They are extremely difficult to spot and identify.

After two years of research, Peleg's team found that perfect synchrony only occurs when a critical mass of individuals is reached. There's no leader or central signal. Instead, each insect copies its neighbors through visual cues, generating a massive pulse of synchronous flashes. Sometimes, synchrony lasts up to 30 minutes. The true breakthrough, however, was their discovery of a mathematical phenomenon known as a "chimera state."

A chimera state occurs when part of a connected group synchronizes while another part remains out of sync—order and chaos coexisting within the same system. In laboratory settings, scientists have observed this phenomenon in the brains of sleeping dolphins: one hemisphere rests while the other stays alert to prevent drowning. But until recently, such emergent behavior had never been documented in the wild, let alone seen with the naked eye. Over two summers, Peleg's team repeatedly observed a subgroup within the swarm syncing to a different rhythm. How an insect the size of a fingernail can break from the collective while still cooperating remains a mystery. Lynn Faust, one of the world's leading firefly experts, suspects these subgroups may be females responding en masse. If she's right, then it wouldn't be a chimera state after all, because males and females would represent different cohorts. But it would raise even bigger questions: Why would females sync with one another? And how?

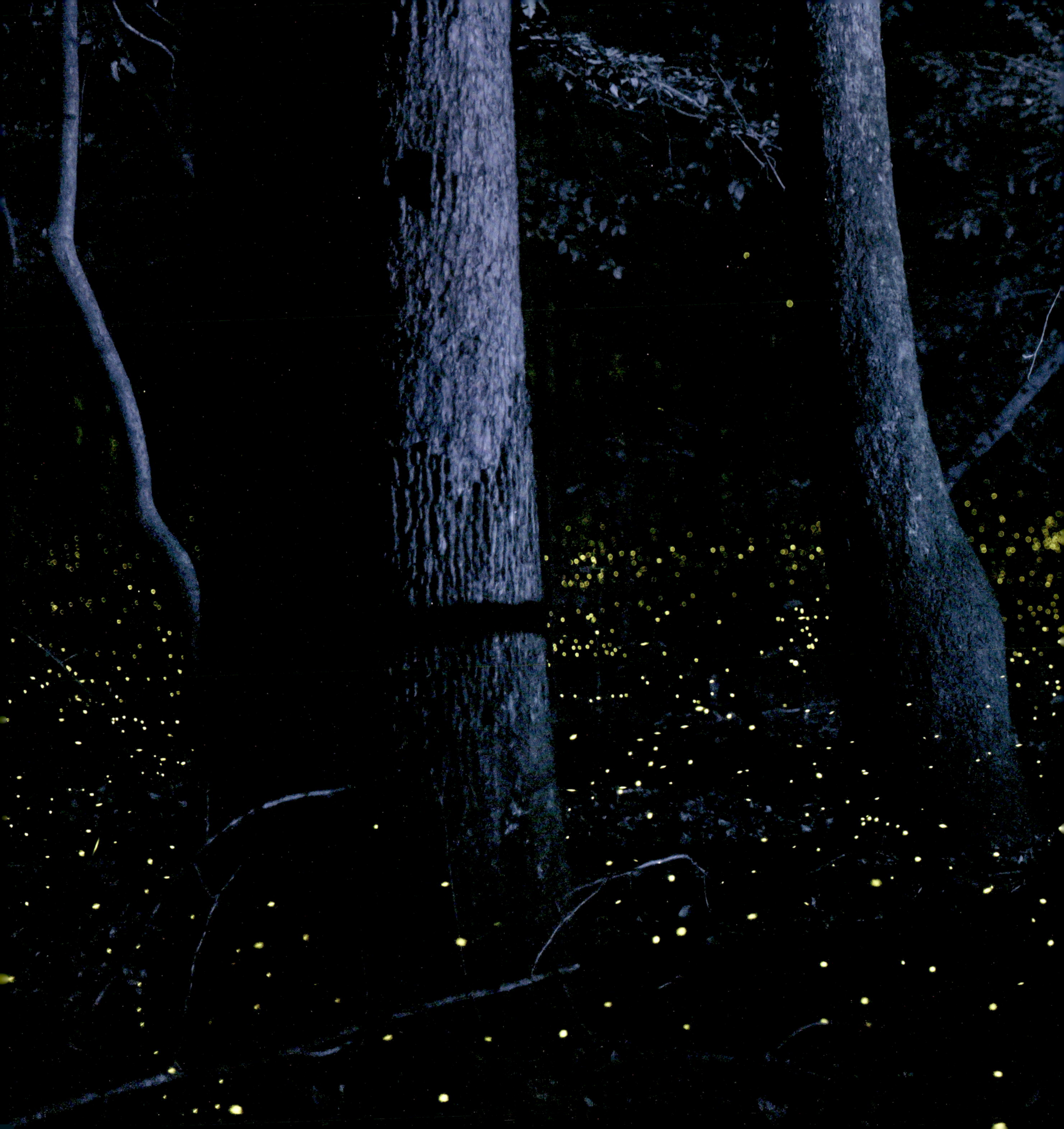

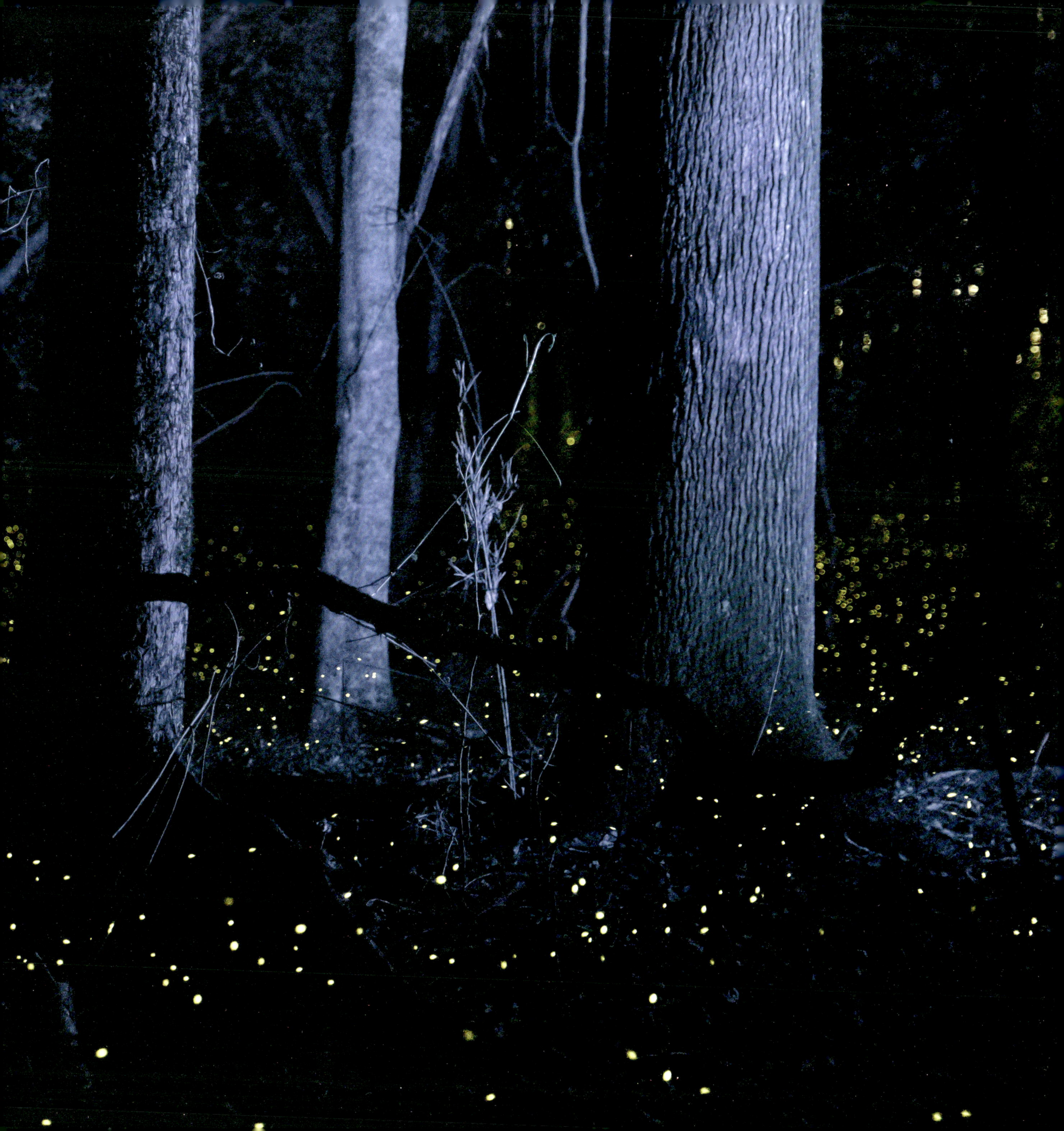

More time under Congaree's old-growth canopy will be required to find out—something Peleg and her team don't seem to mind at all.

The group dynamics behind this phenomenon are mind-bending. Fireflies rely on intact canopy, dark skies, moist undisturbed soils, and thousands of neighbors to reproduce. There are so few places left that can meet those conditions.

I live just two miles from a bustling downtown, but I'm lucky. From my backyard, you can still see stars silhouetted against hickories, poplars, and oaks. On summer nights, the babble of the creek and hooting of barred owls is overtaken by a crescendo of cicadas.

Tonight, my five-year-old stayed up way past bedtime, wedged between the blinds and the pane. Ramrod-straight in dinosaur pajamas, his hands gripped the sill as the indigo dusk spilled into his room. It felt like stepping into a Norman Rockwell painting. He counted firefly flashes until nature called: "Forty-one, forty-two, forty-three . . ." I took over the count.

Maybe next year he'll join me at Congaree. But for now, he's perfectly content watching our own fireflies light up the backyard. Yes, May and June can be buggy, but a few welts are a small price to pay to preserve the wonder outside his window.

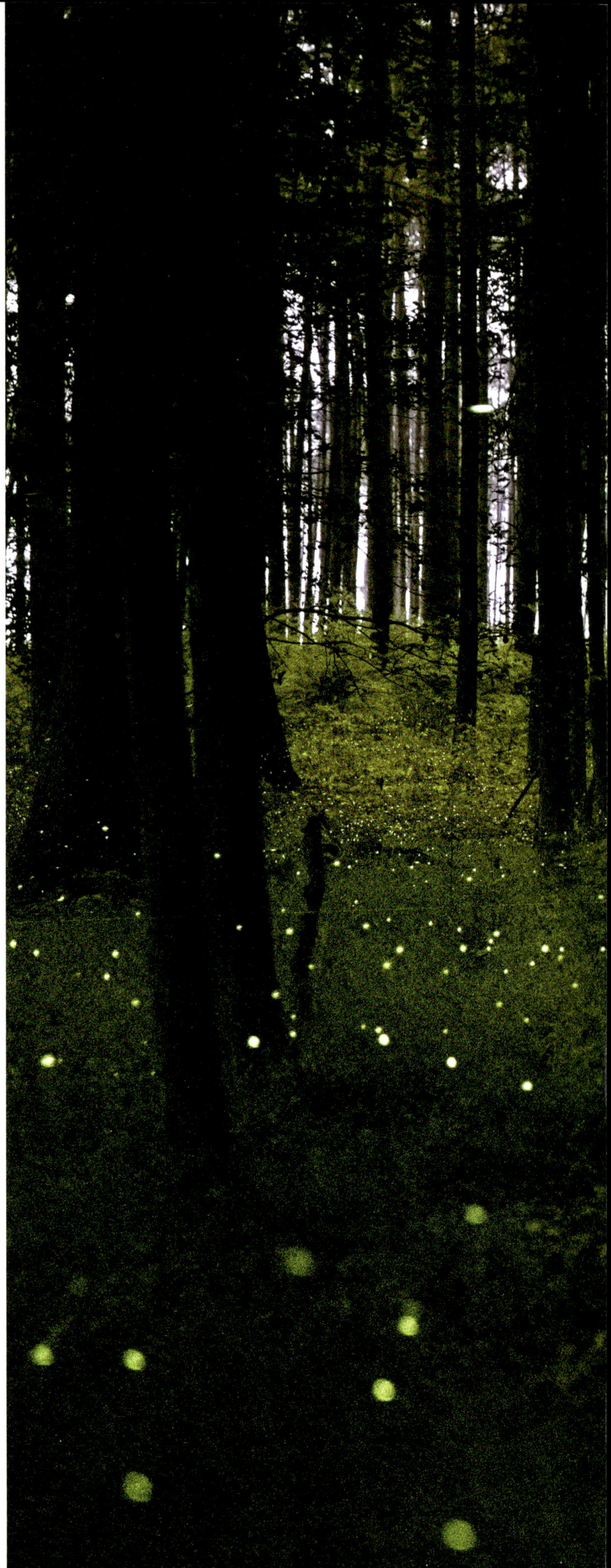

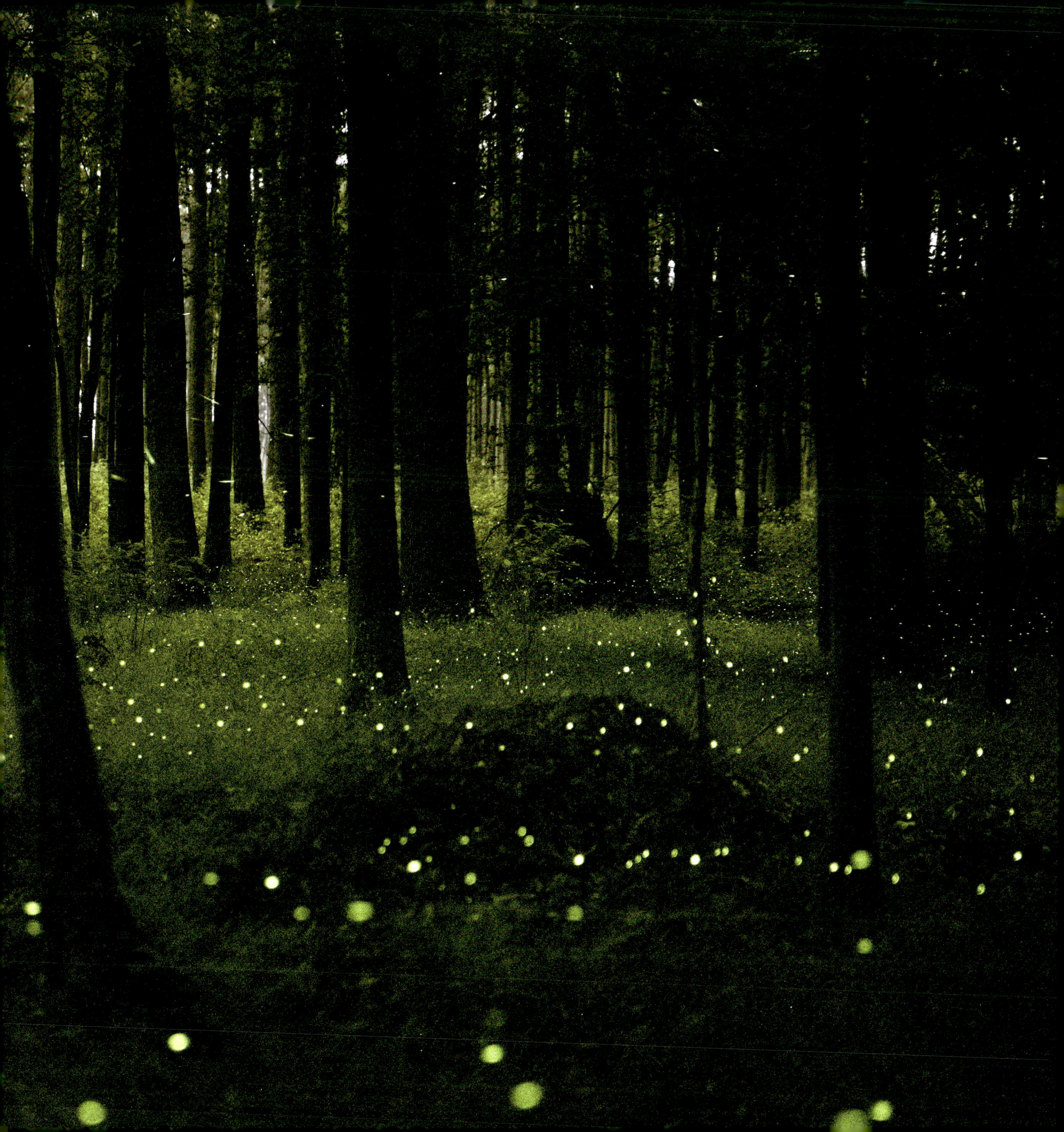

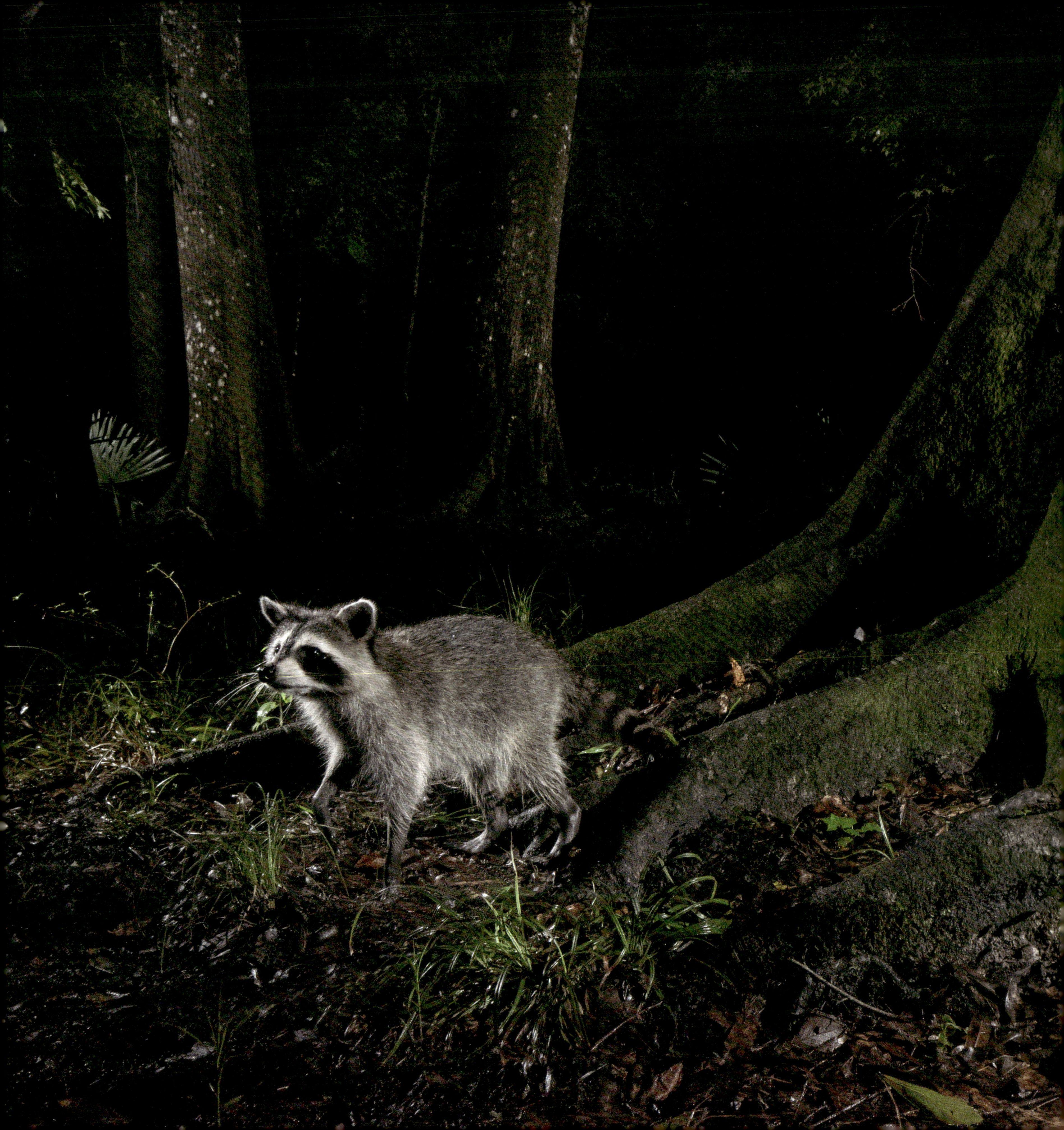

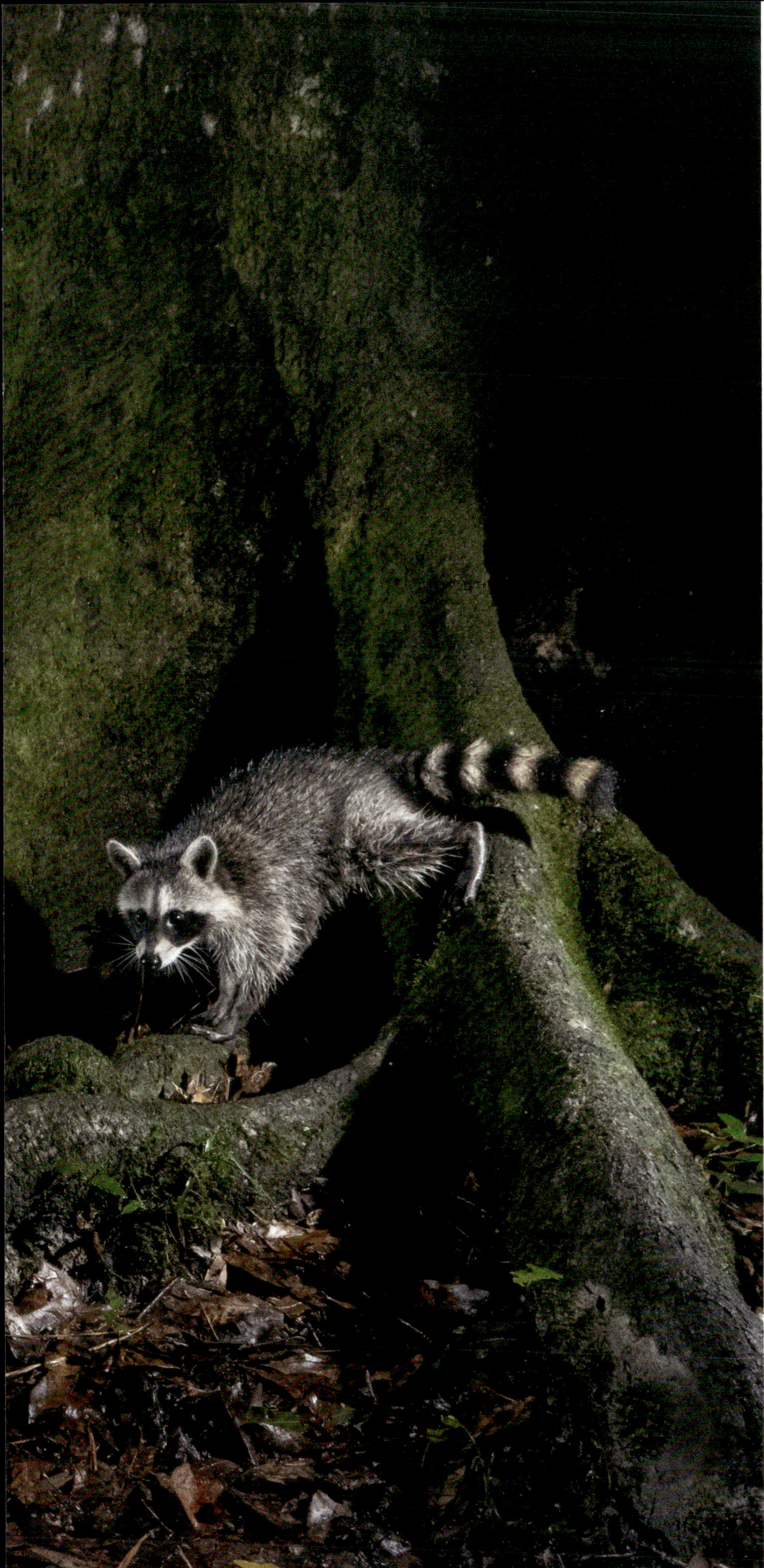

After dusk, raccoons emerge from their dens, often in hollow trees, to scavenge for crayfish, frogs, and snakes.

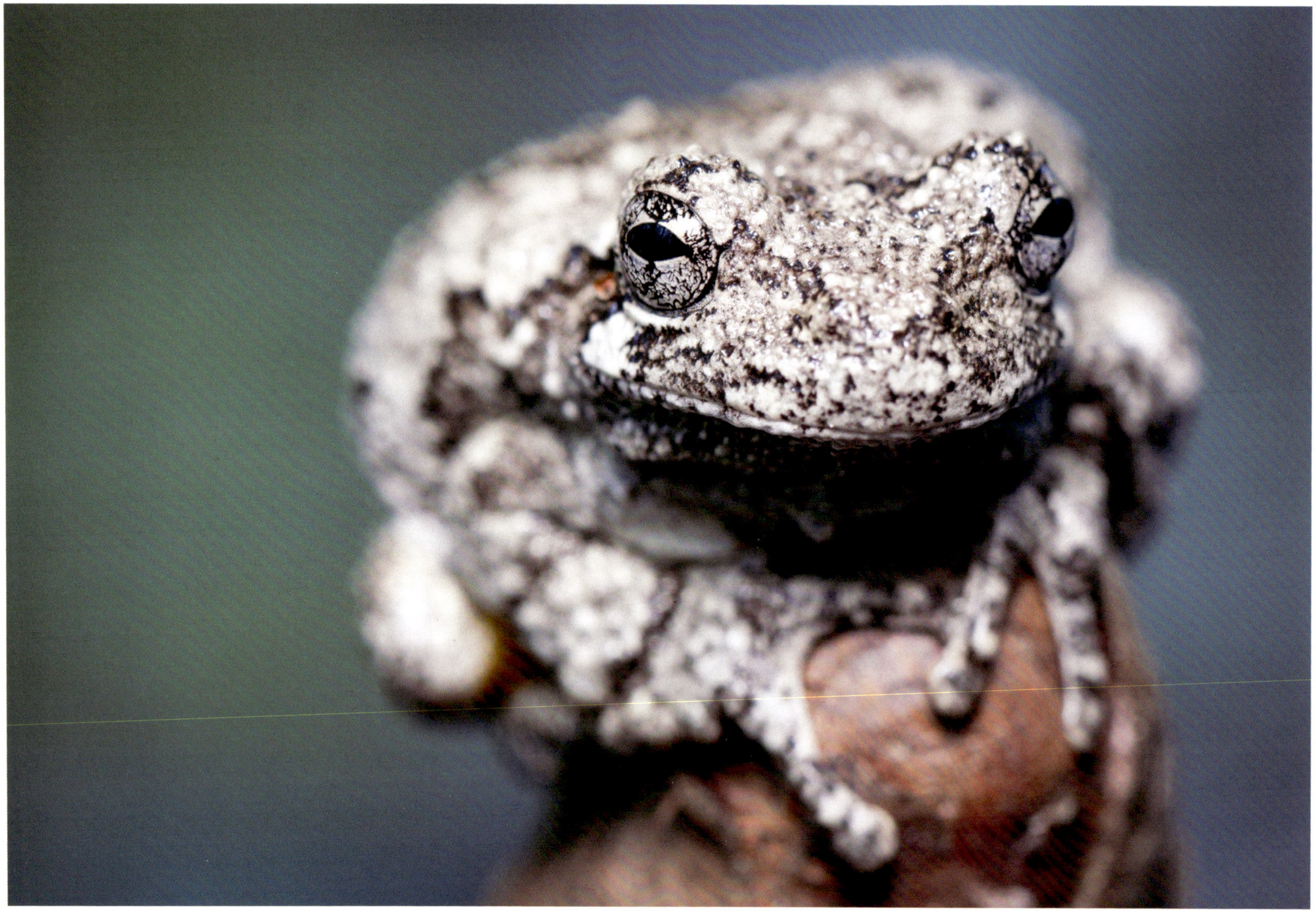

Well-camouflaged and mostly active at night, gray tree frogs blend seamlessly into bark and leaves; they are heard more often than seen.

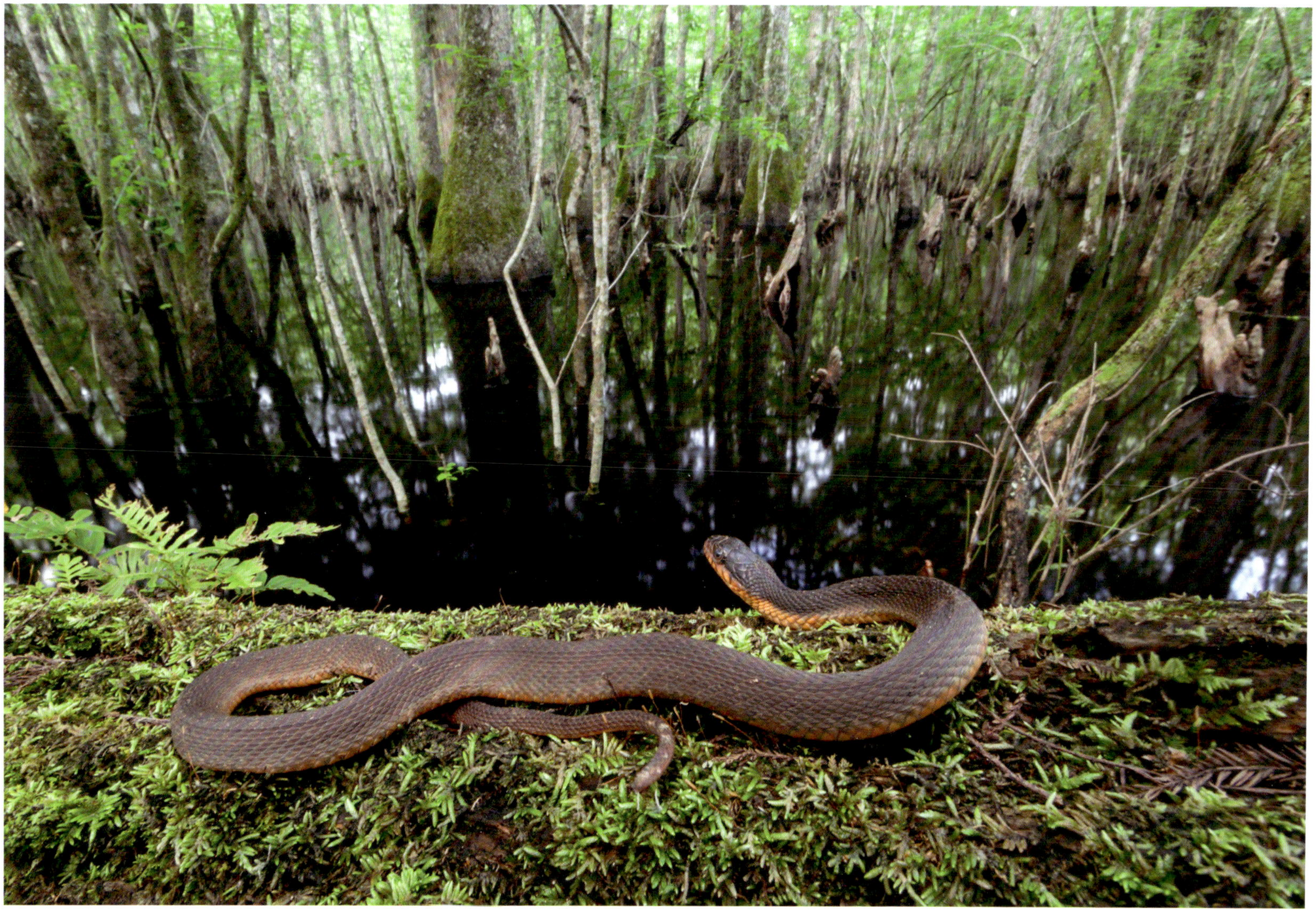

A rare sight above the surface, a nonvenomous red-bellied watersnake basks before sliding back into the swamp to hunt for fish and amphibians.

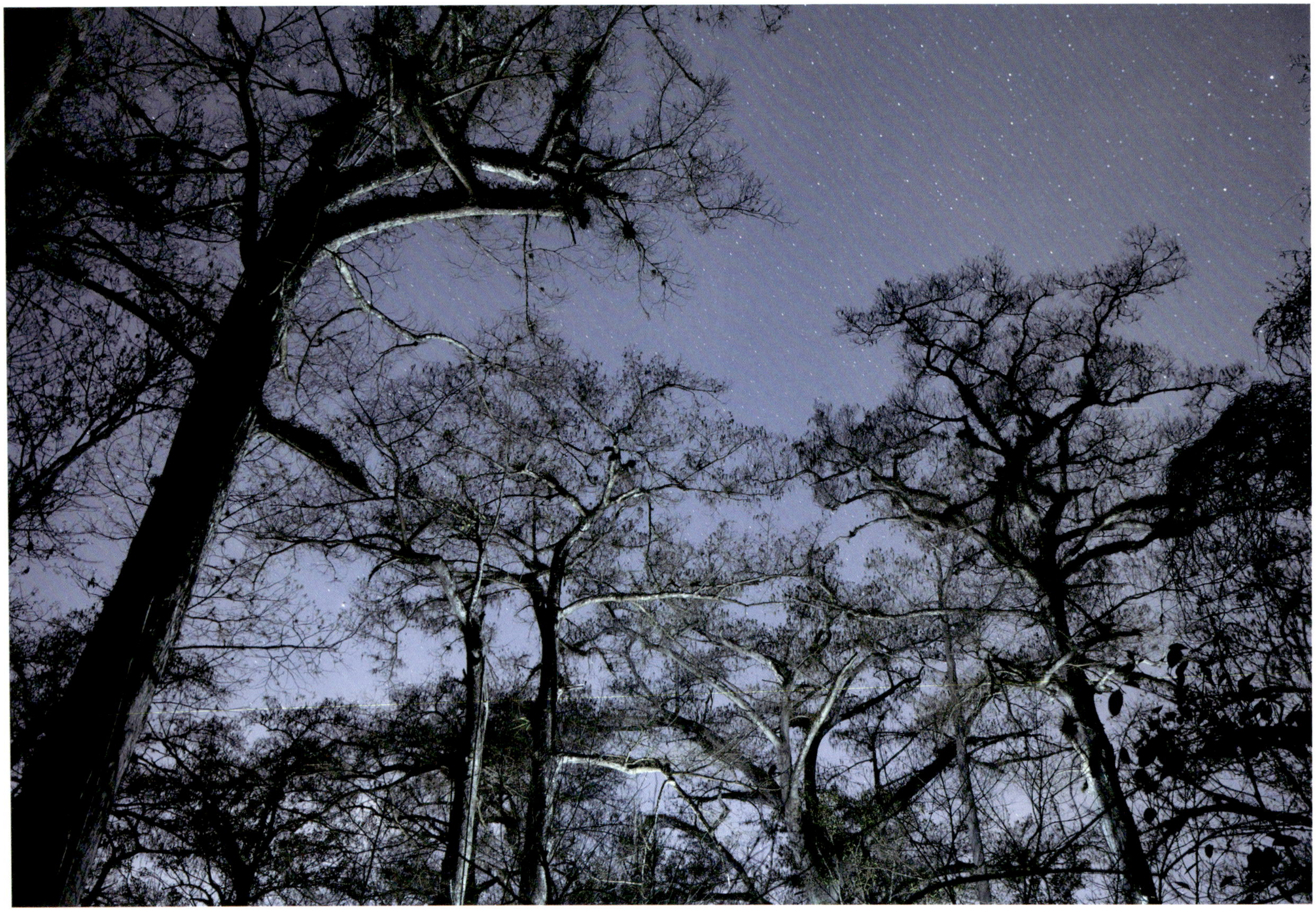

Many cypress around the world are evergreen, but bald cypress gets its name because it loses its leaves in the winter.

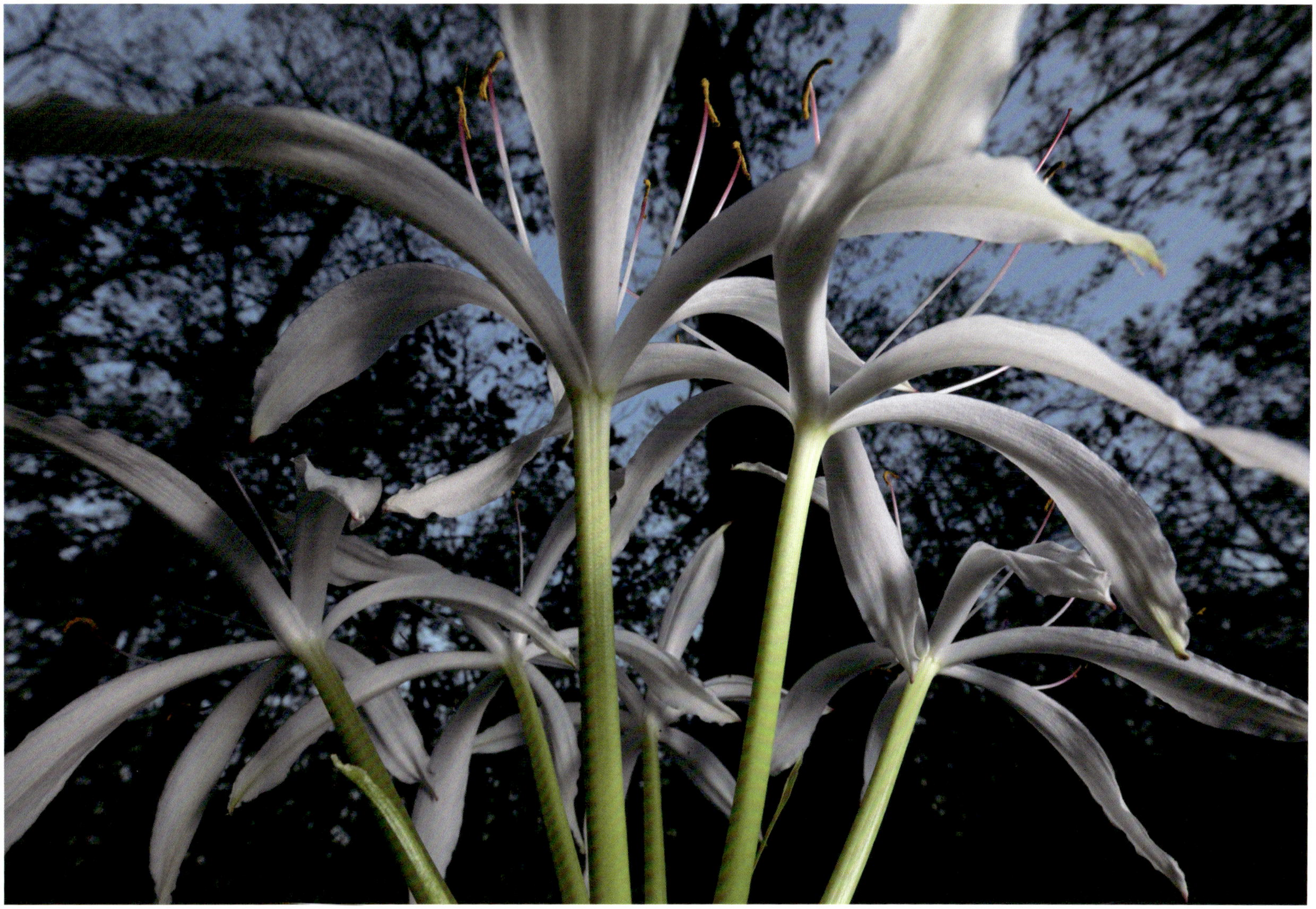

Using long, strap-like leaves to photosynthesize in low-light conditions, swamp lilies' bright white flowers and fragrant nectar attract nocturnal pollinators like hawkmoths.

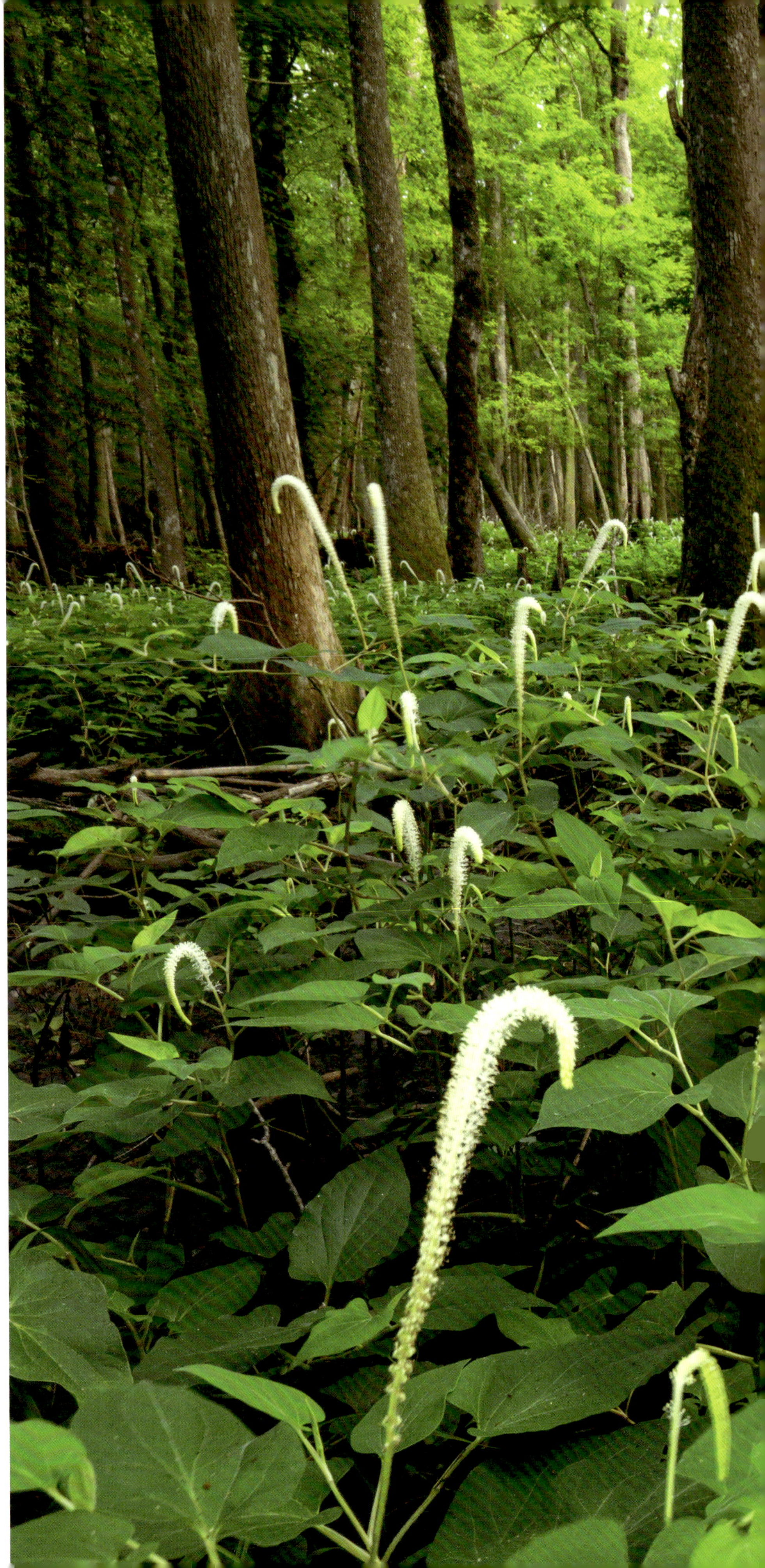

Lizard's tail proliferates in the wake of fallen trees where increased light and reduced competition create ideal conditions for growth in saturated soils.

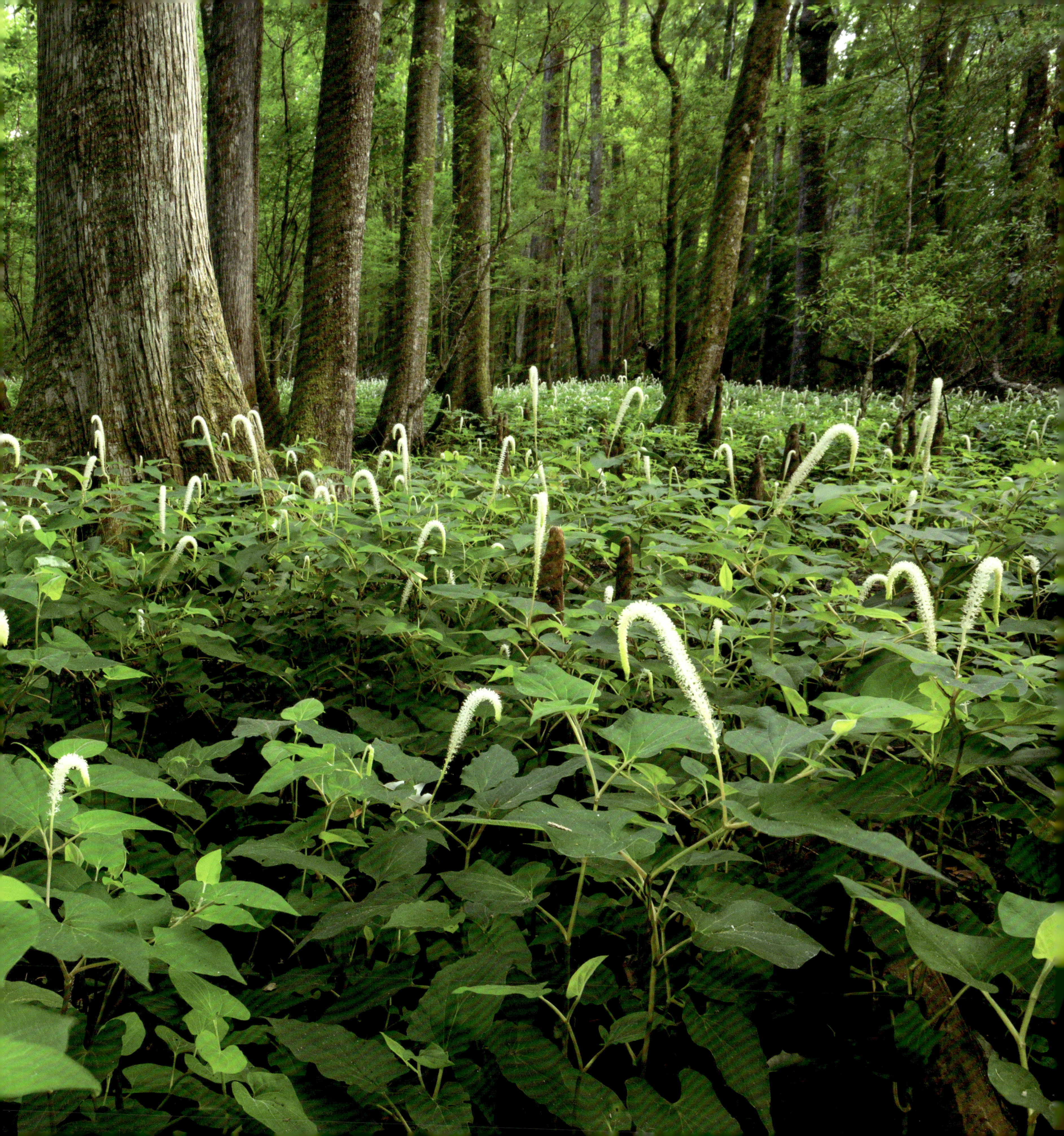

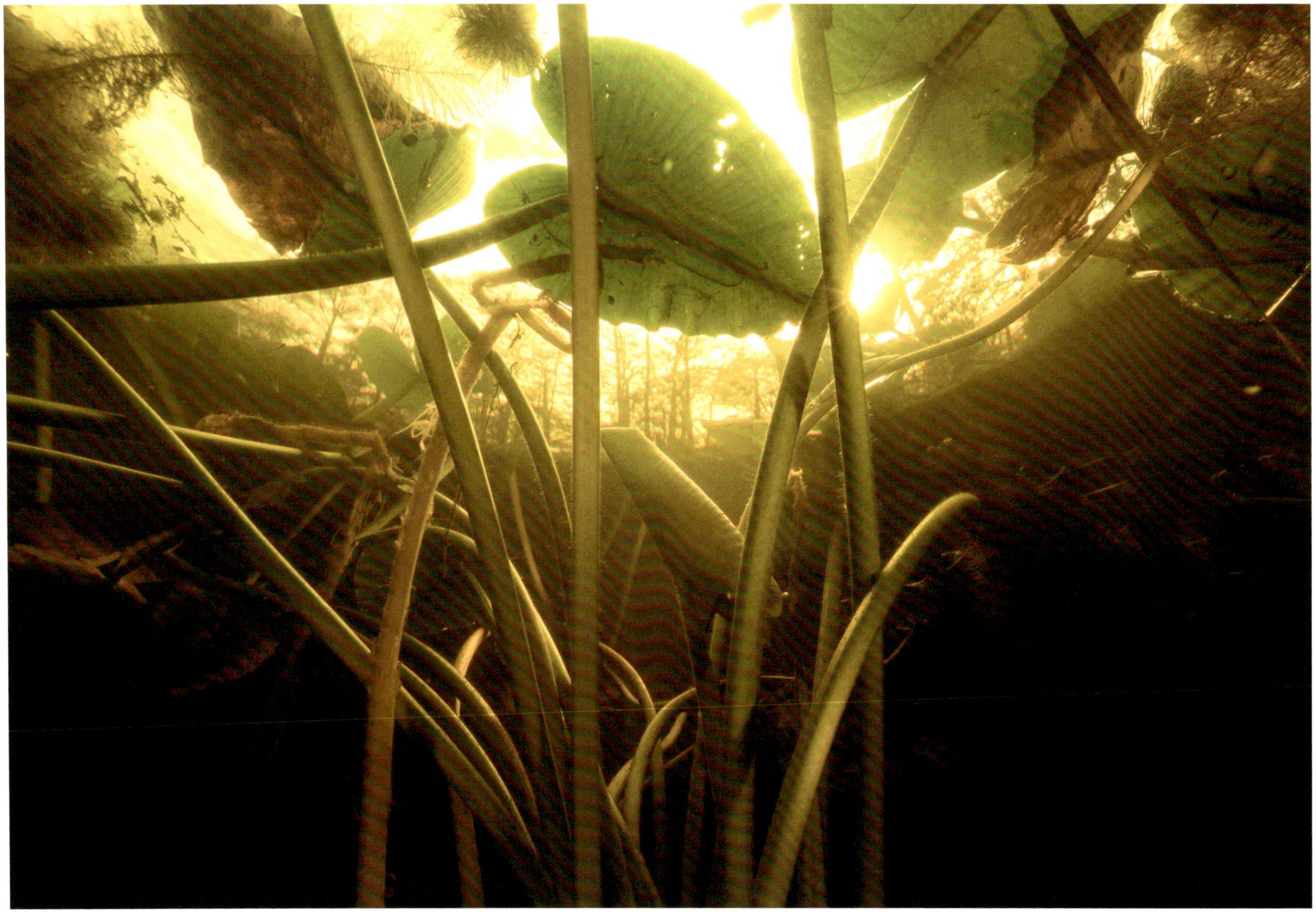

Beneath the inky waterline of a gator hole, spatterdock arches and twists from the peat substrate to reach the surface.

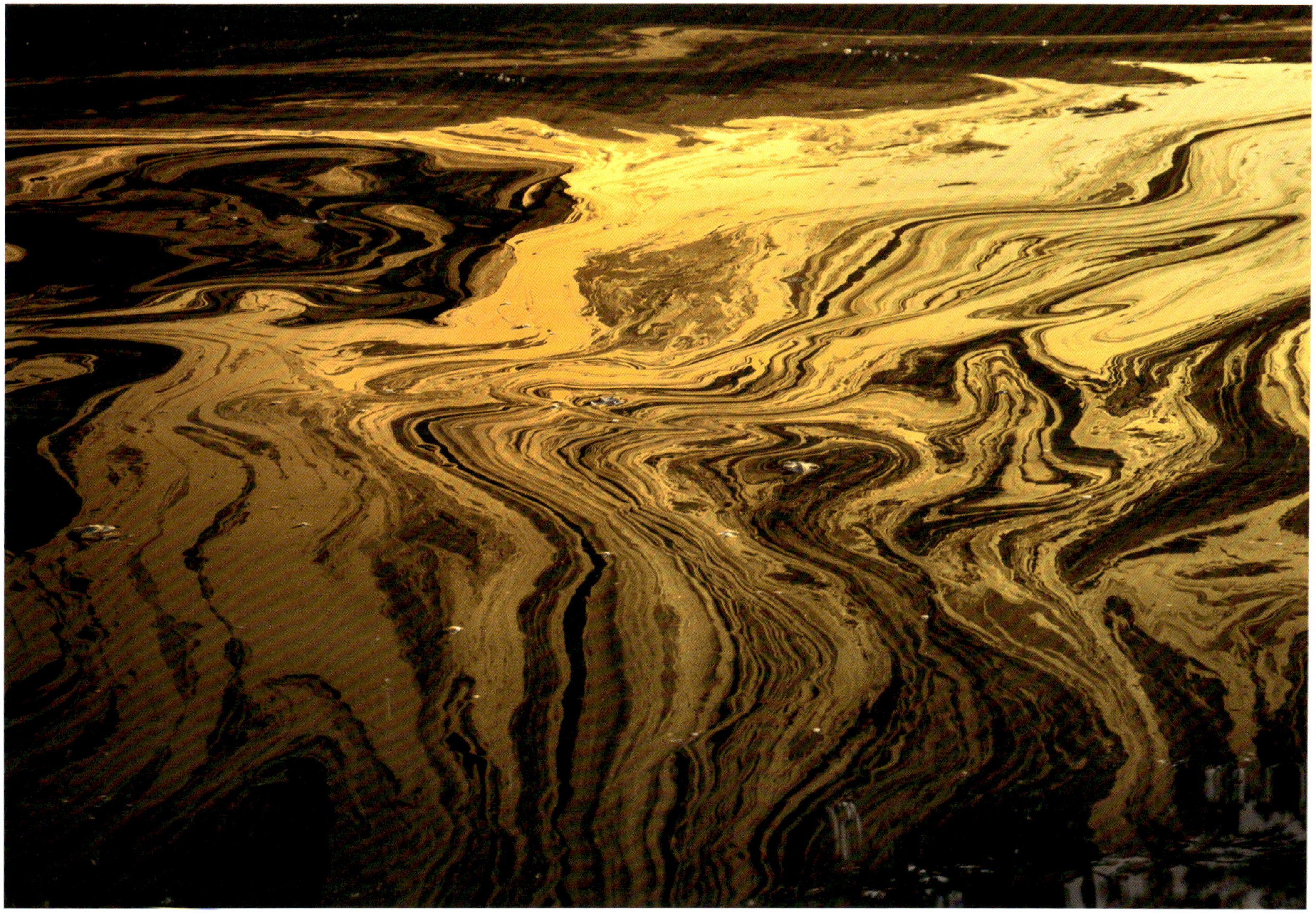

Draining thousands of acres of flowering trees each spring, a marbled river of pollen forms—its tiny grains pack a nutritional punch, feeding aquatic life and releasing nutrients as they decompose.

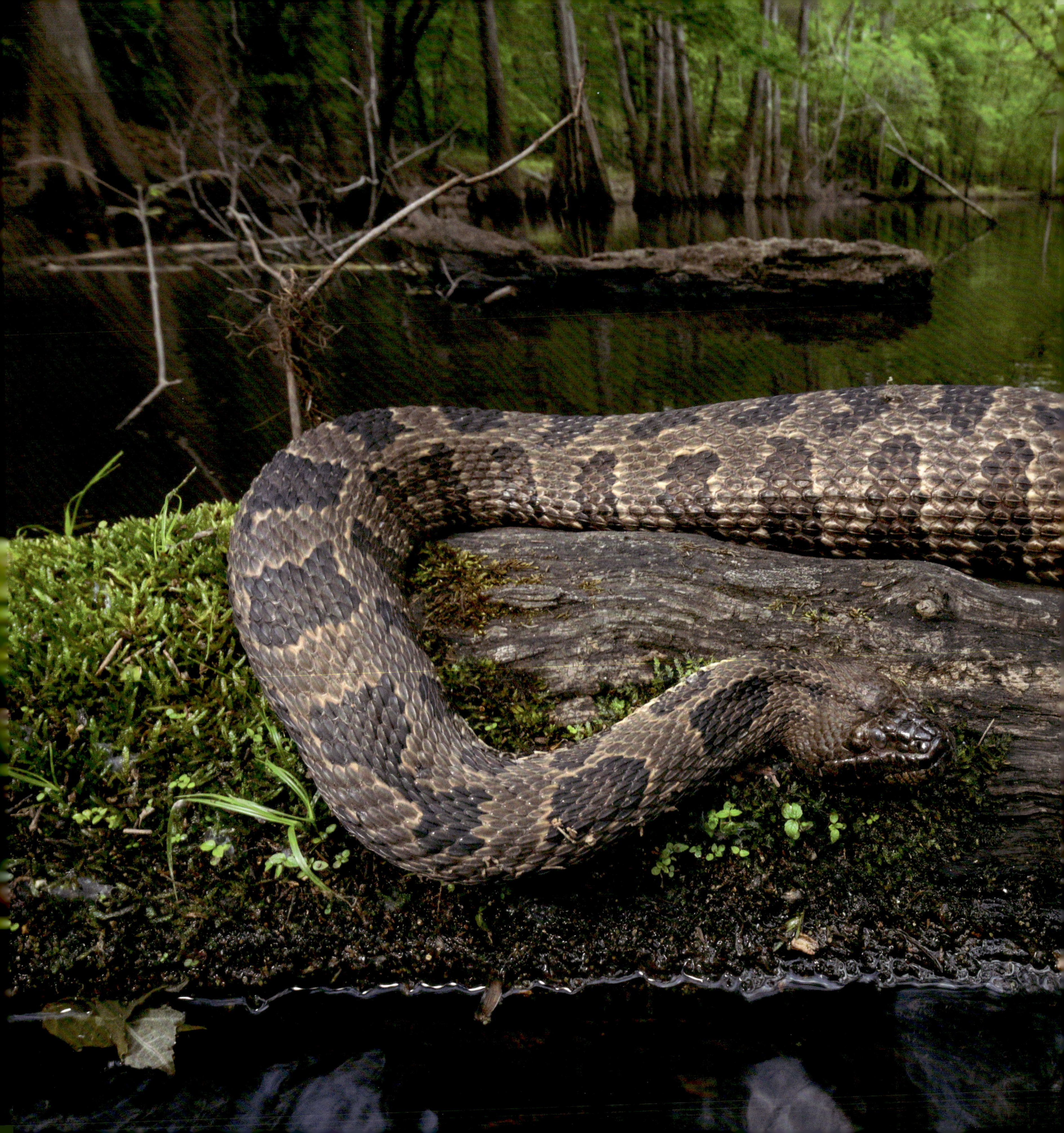

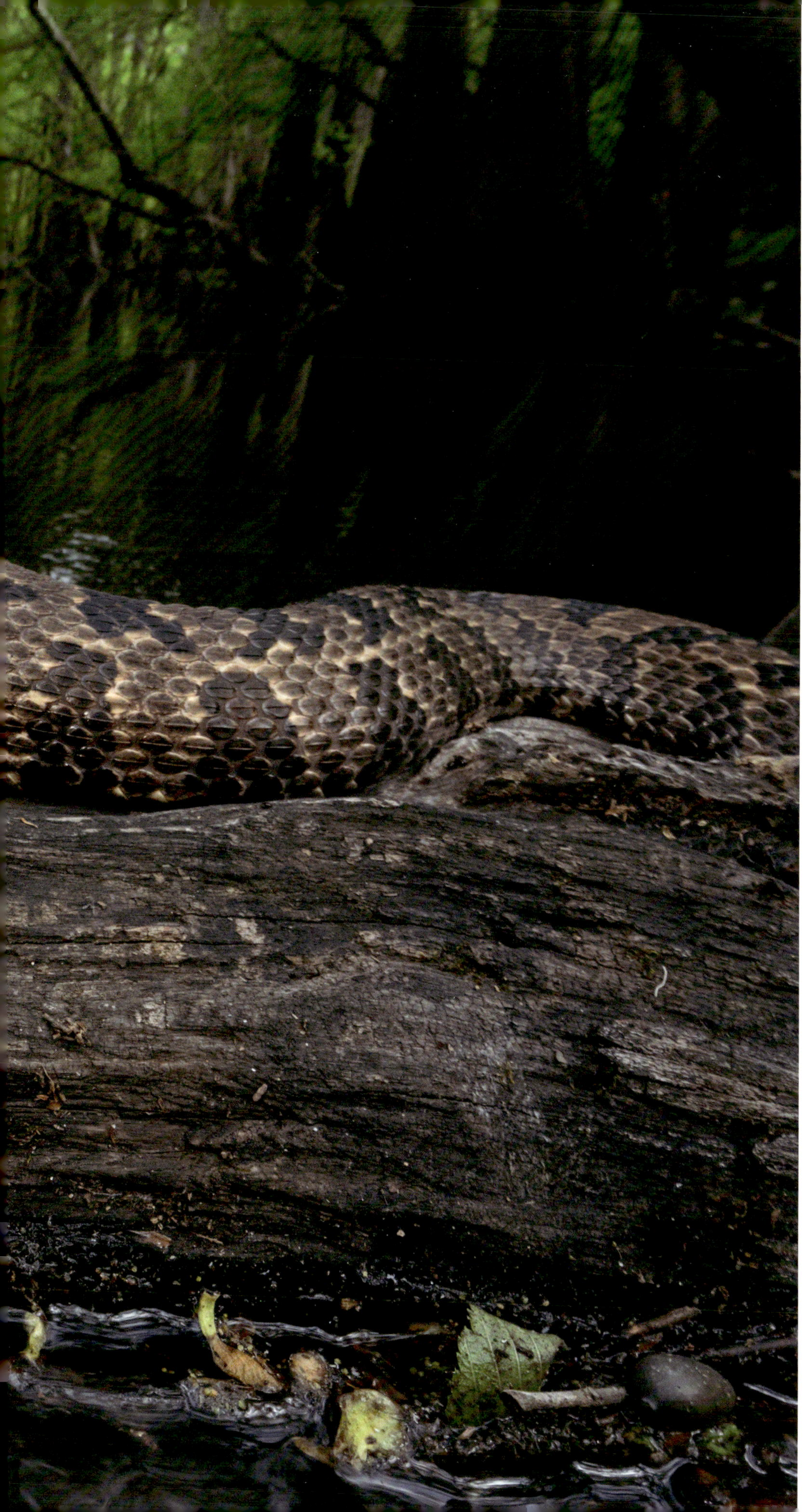

Often mistaken for venomous cottonmouths, the nonvenomous brown watersnake is a regular denizen of the swamp, where it preys heavily on fish—its swollen belly here a clear sign of a successful hunt.

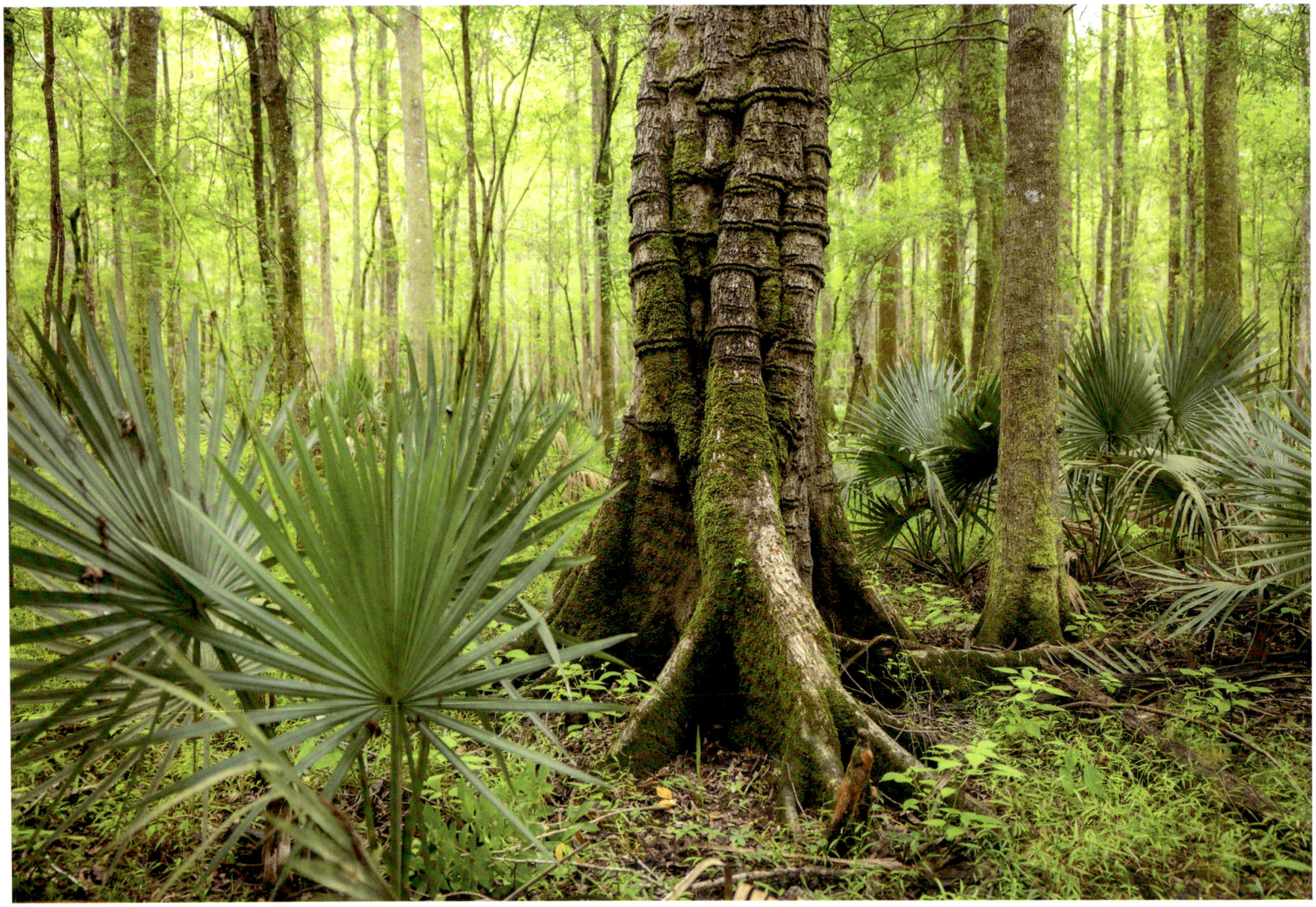

Old forests reveal generational patterns—on the bark of a maple, the neatly drilled rows of a yellow-bellied sapsucker mark the seasonal visits of this migratory woodpecker to the swamp.

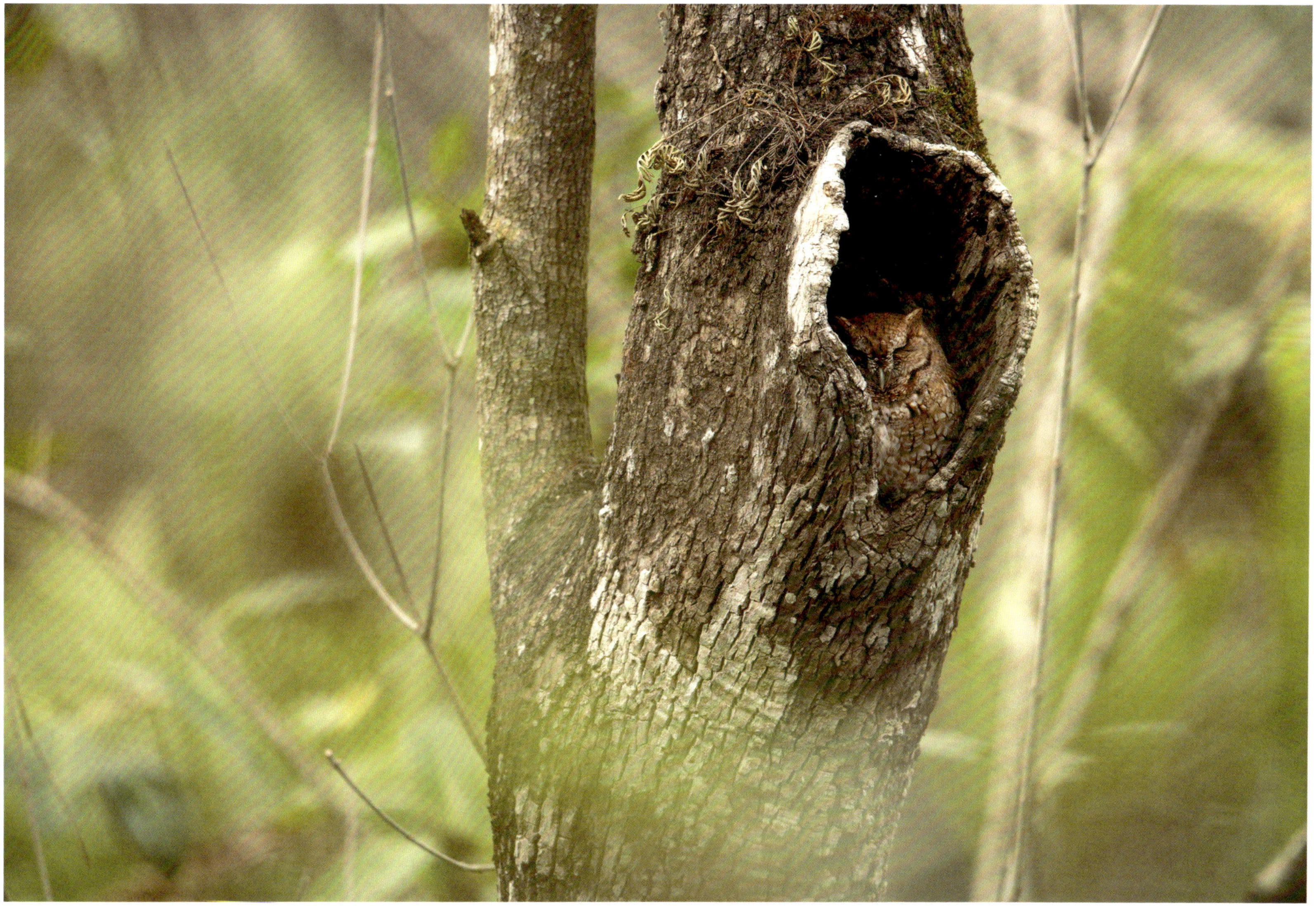

Blending seamlessly into tree bark by day, eastern screech owls come alive at night, their haunting trills echoing through the swamp as they defend territories and search for mates from hollow trees.

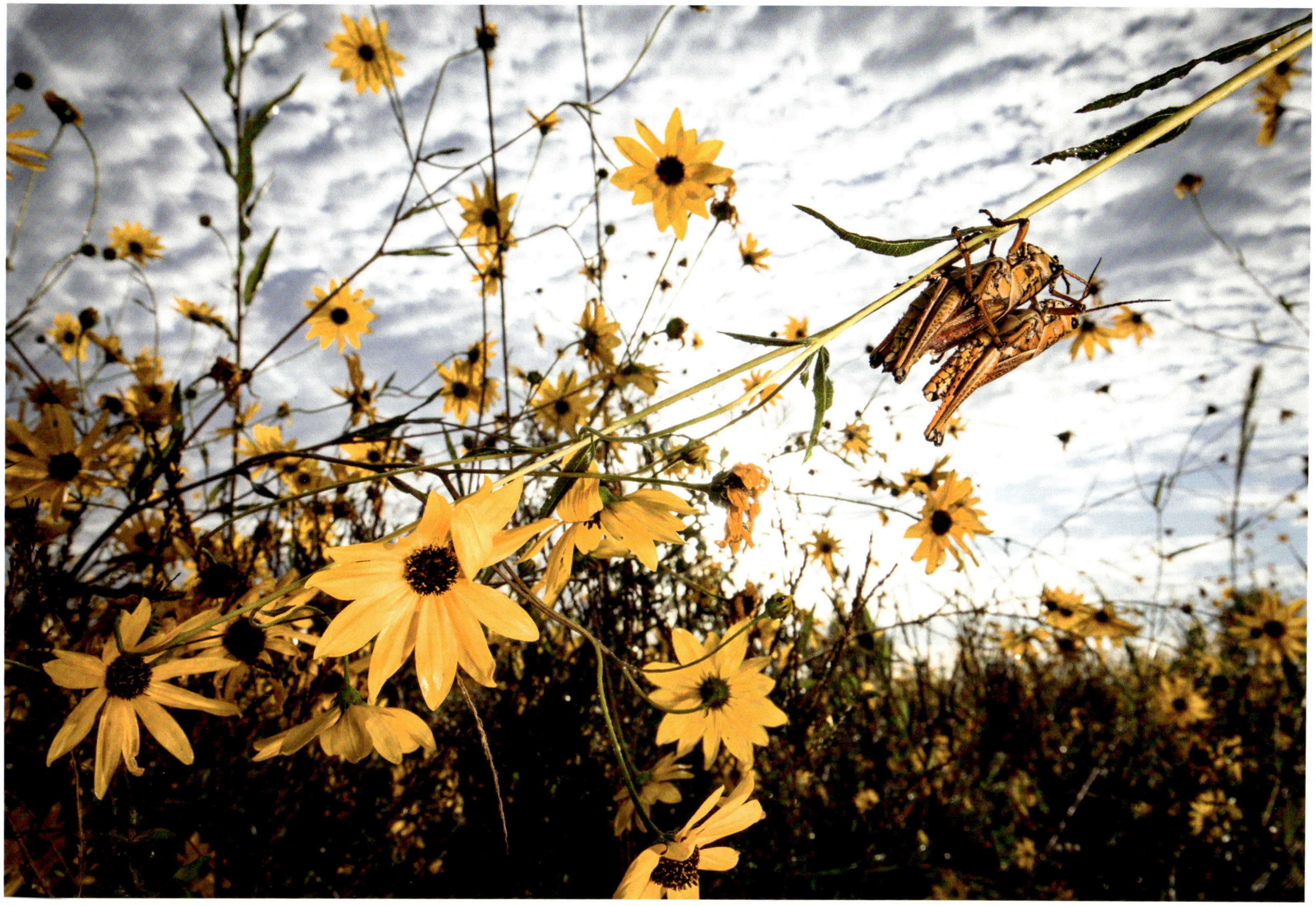

Mating eastern lubber grasshoppers rely on bright warning colors and chemical defenses to deter predators; because of their toxic taste very few predators dare to eat them.

FOLLOWING PAGE

A grove of cypress knees can represent the root systems of a dozen or more mature trees—they weave together like a dense fabric matrix, each root distinct yet interlaced, firmly anchoring the trees to one another during fierce storms.

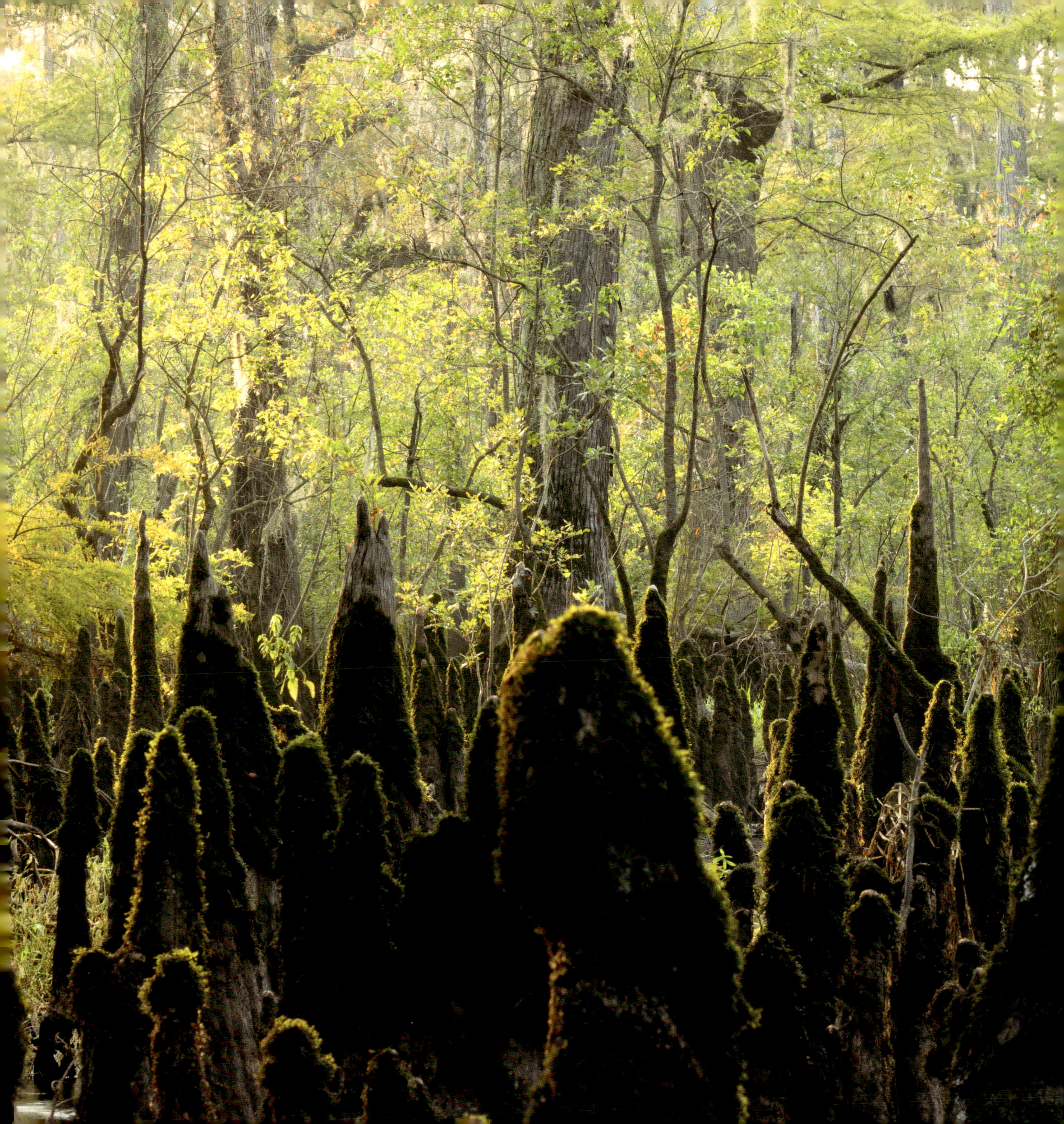

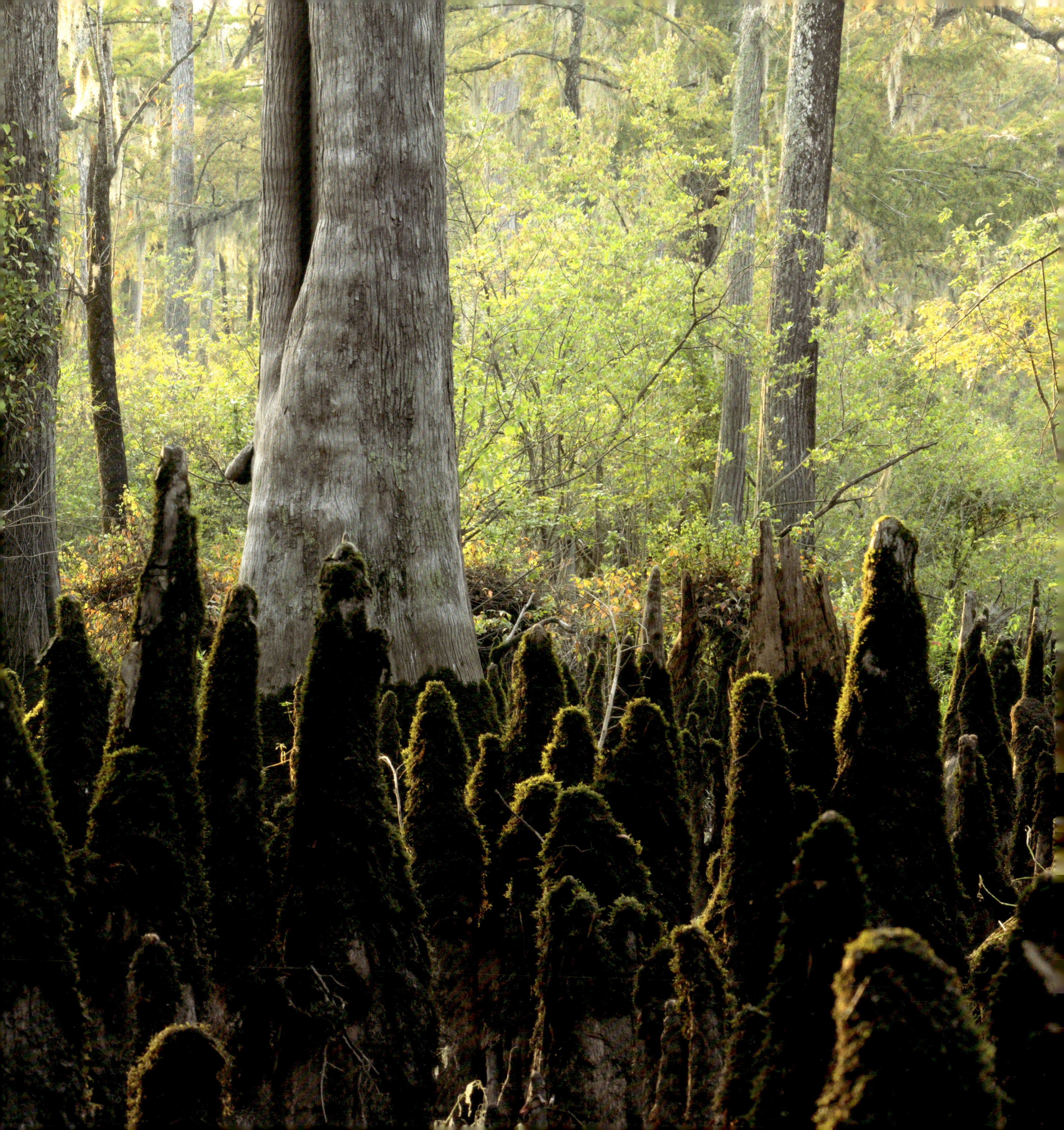

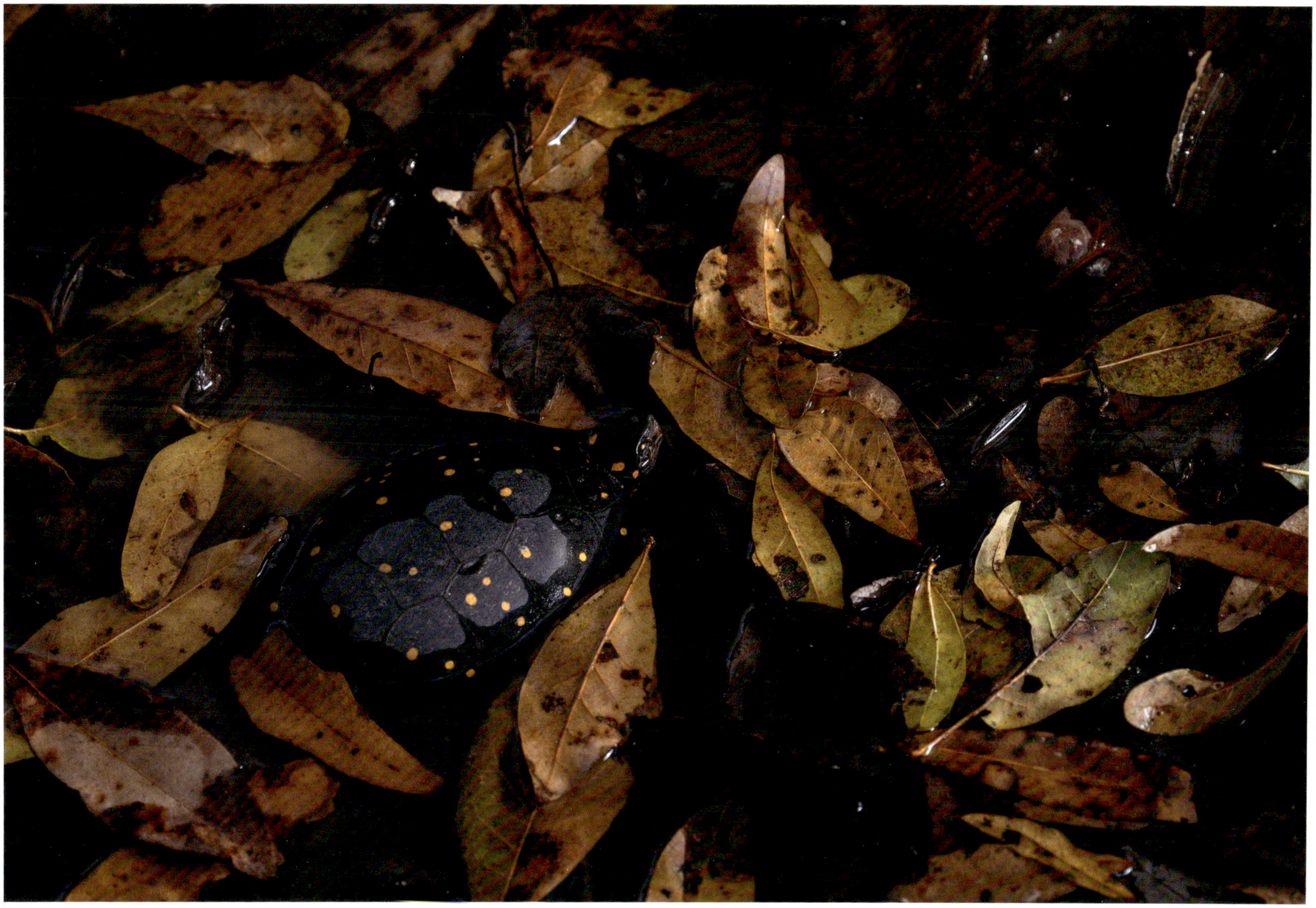

Spotted turtles, which brumate buried in mud through winter, are threatened partly because their distinctive yellow spots make them attractive targets for the illegal pet trade.

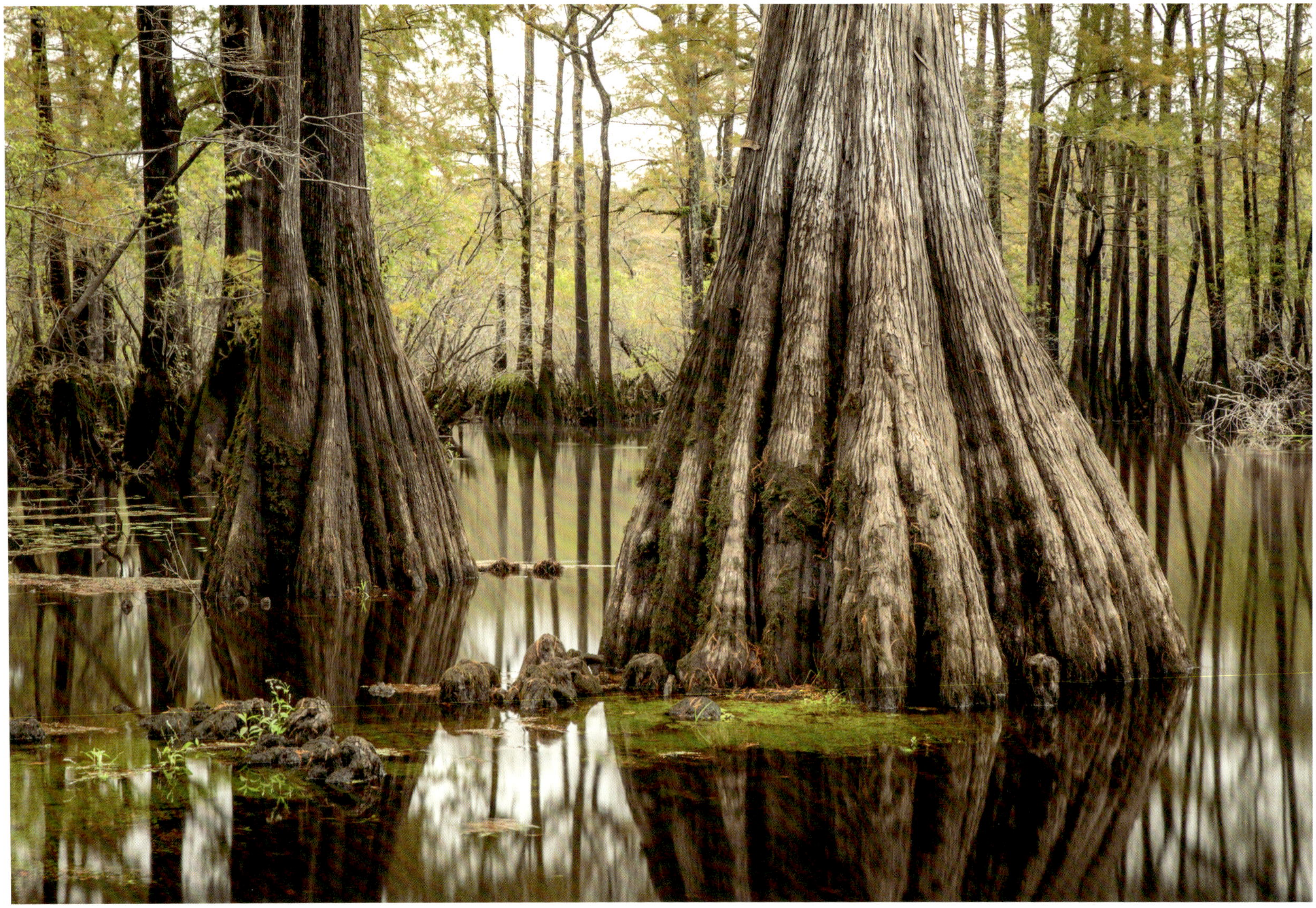

Trees in areas with fluctuating water levels and strong flows develop more pronounced buttress flares, which stabilize them in soft, shifting soils and resist the force of currents.

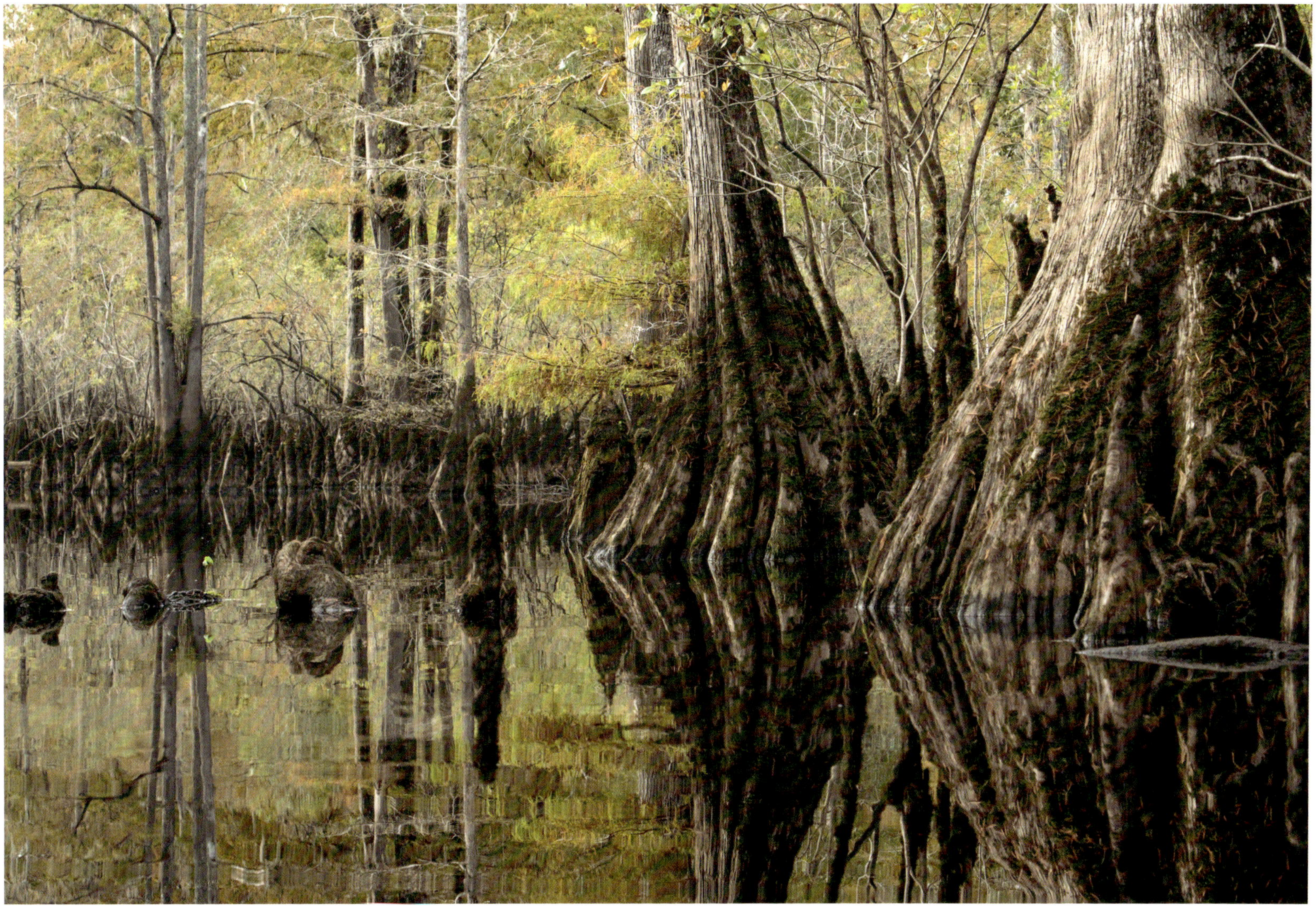

Like other deciduous trees, bald cypress shed their needles in fall
to reduce water loss during winter dormancy.

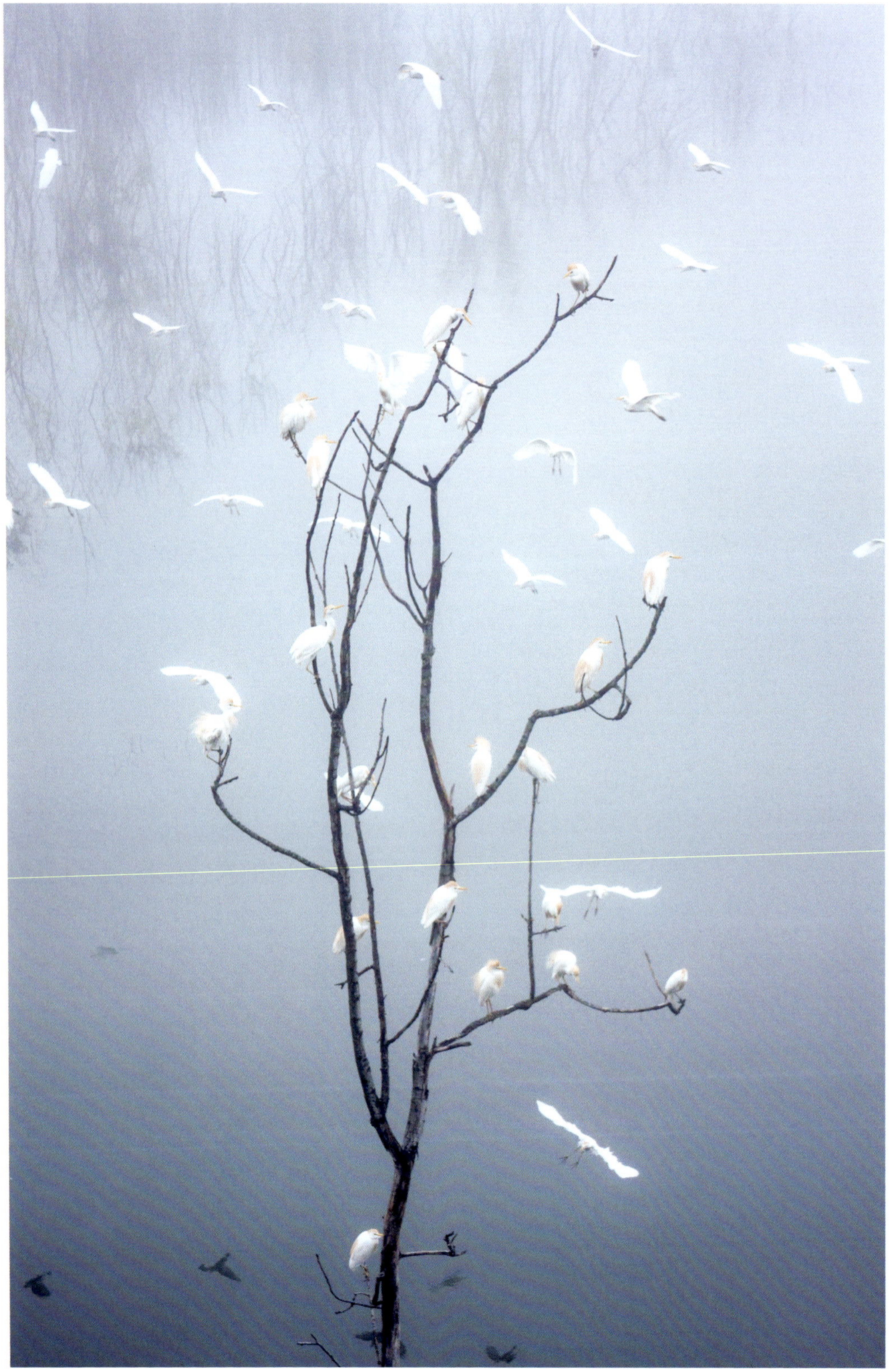

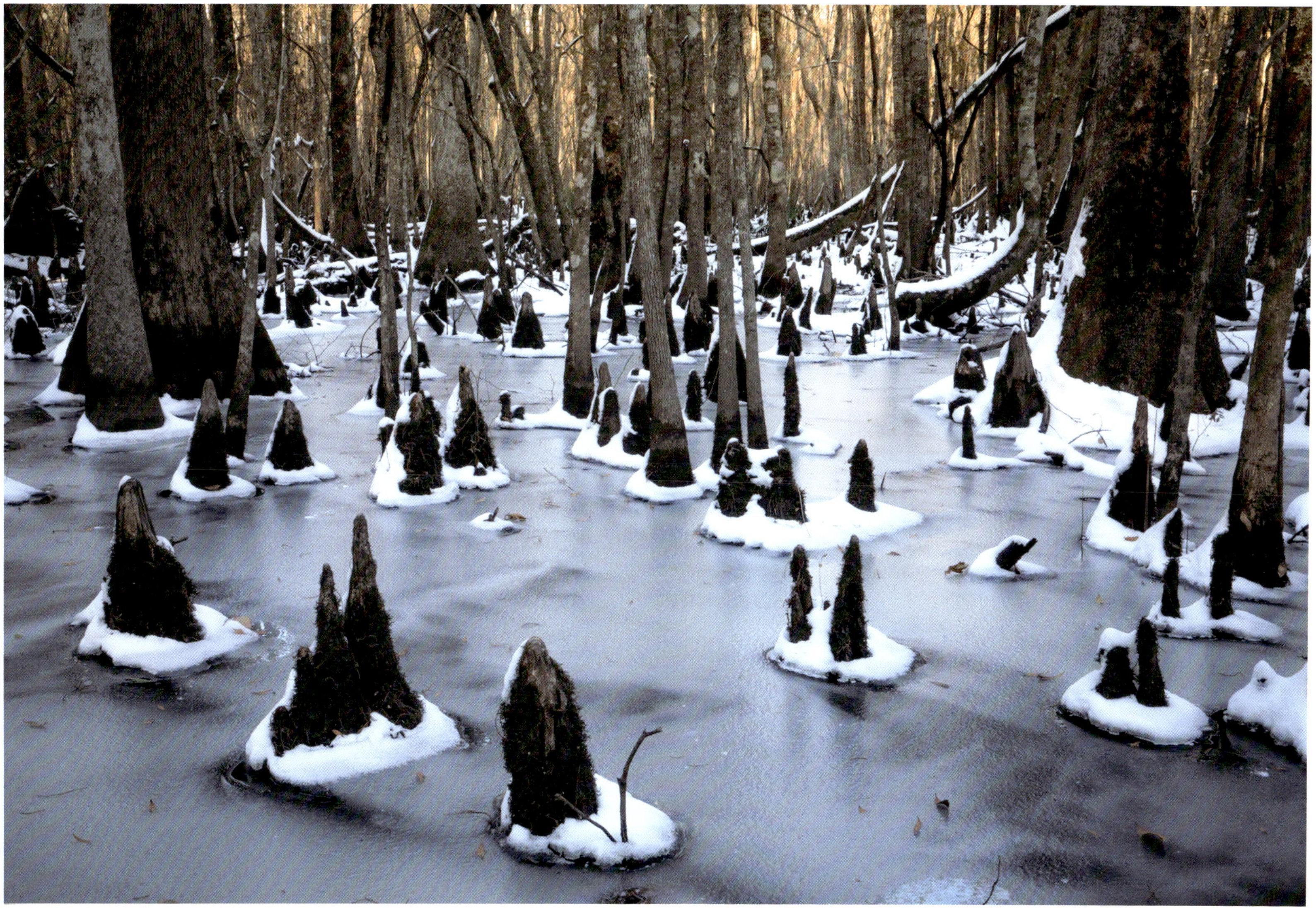

In January of 2018, a bomb cyclone dropped six inches of snow on Francis Beidler Forest, further testing the resilience of the old-growth swamp and its inhabitants.

PREVIOUS PAGE

On the edge of a wetland, cattle egrets roost near their nests, turning a leafless tree into a canopy of white, feathered foliage.

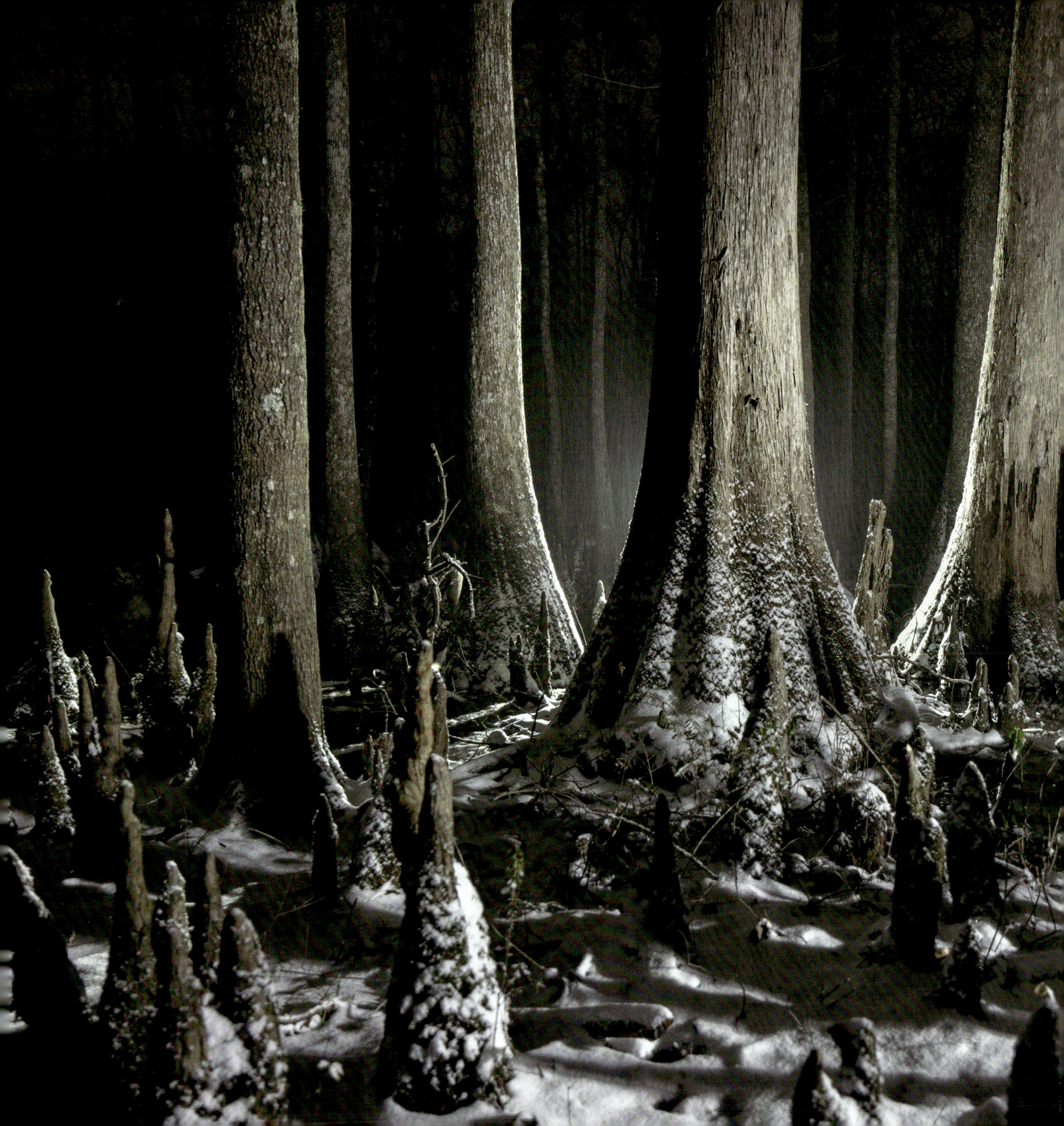

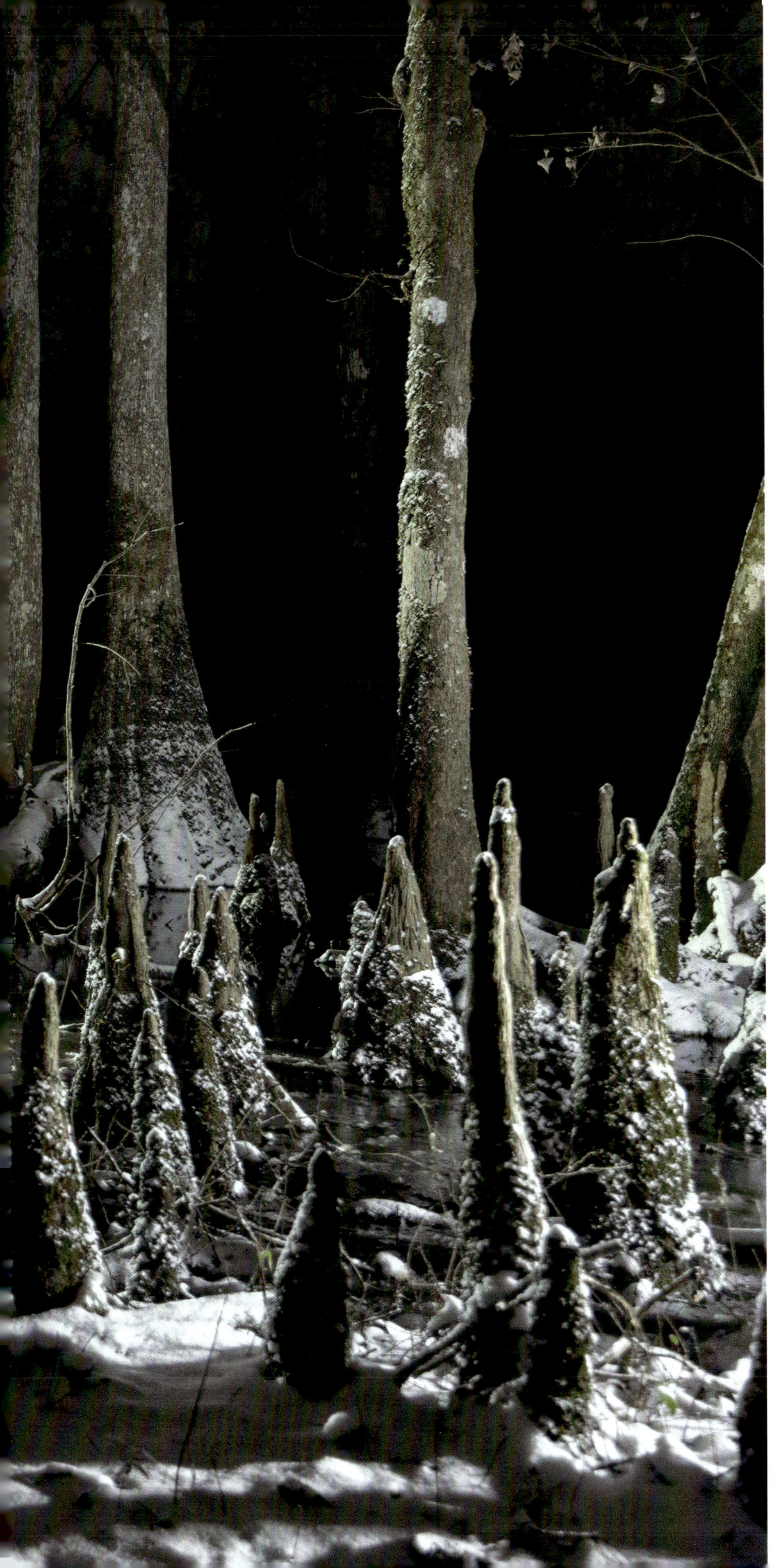

Seven years later, in 2025, snow returned to the swamp, accumulating five inches in the middle of the night.

AFTERWORD

JOEL K. BOURNE JR.

It's safe to say that bald cypress trees have been around for a very, very long time. Far longer, in fact, than the *Homo sapiens* on whom their fate now depends. The first members of the *Taxodium* genus appeared in the late Jurassic some 150 million years ago along with all our favorite dinosaurs. Over the course of a few epochs they'd spread throughout North America, Europe, Asia, and the Arctic. By the time the first Europeans crossed the Atlantic the iconic swamp species' range had shrunk to the coastal plain of the continent from what is now Delaware to Texas and up the Mississippi basin to southern Illinois.

The bulk of the trees, however, lay in the hot, humid, swampy South from eastern North Carolina to Georgia and nearly all of Florida and Louisiana—some 40 million acres. In places, early explorers found a virtual fortress of giant trees 12 feet in diameter and up to 150 feet tall along the frequently flooded swamps and river systems of the region. These tough, rot-resistant, flood-resistant, fire-resistant trees averaged 600 years old, with many older than 1,000. A North Carolina forester once told me that it takes a bald cypress 500 years to be born, 500 years to live, and 500 years to die. Thanks to Dr. David Stahle we now know they can live nearly twice that long.

Unfortunately, the same qualities that make the species so hardy made them targets of the lumber industry, while the lucrative cotton market in the South made the clearing and draining of cheap swamp land extremely profitable, especially with government subsidies. Bald cypress forests once covered as much as a third of Louisiana. Today they cover little more than 1 percent, typical of their fate in the rest of the South. Once America's Amazon replete with its own rare and colorful species, the virgin cypress forests remain only in a few protected pockets, most of which appear in these pages.

Aside from the unique beauty of these primordial swamps, the growth rings of these old trees form one of the longest and most accurate climate records known to science. It's like a farmer's annual report of his growing season carved in wood. As one dendrochronologist said, "When a tree tells you it was dry in 1600, it was dry in 1600." But while the old trees open a window into our climate past, their younger second- and third-growth siblings closer to the coast are teaching us an equally important lesson about our climate future. Even though bald cypress are among the most resilient trees on Earth, cypress forests are now dying in droves along the coastline from Delaware to Texas, leaving bone white skeletons in their wake.

Called "ghost forests" by scientists, these dead and dying trees are essentially billboards for climate change, as rising seas push saltwater deep into once freshwater ecosystems. Although bald cypress are more salt tolerant than the ashes, oaks, and tupelos that share their forested wetland home, they can't survive long with more than 2 parts per thousand (ppt) salt in their water. The Atlantic Ocean can exceed 35 ppt, and the level of the ocean is rising faster along the eastern seaboard than almost anywhere else on the planet. Sea level in Wilmington, North Carolina, some 50 miles from the Black River Preserve, has risen about 12 inches since 1950 and is projected to rise at least another foot by 2050. Deepening harbors and coastal river channels, damming rivers, draining aquifers upstream, even droughts often exacerbate the salinity issue.

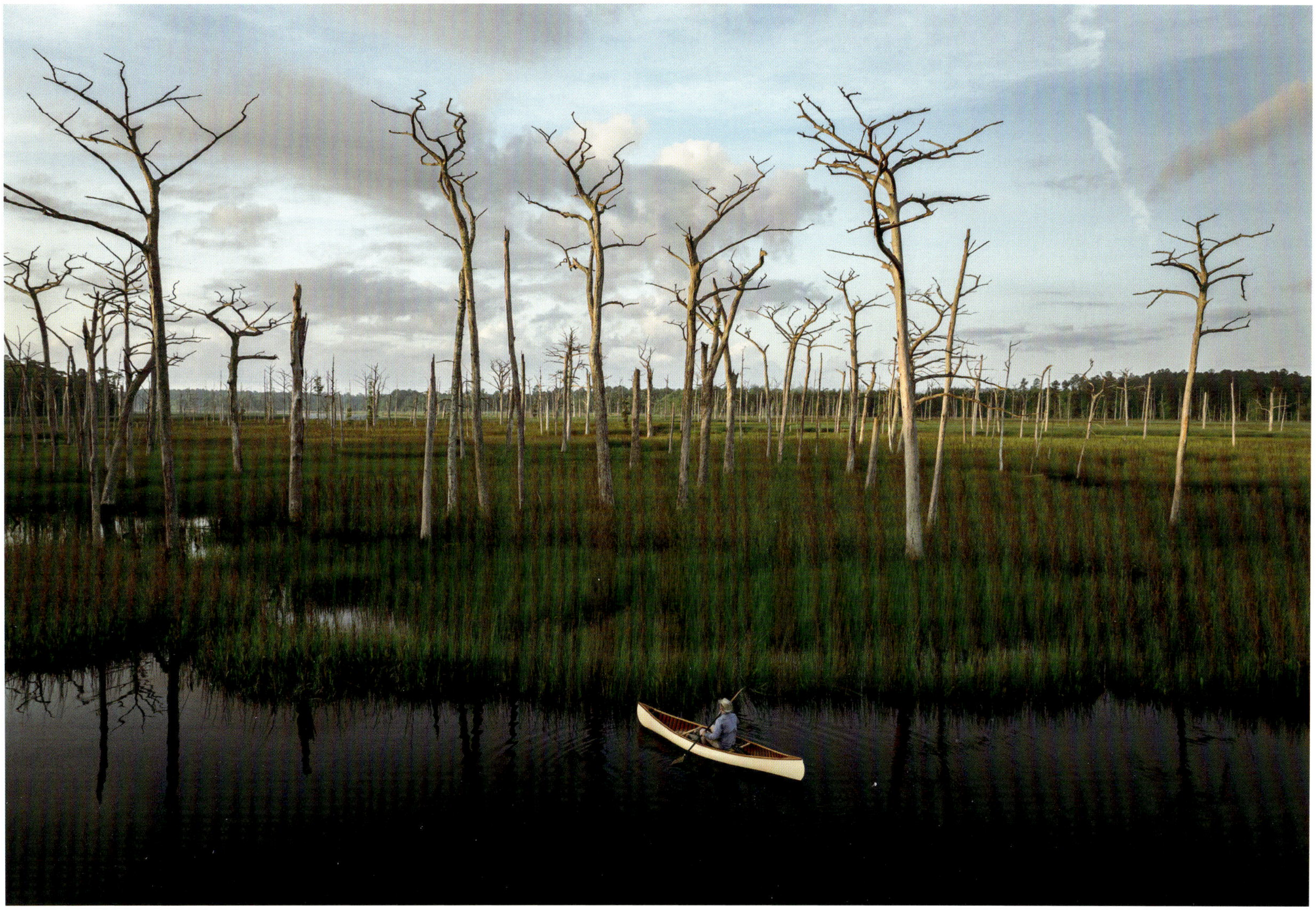

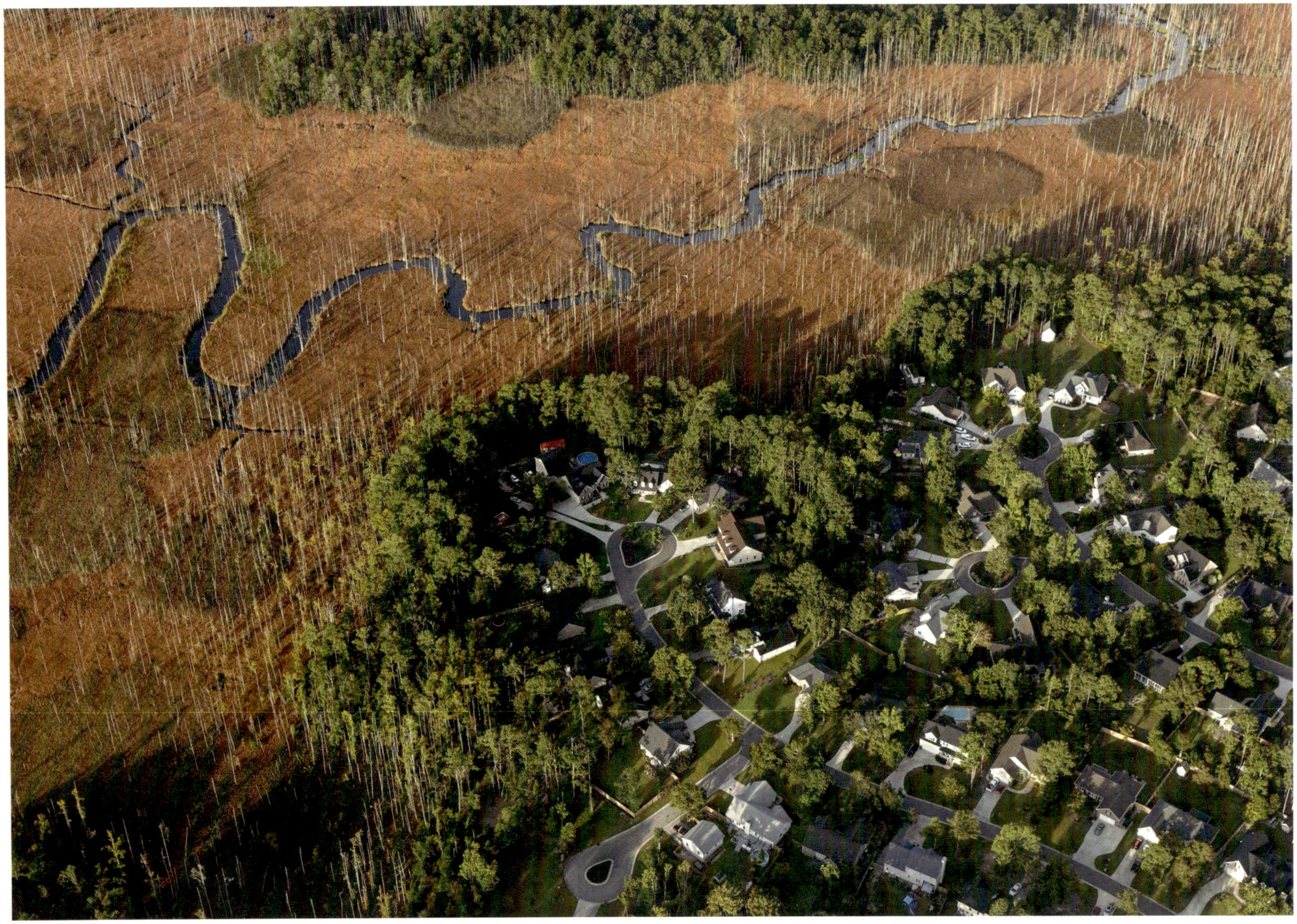

The Black River trees aren't currently threatened by saltwater; the river remains a quintessential blackwater stream. But farther downstream in the Lower Cape Fear River watershed, at least 800 acres of forested wetland have turned into salt marsh since the 1950s as the water has become more brackish, according to recent research from the University of North Carolina at Wilmington. Once annual average salinity hits the 2 ppt mark, the conversion from forest to marsh becomes inevitable.

Cape Fear's ghost forests, which can be seen from area bridges, are a microcosm of a much larger trend. A recent study by researchers at the University of Virginia and Duke University using satellite imagery found that the Gulf Coast and Atlantic coastal plain lost more than 5,000 square miles, or 8 percent, of forested coastal wetlands between 1996 and 2016. That's a Connecticut-size swath of forest that is now mostly salt marsh and scrub. And almost 270 square miles continue to disappear each year—more than triple the loss rate of global mangroves, long considered one of the most threatened ecosystems on Earth. The researchers concluded that at that pace, barring widespread protection or restoration efforts, we could lose all our coastal forested wetlands before the century's end.

A region-wide restoration effort isn't a bad idea, especially since we're losing these forests just when we need them most. Bald cypress swamps and forested wetlands provide a plethora of ecosystem services that could provide an important buffer in what is projected to be a hotter and stormier world. First, they are great at filtering out contaminants in our waterways, which are a significant source of our drinking water, so much so they've even been used for advanced wastewater treatment for small towns. They are important conduits for replenishing groundwater aquifers, the other primary source of our drinking water. They are incredibly productive—producing seven tons of biomass per acre per year in one field study in Florida. That's nearly twice as much as the loblolly pine plantations that cover much of the South. And since they are so long-lived and resistant to decay, they can sequester that carbon far longer than the 30 years those pines typically grow before they are cut. They also provide habitat for far more species. In North Carolina alone, cypress swamps are crucial habitat for nearly 50 species of concern, from the cerulean warbler to the four-toed salamander.

Perhaps most importantly for those in the hurricane zone, nothing knocks down storm surge like a forested wetland, and even though they are standing in soft swampy soils, not even the most powerful storms can knock down a cypress grove.

Forest researcher William Conner interviewed for a job at Clemson University's Belle W. Baruch Institute of Coastal Ecology and Forest Science in Georgetown, South Carolina, two weeks after Hurricane Hugo blasted the state in 1989. The Category 4 storm came ashore with winds of nearly 140 miles an hour, damaging some 4.4 million acres of forest and destroying 6.7 billion board feet of sawtimber—enough to build about 660,000 homes. That would have housed almost the entire state of West Virginia at the time.

"When I drove through Francis Marion National Forest, all the pines were flattened to the ground," says Conner, now professor emeritus at the institute. "All the cypress along the streams were still standing. They are incredibly wind-fast, with their buttresses and knees and intertwined root systems. I've only seen two trees blown over in my career, and both were isolated by themselves."

It's a forestry lesson humans should learn. While we focus a lot of attention on magnificently old trees, the true power of the bald cypress is not its ability as an individual to survive the centuries but the forest it creates and anchors around it: the diversity of species, of age, height, new growth and decay, and the complete web of unique life such a forest supports.

The rebuilding has already started. Since Hurricane Katrina flooded New Orleans in 2005, volunteers with the Lake Pontchartrain Conservancy have planted nearly 100,000 bald cypress trees in the area to restore the forests and the flood protection they've lost. The ancient groves in these pages could form the anchors of broader restoration efforts throughout the South, storing carbon, cleaning rivers, storing groundwater, and fighting floods, all while creating biodiversity hotspots that would attract wildlife and humans alike.

Even when bald cypresses die, they are still "giving trees." Eight miles off the coast of Alabama, 60 feet beneath the Gulf of Mexico, lie the intact stumps of an ancient cypress forest submerged by sea level rise that has been storing carbon for some 60,000 years. The ancient stumps are now a reef-like structure chock full of fish, eels, tunicates, sponges, invertebrates, and myriad other marine species.

Coastlines shift. Ice ages come and go. Still, bald cypress endure.

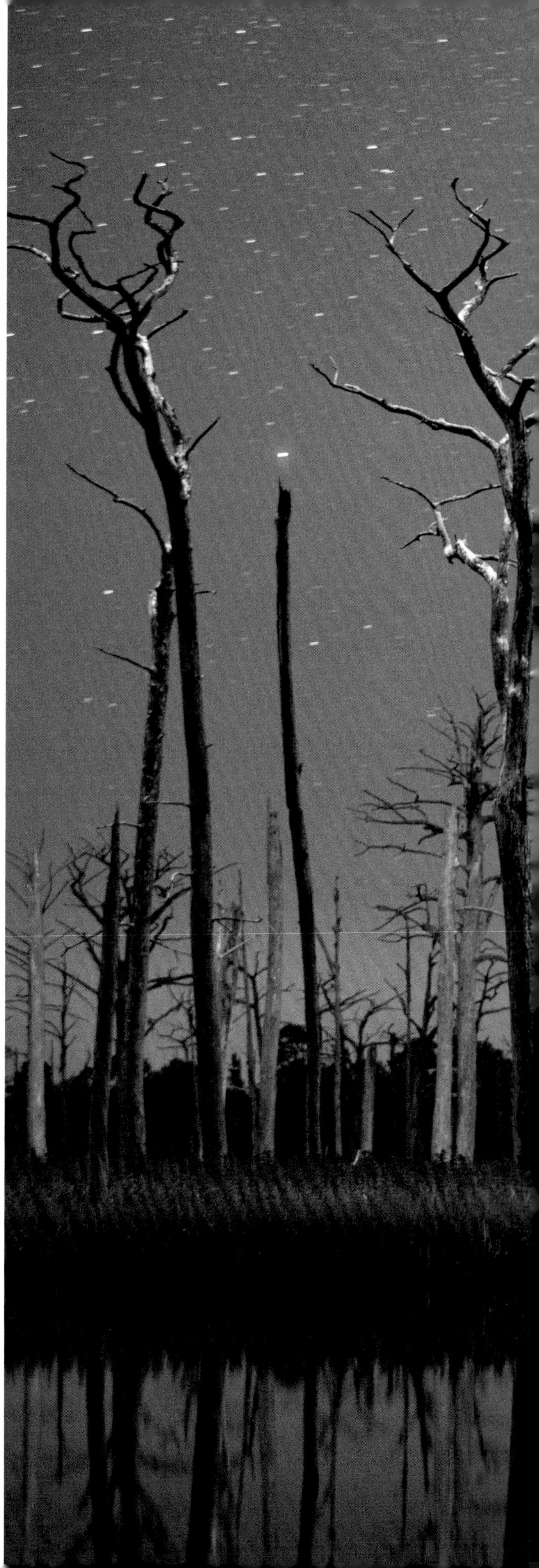

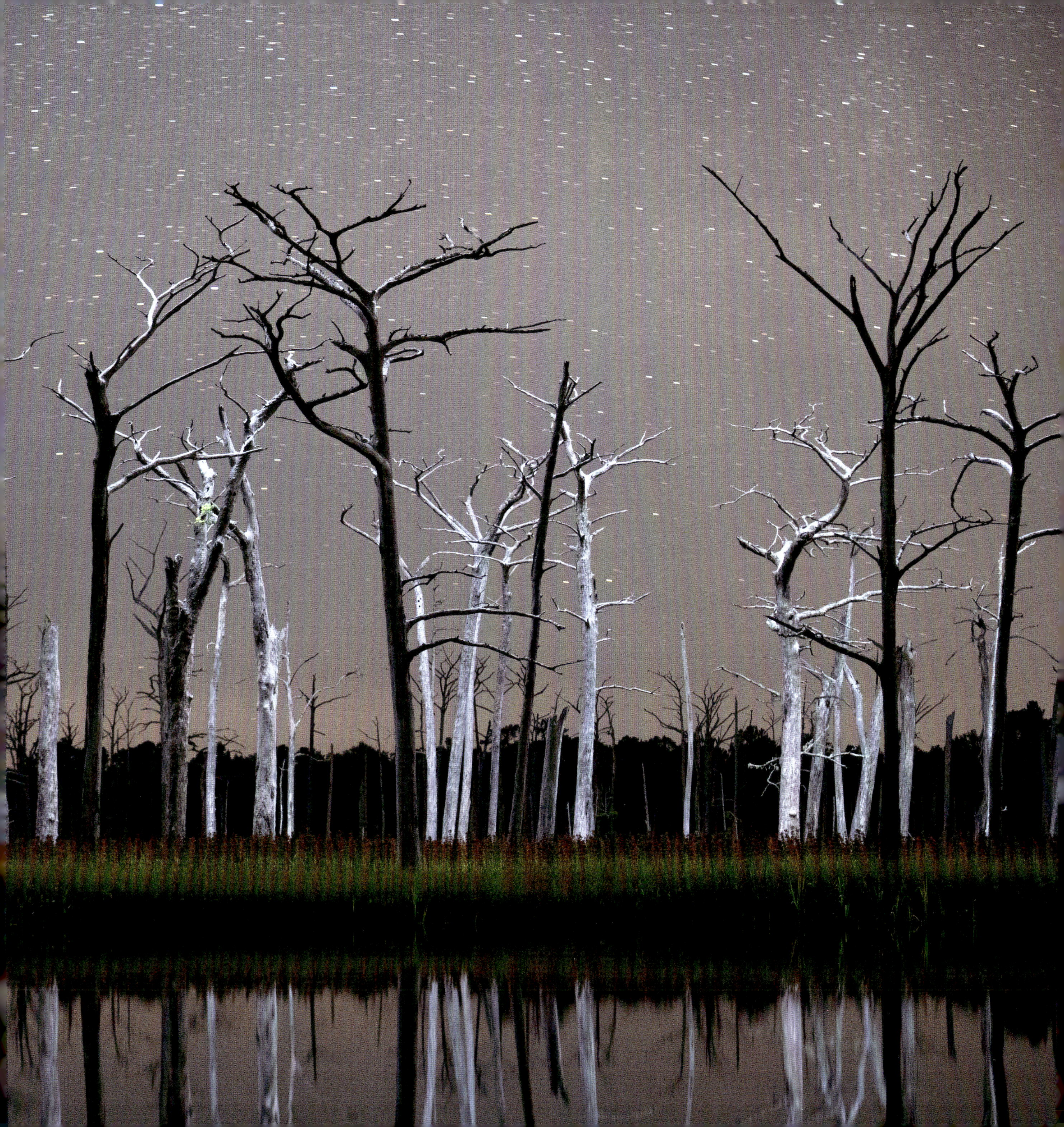

ACKNOWLEDGMENTS

Mike Dawson and Mark Musselman interviewed me for a naturalist position at Audubon's Francis Beidler Forest in 2008. I had just returned to the country after living in Honduras for two years. I was excited about the next step but nervous I wouldn't get the job. Mark confessed years later that midway through the interview, he turned to Mike and said, "What are you doing? Why are we asking more questions? Hire him before he goes somewhere else!"

That seasonal job, under the leadership of legendary conservationist Norman Brunswig, became the conduit for my involvement in the Everglades and, years later, my conservation work in South Carolina's Upstate with Naturaland Trust. It was a major jumping-off point in my life and the fertile ground from which this book sprouted.

Off and on, between 2008 and 2025, I chipped away at this project. But it was the foundation laid at Beidler Forest—and the support of its remarkable staff—that gave me the footing to dream of something larger. Thank you to my Beidler Forest family: Norm Brunswig, Mark Musselman, Mike Dawson, Matt Johnson, Ricky Covey, Barbara Thomas, Nancy Jean Nettles, Anne Shahid, and Jeff Mollenhauer. It is one of the most remarkable places in the South, and it's in good hands.

Funding for a project of this magnitude came in many forms and over six years. Thank you to the National Geographic Society for seeing the value in this local form of exploration, and to Kathy Moran, Kurt Mutchler, and Alexa O'Keefe, and especially to my editor Anne Farrar, who never joined me in the swamp, but she slogged through tens of thousands of images to bring this story to the hallowed pages of *National Geographic* magazine. Thank you to Becky Hale and Mark Thiessen at headquarters for gifting me some studio time and sharing your expertise.

Thank you to Joel Bourne Jr. for pushing the limits of where a journalist will go and for elevating the pressing issues of our time. I'm honored to have your brilliant words in this book.

Deep gratitude to the J. Lyles Glenn Family Foundation—Lyles, Melanie, Francis, Hunter, Joe, and Daniel—who saw the value in this work and provided vital financial support. I wish all grant applications were conducted in person on the North Platte River.

To William Freund at the fStop Foundation—thank you for countless conversations, financial support, always having a fresh supply of PIR sensors and triggers, and for servicing camera traps while I was out of the country. It's incredible what fStop has accomplished since its early days.

Thank you to NANPA and the Philip Hyde Grant for your support, to Frank Beidler IV for continuing your family's generous legacy, and to the International League of Conservation Photographers for stewarding these donations.

Audubon's Corkscrew Swamp Sanctuary was a home away from home for several years. A special thanks to the leadership team who granted access to the swamp and entertained my many ideas in the spirit of discovery. Thank you to directors Ed Carlson, Jason Lauritsen, Lisa Korte, and Keith Laakkonen. Thank you to my good friend Shawn Clem—always quick to pick up the phone—and to the outstanding Audubon staff and network: Allyson Webb, Sally Stein, Lee Martin, Mike Duever, Hayden Deakins, Scott Svec, and

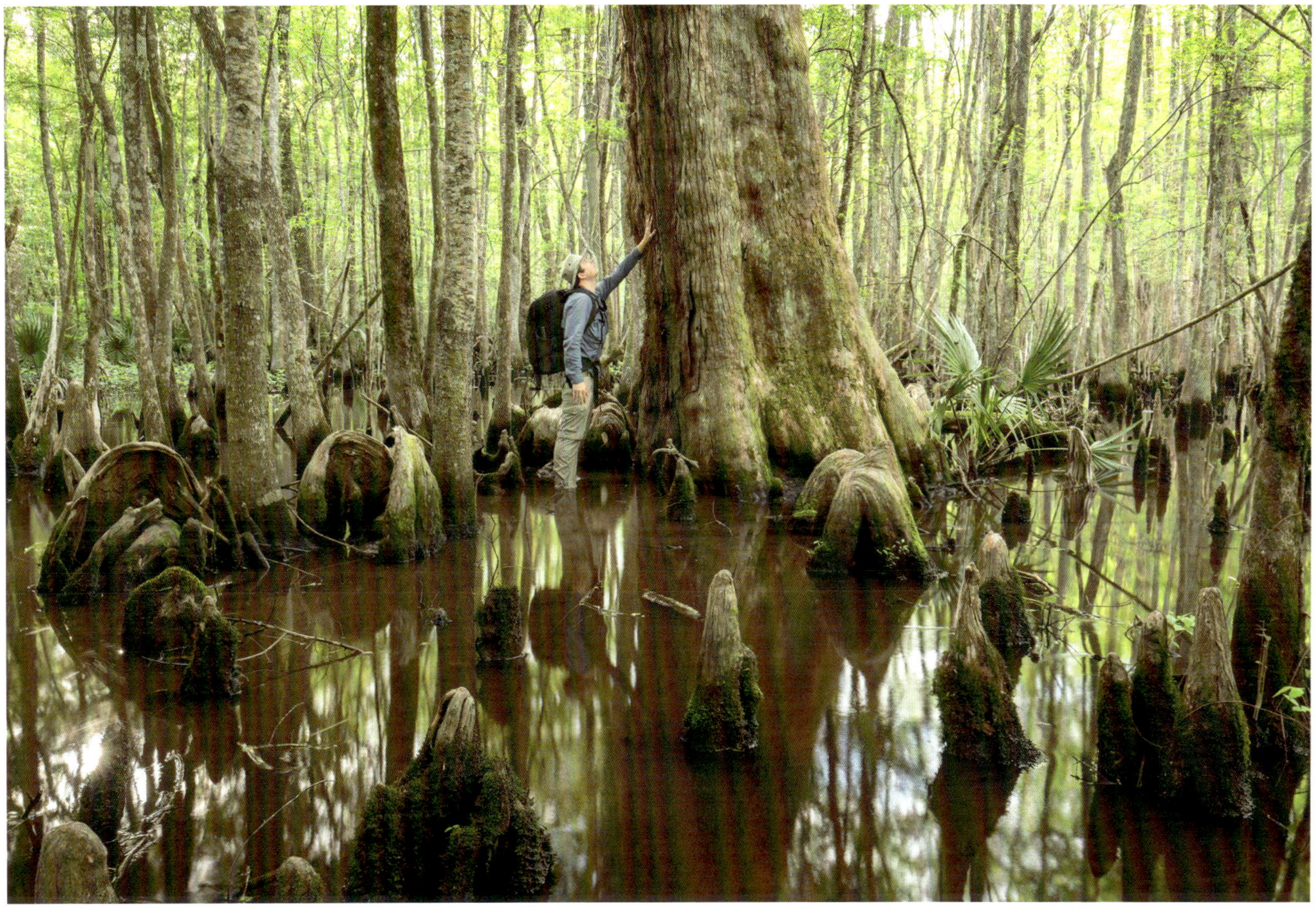

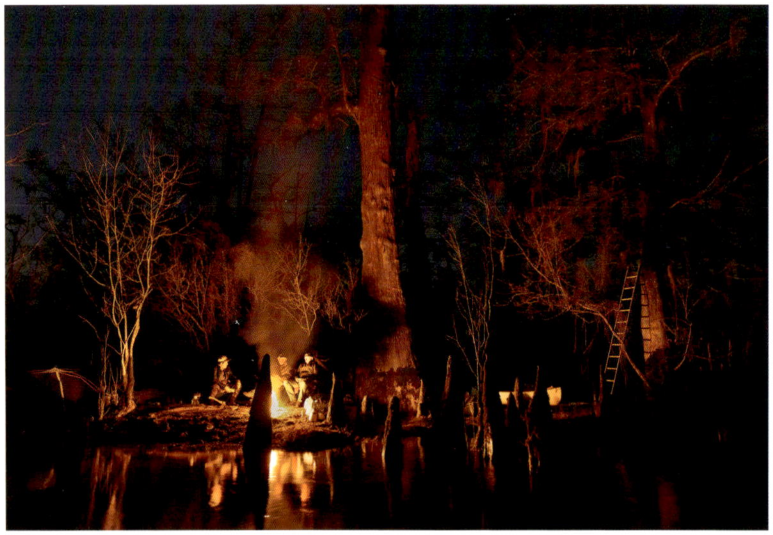

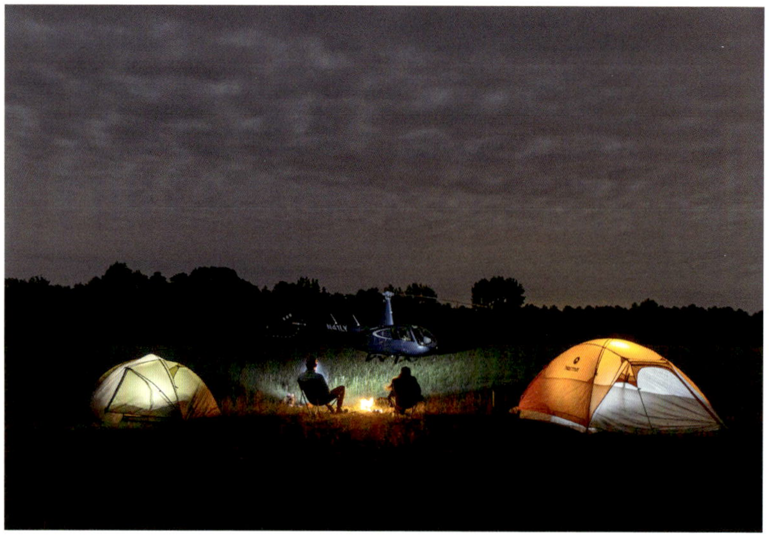

Gio Dachiardi. Thank you to Ralph Arwood for sharing your backcountry knowledge, and to Carlton Ward Jr. for elevating my camera-trap game—and for the many commiserations over failed gear and missed moments.

To my good friend Peter Houlihan, who refused to give up on the hunt for the ghost orchid's pollinator—we shared sweat, hugs, tears, and fear in that swamp, and came out better and closer on the other side. That summer remains one of the most productive and fulfilling of my life.

Thank you to Eric Bendick, Tom Winston, Jeff Reed, Danny Schmidt, and Tori Linder for the film *Chasing Ghosts*—and for enduring everything it took to make it happen.

To rangers Jon Anderson, Greg Cunningham, David Shelley, and Eric Frey of Congaree National Park—thank you for your hospitality and expertise. Kay Lynn Berry, thank you for calling when the gates closed during COVID and trusting me to bring the swamp to the public through images and video. To the UC Boulder team—Orit Peleg, Rafael Sarfati, and Julie Hayes—thank you for letting me document your brilliant work and for the many late calls deciphering your findings. Thank you, Zach Steinhauser, for assisting during the firefly display and for joining me again on the Black River. We've seen some remarkable sights together, and your lighting and company have always been top class. Thank you to John Cely, Graham Norman, and Neal Polhemus for leading trips into the far reaches of the backcountry.

The Black River in North Carolina is one of the most beautiful places on Earth. The Nature Conservancy has done a tremendous service in protecting, restoring, and stewarding these lands. The world owes you a debt of gratitude. Thank you to Katherine Skinner, Angie Carl, Zach West, and Debbie Crane for your trust and vital work.

It was one of the great privileges of my life to be in the swamp with Dave Stahle and Charles Robbins. Camping beneath the oldest trees east of the Rockies and cooking eggs and elk steaks over a fire is a core memory I'll never forget. Thank you for your time, your wisdom, and your candor. I'd follow both of you into any swamp.

On the Sampit River in South Carolina, while on assignment for The Nature Conservancy, Craig Sasser and Maria Whitehead introduced me to my first ghost forest. I toured the former cypress swamps—now marshes—with Jamie

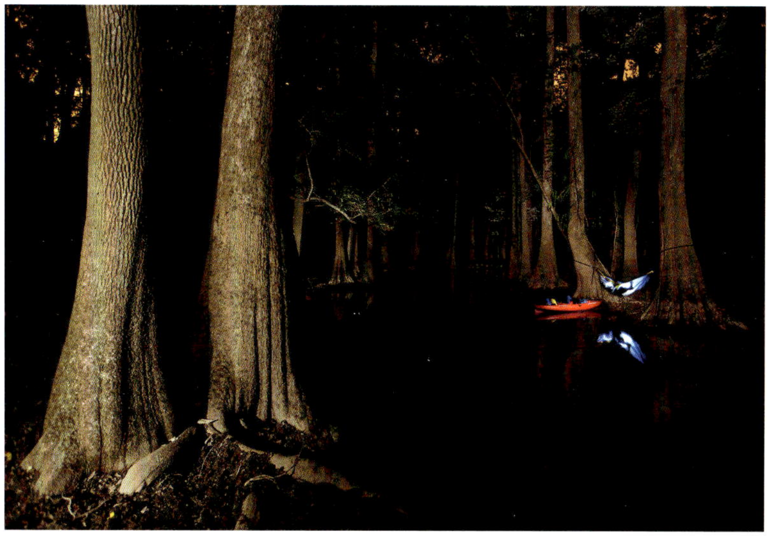

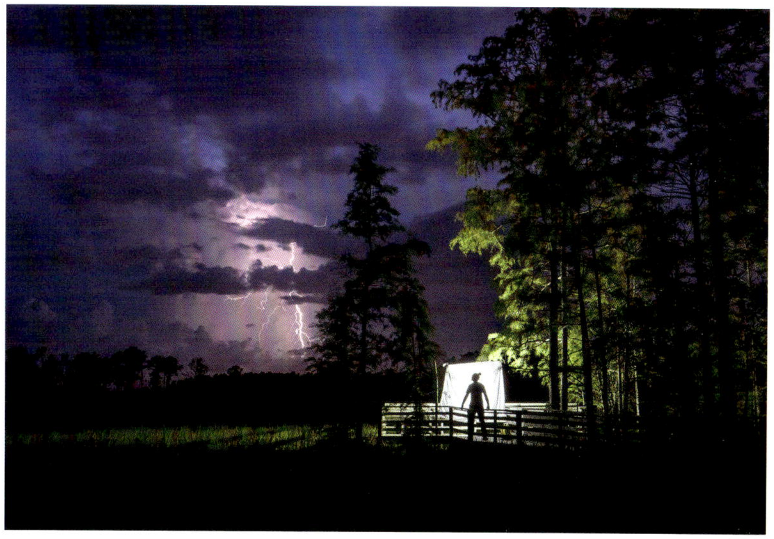

Duberstein and William Conner, who graciously tolerated a barrage of questions. Years later, I returned to the Sampit thanks to Lloyd Weston and Freddy St. Laurent, spending nights trying to make the skeletal trees glow beneath the stars. Freddy, thank you for your generous hospitality.

Thank you to the pilots and captains who took me out and brought me back safely: Gary Lickle, Jeff Farkas, Justin Grady, Mike McDonald, and Robert Searfoss—to whom I owe an apology for nearly throwing up in your pee bottle. Thanks to SouthWings for coordinating volunteer pilots, and to Peter and Marie Buyck for letting helicopter ace Georgina Reinhardt and me create a landing zone on your property. There's nothing more southern than your hospitality toward total strangers, and I'll never forget pound cake by the fire.

Thanks to the Charleston Museum and Matt Gibson for sharing your collections, and to my brother-in-law Raleigh Beasley for assisting with that shoot. Thanks also to Andrei Sourakov at the Florida Museum of Natural History.

To my editors over the years—thank you for your keen eye and thoughtful guidance. You gave these stories wings. To *Audubon Magazine*'s Sabine Meyer, *bioGraphic*'s Steven Bedard, and The Nature Conservancy's Melissa Ryan and Rolaine Ossman—it has been a true pleasure working with you.

I owe a great debt to the friends who ventured into these places with me—whether to hold an umbrella, a strobe, or simply to see what I kept going on about: Will and Greg Stone, Art Nagan, Kalin Stanojev, Adam Chasey, Michelle Robinson, Wes Overvold, Dawson Dunning, Karen Wattam, Darrin Hamlin, Joe Guthrie, and Van Whitehead.

To my parents—thank you for the best possible upbringing and the solid foundation from which I leapt into swamp life. You gave me boundless curiosity and just enough of your work ethic to carry it forward.

And finally, to my best friend, wife, and partner in all things—Hannah. I left Beidler Forest kicking and screaming, not knowing I was on my way to meeting you. You've changed my life for the better in more ways than I can name. Thank you for giving me another wellspring of inspiration and wonder with our two children, McAllen and Hinton, to whom I also owe a great debt for sharing their daddy with the swamp. Thank you for your patience each time I said, "just one more photograph." You really made them sing on these pages.

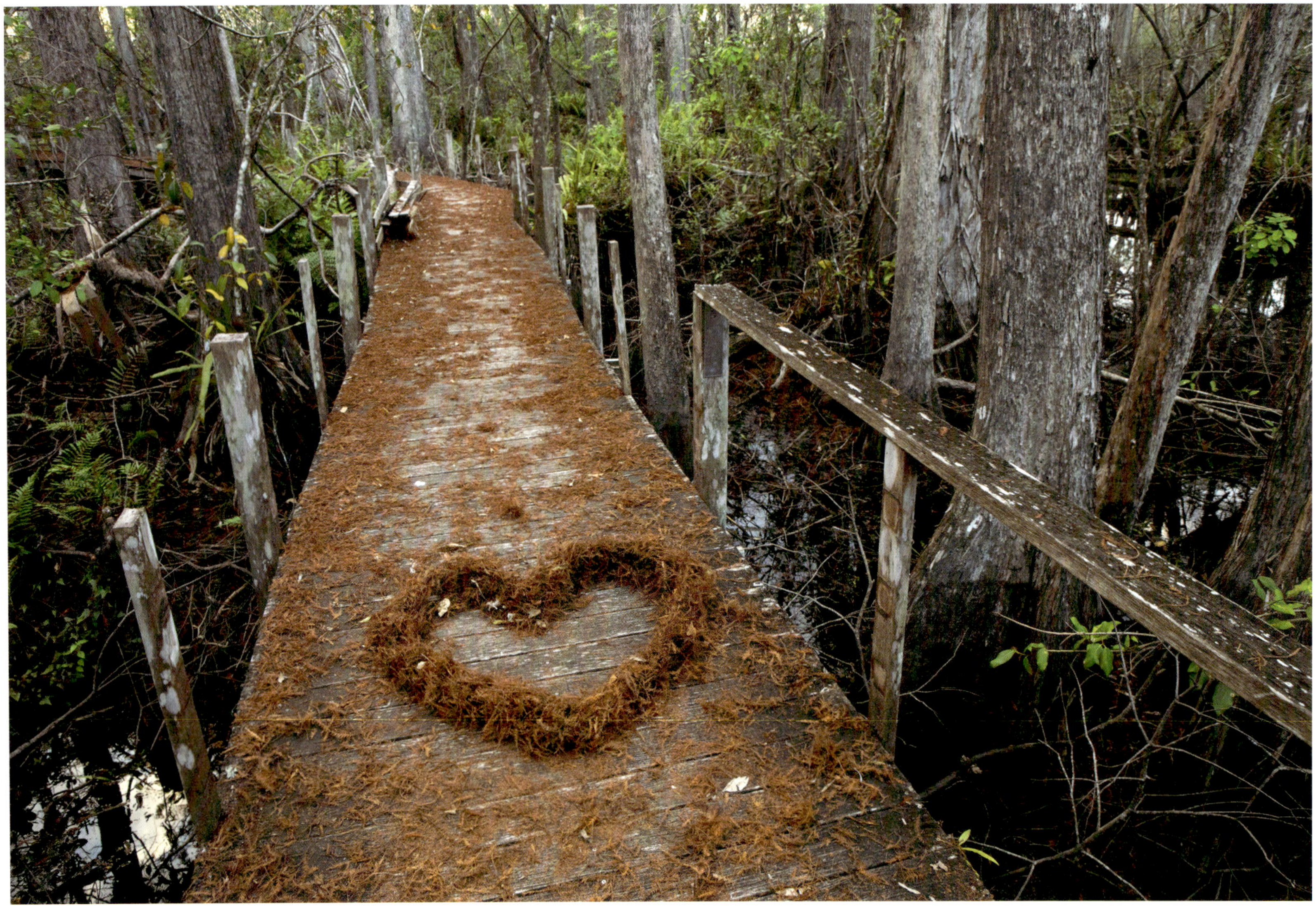

Through countless holidays and birthdays spent deep in the forest, I always found a way to send love home—even on Valentine's Day.

Mac Stone is a National Geographic Explorer and conservation photographer who uses his camera to tell stories about the delicate relationship between humanity and the natural world. Raised among the swamps, springs, and prairies of North Central Florida, Stone developed an early passion for wild places. Today, his award-winning photography and writing reveal the hidden beauty and ecological complexity of wilderness ecosystems across the American South and abroad. His work has been widely published and featured on global stages, captivating audiences through powerful visuals and storytelling. Stone lives in Greenville, South Carolina, with his wife and two children, where he also leads Naturaland Trust, a nonprofit land conservancy dedicated to protecting the region's mountains, rivers, and wetlands for future generations.

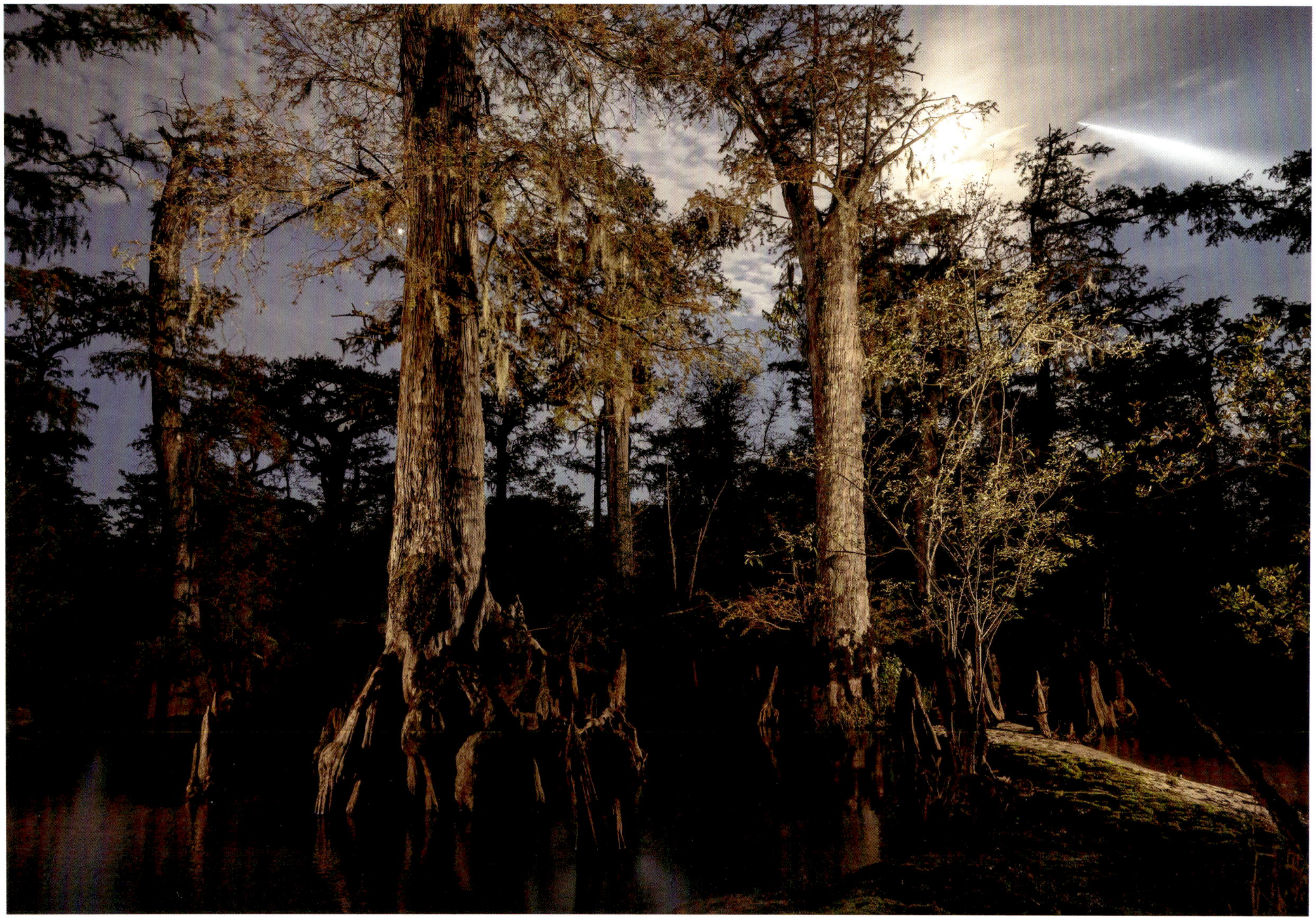

On the evening of September 15, 2021, as the first all-civilian spaceflight soared above the East Coast, its brief arc of light passed over the oldest known cypress trees on Earth—a humbling reminder that while we reach for the stars, there are still ancient mysteries rooted in the swamps below.